THE IMAM OF THE CHRISTIANS

The Imam of the Christians

THE WORLD OF DIONYSIUS OF TEL-MAHRE, C. 750–850

PHILIP WOOD

PRINCETON UNIVERSITY PRESS

PRINCETON & OXFORD

Published by Princeton University Press
41 William Street, Princeton, New Jersey 08540
99 Banbury Road, Oxford OX2 6JX

press.princeton.edu

GPSR Authorized Representative: Easy Access System Europe - Mustamäe tee 50, 10621 Tallinn, Estonia, gpsr.requests@easproject.com

First paperback printing, 2025
Paperback ISBN 9780691222721

The Library of Congress has cataloged the cloth edition as follows:

Names: Wood, Philip, 1982– author.
Title: The Imam of the Christians : the world of Dionysius of Tel-mahre, c. 750–850 / Philip Wood.
Description: Princeton, New Jersey : Princeton University Press, 2021. | Includes bibliographical references and index.
Identifiers: LCCN 2020044606 (print) | LCCN 2020044607 (ebook) | ISBN 9780691212791 (hardback) | ISBN 9780691219950 (ebook)
Subjects: LCSH: Dionysius, of Tel-Maḥrē, Patriarch of Antioch, -845. | Syrian Orthodox Church. | Jacobites (Syrian Christians) | Christianity and other religions—Islam. | Islam—Relations—Christianity. | Christian philosophy—Islamic influences.
Classification: LCC BX179.D56 W66 2021 (print) | LCC BX179.D56 (ebook) | DDC 261.2/7095648—dc23
LC record available at https://lccn.loc.gov/2020044606
LC ebook record available at https://lccn.loc.gov/2020044607

British Library Cataloging-in-Publication Data is available

Editorial: Ben Tate and Josh Drake
Production Editorial: Sara Lerner
Jacket/Cover Design: Heather Hansen
Production: Danielle Amatucci
Publicity: Kate Hensley and Amy Stewart
Copyeditor: Kathleen Kageff

Jacket/Cover Credit: From *Ms. Syr. 559, a Lectionary of the year 1219* © Biblioteca Apostolica Vaticana

This book has been composed in Arno

CONTENTS

ACKNOWLEDGEMENTS

THIS BOOK was the product of a British Academy Mid-career Fellowship that I held 2018–19 at Aga Khan University, Institute for the Study of Muslim Civilisations. I would like to thank everyone at the Institute, especially the dean, Leif Stenberg, for their convivial support.

My thinking on Dionysius of Tel-Mahre was first stimulated by a workshop on elites in the caliphate that was organized by Stefan Heidemann and Hannah Hagemann at Hamburg for the ERC project 'The Early Islamic Empire at Work'. Here I presented an early version of what became chapter 3 of this book, and the discussions I had there were very important for thinking through my ideas.

I also benefited from my involvement with Petra Sijpesteijn's Leiden ERC project, 'Embedding Conquest: Naturalising Muslim Rule in the Early Islamic Empire (600–1000)', where I presented an early version of chapter 4. Audiences at Oxford, Cambridge, London, Frankfurt and Milan provided feedback on many aspects of the work.

Peter Van Nuffelen, Maria Conterno and Marianna Mazzola kindly shared with me their work on the fragments of Dionysius and I am very grateful to them indeed.

I should like to show my particular thanks to Hannah Hagemann and Phil Booth, who read the entire manuscript of the book and made many valuable suggestions. I would also like to thank Averil Cameron, Andrew Marsham, Liza Anderson, Chip Coakley, David Taylor, Salam Rassi, Ed Hayes, Ed Zychowicz-Coghill, Fanny Bessard, Jan van Ginkel, Srecko Koralija, Daniel Hadas, James Montgomery, Andy Hilkens, Peter Sarris, Jack Tannous, Ben Tate, Sara Lerner, Hanna Siurua, Greg Fisher, and the anonymous reviewer from Princeton University Press.

Finally I should like to thank my family for their enduring love and kindness: My parents, George (1930–2000) and Felicity, who nurtured my love of history; my brother Stephen, who has brought out the best in me; my children,

Charlotte, Jamie and Max, for keeping me on my toes; and my wife, Katherine, for everything.

An earlier version of parts of chapter 3 was published as 'Christian Elite Networks in the Jazira, c. 730–840', in H.-L. Hagemann and S. Heidemann (eds.), *Transregional and Regional Elites: Connecting the Early Islamic Empire* (Berlin: De Gruyter, 2019), 359–83.

Parts of chapter 4 were published as 'Christian Authority under the Early Abbasids: The Life of Timothy of Kakushta', *Proche-Orient Chrétien* 61 (2011), 258–74. They are reproduced here by kind permission of the publishers.

Where Arabic terms have been included in Syriac sources, I have presented them here as if transliterated from Arabic, rather than attempting to preserve the (eccentric) Syriac spelling.

I have not included diacritics for proper names and titles in the main text. Full transliterations are provided in the bibliography.

The *Chronicle* of Michael the Syrian is a significant source for this book. I have provided references to Chabot's publication, which is widely available. However, Chabot published a black-and-white photograph of a manuscript that he commissioned in 1888. A superior text is now available in the form of a high-resolution digital photograph from an earlier manuscript of Michael's *Chronicle*, which had been held in Aleppo. This manuscript was produced in 1598 and was the model for the manuscript that Chabot commissioned. A high-resolution digital photograph of the Aleppo manuscript has been published by Gorgias Press, as the first volume of a series of texts and translations of Michael's *Chronicle*. It is much easier to read than Chabot's text and preserves the rubrication and marginal notes. Sebastian Brock provides a useful conversion table in volume 11 of the Gorgias Press series 'Texts and Translations of the Chronicle of Michael the Great'. This table allows references to Chabot's text to be converted to the Aleppo text. I have not seen any substantial differences between the two texts, though Chabot's text employs more frequent abbreviations for common words.

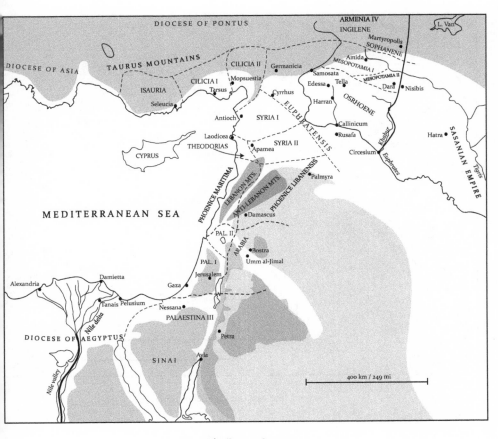

MAP 1. The Roman Levant c. 550

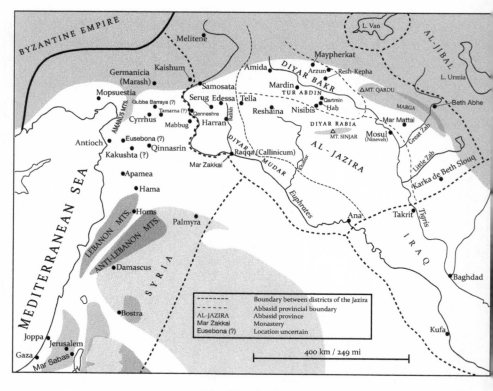

MAP 2. The Abbasid Caliphate c. 800

THE IMAM OF THE CHRISTIANS

Introduction

AFTER A LONG CIVIL WAR, the Abbasid caliph al-Ma'mun established his rule in Baghdad, the city that had been built by his ancestor al-Mansur some fifty years before. The Christians of the Levant had endured oppression from a series of local warlords in the course of this conflict. The establishment of the caliph in Baghdad offered them new opportunities to seek the patronage of central government. But this patronage came with strings attached. For any Christian leader to win the ear of the powerful, he would also need to present himself and his co-religionists as loyal and useful supporters of the new status quo.

Al-Ma'mun's reign was experimental in many ways. The new caliph toyed with designating a successor from outside the Abbasid family, the Shia imam 'Ali al-Rida. And he would be notorious in later Sunni circles for forcing Muslim scholars to agree to that the Quran was uncreated. But from a Christian point of view, his most disturbing innovation was to decree that small groups of non-Muslims could secede from their traditional leaders (Christian patriarchs and Jewish exilarchs) without penalty and nominate their own leaders. Until this point the caliphal government had tended to endorse the leadership structures of a small number of Christian confessions, all of which could trace their histories back to before the Islamic conquests of the seventh century. But al-Ma'mun's innovation threatened to alter this arrangement quite radically, and allow any disaffected Christian bishop to secede from obedience to the patriarch and from the wider structures of his confession.

This book focuses on the life and times of Dionysius of Tel-Mahre. Dionysius was al-Ma'mun's contemporary and a client of his general 'Abd Allah ibn Tahir. It was partly thanks to 'Abd Allah's support that Dionysius was able to retain the patriarchate, in the teeth of the complaints of rivals. And Dionysius' links with 'Abd Allah allowed Dionysius to act as a representative of the caliph in Egypt. These connections made Dionysius much more prominent and secure than most of his predecessors. One major strand of this book is how Christian institutions were strengthened by the support they received from the caliph's government. In an era when the reach of government was becoming deeper and more effective, in such fields as taxation, the judiciary and the recruitment of a standing army, Christian leaders were able to gather tithes and issue legislation, facilitated by official support in the recognition of an official patriarch and the use of coercion against recalcitrant clergy.

The transformations of this period that resulted from the closer connection of Muslim government and Christian church were not only political and economic; they were also cultural and intellectual. When al-Maʾmun was on the cusp of allowing a proliferation of non-Muslim authorities, Dionysius tells us that he preserved the authority of the patriarchate by drawing an analogy between himself and al-Maʾmun as both being imams. Dionysius' attempts to draw on the cultural and political thought of the Muslim elite are the second major strand of this book.

The notion of an imam was a central feature of the political thought of the Abbasid family. The title 'imam' had been used to designate the rightful caliph in exile in the era before the Abbasid revolution against his 'tyrannical' Umayyad predecessors. And it had been used in a similar fashion to assert al-Maʾmun's legitimacy during his civil war with his brother. But often the term 'imam' was simply used as a synonym for 'caliph'; i.e., the ruler of the state. The jurist Abu Yusuf conceives of the imam as the proper object of all Muslim obedience: to obey the imam is obey God.[1] In addition to having this political meaning, the term 'imam' could also carry a lower-order meaning to refer simply to a prayer leader, who stood in front of a congregation in a mosque.

Dionysius uses the Arabic term 'imam' in his Syriac account of his audience with al-Maʾmun. In so doing he develops the meaning of the term to assert a political role for the Christian patriarchate within the caliphate. As imams, he allegedly told al-Maʾmun, patriarchs exhorted their congregations to peace and obedience. He stresses that this did not mean that he challenged al-Maʾmun's authority in such matters as capital punishment. Rather, Dionysius asserts that his authority had the same legitimacy as the caliph's, in that it flowed from the consent of his co-religionists, and that, like the caliph, the Christian imam assured the good order of the realm.[2]

1. Duri 2011: 49.
2. MS XII. 14 (IV, 519 / III, 68–69).

This justification for the authority of a Christian patriarch would also serve as a mandate for the caliph's troops to intervene against Dionysius' opponents. One of Dionysius' rivals, Abraham of Qartmin, known as 'Abiram', objected to Dionysius' omission of a traditional prayer. Dionysius represents this act of dissent as an affront to his role as imam, guaranteeing the good behaviour of the Christian masses.[3] Dionysius' self-fashioning as imam was both a defence of the status quo before the caliph and an excuse for an intervention against his rivals that was quite novel, and it gave him a power that few of his predecessors had enjoyed.

We are reliant on Dionysius himself for these statements. Naturally, we cannot know whether he really did say these things in front of the caliph. But it is striking that he expected the readers of his Syriac history to see the different resonances of the Arabic term. He seems to have envisaged a sympathetic audience that was already immersed in the elite Islamicate culture of the caliphate.

Marshall Hodgson defined 'Islamicate' as a 'social and cultural complex associated with Islam and Muslims . . . even when found among non-Muslims'.[4] I find the term useful here for describing the transfer of terminology from Muslims to non-Muslims in the caliphate, which allows us to recognize that Christians and Jews remained unconverted and bore different political rights from Muslims (and were therefore not 'Islamic'), but they were increasingly distinct from co-religionists in Byzantium and Francia, in terms both of their historical self-fashioning and of church governance and doctrine. This book describes how interactions with the caliphal government that was growing in power produced a distinctively Islamicate church.

This reuse of ideas of Islamic origin by a Christian leader illustrates the close links between Dionysius and Muslim rulers and intellectuals. But it also shows us that he considered it advantageous to replicate and adapt Islamic discourses for his own goals: to protect the rights of his co-religionists and to assert his own right to rule over them.[5] Moreover, the two phenomena that

---

3. MS XII. 12 (IV, 509–10 / III, 56).

4. Hodgson 1974: I, 59. Ahmed 2016: 157–70 observes several problems with Hodgson's model, especially the priority it gives to 'interior religion' and its implicit downgrading of mere culture. Ahmed fears that this distinction gives ammunition to those who wish to prioritize Salafist interpretations over 'Asian' forms of Islam.

5. Weitz 2018: 3–5 comments that studying the involvement of subaltern elites in adapting imperial ideas and institutions is an underexploited approach in the historiography of the

I discuss—the changes in the church as an institution and the changes in the way in which Christian leaders expressed their worldview—were connected. Christians were being asked to acknowledge the clergy (as opposed to lay aristocrats) as their leaders, to pay money in tithes and to accept collaboration with the state. These demands were rendered palatable because of the clergy's claim that they acted as an effective advocate of Christian rights before Muslim rulers at the same time as they asserted social boundaries between Christians and Muslims on an everyday level.

The Parting of the Ways?

Much recent scholarship has stressed the vagueness of boundaries between Muslims and others in the first centuries of Islam. One strand of this scholarship has highlighted the involvement of Christians in the earliest stages of the development of Islam. Scholars such as Guillaume Dye, Karl-Friedrich Pohlmann and Carlos Segovia have identified possible Christian contexts for the composition of parts of the quranic corpus.[6] Others, including Angelika Neuwirth, have pointed to the use of Christian concepts and vocabulary by the Quran's composer(s) that might have made it more attractive or comprehensible to Christian audiences.[7]

Fred Donner has taken a rather different approach by suggesting that Christians and Jews were a part of the believers' movement alongside converts from Arabian polytheisms. He argues that they remained so until the time of ʿAbd al-Malik (r. 685–705), whose deliberate and public anti-Trinitarianism was directed toward Christian members of the movement. It was only at this point, Donner asserts, that we can speak of Islam as a religion distinct from a more ecumenical believers' movement.[8]

A second strand of recent scholarship has seen Islam, Christianity and Judaism as distinct religious traditions but emphasized the porosity of their boundaries and the ease with which ideas and practices flowed between them. Shared rituals provide some of the most striking examples. Muslims continued to practice common rituals with their Christian neighbours, such as 'sniffing the

Islamic world, which tends to be interested in non-Muslim populations only through the lens of 'tolerance'.

6. Dye 2014; Dye 2011; Pohlmann 2013; Zellentin 2013; Segovia 2019.
7. Neuwirth 2010; Neuwirth 2014: esp. 25–26.
8. Donner 2010.

breeze', the Egyptian spring festival,[9] or the great feasts of Christmas, Easter and Pentecost.[10] Jack Tannous and David Taylor have noted the continuation of rituals of baptism (the baptism of St. John), which was used to protect children from the power of demons, among Muslims even into the twelfth century.[11]

Scholars of intellectual history can point to further examples of interconfessional exchange. Josef van Ess and Sidney Griffith have highlighted the role of *kalām* ('the science of dialectical speech') in the Islamicate world of this period. This was a method of debate that sought to elucidate the nature of God and moral questions on the basis of rational arguments, without presuming the primacy of any specific scripture. The prevalence of kalām produced a relatively open environment in which Jews, Christians and Muslims (as well as freethinkers, Zoroastrians, dualists and Manichaeans) could all engage in joint discussion.[12]

The *mutakallimūn* were not moral relativists, and they aimed to convince others of their own persuasive version of the truth. But the existence of a shared culture of debate, conducted in Arabic, facilitated the spread of ideas among thinkers of different religious traditions.[13] As Garth Fowden has argued, the so-called Abrahamic traditions were united by Aristotle much more than they were by Abraham.[14]

The prestigious role of Christians in the translation movement from Greek to Syriac to Arabic has long been known,[15] but Sidney Griffith also highlights the degree to which Christian translation and use of the Bible were themselves influenced by quranic language.[16] In a world where intellectuals refined their

9. Mas'udi, *Muruj*, II, 70. Cf. II, 364.

10. Mas'udi, *Muruj*, III, 405; Muqaddasi 182–83 / 153.

11. Tannous 2018: 375–76 and Taylor 2015.

12. Cook 1980; Griffith 2007 (and Griffith 2002a–g); Becker 2003: 390–91; van Ess 2006; Keating 2006: 8–9; Beaumont 2018a. Van Ess 2017 discusses the origins of kalām at 55–64 and surveys the presence of diverse religious groups (and religious ideas) in the 'salon culture' of Baghdad at 488–536. For Zoroastrians in religious discussions, see de Jong 2016: 230. Treiger 2014a stresses the origins of kalām in Christian Christological discussion. The importance of arguments from first principles in kalām may be partly the result of different communities' refusal to accept one another's scriptures because of rival accusations of tampering (*taḥrīf*) (cf. Hayek 1986: 39). On 'freethinking' in Baghdad, see S. Stroumsa 1999.

13. Rudolph 1994; Moss 2016b; Hughes 2015: 91–95.

14. Fowden 2014. Cf. also D. King 2013 and D. King 2014.

15. Gutas 1998; Troupeau 1991.

16. Griffith 2013.

positions in order to defend the superiority of their religious traditions, they also borrowed the ideas and expressions of their interlocutors to make their defences more persuasive.[17]

Both of these two scholarly trends—the focus on a Christian presence within the caliphate and the emphasis on the blurred boundaries between religious communities—can be seen in the work of Michael Penn. Penn has noted that Christians writing in Syriac in the Middle East rarely recognized that their seventh-century conquerors had a distinctive religion.[18] Even in the Abbasid period, he observes, some Christian authors minimized the distinctions between Islam and Christianity.[19] And authors such as Jacob of Edessa who sought to demarcate the different communities mostly spoke to deaf ears in addressing non-elite community members who did socialize with outsiders, whether Muslims or heretics.[20] Indeed, moral legislation can more readily provide evidence of the presence of perceived social 'problems' than prove that these problems found effective solutions. Penn argues that the ways of Islam and Christianity had not fully parted even by the ninth century.[21]

However, as Yonatan Moss points out in a review, it is unclear when Penn thinks the ways did part, and when we might speak of distinct Muslim and Christian religious communities or meaningfully use the words 'Muslim' and 'Christian' to describe historical individuals.[22] The fact that sources do not report, or choose to underplay, differences in practice or that members of religious communities shared ideas and practices does not mean that boundaries between communities did not exist. As Luke Yarbrough observes, Penn draws an analogy between the study of Judaism and Christianity on the one hand and the study of Christianity and Islam on the other.[23] But Penn's analogy fails to convince, both because Islam was a religion of the conquerors (who had the motivation and the means to assert their distinctiveness from the conquered) and because the seventh-century Near East already had a model of

---

17. Griffith 2002a–g and Beaumont 2018b. Griffith 2018: 3 comments that although Christian apologists did not treat the Quran as a canonical scripture, they quoted from it to support Christian teachings and used it as a source of 'felicitous Arabic expression'.

18. Penn 2015a: 53–63.

19. Penn 2015a: 74–96.

20. Penn 2015a: 66–70, 145–48, 151–52, 164–65.

21. Penn 2015a: 182.

22. Moss 2018.

23. Yarbrough 2016b. Also see Tannous 2018: 396.

discrete religious communities in the legislation of the Christian Roman empire, which could be imitated by its successors.

Creating Distinct Communities

Much of the recent scholarship that I have described here responds to two welcome developments in the study of religion and in the representation of the relationship between 'Islam' and 'the West'. The first is the turn away from seeing religious traditions as essentialized categories. Scholars are increasingly reluctant to speak simply of religions, as if they were static things born from the heads of prophets. Rather, religions are phenomena that are constantly 'in the making'.[24] They are also continuously linked by shared texts and narratives, which, in the case of the 'Abrahamic' religions in particular, serve as bridges for the transmission of ideas from one tradition to another.[25]

The anti-essentialism of approaches in religious studies in the late twentieth century is connected to the second development, namely growing efforts to chart the shared cultural legacies of 'the Muslim world' and 'the West', even to the point of breaking down the coherence of these two zones. Richard Bulliet's coinage of an Islamo-Christian civilization is a good example of this approach for its emphasis that Christendom and 'Islamdom' were far more similar to one another than they were to other political-cultural systems.[26]

Nevertheless, I follow Tom Sizgorich in stressing that something that monotheist traditions also had in common was their use of a series of social technologies that differentiated adherents of different religions into distinct communities and organized these into hierarchies. Figures such as John Chrysostom in fourth-century Antioch and Ahmad ibn Hanbal in ninth-century Baghdad underscored the need to keep outsiders and their ideas at a circumspect distance, even when the government granted these outsiders rights and legal protection.[27]

Chris Wickham, writing about conversion to Christianity in the Middle Ages, has recorded similar kinds of constraints in the area of institution building. He argues that the first stage of conversion, in which individuals accept a new religious identity, is fairly tolerant of older beliefs. But this tolerance is followed,

---

24. This literature is now very large, but see Nongbri 2013.
25. Cf. Gregg 2015.
26. Bulliet 2004.
27. Sizgorich 2012.

maybe generations later, by the development of church institutions that both police belief and enforce rules on tithing and marriage. This is the point at which some ideas are identified as having foreign origins and are censored.[28] Anthropologists have referred to this process as 'anti-syncretism', in which individuals' beliefs and practices are aligned to their public religious identities.[29]

Though people did share ideas and practices between religious traditions, some religious traditions also constituted themselves as distinct communities. Such communities were led by religious elites who generated revenues and redistributed them as charity according to criteria they themselves controlled.[30] These definitions of the 'deserving poor' might encourage community members to obey the strictures of a religious elite. Community members were bound by rules to limit social contact with and marriage to outsiders.[31] Such restrictions ensured that property remained within the community and hindered the ability of community members to make alliances with outsiders that might undermine the importance of its leaders. Without the ability to control marriages and revenues in this way, religious communities could not have persisted from generation to generation.

The existence of boundaries between communities was not a natural or inevitable development. After all, the use of practices from multiple religious traditions to mark different life stages or to govern different aspects of an individual's life has long been accepted in several East Asian societies.[32] Instead, we have to see the emergence of distinct confessional communities as the result of interaction between models and institutions present in the late Roman period on the one hand and the incentives and constraints provided by the caliphate on the other.

28. Wickham 2016.

29. Shaw and Stewart 2003.

30. For the control and definition of charity as a central feature of episcopal power, see Patlagean 1977; Norton 2007: 188; Benga 2013: 551; Brown 2002. For the significance of the Muslim charity tax (zakāt) and the gradual annexation of its collection and distribution by muḥaddithūn such as the followers of Ibn Hanbal, see Salaymeh 2016: 344; Mattson 2003: 39–40.

31. Here I draw on the broad literature on group maintenance in modern and contemporary studies, e.g., Gordon 1964; van der Berghe 1987; Goody 1976; Kalmijn 1998; van Leeuwen and Maas 2005.

32. Gellner 1997. See also Liu 1988: 175 for the incorporation of local cults into Chinese Buddhism and Palumbo 2015 for Taoism and Buddhism as two poles on a spectrum of belief in fourth-century China.

Clerical Leadership

It is important to recognize there was no single 'Islamic' response to religious and cultural diversity.[33] The Quran does conceive of humanity as divided into confessional communities, of which the Jews, the Christians and the Muslims are the most prominent.[34] And it conceives of pre-Muhammadan prophets as lawgivers, in the sense that they issued rules for their followers, as the Quran and the Torah both do to some extent.[35] These quranic presumptions may have encouraged Muslim rulers to classify conquered populations according to confessional identity and to endorse clerical leadership of these communities. Nevertheless, it is not clear that such expectations directly determined how non-Muslims were governed and classified in the Umayyad period, for instance. Nor is the meaning of the Quran's vague and often contradictory statements on the subject self-evident.[36] Neophyte Edelby has suggested that lawgiving by Christian patriarchs was a response to the quranic expectation that each religious community should have its own law.[37] But we might also argue that patriarchal lawgiving represents a continuation of pre-Islamic traditions of canon law and of bishops' official roles as judges and arbitrators in the Roman period.[38]

33. Dorfmann-Lazarev 2008: 75 gives this impression by describing the installation of a system of rules in the seventh century that lasted 'from the Muslim conquests to 1922'.

34. Karamustafa 2001 comments that the Quran's acceptance of multiple *ummāt*, defined by their respective religious traditions, is a peculiar combination of human dissent and divine preference (discussing Q 2:213, 16:120). W. Smith 1991: 81–86 argues that 'Islam' was unusual in launching into a world that already had traditions with a developed self-consciousness, a context that is reflected in the Quran's division of humanity into different 'religions' and its conception of 'Islam' as a closed system.

35. Van Bekkum 2007 discusses the Karaite treatment of the Torah as a source of law, which responded to Muslim expectations of prophets' acting as lawmakers but also undermined Rabbinic claims that the Talmud should be a source of law.

36. Donner 2011 argues that several of the state's administrative functions were retrospectively identified with terms used in the Quran that had originally lacked this specific sense. One example may be the use of the term *jizya* for the poll tax. The term *jizya* is associated in the Quran with the humiliation of the payers, but the poll tax in the caliphate may not have originally carried this association. Cf. Legendre and Younes 2015.

37. Edelby 1950–51. Simonsohn 2016b: 236 (citing earlier literature) suggests that in the eighth and ninth centuries Christians developed legislation that was more explicitly rooted in religious sources in response to Muslim expectations.

38. Humfress 2007: esp. 34–35, 155–71.

Alan Walmsley argues that 'rather than enervating Christian society, Muslim rule strengthened Christian communities and their leaders as they responded to new challenges and opportunities, encouraging them to become increasingly self-reliant, reinforcing self-identity and building a new cultural orientation'.[39] This is true up to a point. I certainly concur that the period following the conquest created new opportunities for minority groups and that Christians began to write in Arabic. But we should not take for granted the particular type of Christian leaders that arose or the kind of social identity that they attempted to reinforce. Clerical authority sometimes came at the cost of the authority of non-Muslim lay aristocrats. Furthermore, behind the general term 'Christian' lurk a number of competing confessions, only some of which were granted influence or recognition by the caliphal state.

A glance at the historiography of South Asia helps to illustrate how traditional leaders can play a key role as native informants for rulers and, in the process, exclude the narratives of others, contributing to the reclassification of religion. Historians of British India have highlighted the extent to which 'Hinduism' is a product of Muslim and Christian expectations of a religion as a discrete entity with its own scripture, on the model of the Bible or the Quran. But the classification of diverse beliefs and practices in different parts of India as 'Hinduism' also provided an opportunity to Brahmins who could articulate the common features of this Hinduism to their rulers. The reclassification of the religious landscape was thus not solely an imperial imposition but also the elevation of certain Sanskrit texts and Brahmin clergy as embodiments of the 'Hindu tradition'.[40]

Both Jews and Christians possessed institutions that supported community members with welfare and education and that restricted, or attempted to restrict, social interactions with those outside the community.[41] Nevertheless, it is important to recognize that clerics and intellectuals effected a redefinition of non-Muslim religions that responded to Muslim expectations but did so in a way that was varied and innovative.[42] For instance, centralized rule by the patriarchs of Antioch and Alexandria was portrayed as an intrinsic part of the

39. Walmsley 2007: 124.

40. Bayly 1988: 155–58, esp. 156: 'Traditional India was not a rigid society. It was British rule which made it so, codifying many localised and pragmatic customs into a unified and Brahminised "Hindoo Law" and classing people into immutable castes'. Cf. R. King 1999; Nongbri 2013: 109–17.

41. See further discussion in chapter 6.

42. Some non-Muslim religious traditions underwent much greater redefinition in response to Islamic expectations of religion and prophecy. See, for instance, van Bladel 2009: 234–37 for

Christian religion, which the caliph was obliged to support because of the agreements of his predecessors.[43]

One effect of the ability of patriarchs such as Dionysius to establish close links to the caliph and to speak on behalf of Christianity was that it isolated groups who might have called themselves Christians but who did not acquire this kind of access. Both Marcionites and Manichaeans held cosmological ideas that were quite unlike those of Nicene Christians (that is, of the mainstream confessions of both the Roman world and the caliphate). They also used very different scriptural canons. Both groups nonetheless called themselves Christians.[44] The fact that Arabic sources do not call them Christians is, in part, due to the success of other, more numerous and influential groups in appropriating exclusively the identity of the Christians who are accorded rights and status in the Quran.

By a similar token, the influence that Dionysius and his fellow patriarchs were able to wield at the Abbasid court and the revenues they were allowed to collect as a result from their co-religionists were substantial incentives toward the merger of smaller groups whose leadership did not enjoy such benefits. A very nearly successful attempt at union between the Julianists and the Jacobites may be an example of this process from the early Abbasid Jazira.[45]

Hierarchy and the Insecurity of Minorities

The authority granted to clerical leaders is sometimes represented as a sign of the tolerance embodied by Islamic methods of governing diverse societies, especially in the Abbasid and Ottoman periods.[46] But we should

---

the emphasis of Harranian 'pagans' on their following of Hermes as a monotheistic prophet who provides a *sunna* and a *sharī'a* and constitutes the Harranians as a *milla*.

43. I discuss this type of representation in chapter 8.

44. The sixth-century Syriac *Life of Aba*, 3, suggests that the term 'Christians' (*krīstyanē*) was used in one part of northern Iraq to refer to Marcionites rather than Nicene Christians; see the discussion in Fiey 1970b. For Mani as 'apostle of Christ', see Sundermann 1991, and for Manichaeans as 'true Christians', see Lieu 2007: 291. Both groups were sufficiently significant to merit refutations by John of Damascus and the patriarch Timothy I in the eighth century (Griffith 2016: 35; Briquel-Chatonnet et al. 2000: 9) and by 'Ammar al-Basri and Moses bar Kepha in the ninth (Hayek 1986: 42; Vööbus 1975).

45. See chapter 3.

46. Edelby 1950–51; Barkey 2005. Barkey and Gavrilis (2016) explicitly consider the Ottoman *millet* system a product of the 'pact of Umar'. Tas 2010: esp. 499 sees it as stemming from the religious pluralism of the seventh-century Constitution of Medina. The two latter claims are examples of wishful thinking.

remember that clerical powers were predicated on an arrangement that kept non-Muslims unarmed and inferior to Muslims in the confessional hierarchy, both of which were important mechanisms in enabling a small number of conquerors to maintain control over very large non-Muslim populations.[47]

Writing of the late Roman empire, Michael Maas has argued that the management and classification of ethnic and religious diversity was a key element in the maintenance of empires through hierarchies within an empire's borders and binary divisions vis-à-vis absolute outsiders.[48] 'Tolerance' of ideas and practices could be an element in what Brian Catlos calls an 'authoritarian toolbox'; it could be used to encourage minority groups to endorse a hierarchy in which they were placed in the middle and to share in collective prejudice against outsiders who were not deserving of such tolerance.[49]

In the case of the caliphate, Lena Salaymeh suggests that we might think of Jews and Christians as 'semi-citizens', dependent on the government for protection and recognition.[50] They were officially superior to religious outsiders (such as Manichaeans or pagans) or political enemies (such as the Romans), and they were accorded rights and legal protections. But they could also be rhetorically associated with these external groups in order to demonstrate the precariousness of their position in society. For instance, al-Jahiz accuses Christians in Baghdad of introducing ideas from Manichaeism or 'pagan' philosophy that disturb and confuse innocent Muslims.[51] Likewise, authors of *futūḥāt* works, such as Azdi, describe Christians in Syria as *mushrikūn*, the term used in the Quran for the 'polytheist' opponents of Muhammad among the Quraysh, who reportedly associated other deities with God. The futūḥāt works draw on this binary language and condemn Christians for their veneration of the cross and their prideful resistance to the Muslims.[52] Finally,

---

47. For comments on the Ottoman situation, critical of attempts to use this in modern multicultural debates, see B. Turner 2013: 287. Braude 2014 stresses that there were many different *millet* 'systems'.

48. Maas 2003. Cf. Schott 2008: 10–11; Lyman 2003.

49. Catlos 2014: 864.

50. For 'semi-citizenship' in the caliphate, see Salaymeh 2016.

51. Al-Jahiz, *Refutation of the Christians*, 4.7. See also discussions in Chokr 1993: 58–61; Gibson 2015: 124–25, 134, 189.

52. E.g., Azdi, *Futuh al-Sham*, 107, where ʿAmr ibn al-ʿAs writes to Abu ʿUbayda al-Jarrah after the conquest of Damascus that God will never allow disbelievers to overcome believers. For the cross as a (useless) battle standard at Yarmuk, Azdi, *Futuh al-Sham*, 220.

Dionysius of Tel-Mahre is very conscious of Muslim attempts to conflate Mesopotamian Christians with the Romans. He stresses that Mesopotamian Christians are the descendants of those conquered people who concluded a treaty with the Muslims and were promised religious rights and security in return for laying down their arms and paying taxes.[53] Dionysius' anxiety reflects the fact that not all Muslim elites felt that Christians deserved these protections: to some they were simply a defeated people whose role was to labour for and pay taxes to their conquerors.[54]

These three ninth-century examples all illustrate that some models of Muslim–Christian relations entailed a hierarchy in which Christian religious practice was tolerated and Christians were protected as long as they obeyed certain conditions. On the other hand, the narratives of conquest and the description of Christians in the Quran were sufficiently malleable that some Muslims could simply collapse humanity into a binary of Muslims and non-Muslims, which could be equated to the binaries of pure and impure, believer and nonbeliever, and conqueror and conquered. I believe that the insecurity of categories helped to keep Christian representatives as clients of the caliph's patronage and supporters of his rule, since it was ultimately the caliph's intervention that ensured that Christians' rights were protected in practice.

Writing about Minorities in the Caliphate

There is a temptation to write in general terms about the relationship between Muslims and non-Muslims within the caliphate. This is certainly a feature of several classic works on the treatment of non-Muslims that tend to conflate the experience of different Christian and Jewish confessions (while often ignoring the experience of Zoroastrians and Manichaeans).[55]

---

53. Discussed in chapter 7.

54. E.g., MS XII. 9 (IV, 499 / III, 36), where Tahir's governor in Edessa rejects the citizens' complaints when troops are billeted on them: 'Why do you complain to me[,] Christians? In the time of the Romans you lived off this land while our ancestors wandered in the desert. . . . Now [that] we have seized this land from the Romans by our swords, why do you find it so difficult to leave it? . . . Pay the tribute and shut up'.

55. Fattal 1958; Tritton 1930. Note the comments of R. S. Humphreys (1988: 257–58) on the ahistorical approach of these works. For Zoroastrians, see Choksy 1997, Savant 2013 and the important article of de Jong 2016. For Manichaeans, see Chokr 1993 and Reeves 2011.

In this book I attempt to differentiate between various confessional groups as well as between divergent social classes and regional experiences. One advantage of the chronicle sources and saints' lives that I employ in this book is that they often offer fine-grained detail, which allows us to escape the trap of generalizing about non-Muslims *tout court*, an approach that ignores differences among communities and change over time. These sources also allow us to track their authors' varied kinds of self-fashioning: sometimes the 'we' of the text is an ethnic group (Suryaye as opposed to Armenians, for instance) or the inhabitants of a region (the people of the mountain) rather than explicitly a religious group.[56] And they can reveal how the same word is used differently across time and space, sometimes even within the same source. Nevertheless, these sources do not present us with the unfiltered experiences of any given sector of the population. Rather, they are often interventions by sectarian entrepreneurs, who seek to present the past to engender behaviour in the present and/or to exclude groups or individuals from the collective identity that the authors imagine for their readers.

In this book I have chosen to write chiefly about the Jacobites, the Miaphysite confession that owed allegiance to the patriarch of Antioch and that chiefly employed Syriac as a liturgical language. My main source is the *Chronicle* of Michael the Syrian, a twelfth-century Jacobite patriarch, which embeds the work of the earlier Dionysius of Tel-Mahre.[57] I will make some comments shortly on the Christian confessions of the Middle East, on the terminology used to describe them and on my primary sources, especially on how we might identify Dionysius' work. But I should stress that my immediate purpose is to investigate how Dionysius and near-contemporary historians in the Jacobite tradition imagined their environment and to demonstrate that they were overwhelmingly concerned with the internal affairs of the Jacobite church and with their relationship to Muslims and their government. They do mention some other minority communities (the Melkites and the Maronites in particular), but this interest is secondary. I invoke examples from other communities for two purposes: in order to clarify causation in the Jacobite case and to show how Jacobites used the example of other communities in their own self-fashioning.

56. I discuss this vocabulary in chapter 9.

57. On Michael in general, see Weltecke 2003 and, more briefly, Weltecke 2010 and van Ginkel 2006.

The Miaphysites in the Sixth Century

The Jacobites were the most numerous and significant Miaphysite confession of the Middle East in the eighth century. Miaphysitism is a Christological position that asserts Christ's united human and divine nature, and many of its adherents have found it difficult or impossible to accept the Christological statements of the 451 council of Chalcedon.[58] Miaphysitism was briefly an imperial orthodoxy under the emperor Anastasius (491–518), and it was championed by the patriarch of Antioch Severus (d. 538), as well as by several sixth-century Syriac-speaking theologians, such as Philoxenus of Mabbug (d. 523).[59] Anastasius' successors Justin I (518–27) and Justinian (527–65) reasserted Chalcedonianism as the imperial orthodoxy, and Severus was exiled to the Egyptian desert. Nevertheless, Justinian and other sixth-century emperors did make several substantive attempts at union and tended to treat the Miaphysites as schismatics rather than simply heretics. There was periodic use of force against recalcitrant monks and clergy, and this was sometimes represented as persecution by Miaphysites, but the imperial court continued to be a source of (indirect) patronage and arbitration for Miaphysites, especially in Constantinople. It was against the background of this oscillating government policy that the missionary bishops John of Tella (d. 538), John Hephaestu and Jacob Baradeus (d. 578) ordained priests and consecrated bishops in an independent Severan Miaphysite hierarchy in the Levant, the Aegean and Anatolia.[60]

There is a tension in the attitudes of Severan Miaphysite authors of the sixth century toward the Roman emperor and the Chalcedonian churches. On one hand, emperors such as Marcian (450–57), who convened Chalcedon, and Justinian were sometimes reviled as persecutors.[61] But on the other hand, there was real hope for reconciliation, and Miaphysites such as John of

58. For Miaphysite Christology, see Lebon 1909 and Grillmeier and Hainthaler 2013. Winkler 1997 played a major role in popularizing the term 'Miaphysite'. Horn 2006: 8–9 prefers 'anti-Chalcedonian', but I avoid this because some Miaphysite churches did accept the disciplinary canons issued at Chalcedon, even if they rejected its Christology. Blaudeau 2016 discusses the debate on the theological terminology and summarizes the older literature.

59. On Severus, see Alpi 2009; Menze 2008: ch. 1. On Philoxenus, see Michelson 2014.

60. I sketch this narrative in Wood 2010: 167–70. See also Grillmeier and Hainthaler 2013: 187–91. There were other, non-Severan Miaphysite churches as well. The Julianists were the most prominent in our period.

61. Wood 2018b.

Ephesus (d. 588) conceived of the movement as 'an orthodoxy in waiting'. People accepted communion, attended services and visited pilgrimage sites in churches of the 'wrong' confession.[62] A number of significant Miaphysite intellectuals did cross over to the Chalcedonians in the late sixth century,[63] and Monenergism, the early seventh-century compromise formula, was briefly successful in reconciling substantial numbers of Miaphysites to accept communion with Chalcedonians.[64] In the sixth century the boundaries between Miaphysites and Chalcedonians were often blurred in practice, even if episcopal and priestly hierarchies diverged by about 600.

The Jacobite Church in the Seventh and Eighth Centuries

The history of the Miaphysites after the Arab conquests is frequently very obscure. The parts of Michael's *Chronicle* that discuss the Jacobite church are often limited to brief biographies of the patriarchs. Hagiography is particularly important for our understanding of the period circa 630–740, for which it provides localized insights into the experience of different Jacobite communities, especially in former Roman Mesopotamia.[65]

The Jacobite church of the seventh and eighth centuries was ruled by a patriarch of Antioch who claimed to be a successor of the patriarch Severus. But though the patriarchs retained the title of Antioch, they never ruled from the ancient capital of Roman Oriens and instead resided at rural monasteries in Syria and Mesopotamia.[66]

The role of the patriarchs was, in theory, to uphold the church's orthodoxy and the canons.[67] In practice, however, the patriarchs did not seek to regulate

62. Wood 2010: 166–73; Wood 2018b. Cf. Mikhail 2016: 178–80 on Egypt.

63. See Van Nuffelen forthcoming for the examples of Probus and John in the late sixth century. Another example is the Severan Miaphysite patriarch Paul the Black; see Brooks 1929 and Blaudeau 1996.

64. Moorhead 1981; Meyendorff 1989: ch. 10; Booth 2013a: 206–8; Haldon 2016: 37.

65. See chapter 1.

66. Hage 1966: 10–11. Note the useful list of monasteries in Hage 1966: 107–9. The two main surveys of Jacobite church structures in the caliphate are Hage 1966 and Nabe-von Schönberg 1977. Both suffer from a failure to recognize change over time, rooted in a lack of source criticism. And their division of material at the reign of Cyriacus means that they cannot trace important changes in attitudes across the period 750–850. Nevertheless, I have benefited from both books' clear exposition of the evidence.

67. Hage 1966: 14; Nabe-von Schönberg 1977: 12.

the church by issuing their own canons until the end of the eighth century, which is a sign of the church's greater centralization under the Abbasids. The patriarchs travelled widely to free prisoners, petition the caliph, investigate accusations against incumbent bishops and convoke synods.[68]

Occasionally patriarchs were appointed after being senior bishops. But it was not uncommon for unordained monks to be elected as patriarch and pass through all ranks of ordination on successive days, as occurred in the cases of George of Beltan and Dionysius.[69] Several patriarchs had served their predecessors as archimandrites or *syncelloi* (chief administrators), and this pattern may have allowed standing patriarchs to wield some influence over their succession.[70]

Unlike the church of the fourth century, the Jacobite church required that all bishops be monks.[71] In practice, patriarchal elections were dominated by a small number of monasteries. The most significant in the seventh century were Gubba Barraya ('the outer cistern') near Cyrrhus in northern Syria and Qenneshre ('the eagles' nest') also in northern Syria. Qenneshre was the most significant of these, and in the period 591–845 monks of Qenneshre held the patriarchate for 136 years.[72] After about 740 these two monasteries were joined by several others, all, not coincidentally, near to new political centres: these were Qartmin in the Tur Abdin (the modern monastery of Mor Gabriel), as well as the monastery of the Pillars and the monastery of Mar Zakkai, both in Raqqa.[73] The latter two had been dedicated in the sixth century but flourished in the conditions of mid-eighth-century caliphal patronage. Finally, the monastery of Mar Mattai near Mosul also deserves mention in this context because

68. Hage 1966: 18. Debié 2015a: 145–46 summarizes the itinerary of Dionysius himself.

69. Nabe-von Schönberg 1977: 10.

70. Hage 1966: 13. MS appendix III: V, VII.

71. A clear statement is given in Ibn Jarir 31, 101.

72. Tannous 2018: 171.

73. Honigmann 1954: 52. Palmer 1990 is focused on the monastery of Qartmin. For the foundation of the monastery of the Pillars by Justinian's wife, Theodora, see MS XI. 5 (IV, 414 / II, 420). The monastery was burned by the rebel Nasr ibn Shabath during the fourth fitna (MS XII. 7 [IV, 494 / III, 24]), but it recovered sufficiently for Dionysius to be ordained deacon there (MS XII. 10 [IV, 503 / III, 43]). The monastery of Mar Zakkai was also a sixth-century foundation whose monks had been persecuted by the Chalcedonians but which had also hosted several early Miaphysite synods. For two mosaic inscriptions in verse at Mar Zakkai, see Brock 2009: 292. Both monasteries continued to produce numerous bishops throughout the period under consideration.

of its significant influence over sees in Iraq. Chapters 2, 4 and 5 consider the changing fortunes of these monasteries under Abbasid rule.

These monasteries also stood out as important intellectual centres. The Church of the East patriarch Timothy envied the library of Mar Mattai.[74] Seventh-century Qenneshre was probably the place where translations of Greek philosophy and patristic theology were made for later generations of Syriac-speaking clergy.[75] In addition to being Dionysius of Tel-Mahre's home monastery, Qenneshre also trained the famous intellectuals Jacob of Edessa, Severus Sebokht and Thomas of Harkel.[76] Monasteries were significant scribal centres in this period, and manuscript copies were an important (and expensive) output of monastic intellectual life. One theme of Dionysius' history writing is Qenneshre's rivalry with the other great monasteries, sometimes expressed through Qenneshre's claims to an intellectual heritage and through denigration of the ignorance of his competitors.[77]

The Jacobite church of the eighth and ninth centuries contained three regions that the chronicles register as politically active. The first of these was Mesopotamia, which corresponds roughly to the Arabic Jazira. Wolfgang Hage has aptly described it as the 'hinge' of the church: it encompassed the cities of Edessa, Harran, Amida and Reshaina, whose bishops were all significant players in the election of the patriarch and where many of the major synods of the church were held.[78] Edessa, in particular, could draw on a prestigious history as a centre of Syriac scholarship in the Roman period and as the capital of the pre-Roman kingdom of Osrhoene.[79] Dionysius himself was the scion of several Edessene aristocratic families, the Gumaye and the Rusafaye.[80] However,

74. Barsoum 2003: 359. For Timothy's letter (Letter 43), see Tarán and Gutas 2012: 80. The library of Mar Mattai features prominently (if polemically, as a trove of magical spells) in the *Life of Rabban Hormizd*, 94/190.

75. D. King 2013; Tannous 2013; Tannous 2018: 169–98.

76. Barsoum 2003: 317, 325–28, 334–50; Tannous 2018: 171–72.

77. Michael the Syrian includes biographies of several Qenneshrite intellectuals (X. 24 on Athanasius Gamala; X. 26 [IV, 391 / II, 381] and BH HE I, 267 on Thomas of Harkel; XI. 7 on Severus of Samosata; a brief note on Severus of Sebokht at XI. 8 [IV, 423 / II, 433]; and XI. 15 and BH HE I, 289–91 on Jacob of Edessa). The bias in favour of Qenneshre in modern histories of Syriac thought may ultimately reflect our reliance on Dionysius and the traditions of his monastery.

78. See the list of synods in Hage 1966: 110–11 and Mounayer 1963.

79. Millar 2015d; Millar 2015e; Wood 2010: chs. 3–4.

80. See chapter 1.

the period under study witnessed serious challenges to Edessa's primacy with the new political prominence of Harran, which served briefly as the Umayyad capital, and Maypherkat, which was deliberately promoted by its bishop Athanasius Sandalaya.[81]

Raqqa, the capital city founded by Harun al-Rashid (786–809), was also the most significant Jacobite centre in the Jazira (and in the caliphate) throughout the period circa 780–880. Al-Rashid's foundation incorporated the ancient city of Callinicum as well as the military colony of Rafiqa.[82] Raqqa was the site of synods and the consecration of patriarchs, and influence with the Arab governors of Raqqa was central to patriarchal authority. Three of the four patriarchs who ruled in this period were from Raqqan monasteries.[83]

The second of the Jacobite church's active regions was Syria, which, in the usage of the chronicles, corresponds to the lands west of the Euphrates. However, we should note that Jacobite monasteries tended to be distributed inland, and the major cities of Roman Syria, Antioch and Apamea, remained in Chalcedonian hands. The official residence of the patriarch lay in the monastery of Eusebona, on the outskirts of Antioch (though Raqqa seems to have been much more important in practice).[84] There were also Jacobite sees further to the south, in Damascus and Jerusalem, but we hear very little of the activity of their bishops. This silence may be explained by the fact that most of our sources were produced in a small number of significant monasteries, and places without connections to these nurseries of patriarchs fell outside the sources' interest.

The third region that I discuss is Iraq. It is sometimes referred to in Syriac as 'Beth Parsaye', the land of the Persians, because it was the portion of the Jacobite church that had lain in the former Sasanian empire.[85] A Jacobite presence had been established here through refugees fleeing Roman persecution and through missions that targeted the Arab groups that lived between the Roman and Persian empires, as well as settled populations.[86] The most

81. See the discussion in chapters 2 and 4.

82. Heidemann 2006, 2011 and 2016 set out the economic context for the creation of the Raqqa conurbation. Eger 2014: 154–57 observes that Raqqa and the Balikh valley are unusual in having a higher settlement density under the Abbasids than in the late Roman period.

83. Note MS appendix III and the biographies in BH HE I.

84. MS XII. 11 (IV, 507 / III, 49).

85. E.g., MS XI. 14 (IV, 488 / II, 498).

86. Fiey 1970a: 127–30; Grillmeier and Hainthaler 2013: 192–95.

significant sees in this region were Takrit in central Iraq, whose bishop held
preeminence over the other bishops of the east, and Mosul, whose Jacobite
bishop traditionally resided in the monastery of Mar Mattai. A Jacobite bishop
was also appointed for Baghdad soon after the foundation of the city. Most of
the Jacobite bishops of the east were appointed by the bishop of Takrit, and
Takrit's degree of autonomy from the patriarch of Antioch was a recurrent
bone of contention.[87] This part of the Jacobite community was the first to use
Arabic as an intellectual and liturgical language, often alongside Syriac, and
this may be one reason for the flourishing of Takritian Jacobite intellectuals in
the ninth century.[88]

Finally, we will also be tangentially concerned with the Jacobites' relations with Miaphysites in Egypt, known locally as Theodosians.[89] The
Miaphysite patriarch of Alexandria was the only other Miaphysite patriarch
in this period besides Antioch, and the mutual recognition of the two patriarchs was a major factor in assuring the legitimacy of both. Miaphysite
churches in Nubia and Ethiopia were notionally subject to the patriarch in
Alexandria.[90] Syrian Jacobites were heavily involved in Egyptian affairs
around the turn of the seventh century, when the patriarch Damian of Alexandria may have controversially attempted to unite the two patriarchates
into a single authority.[91] But these links became more attenuated after the
Arab conquests, and it is only from about 740 that we see the reestablishment of regular contact between the patriarchs.[92] The close relationship
between the Theodosian and Jacobite churches is a particularly marked feature of the reign of Dionysius, and Dionysius' account of his own visit to
Egypt is a key feature of his history.

87. See the discussion in chapter 5. For Jacobites in Khurasan and Segestan, see Fiey 1973.

88. Vollandt 2015: 30–32.

89. For Theodosius of Alexandria (d. 567), who was styled the 'ecumenical patriarch' of
the Miaphysites, see Wood 2010: 181–82; Winkler 1999; Grillmeier and Hainthaler 1996:
53–59.

90. For Christianity in Nubia and Ethiopia, see Grillmeier and Hainthaler 1996: 263–335 and
Mikhail 2016: 191–203.

91. Blaudeau 1997.

92. I address aspects of the renewal of links between the patriarchs in chapter 7. One exception to the pattern stated here is the election of the Syrian Simeon: History of the Patriarchs,
Patrologia Orientalis (PO) 10:28. Mikhail 2016: 193 discusses the influence of Syrian theological
terminology in Egypt. Contact between Antioch and Alexandria in the seventh to ninth centuries is the subject of a forthcoming article by Phil Booth.

Chalcedonians and the Church of the East

Three other Christian confessions also enter the story: the Melkites, the Maronites and the Church of the East (sometimes referred to as 'Nestorians'). Both the Melkites and the Maronites were Chalcedonians, the confession that had been the Roman imperial orthodoxy since 512. Chalcedonians are Dyophysites, who believe in the dual human and divine natures of Christ. In various versions, Chalcedonianism continued to be the faith of the emperor, and there were Chalcedonian patriarchs in Rome, Constantinople, Alexandria, Antioch and Jerusalem. So in addition to being a significant force in the Middle East, especially in Palestine and the region of Damascus, Chalcedonians were also the only Christian confession to be in communion with Christians in the far west.[93] What is more, they, like the Jacobites, had colonies in Iraq and in places further east, extending into Central Asia.[94]

Chalcedonians had traditionally used Greek as a liturgical language in the eastern Mediterranean, but many Middle Eastern sees also employed Syriac. Hellenophone Melkite communities were among the first Christian populations to shift to Arabic, and the first places in the Levant in which Christians used Arabic as a literary language were the Chalcedonian monasteries of Sinai and Mar Sabas in Palestine.[95] However, there continued to be Melkites who used Syriac, especially in Edessa, and the Melkite monasteries on the Black Mountain near Antioch housed Syriac scriptoria.[96]

Chalcedonianism was splintered in the seventh century by two attempts at compromise formulas by the emperor Heraclius (610–41). In the aftermath of his victory over the Persians, Heraclius' patriarch Sergius (d. 638) proposed two Christological initiatives, Monenergism and Monotheletism, which sought to bridge differences between different movements among the Chalcedonians and the Miaphysites by asserting that Christ's natures enjoyed a single united energy or a single united will. This compromise was, initially, very successful in winning over both Chalcedonians and Miaphysites in the Levant. But it shattered as Heraclius and his successors faced defeat by the

---

93. D. Reynolds n.d.; Griffith 2008a: 138; Griffith 2008b.
94. Nasrallah 1976.
95. Vollandt 2015: 27–28; Eddé, Micheau and Picard 1997: 94, 100–101, 152–54; Griffith 2002g.
96. Possekel 2015; Thomson 1962 and Mouterde 1932 on Edessa; Brock 1990 on the Black Mountain.

Arabs and Monotheletism was eventually abandoned at a council in Constantinople in 680/81.[97]

The Chalcedonians who followed the post-681 orthodoxy were known as Melkites ('followers of the king'), whereas those who opposed it and continued to adhere to Monotheletism were known as Maronites, after the famous monastery of Mar Maron in central Syria.[98] By the ninth century, the Melkites were clearly the dominant group, and Muslim historians of the time tend to divide the Christians into three groups, the Melkites, the Jacobites and the 'Nestorians', often ignoring smaller groups such as the Maronites and the Julianists or discussing them separately.[99]

The third major confession of the Middle East was the Church of the East, which had been the main Christian confession in the Sasanian empire. It adopted a heavily Dyophysite theology that could sometimes be reconciled with Chalcedon. Christians in the Sasanian world had suffered periodic persecution at the hands of the shahs, but this was interrupted by various experiments by the shah to give a measure of authority to the bishop of Seleucia-Ctesiphon and to try to influence the behaviour of Christians through church institutions.[100] The bishops of Seleucia-Ctesiphon are normally referred to as catholicoi, nominally autocephalous leaders of a part of the patriarchate of Antioch, but from the mid-sixth century onward they began to style themselves patriarchs, that is, of the same rank as Antioch, Constantinople and Alexandria.[101]

The Church of the East was probably the greatest beneficiary of the dissolution of the frontiers between Rome and Persia and the creation of a new capital in Baghdad. After the seventh century the church created new sees outside its traditional territory, both in the west (in Jerusalem, Damascus, Edessa and Egypt) and in the east (in Khurasan, Central Asia and China).[102] The church

97. See Booth 2013a and Jankowiak 2009 for their detailed discussions of these controversies.

98. Griffith 2008b: 218. For the appropriation of the term 'Melkite' as a polemical term that was accepted by the community (as referring to Christ as king of heaven, rather than the Roman emperor), see Treiger 2014b. Dionysius tends to refer to the 'Melkites' of his own day as Chalcedonians, but I have not followed his usage because the Maronites were also Chalcedonians.

99. Mas'udi, Muruj, II, 282; al-Jahiz, Refutation of the Christians, 4.27; Biruni 282; Conrad 1981: 97. For Mas'udi's separate discussion of the Maronites, allegedly drawn from one Qays, a Maronite historian, see Tanbih, 211–12, 217–18.

100. Wood 2013.

101. Macomber 1968: 194–97. Cf. Fiey 1967.

102. Dauvillier 1948: esp. 273–74 on the western sees; Wood 2013: 237–38.

transferred its patriarchate to Baghdad as well, and it was successful in preventing other confessions from establishing clergy above the rank of bishop in the city.[103] Like the confessions of the Levant, the Church of the East employed Syriac as a scholarly and liturgical language, written in its distinctive 'eastern' script, but this was increasingly supplemented by Arabic in the second half of the eighth century.[104]

The Term 'Jacobite'

I employ the term 'Jacobite' to denote Miaphysite Christians under the patriarchate of Antioch. This appellation differentiates them from Miaphysites in Egypt and Armenia, but it includes Miaphysites in Iraq who also fell under Antioch's authority (and are of interest to the West Syriac historians I discuss). It also distinguishes them from other groups of Miaphysites who had rejected Severus' theology, such as the Julianists, who enjoyed a following in Syria, Iraq, Armenia and Arabia.[105]

The term Jacobite derives from the missionary Jacob Baradeus, who was responsible for consecrating a Miaphysite patriarch of Antioch after a substantial hiatus. It is the standard term used for Miaphysites in the patriarchate of Antioch by many medieval commentators in Arabic, both outsiders[106] and 'Jacobites' themselves.[107] It has also become part of the normal terminology of modern scholarship in Christian Arabic.[108] One of the advantages of this term is its stress on the crystallization of a distinct historical tradition and church institutions after the end of the Roman empire. Another is its clear differentiation of this group of Miaphysites from others.

---

103. For the ability of the Church of the East to block Melkite attempts to place a patriarch in Baghdad, see Fiey 1980: 129–30. In the tenth century the major coup by the Church of the East was to be recognized as the final court of appeal for all Christians in the caliphate, leading Fiey to refer to it as the unofficial second religion of the caliphate (Fiey 1980: 29, 208–10). For the appropriation of the originally polemical term 'Nestorian', which came to be used as a non-controversial autonym in Arabic, see Rassi 2015: 158–62.

104. Vollandt 2015: 33. For the evolution of eastern Syriac script out of the monumental *estrangela* script used at Edessa, see Briquel-Chatonnet 2001.

105. Jugie 1937. For Julian of Halicarnassus and his rivalry with Severus, see Moss 2016c.

106. See, e.g., Mas'udi, *Muruj*, II, 329; Biruni, 282.

107. See, e.g., the Jacobite Takritian Ibn Jarir. Khoury-Sarkis 1967: 308.

108. Griffith 2008a; Griffith 2013; Platti 2015; Thomas 2008; Roggema 2009.

We should also note that the term 'Jacobite' is attested as an autonym in Syriac as well as in Arabic. It is used by John of Ephesus in his *Ecclesiastical History* to refer to the party of Miaphysites that was supported by Jacob during a schism in the late sixth century. By the following century, it could be applied to the whole confession in the Levant. A Syriac *Life of Jacob Baradeus*, falsely attributed to John of Ephesus, reports:

> When the heretics and the orthodox met, they would ask, 'Who are you?' and the orthodox would answer, 'We, for our part, are of the faith of Jacob, the first apostle (who was termed the brother of Our Lord in the Flesh), which this divine Jacob also proclaims to us', while the adversaries would answer, 'Of the faith of Ephrem of Amida [a famous Chalcedonian persecutor of the sixth century]' . . . and hence throughout Syria and in the lands of Persia and of the Armenians[109] the expression 'We are of the faith of Jacob' became current, and in Alexandria and in Egypt 'We are of the faith of Theodosius'. Hence, on this account, believers in Egypt were named Theodosians and the Suryaye were called Jacobites.[110]

This account recognizes that 'Jacobite' had become a widespread term for the confession. It is understandably defensive, because only heretical groups were generally known by the name of a founder; accordingly, the author refers to his own group as 'the orthodox'. Use of the term for Levantine Miaphysites seems to have been sufficiently widespread at the time of writing that the author provides an additional etymology for it, linking it to Jacob the lesser, brother of Christ, to blunt any potential criticism that the Jacobites were followers of a heresiarch.[111] Dionysius places the term 'Jacobite' in the mouth the

109. The author may refer here to communities in Armenia that fell under the patriarch of Antioch rather than under the Armenian catholicos at Dvin. For these communities, see Honigmann 1954: 114.

110. John of Ephesus, *Lives of the Eastern Saints*, PO 19:256. This text was written between 628 and 741, when it was copied in the monastery of Peshilta in the Jazira (Saint-Laurent 2015: 99). Given the absence of allusions to Muslims I would veer toward a seventh-century date. Saint Laurent 2015: 105–7 suggests that the text attributes to the Jacobites *in general* the saint's holy poverty.

111. For parallels in the appropriation of originally polemical terms for Melkites and Nestorians, see Treiger 2014b and Rassi 2015: 158–62, respectively. The term 'Theodosian' is attested as an autonym for Egyptian Miaphysites in the *History of the Patriarchs*. However, in the long term, Muslim governments tended to recognize only Jacobites, Melkites and 'Nestorians' as Christian confessions, forcing Egyptian Miaphysites to present themselves as Jacobites. Given

caliph al-Ma᾽mun, a patron to whom he was sympathetic, so he does not seem to have found the term polemical and recognized its common currency as a public term for the community.[112]

Some scholars have preferred to use the terms 'West Syrian' or 'Syrian Orthodox' to describe the group that I call Jacobite. These terms use the regional or ethnic adjective 'Syrian' to describe a confession (in the manner of early modern and modern Orthodox churches, like Russian Orthodox or Bulgarian Orthodox). Implicitly, this usage also stresses the use of the Syriac language. The relationship between language, region and ethnicity was debated in antiquity, and much of the surviving source material is in Syriac, which was also the main liturgical language. But the church does not map neatly onto the Syria of either Roman or caliphal administrative geography (with capitals in Antioch and Damascus, respectively, both of which were Chalcedonian centres).[113] Nor were all Levantine Miaphysites speakers of Syriac: others spoke Greek or Arabic, and it is not clear which ethnonym they might have used for themselves. The term 'Syrian Orthodox' is attested in sources of the period, but very rarely,[114] and I avoid it here because its conflation of ethnicity, religion, language and confession mostly belongs to a later period. I use the term 'West Syriac' to refer to literature that was written in western Syriac scripts but transcended the confessional boundaries of Jacobites, Melkites and Maronites.[115]

The Sources

My discussion draws mainly on the Syriac history of Dionysius of Tel-Mahre, which does not survive independently but is quoted extensively in medieval compilations, especially the *Chronicle* of Michael the Syrian. Dionysius was the Jacobite patriarch during the reigns of the caliphs al-Ma᾽mun and al-Mu῾tasim (833–42). He was a monk from Qenneshre, the famous nursery of patriarchs and centre of scholarship. But he was elected patriarch without any former ordination. At the death of the patriarch Cyriacus, the assembled

---

that Jacob Baradeus had no connection to Egypt, this renaming spawned various attempts to identify the Jacob after whom they were named; see Seleznyov 2013.

112. MS XII. 14 (IV, 518 / III, 67) and MS XII. 12 (IV, 510 / III, 57).

113. Note the useful maps in Frend 1972 for the situation in the sixth century.

114. See, e.g., *Life of Theodota*, 115.

115. Baumstark 1922: 335–43 surveys the Syriac literature of the Melkites and the Maronites, which is ignored entirely in some surveys (e.g., Ortiz de Urbina 1965).

bishops had been considering Mar Atunos, a learned theologian and biblical commentator, until a bishop named Theodore of the monastery of Mar Jacob of Kaishum recommended the young Dionysius, who had been staying at the monastery for two years.[116]

Dionysius does not tell us directly why he was selected as patriarch, and he hides behind a protestation of modesty. But in the course of his narrative he highlights his close relations with al-Ma'mun, his good command of Arabic and his knowledge of Islamic culture more generally, and it may be that he believed that these diplomatic skills made him peculiarly suited to the role. Connected to these skills was Dionysius' own aristocratic background as the scion of the Rusafaye and Gumaye families of Edessa, whose fortunes he charts in his history.[117]

Dionysius composed a chronicle in sixteen books, which covered the period from 582 to 842, up to the deaths of the Byzantine emperor Theophilus and the caliph al-Mu'tasim. Eight of the books were devoted to ecclesiastical history, and these were probably placed before the secular sections.[118] This innovative division of material was highly influential for Dionysius' medieval successors, who praised him for his reliability.[119] Rudolf Abramowski, whose 1940 work is the only monograph on Dionysius, describes him as a Syriac Thucydides for his complex vision of the politics of his own day.[120] Yet Dionysius, like many other Christian authors from the caliphate in the eighth and ninth centuries, has not been included alongside seventh-century figures such as Ishoyahb of Adiabene (d. 659) or Jacob of Edessa (d. 708) in academics' general knowledge of Christianity in the Near East.[121]

116. MS XII. 10 (IV, 502 / III, 41). Qenneshre had been pillaged a few years earlier, which is why Dionysius had been at the monastery of Jacob of Kaishum: MS XII. 11 (IV, 597 / III, 49).

117. For further discussion, see chapters 1–2.

118. Palmer et al. 1993: 86–87. There are general treatments in Wright 2001: 196–200, which gives a clear narrative, though Wright wrongly thought that the *Chronicle of Zuqnin* was a short recension of Dionysius' history; Hoyland 1997: 416–19; Barsoum 2003: 386–87; Hilkens 2018: ch. 19; and Debié 2015a: 143–49. Tel-Mahre has been identified as Tell Sheikh Hasan, a site on the Balikh River some forty kilometres south of the modern Turkish-Syrian border. It may have been a village owned by Dionysius' family (Debié 2015a: 144).

119. Weltecke 2003: 197–208.

120. R. Abramowski 1940: 116.

121. See, for example, the distribution of entries in the *New SCM Dictionary of Church History* (Benedetto 2008).

In the preface to his text, Dionysius provides important details on his own sources and models. He addresses the work to his spiritual son, John the metropolitan of Dara, who, he says, has been trained in orthodoxy 'from the softening of [his] fingernails to the whitening of [his] hair':

> Although wise men have written about the earliest times, from the beginning of Creation until the time of Constantine the believing king, and told about the making of creatures and the succession of generations since Adam and the number of their years and about the kings who have ruled and the size of their territories, their writings are not termed histories but chronographies, that is time writings, such as those made by Josephus, Andronicus, Africanus, Annianus, George of Raggath, John of Antioch and Eusebius son of Pamphilus [of Caesarea].
>
> The first to write ecclesiastical history, on the other hand, was the same Eusebius, followed by Socrates, Sozomen, Theodoret, Zachariah [of Mytilene], Elijah, John of Asia [of Ephesus] and last of all the priest Cyrus of Batna.
>
> Other men charted the succession of the years; I mean Jacob of Edessa and John the stylite of Litarba.
>
> Narratives resembling ecclesiastical history have been written by Daniel son of Moses of Tur Abdin,[122] John son of Samuel of the western region [i.e., Syria and the coast?],[123] a certain Theophilus and Theodosius, metropolitan of Edessa.[124] But those whom we have just mentioned made their narratives in a brief and fragmentary way, without preserving either chronological exactitude or the interrelatedness of events. One of these writers was Theophilus of Edessa, a Chalcedonian who regarded it as his birthright to loathe the orthodox. His presentation of all events that involved one of our number is fraudulent.
>
> So we will start with traditional practice and begin where Cyrus of Batna left off; we shall . . . take from this man some details here and there from parts which are reliable and do not deviate from the truth.[125]

---

122. Barsoum 2003: 352.

123. Baumstark 1922: 273. Cf. Brooks 1906.

124. Debié 2015a: 144 notes that this Theodosius was Dionysius' brother and, like him, a monk of Qenneshre. He was highly trained in Greek, Syriac and Arabic and, like Dionysius, was a client of the general ʿAbd Allah ibn Tahir and the caliph al-Maʾmun. He served the patriarch Cyriacus in Iraq and accompanied his brother to Egypt. See further below.

125. MS X. 20 (IV, 378 / II, 357–58). Translation in Palmer et al. 1993: 91–92.

Dionysius is not, technically speaking, providing a list of his sources here but rather commenting on the different ways in which writing about the past has been undertaken and which of his predecessors he proposes to follow.[126] He may have also used Arabic[127] and Greek[128] sources as well as other Syriac texts.[129] I read his preface as a statement that he draws his model from the ecclesiastical historians from Eusebius to Cyrus of Batna, and this determines his starting point. He is aware of other writers who have been active more recently and who have composed chronological tables (like Jacob of Edessa) or more fluent narratives (like Daniel of Tur Abdin). But he differentiates historians such as Daniel from ecclesiastical historians proper because the former, in his view, are not concerned with chronology or with relating events to one another. Dionysius seems to have taken pride in his ability to link events that took place at different times, to track long-term trends and to use

126. Palmer et al. 1993: 92.

127. Anthony 2010 discusses Dionysius' use of an Arabic Muslim source on the assassination of Umar I. Yarbrough 2016a: 190 indicates that he used an Arabic Muslim source on Umar II. Conterno 2014 suggests that some of the material shared by Dionysius, Agapius and Theophanes Confessor derives from an Arabic Muslim source rather than from Theophilus of Edessa. Debié 2015b: 379 argues for Dionysius' use of a Muslim Arabic source on the conquest of Cyprus (which has been transmitted by a Christian intermediary) and Muslim Arabic sources on the deaths of the caliphs Uthman and Yazid I.

128. Among these is a Greek source critical of the emperor Nikepheros: MS XII. 15 (IV, 530 / III, 70); see the discussion in Dickens 2010: esp. 16–18 and Hilkens 2018: 270. Debié 2015b: 378 argues for Dionysius' use of several Greek sources for the seventh and early eighth centuries. One is an account of the reigns of Heraclius and Constans II. This is shared with Theophanes and is well informed about matters in Constantinople as well as the frontier. A second is an account of Constantine IV deposing his brothers that Theophanes did not share.

129. Dionysius may have had access to Syriac documentary sources such as letters (e.g., the letter to Severus bar Mashqa in XI. 14) or synodical lists (e.g., the union with the Armenians in XI. 20). Brooks 1906 identifies a source that Dionysius shares with the ninth-century Greek historian Theophanes that extended to 746. Because of its Jacobite slant, Brooks suggested that this might be John son of Samuel, but this is speculative. Debié 2015b: 378 suggests that John son of Samuel is the author of material that describes natural disasters in northern Syria, the fall of Arwad to the Arabs and the succession of bishops in Apamea. Brock 1973: 337 notes the use of a Syriac account of Maximus the Confessor attributed to one Shem'un of Qenneshre (drawing on Syriac Maronite sources), by both X1234 and MS. Both chronicles probably obtained their knowledge of Shem'un through Dionysius.

chronological tables to situate and interrelate the various sources that were available to him.[130]

Dionysius gives special prominence to Theophilus of Edessa. Theophilus was a Maronite[131] who had written a history while serving as an astrologer at the court of al-Mahdi.[132] Dionysius objects to his treatment of Jacobite affairs, but if the 'man' in the final paragraph does indeed refer to Theophilus, Dionysius also seems to feel the need to apologize for making such extensive use of him.

Given that Dionysius presents himself as a continuator of Eusebius, whose ecclesiastical history celebrated the conversion to Christianity of the Roman emperor Constantine, it is worth stressing how disinterested he is in the ecclesiastical history of the Roman empire of his own day. Dionysius' ecclesiastical history is restricted to the caliphate, to the Miaphysite sees of Antioch and Alexandria (perhaps with occasional glances to other confessions, but always located in the caliphate). It is hard to discern how Dionysius dealt with the aftermath of the Arab conquests and the separation of ecclesiastical politics in the caliphate from the influence of the Byzantine emperors. It may be that Michael's *Chronicle* preserves an editorial statement from Dionysius, located around 720 in his text, in which he explains his omission of the succession of the patriarchs outside the caliphate with reference to their persecution of the Miaphysites, the political boundaries that now separated the churches and the descent of the Byzantine church into deeper heresy.[133] I intend to discuss the seventh-century material in Michael's *Chronicle* in future work.

We should always bear in mind that we do not have a discrete text for Dionysius' history.[134] The attribution of material to Dionysius is often a matter of opinion, based on the reuse of his work by four medieval historians: Bar Hebraeus (in part 1 of his *Ecclesiastical History* and in his *Secular Chronicle*), the author of the *Chronicle to 1234* (for which only the secular part is fully extant), Elias of Nisibis (who draws notices on Jacobite ecclesiastical history after 754

130. Palmer et al. 1993: 88–89 and 93.

131. Wright 2001: 163–64.

132. On Theophilus, see Hoyland 2011, but note the objections to Hoyland's attempts to attribute material to him in Conterno 2014, Papaconstantinou 2013 and Debié 2015a: 27–31 and 139–42. There is a summary of the state of the debate in Hilkens 2014: 363–66.

133. MS XI. 18 (IV, 452–54 / II, 486–87). This passage is translated in Palmer et al. 1993: 93–94, which attributes it to Dionysius. I also discuss it in Wood 2019.

134. One fragment survives, translated in R. Abramowski 1940: 19, in which Dionysius describes heresy in the late sixth century.

from Dionysius)[135] and, most importantly, Michael the Syrian in books 10 to 12 of his *Chronicle*.[136] These compilers may have added their own observations to their sources[137] and are likely to have drastically abbreviated their material in many instances.[138] Finally, there is also the possibility that the fragmentary *Chronicle to 813* is also a summary of Dionysius, since it covers a similar mix of Jacobite ecclesiastical history and the political history of the Jazira and Byzantium.[139]

Even when material in the medieval compilations does seem likely to derive from Dionysius, we cannot be sure whether it has been summarized by the medieval compiler himself or by an intermediate source.[140] One possible candidate for such an intermediate source, which was used by Bar Hebraeus, the *Chronicle to 1234* and Michael the Syrian is the *Chronicle* of Ignatius of

135. Elias of Nisibis 175/83 is the first use of Dionysius (the death of the patriarch Iwannis). Elias also quotes Daniel of Tur Abdin ('son of Moses') for the election of Athanasius Sandalaya (168/80) and the entry of Marwan II into Damascus (170/81). Unfortunately, there is a lacuna in our manuscript of Elias that covers the reigns of Cyriacus and Dionysius, i.e., where one would expect him to have made greatest use of Dionysius.

136. On Michael and Bar Hebraeus in general, see Debié 2015a: 149–55; on Michael, see also Weltecke 2003: esp. 44, 163–78 for the innovative layout of the text into columns treating ecclesiastical history, secular history and natural disasters. Hilkens 2018 discusses the *Chronicle to 1234*.

137. This is a marked feature of Bar Hebraeus' histories in particular. Note, for instance, his eyewitness testimony on the gates of Rafiqa (BH Chron 124/160) and his statement that the people of Cyrrhus had converted to Islam, which seems to reflect the situation of his own day rather than that of the ninth century (BH HE I, 337). He also retrojects the term 'maphrian' onto the leaders of the eastern Jacobites, an anachronism that conceals the many different titles that were (sometimes controversially) employed in the period under study.

138. Van Ginkel 1998 observes that in the third part of John of Ephesus' *Ecclesiastical History*, which is extant and allows us to trace Michael's editing methods, Michael has reduced the length of the material by about 80 percent. Michael also removes references to the Tritheist movement, which was significant only in John's own lifetime.

139. All the scenes in the *Chronicle to 813* are attested in Michael, though the former is often less detailed. There are some changes of emphasis: the *Chronicle to 813* is more critical of patriarchs who held diplomas, for instance. The *Chronicle* is dated paleographically to the tenth or eleventh century, and the fragment as we have it lacks both a beginning and an end. See further Brooks 1900.

140. Palmer et al. 1993: 89–90. Mazzola 2017: 446 describes the working methods of these compilers, 'selecting, excerpting, possibly shortening or modifying the excerpts and finally organizing the excerpts in a new composition according, respectively, to thematic and chronological criteria'. Michael, Mazzola suggests, was happy to use earlier authors' abbreviations if they suited his purposes.

Melitene, who claims to have used the chronicles of Jacob of Edessa and Dionysius but to have supplemented them with Greek sources.[141]

Nevertheless, in spite of this ambiguity there are two reasons that we can be relatively hopeful about the possibility of attributing material to Dionysius. First, there are a number of fragments for which we do possess Dionysius' *ipsissima verba* through direct quotation, where later compilers have identified the authorship of scenes that are known in greater detail in other compilations or where sections in the first person allow us to establish authorship. Van Nuffelen, Conterno, and Mazzola have organized these, and they are repeated here in the list of fragments of Dionysius of Tel-Mahre in the backmatter.[142]

From these extracts we can be sure that Dionysius began his history with an account of the schism between Antioch and Alexandria in the late sixth century and their reconciliation at the union of 616. He also dedicated a detailed discussion to the elections of Iwannis II and his successor, George of Beltan, during the anarchic conditions that surrounded the fall of the Umayyad caliphate about 750.

Unsurprisingly, Dionysius also recounted a number of scenes from his own life that are quoted directly by Michael.[143] He was perhaps most valued as a witness to the events of his own lifetime that were taken as models for later patriarchs. These include his own election, his conflicts with the monks of Gubba Barraya and the bishops of Takrit, his meeting with al-Ma'mun, his visits to Egypt and his discussion of the meaning of the name 'Syria'.

Second, we can observe from the texture of Bar Hebraeus, Michael and the *Chronicle to 1234* alike that their detailed narratives stop abruptly around Dionysius' death; they are not able sustain a continuous level of narrative into the

---

141. See MS XIII. 1 (IV, 546 / III, 115) for Ignatius' statement that he has used Jacob and Dionysius 'without altering them in any way' (cf. Hilkens 2018: ch. 21). Ignatius' secular history ran from Constantine to his own day. However, Michael does not offer the succession of the bishops of Melitene until 869, which may imply that he did not make use of Ignatius for the ecclesiastical part of his *Chronicle* before this point. Michael and X1234 share a source on Roman imperial and Jacobite ecclesiastical matters from 842–1089, which is probably Ignatius (Hilkens 2018: 294). X1234 may receive material from John of Ephesus through Ignatius' abbreviations, as well as using John directly: Hilkens 2018: 174. On Ignatius in general, see van Ginkel 2010. Michael also drew directly on an otherwise unknown account of the Arab conquest of Syria by one Guria, which may be a seventh-century composition: I discuss this further below, in note 161.

142. Van Nuffelen, Conterno and Mazzola n.d.

143. R. Abramowski 1940: 26. In many cases Elias of Nisibis indicates passages extant in Michael as being Dionysian.

middle of the ninth century. This disconnect indicates that the medieval compilers did not have access to any substantial histories for the ninth century other than that of Dionysius. This hypothesis seems to be confirmed by the fact that the medieval compilations do not name any historians between Dionysius and Ignatius. Rudolf Abramowski is likely to be correct when he comments that Ignatius' coverage of the late ninth and tenth centuries was very scant indeed.[144]

Michael the Syrian's *Chronicle* is by some margin the most detailed of the three sources, and I use it most intensively. I focus on the ecclesiastical history of the early ninth century, both because this period offers the richest evidence and because this material is most likely to be Dionysian.[145] On the basis of the dramatis personae, the changing agendas of the author(s) and the density of the material, we can summarize the ecclesiastical history content in Michael as follows:

Section 1: The schism and union between Antioch and Alexandria and the attempted union between Heraclius and the Jacobite patriarch Athanasius Gamala, circa 585–640
Section 2: The succession of Jacobite patriarchs, 640–740
Section 3: The anarchy in the church during the Abbasid revolution and the dominance of the Qartminite patriarchs, 740–70
Section 4: The centralized patriarchates of George, Cyriacus and Dionysius, 770–840

Section 1 makes use of multiple sources, some of which are more focused on the upper echelons of the Jacobite hierarchy whereas others centre on local affairs in the city of Edessa. It is uncertain what of this material can be associated with Dionysius aside from the account of the schism with Egypt.

Section 2 is markedly more sparse: Michael draws heavily on non-Jacobite narratives in order to cover this section and tends to offer only very brief narratives of the deeds of the Jacobite patriarchs themselves.[146] Section 2 also includes accounts of the martyrdoms of Christian Arabs at the hands of

---

144. R. Abramowski 1940: 17. MS XIII. 1 (IV, 544 / III, 112) observes Ignatius' lack of interest in the Arabs, which also makes it unlikely that the secular material in books 11 and 12 of Michael, which covers the Abbasid revolution and the fourth fitna, have passed through Ignatius.

145. Bar Hebraeus is much more brief and also more closely focussed on the Jacobite patriarchs themselves. He covers the same period as books 11 and 12 of Michael in twenty-two pages of Wilmshurst's translation.

146. A comparison with Bar Hebraeus shows that this sparseness is most likely not the result of heavy editing; rather, the relevant sources were simply unavailable to later compilers.

al-Walid as well as saints' lives, including several of Qenneshrite monks. The latter are likely to be Dionysian, since Dionysius too was a monk of Qenneshre, and the life of the holy man Severus of Samosata is explicitly identified as Dionysian by Michael.

Section 3 is also multivocal, and it charts the rapid changes in the alliances of the upper echelons of the church in the last years of the Umayyad reign and the early years of the Abbasid one. The caliphs Marwan II and al-Mansur seem to have been especially willing to intervene in church elections. This period saw the brief relocation of the caliphal capital to Harran on the edge of the Jaziran steppe. The multivocality of the material also suggests that histories were being written as the contentious events were taking place, which accounts for the rapid changes in the identification of heroes and villains that later editors found hard to work with. Unlike section 2, section 3 provides extensive detail on the internal workings of the Jacobite church. I believe that many of the 'narratives resembling ecclesiastical history' that Dionysius refers to come from this period. The rejection of many of the patriarchs of this period as anti-patriarchs in Michael's text is probably linked to the Qenneshrite bias of the sources and/or their transmission through Dionysius. It is possible that Michael is consulting some of these sources directly, without using Dionysius as an intermediary, but Dionysius names two sources, Daniel and John son of Samuel, who cover this period, so I think it likely that much of this material came through Dionysius. I draw on this section in chapter 2.

Section 4 accounts for the lion's share of identifiable fragments of Dionysius' own writings. It reflects his testimony on his own reign, which, of course, we should not read as the unvarnished truth. It also contains reflections on the reigns of George and Cyriacus as orthodox predecessors, though Dionysius also tacitly criticizes both men. Dionysius mentions his own (older?) brother, Theodosius of Edessa (d. 832), as one of his sources. Given that Theodosius was appointed by Cyriacus, Dionysius may rely on Theodosius for his inside knowledge of Cyriacus' policy and his itineraries.[147] Dionysius concludes the ecclesiastical part of his history with his reconciliation of competing factions

---

147. BH Chron 137/177 reports that Theodosius was with Cyriacus during the siege of Raqqa, when he and the patriarch were forced to eat rice bread (apparently a sign of their hardship). BH HE I, 363 mentions that Theodosius was Dionysius' brother and refers to Theodosius' command of multiple languages. He made numerous translations from Greek, including questions and answers submitted to Theodosius of Alexandria, and he was a friend of the philosopher Anton of Takrit. Debié 2015a: 568–69.

in Iraq in 834 and his defeat of the schismatic monks of Gubba Barraya in 836, both of which were defining features of his patriarchate.[148]

As noted earlier, not all the material for this period in the medieval compilations is necessarily Dionysian. In particular, the reports on the bishops of Takrit that Bar Hebraeus includes in his *Ecclesiastical History* without naming his source are likely to come from an archive in Takrit rather than a source in Syria or the Jazira.[149]

Several notices in Michael are drawn from non-Jacobite church traditions. Michael gives a detailed history of the Maronites that ranges from the late sixth to mid-eighth century that was composed in Maronite circles.[150] Michael also draws on sources from the Church of the East[151] and the Chalcedonians[152] and describes a union between the Jacobites and the Armenians at Manzikert in 724.[153] And in the seventh- and eighth-century narrative he describes the sufferings of the Christian Arabs.[154] In all these cases I think we have to remain agnostic about whether the material was in Dionysius' history.[155] None of these scenes obviously anticipates the main themes of the passages that are

148. MS XII. 18 and 19.

149. Schrier 1991: 71.

150. MS XI. 9–12 (on the career of Maximus the confessor and its aftermath); MS XI. 20 (IV, 458–61 / II, 492–96) (on the conflict between Maximites and Maronites in Aleppo); MS XI. 23 (IV, 467 / II, 511) (on the persecution of the Maronites by Theophylact bar Qanbara). These are surveyed in Gribomont 1974 and Brock 1973 and discussed further in Wood 2019. There appears to be a core discussion of the foundation of Monotheletism and Maximus' opposition, followed by sympathetic accounts of the fate of the Maronites in the eighth century, occasionally with a Jacobite gloss.

151. On the foundation of the Jacobite monastery of Mar Hanania by a monk of Mar Mattai, which draws on an otherwise unattested chronicle composed by one Denahisho`: MS XII. 6 (IV, 489 / III, 20). For the role of the Bokhtisho family in a contested election in the Church of the East, see MS XII. 19 (IV, 533 / III, 94).

152. The mutilation and exile of a Melkite patriarch by al-Walid II in 745: MS XI. 22 (IV, 464 / II, 506). This is a mistake for Peter, bishop of Damascus. MS XII. 20 (IV, 536–37 / III, 98–100) describes controversies following the death of Job, Melkite patriarch of Antioch.

153. MS XI. 22 (IV, 492–500 / II, 457–61). This text quotes from the documents signed at the meeting, including episcopal lists. Detailed episcopal lists of this length are not a feature of the material known to be Dionysian.

154. Especially MS XI. 17 (IV, 451–52 / II, 481). Passing references suggest that Christian Arabs had been a significant element of the Jacobite community in the eighth century: see discussion in Wood 2019.

155. Some of these passages are found in BH, HE I (e.g., 333 on the monastery of Mar Hanania; 301 on the Armenian synod and 277 on the career of Maximus), but it is possible that Bar Hebraeus took this material from Michael rather than from Dionysius.

known to be Dionysian. If he did include them, then he would have extracted them from histories or documents known to him, but this could also be the work of Michael himself.

On the other hand, Dionysius refers to a number of his predecessors and their rivals in his description of his own meeting with al-Maʾmun in Baghdad, so it seems likely that these were covered in his history. They are Sergius Zakunaya and Severus bar Mashqa; Denha II of Takrit and Julian the Roman; Ishaq and Iwannis II; John of Callinicum and David of Dara; and George of Beltan and Abraham of Qartmin and Cyriacus.[156] In addition, given the sudden disappearance of any substantive narrative after Dionysius' death, I speculate that much of the narrative that concerns Dionysius and his predecessors Cyriacus and George (i.e., much of book 12 of Michael) is also likely to be Dionysian.

The secular history found in Michael the Syrian is often found in a less abbreviated form in the Chronicle to 1234, which led Andrew Palmer to argue that the latter provides the most complete attestation of Dionysius' secular writings.[157] Certainly, material that is shared by the Chronicle to 1234 and Michael does seem more likely to be Dionysian.[158] It is notable that this secular material rarely shows any overlap with the ecclesiastical history, which may support Rudolf Abramowski's suggestion that Dionysius worked with quite distinct source bases to compose the two sections of his history and that the relationships between the two that do occur are Dionysius' own interventions.[159]

The secular material in Michael and the Chronicle to 1234 is not restricted to military and political events; it also includes records of solar eclipses and natural disasters. These disasters are treated not simply as raw facts but rather as indications of God's response to humankind's actions. For instance, it is no coincidence that Michael records numerous natural phenomena around major

156. MS XII. 14 (IV, 516–17 / III, 65).

157. In addition to Palmer et al. 1993, note Ortiz de Urbina 1965: 220. Hoyland 2011: 13 n. 43 observes that X1234 includes material from Islamic sources that is absent from Michael and was probably absent from Dionysius too. X1234 seems much more interested than Michael was in military narratives and thus preserves them more completely. On the other hand, X1234's longer military narratives may also involve the supplementary use of Arabic sources (e.g., Hilkens 2018: 290).

158. Hilkens 2018: 283–90. Parts of the narrative set in the Jazira are particularly strong candidates. At 272 he suggests that the author of X1234 and Michael used the same manuscript of Dionysius because of common spelling mistakes.

159. R. Abramowski 1940: 24.

political events such as the Abbasid revolution: they constituted data by which to interpret the wider eschatological significance of contemporary events.[160] The secular material can be divided as follows:

> Section 1: The last war between Rome and Persia and the invasions of the Rashidun caliphs
>
> Section 2: The frontier wars between the Arabs and the Byzantines and the internal politics of Byzantium and the caliphate
>
> Section 3: The events of the fourth *fitna* in Syria and Mesopotamia
>
> Section 4: The wars of Theophilus and al-Muʿtasim

Section 1 draws on narratives from the time of Heraclius that originate in sources in favour of the Roman government. But these are mixed with other material that describes Roman war crimes during the Romans' retreat from Syria and depicts the Muslim conquerors as liberators. The latter type of material uses many of the tropes of the Arabic *futūḥ* literature, and it may have been composed by an author who was familiar with it, if only through oral sources.[161]

Section 2 is a military and political history of Byzantium and the caliphate until the death of al-Rashid. Much of this material is similar to that reported by the Greek historian Theophanes and by the Melkite Arabic historian Agapius of Manbij. Robert Hoyland has referred to these texts as deriving from a 'Syriac common source', a body of material that was transmitted between Byzantium and the caliphate and that draws on perspectives internal to both empires. He has tentatively suggested that this common source might be identified with Theophilus of Edessa.[162] This identification is broadly compatible with Dionysius' own statement that he drew on Theophilus while ignoring his comments on the Jacobites: he may have considered it safe to use Theophilus for military and political history. Nevertheless, only one statement is explicitly

---

160. MS XI. 22 (IV, 464–66 / II, 506–8).

161. It is especially hard to discern what parts of this section might be Dionysian. Dyakanov 1912 argued that the ecclesiastical historian Cyrus of Batna extended his history into the reign of Heraclius. Cyrus may have been used as a source by Dionysius as well as being used directly by Michael. The introduction to the Armenian translation of Michael's *Chronicle* also reports that Michael used the work of one Guria, an otherwise unknown historian who described the period from Justin to Heraclius as well as the Arab conquests (translated by Chabot in MS I, 2). The name Guria may be a mistake for 'Cyrus' by the Armenian translator. It is possible that the strong sense of the Romans as heretics and persecutors in this section should be attributed to Guria or Cyrus rather than to Dionysius. I hope to discuss this material in future work.

162. Hoyland 2011.

attributed to Theophilus (by Agapius), and none of my arguments here relies on attributing material to Theophilus.[163]

Section 3 is a very detailed local history of battles in Syria during the fourth fitna, the civil war fought between al-Amin, based in Baghdad, and al-Ma'mun in Merv. The war itself took place 811–19, but the disruption persisted in Syria and Egypt until about 827. The section covers the rebellion of the Arab chieftain Nasr ibn Shabath and the raids of Kurdish bandits on the monastery of Qartmin. It also includes Dionysius' eyewitness account of the siege of Edessa and probably draws on a number of contemporary oral reports. For Dionysius, this section provided an opportunity to showcase the achievements of his patron 'Abd Allah ibn Tahir as well as describe the events of his own lifetime. I discuss these events in chapter 7.

Section 4 contains the same kind of material as does section 2, but it is set in the era of al-Mu'tasim and Theophilus, who reigned at the end of Dionysius' lifetime. I read this section as Dionysius' continuation of the kind of secular history that he had received from earlier authors, except that he supplements it with a record of the exactions of al-Mu'tasim on his subjects.

Given Dionysius' intense antipathy to al-Mu'tasim, we should probably read Dionysius' positive depiction of al-Ma'mun in this context, where, in retrospect, al-Ma'mun's reign seemed like a golden age of good relations between patriarch and caliph. Some of the last events that Dionysius refers to at the end of his history are dated by the *Chronicle to 1234* to the reign of al-Wathiq (842–47), so it seems likely that he composed the secular part of his history later than the ecclesiastical part, which concludes about 836. The later completion date for the secular history may also account for the change in tone in the conclusion: whereas Dionysius concludes his ecclesiastical section with his defeat of his opponents, the history as a whole ends with a lachrymose final statement in which Dionysius searches for God's purpose in humankind's actions.

Summary of Argument

I focus my discussion here on the late eighth and early ninth centuries. This material is much more likely to have been written by Dionysius himself, and the bulk of my discussion deals with Dionysius and his immediate predecessor, Cyriacus of Takrit. It also illustrates key features of an Islamicate church,

---

163. Agapius, PO 8:525.

namely the caliphal endorsement of the patriarch and the patriarch's participation in the wider debates of the caliphate around political and religious authority and the rights of *dhimmīs* (protected peoples).

In chapter 1, I make the case that the seventh century did not see the immediate disappearance of the landowning elite in the Levant. Indeed, the melt-
ing away of the Roman state created opportunities for this aristocracy to en-
rich itself. It was only as the tax structures of the new state began to bite that
the aristocrats were forced to find new avenues to power and influence, such
as state administration or church hierarchy. Even then, Christian landed aristocracies endured into the ninth century.

In chapters 2 and 3 I chart the gradual changes in attitude toward collaboration between church and state, using the layered texture of Michael's *Chronicle*
to show that different historians took very different stances on the same practices, even though they worked within the same historical tradition. In particular, I examine the new significance of the church as a revenue-raising organization. The patriarch started to be legitimated by the caliph with a special
diploma and was able to call on caliphal support against oppressive Muslim
governors or Christian opponents within the church.

In chapters 4 and 5 I present more detailed case studies of how the establishment of a new administrative geography and new political and economic
centres affected the relationships among important loci of Christian life.
I argue that the eastward drift of the caliphate's centre of gravity marginalized
significant Christian sites in Syria, such as the city of Cyrrhus and the monastery of Gubba Barraya. At the same time, the changes benefited sites in the
east, such as the city of Takrit, whose powerful trading network underpinned
the development of new elites that wielded significant power within the
church, especially after the election of a Takritian patriarch.

Chapter 6 turns away from chronicle sources to examine liturgical commentaries and patriarchal legislation. I contend that this material is taken for
granted in the ecclesiastical and political history of the chronicles, but it allows
us to see how the liturgy created a self-contained, self-sustaining worldview in
which Muslim military success was irrelevant to the soteriological purpose of
the church and Christian history was focused on the events of Christ's life.
I also argue that the legislation of the period reveals the increasing administrative sophistication of the church's revenue raising and its intervention in the
arrangement of marriages and betrothals. I suggest that in regions that saw the
settlement of powerful, militarized Arab groups, the heads of Christian

households would have welcomed the church's policing of marriage to outsiders.

The final three chapters discuss ways in which Dionysius reproduced and altered elements of Islamic political thought to legitimate his own position. Chapter 7 examines the political conditions of the civil war between al-Amin and al-Maʾmun, the so-called fourth fitna. Al-Maʾmun defeated his brother using troops from Khurasan in the east of the caliphate, and the war created further opportunities for easterners under the caliph's patronage. This chapter shows how Dionysius presented himself as a servant of the caliph and highlights the importance of his alliance to the Khurasanian general ʿAbd Allah ibn Tahir, whose influence enabled Dionysius to overcome his enemies within the church. The final part of this chapter considers Dionysius' representation of *dhimma*, the contract between Muslims as the conquerors and Christians as the conquered, and the criticisms that he levels against Muslim troops in Egypt, whom he accuses of having transgressed Islamic norms of justice.

Chapter 8 focuses on Dionysius' showpiece, his own account of his encounter with al-Maʾmun. Al-Maʾmun had threatened to reorganize the way in which religious minorities were governed and to allow even very small groups to select their own leaders and representatives to government. This plan was a source of serious concern for a patriarch such as Dionysius, and he was thus forced to make a case to the caliph why the Christians should not be treated in this manner. His strategy was to argue that he, like the caliph, was an imam, elected by his people and not chosen by descent like the leaders of the Jews and the Zoroastrians, and that patriarchal leadership was an intrinsic part of Christianity that Muslim rulers were sworn to protect.

Chapters 9 deals with the ways in which Muslim rule changed Jacobite conceptions of the past. It analyses Dionysius' innovative discussion of the relationship between language, ethnicity and ancient history, which was highly influential for his successor Michael the Syrian. I chart the use of ethnic language in John of Ephesus, the *Chronicle of Zuqnin* and Dionysius. I situate their changing usage in the context of immigration by new ethnic groups and the development of a discourse of ethnicity that emphasized kingship. I also consider the existence of a second discourse of ethnic prestige, namely scientific achievement, which Dionysius was probably aware of but deliberately avoided because of its pagan connotations.

However, the impressive and creative reworking of Islamic thought for Christian purposes was dependent on the continued strength and support of the central government. The centralization of the church under Cyriacus and Dionysius was a product of good relations with the caliphs. But when al-Ma'mun died and was succeeded by his brother al-Muʿtasim, the latter's war against Byzantium meant that the Christians of the caliphate also came under suspicion. The reign of the new caliph led to the unravelling of Dionysius' political position, which had sustained his innovative cultural and intellectual stance during the reign of al-Ma'mun.

1

Lay Elites under Arab Rule

BY THE STANDARDS of the preindustrial world, the later Roman empire was a highly interventionist state. High levels of taxation were used to pay for a large standing army, which had dramatically increased in size after the invasions of the third century. Imperial fleets transported grain from Egypt, Africa and Sicily to feed massive capital cities at Rome and Constantinople.

This interventionism could place the Roman state at odds with its own aristocracy, since the latter possessed substantial resources that were potentially taxable. The aristocracy held massive wealth on an international scale and extracted revenue from tenants on its land, as well as from the sale of cash crops such as wine and oil.[1] Large disparities in wealth meant that the aristocracy was well placed to benefit from periods of economic insecurity, because such periods offered opportunities to acquire the lands of free peasants who had become impoverished.[2]

The Roman state used the aristocracy as a service elite to undertake functions such as the maintenance of civic infrastructure and the collection of taxes. Such employment generated an intrinsic tension, since the men who were supposed to act on behalf of the state might also privately seek to take advantage of their position by offering tax exemptions to their clients or even suborning parts of the army to police their private estates. When the state was strong and felt able to pick and choose among its supporters, it could oppose such practices directly. In the 540s, Justinian complained in his legislation about the massive tax evasion of the Egyptian aristocracy and the accumulation

1. Wickham 2005: 153–302; Sarris 2006; Banaji 2001.
2. Sarris 2006: 183–84 discusses how offers by aristocrats to help peasants pay for irrigation or avoid taxes through a fictive transfer of ownership could lead to the real transfer of property in the long term. See also Woolf and Garnsey 1989: 163–64.

of armed retinues by the magnates of Cappadocia.[3] But at other times, corrupt behaviour was simply represented as natural and inevitable.[4]

The available evidence for the Sasanian world does not afford the level of detail that the Roman legal codes and the Egyptian papyri do. But we can see a similar tension in the narrative sources on the late Sasanians, which depict a state that relied on the aristocracy to enforce its writ, but which acknowledge that the same aristocracy could also seek to acquire land from the peasantry or abuse its role as an agent of the state. Sasanian aristocrats certainly appreciated the rewards provided by the state, but they could also oppose or topple a shah who tried to curtail the rights of their houses.[5]

We get a good indication of the three-way relationship between the state, the aristocracy and the peasantry when one of these actors was removed. John of Nikiu, writing in the 690s but drawing on earlier sources, reports on the behaviour of Roman aristocrats in the Egyptian Delta during the period of disruption in the late sixth and early seventh centuries. In the absence of a strong Roman state, they raised private armies, besieged the cities of their rivals and increased the taxes they imposed on the peasantry.[6] In other words, the immediate effect of the removal of the state was the freedom of the former service elite to use the local powers of the state to their own ends and for their own enrichment.

This chapter uses letters and saints' lives to chart how many aristocracies benefited from the collapse of the Roman and Sasanian empires before the caliphs started to reassert their authority and demand higher taxes in the eighth century. Nevertheless, non-Muslim landed aristocrats persisted in many areas. What changed, I argue, is the increasing premium on good relations with Muslim patrons who might protect these elite interests.

Aristocrats in the Seventh Century

After the Arabs removed the previous administrations in the Near East, local aristocrats, working on behalf of the new rulers, took the opportunity to charge additional taxes for their own benefit or to claim the crown lands of the

---

3. Sarris 2011a: 152–53; Sarris 2006: 162–75.

4. Sarris 2006: 223. Crone 1989b: 68–69 offers parallels to China and Vietnam.

5. Banaji 2016: 179–83.

6. John of Nikiu 120.29 and 121.6 describes the exactions of one Menas, who had been appointed prefect of Lower Egypt by Heraclius and was retained in the post by the Arabs. John accuses him of enforcing labour corvées on the Christians and increasing the already high taxes demanded by the Muslims, presumably to line his own pockets. For the activity of private armies during the early seventh century, see John of Nikiu 108.3.

old Sasanian empire for themselves.[7] Arab settlement in the seventh century was mostly restricted to a small number of new garrison cities (*amṣār*), and the territories beyond these cities were relatively unsupervised by the Muslim state.[8] Aristocrats seem to have been given relatively free rein, whether or not they had converted to Islam, in what Chase Robinson has termed the 'Indian summer' of the Sufyanid period.[9] We should not presume that this implied a golden age for the peasantry; it merely meant that much wealth was being consumed locally by aristocrats rather than being passed on to a central government.

What was this wealth spent on? To some degree, the post-Roman elites of the caliphate may have taken on some of the roles of the state that the caliphate did not initially fulfil, such as the minting of low-denomination coinage.[10] Money was also likely spent on lavish consumption that is not archaeologically visible, such as food or textiles. Dionysius of Tel-Mahre accuses his ancestors of squandering a fortune on fine horses and hunting dogs.[11] But wealth was also channelled into expensive display architecture. In the former Roman world, churches are the most prominent example.[12]

Archaeological surveys in several parts of the Levant have highlighted the continuation of church building throughout the seventh century. Nessana, for instance, saw two massive churches built in that century, both larger than any of their sixth-century predecessors.[13] The Transjordan witnessed the building of a range of churches in rural locations such as Madaba and Umm el-Jimal, often decorated with lavish mosaics.[14] Palestine acquired some eleven new constructions in this period.[15] In the Tur Abdin there was likewise a spate of construction of rural churches and monasteries.[16] In both Palestine/

7. Morony 1984: 115 and 205.

8. Kennedy 2006; Whitcomb 1994.

9. Robinson 2000: 57 and 171.

10. Bates 1994: 393–94 suggests that Arab-Byzantine coinage was produced by bishops, but it could equally have been generated by lay aristocrats. For an example of local coin production in Cyrrhus, see Schulze 2017.

11. MS XII. 4 (IV, 485 / III, 14).

12. Cf. Whittow 1996: 91, which observes that the seventh century saw many fine churches built in Armenia but almost none in Byzantium. Whittow explains this difference with reference to the intensive Byzantine tax regime compared to the relative freedom of the Armenian aristocracy.

13. Ruffini 2011.

14. Piccirillo 2002: 227–42; D. Reynolds n.d.

15. Schick 1995: esp. 120; D. Reynolds n.d.

16. Keser-Kayaalp 2013; Keser-Kayaalp 2016; Keser-Kayaalp 2018.

Transjordan and in the Tur Abdin, this period of construction lasted until the last quarter of the eighth century.[17] And though Iraq has not benefited from the kind of archaeological work that has been possible in the Levant, the dates of monastic foundations recorded in the ecclesiastical history of the Church of the East are clustered in the period 580–720, which provides an interesting parallel to the situation in the Levant.[18] These monasteries lay mainly in northern Iraq, but they also included foundations near al-Hira and in Khuzestan.[19]

There are several patterns to this spate of building. The first, as Matta Guidetti has observed, is that church foundations are not apparent in major centres of Muslim settlement such as Damascus or Aleppo;[20] it is a phenomenon associated with secondary settlements and/or with peripheral regions such as northern Iraq or the Tur Abdin. Second, where their identities can be ascertained, the donors of these churches were often private individuals.[21] Whereas in the sixth century the state had been a major builder of churches, by this time the donors were bishops[22] or aristocrats, such as Gadimos, who built the great church at Nessana,[23] or the village chiefs mentioned in inscriptions in the Transjordan.[24] Even where we cannot identify church founders, the building of large numbers of churches in relatively small settlements (as at Ḥaḥ in the Tur Abdin or Umm el-Jimal in the Transjordan) suggests that rivalry between wealthy donors was a more powerful motivation than local need.[25]

The construction of churches in the Islamic period is often studied with the intention of answering questions about the treatment of Christians under

17. D. Reynolds n.d.; Keser-Kayaalp 2018: 203. Reynolds notes that evidence for building in many key sites in Palestine may be obscured by later construction in the Crusader period.

18. This estimate is taken from the history of Amr ibn Matta, who organizes monastic foundations according to the reigning patriarchs of the Church of the East. There are some outliers to this pattern in the fourth century, but I take these to be legendary precursors to the foundation of monasteries in 580–720 under Abraham of Kashkar and his disciples. For Abraham, see Jullien 2008 and Wood 2013: 146–60.

19. Ishodnah of Basra's ninth-century *Book of Chastity* offers a succinct survey of these monastic foundations.

20. Guidetti 2009: 4 n. 39.

21. Keser-Kayaalp 2016: 48.

22. Gatier 2011: 10–11.

23. Ruffini 2011: 220–21.

24. Piccirillo 2002: 231.

25. For Umm el-Jimal, see B. de Vries 1998. For Ḥaḥ, see Keser-Kayaalp 2018: 197.

Muslim rule. Indeed, Robert Schick and Steve Humphreys are correct to observe that the construction and maintenance of churches demonstrates the existence of a wealthy class of Christians who wished to showcase their wealth and their religious credentials to others and/or were committed to the preservation of the Christian character of their towns and villages.[26] Even if it was only a by-product of elite display, competitive giving by Christian aristocrats paid for priests, the upkeep of buildings and the provision of education and food for the poor, and it played a role in making the practice of Christianity an attractive prospect.[27]

However, we can also ask another question about the wave of church construction in the seventh century, namely what it tells us about the relations among the aristocracy, the state and the peasantry—an issue that has been a major concern for historians of the sixth century. An interesting model for the kind of pattern we have seen in the seventh-century Levant is suggested by William Bowden's work on the Balkans in the sixth century. Bowden challenges the tendency of archaeologists and historians to interpret monumental architecture as a sign of 'urban flourishing'. Instead, he argues:

> Monumental architecture represents the ability to control surplus resources, while the prestige that accompanies the activity is based on a universal recognition of the energy that is expended during the process. . . . It does not follow that the greater production of monumental buildings is an indication of the greater production of surplus, but rather it is a sign of the increasing control over the surplus by an emerging elite.

In rural areas, Bowden argues, the institutional church would always have a disincentive to build new churches, since it would seek to balance what churches might bring in with donations with what it might lose in maintenance. But aristocratic donors might have a different perspective on the costs

26. Schick 1995: 124; R. S. Humphreys 2014. Muslim expropriation of churches was unusual and normally restricted to centrally located churches in major cities; it is much more common to see churches abandoned and then converted to domestic use. See Schick 1995: 128–34; Guidetti 2009: 1–6.

27. For an example of how competitive giving was harnessed to create new Christian centres, see the *Life of Ahudemmeh*, 27–28, where the missionary names churches and monasteries after the chiefs of the Arab tribes, who then make donations. See further analysis in Fisher et al. 2015: 350–57. For the role of the church in education and welfare in Egypt in the late Roman and early Islamic periods, see Wipszycka 1972: 110–14.

and benefits of construction, if they saw a benefit simply in the display of their wealth to local rivals and clients in the region in which they were based.[28]

The Tur Abdin

A number of near-contemporary Syriac sources shed light on the behaviour of Christian elites in the Tur Abdin and northern Iraq, in particular their relationship to religious leaders and institutions. Here I draw on letters composed by Ishoyahb of Adiabene, patriarch of the Church of the East (r. 649–59); on a hagiography associated with the monastery of Qartmin, the *Life of Simeon of the Olives* (d. 734); on the *Life of Theodota of Amida*, a peripatetic saint (d. 698) who regularly travelled across the former Roman-Persian border; and on a hagiographic collection set in northern Iraq, Thomas of Marga's *Book of Governors* (written circa 840).

Ishoyahb corresponded with several aristocrats and clergy in the city of Nisibis. His main aims were to exhort the Nisibenes to drive 'heretics' out of the city and to advertise his good connections with the new ruling powers.[29] His call to arms for these aristocrats was based on the presumption that the old political system had collapsed and that the Christian lords of the city could now act independently, to the benefit of their co-religionists. He tells one bishop, Jacob of Shahrzur, that he is surprised that Jacob 'does not demonstrate to the dead authority at once that it is lifeless' by acting in defiance of the civic leaders who had held a role in the Sasanian administration.[30]

Ishoyahb's letters present an ideal of lay aristocrats acting in concert with their clergy and respecting the patriarch's authority. But it may be significant that Ishoyahb's appeal to these aristocrats, who had often supported opponents of the patriarch in the previous generation, is couched in terms of their 'manly valour'.[31] Like the lords of Nisibis, Ishoyahb himself, as well as his successor Giwargis I (r. 661–80), were aristocrats from a Persian-speaking background.[32] It may be that, in an environment in which the state was relatively absent, good relationships with established families were the best guarantee

28. Bowden 2001: 61. On the funding of private chapels and monasteries on Egyptian great estates in the sixth century, cf. Wipszycka 2011: 168; Wipszycka 1972: 27.

29. Ishoyahb III, *Letters*, 225–26. I draw on Payne 2009.

30. Ishoyahb III, *Letters*, 237, with Payne 2009: 402.

31. Ishoyahb III, *Letters*, 222, with Payne 2009: 405.

32. Wood 2013: 225.

of cooperation with church rulings, and the best way to ensure such relationships was electing aristocrats to high offices in the church and advertising their election.

A second testimony to the relationship between aristocrats and religious institutions is drawn from the *Life of Simeon of the Olives*. The holy man Simeon was the son of one Mundhar, a local notable. He first acquired fame by being resurrected from the dead as a boy by the holy man Gabriel of Qartmin after a feast at the monastery.[33] After becoming a stylite at Qartmin, he reportedly healed the famous Persian general Shahrbaraz (d. 628) of a disease and enjoyed good relations with the 'king', Peroz, of Nisibis and the leader of the village of Anḥel, Giwargis. Later on, David, a relative of Simeon's, became part of Shahrbaraz's retinue and discovered a great treasure while out hunting. Simeon used this money to purchase estates and olive groves in the vicinity of Qartmin and then drew on these investments to fund the building of churches in Nisibis, Edessa, Harran and Amida. Subsequently, he is said to have gone to Baghdad (*sic*) and received a diploma that granted the churches he had built immunity from taxation. Finally, he was made bishop of Harran, where he built a mosque out of his great wealth, and where he died in 734.[34]

The Syriac *Life of Simeon of the Olives*, copied in Harran in the 790s, asserts that Simeon was born in 625 and died in 734, but Jack Tannous points out that this is improbable. At any rate, his claimed visit to Baghdad, which was founded only in 762, and his meeting with Shahrbaraz, who died in 628, are obvious anachronisms.[35] Simeon's association with the securing of tax-free status for churches would have generated a clear motivation for the false ascription of foundations to the saint. Nevertheless, the death date of 734 seems to be a relatively secure feature of the text (it is also mentioned in the *Chronicle to 819*).[36] The text's references to virtually independent rulers in Nisibis and Anḥel seem credible. And Tannous suggests that 'Shahrbaraz' is a corruption of the name of one Shahrizar of Shirwan, a regional aristocrat who would have been unknown to a late eighth-century scribe.[37]

I believe that the *Life of Simeon of the Olives* depicts the scion of a local Jacobite elite family who had acquired political connections with more powerful

---

33. *Life of Gabriel of Qartmin*, LXXXIX.
34. Tannous 2016. The text is also summarised in Brock 1979.
35. Tannous 2016: 315–16.
36. *Chronicle to 819*, AG 1045 (17/12).
37. Tannous 2016: 323.

figures bearing Greek and Persian names on both sides of the old border. The reference to the discovery of a treasure may be a way of concealing what was actually a donation from Shahrizar, perhaps because this magnate was a non-Christian (though it could equally describe a real event). We do not have to accept that all the churches ascribed to Simeon were really founded by him, but the lists of investments do suggest that one function of the Simeon narratives was to safeguard the income of a group of churches that were associated with the saint and, by extension, to protect his monastery and his family.

Simeon's precise lineage had been forgotten when the *Life of Simeon of the Olives* was copied in 799; this text portrays him merely as the son of a noble. However, the Syriac *Life of Gabriel of Qartmin*, probably written earlier in the century, calls him the son of Mundhar. It is possible that the story in the *Life of Gabriel* was composed at a time when Mundhar's family was of local significance, but that it had become extinct or insignificant almost a century later.

Our third example comes from the *Life of Theodota*, a lengthy text that describes the saint's wanderings across the old Roman-Persian border.[38] The text evokes a recently conquered borderland, filled with refugees[39] and wounded warriors,[40] in which itinerant outsiders bear uncertain loyalties.[41] The Arabs are mostly notable for their absence: we see Arabs in Amida, where they form part of a crowd that acclaims Theodota's miracles, but the text deals mainly with the indigenous population. They are ruled on the Arabs' behalf by notables who bear Greek names and Roman honorifics. Thus, in one scene, a young man named Sergius, a native of Harran,[42] is sent by an 'illustriya' at Samosata (a corruption of the Roman title *illustris*),[43] to collect a land tax from a monastery and a poll tax from Theodota himself, who is staying at the monastery as a guest. When he arrives, the haughty Sergius is possessed by a demon, and Theodota orders him to return everything that he has seized from the poor and from widows and orphans and to surrender the census document

38. The chief use of the text has been in Palmer 1990–91; Palmer 2006 and Tannous 2018.

39. See *Life of Theodota*, 115, for Jacobite refugees fleeing to a fortress still controlled by Roman troops.

40. See *Life of Theodota*, 126, for a man wounded by an arrow during the siege of Edessa.

41. *Life of Theodota*, 108–9 and 118 (false holy men), 98 (a closet 'Nestorian' in a Jacobite monastery), 106 (a blacksmith who had committed murder). Cf. Palmer 1990: 89, 166.

42. I am not persuaded by the suggestion of Palmer 2006: 118 that he was likely a 'pagan'.

43. Palmer 2006: 127 notes the continued use of some Greek administrative terms in the *Life*, such as *epitropos*.

he has written for the monastery.[44] There is no sense here that the taxes collected might be legitimate or serve some higher function; they are seen simply
as an act of tyranny by the powerful.

Later on in the narrative Theodota is sought out by Eustratios, the illustriya
of Maypherkat, who wants to be blessed by the holy man. The saint hides from
him, perhaps to avoid unmerited fame (a common *topos* in hagiography) or
perhaps to avoid sanctioning a man who seemed corrupt (because of his oppression of the poor) or heretical (if we assume that individuals bearing Greek
names were Chalcedonian).[45] However, he is happy to bless the illustriya of
Dara and his family, after which the official offers to pay Theodota's poll tax to
the Arabs.[46] Shortly before Theodota's death, the saint commands this same
illustriya to build a monastery.[47]

The apogee of Theodota's career comes when he reluctantly accepts election as bishop of Amida by the patriarch Julian (r. 688–708). In the course of
his tenure, he is responsible for the miraculous abundance of food during a
time of drought and famine[48] and is respected by all sections of society.[49] He
is noted for his ability to discern sins, to exorcize the possessed, and to bring
down curses on those who defy him and his interpretation of God's wishes. It
is in recognition of these miraculous abilities that the Arab governor of the
east orders that 'the laws of the city of Amida and all the region be given into
the hands of that trustworthy man who is made Bishop in it. For I have heard
that he is no respecter of persons. On account of this, I have given the regula-
tions of the Christians into his hands'. As a result, according to the *Life of
Theodota*, 'the fear of the Blessed One was upon all the people; and on the chief
men and administrators and those who stand before the officers of the ruler
of this world'.[50]

The *Life of Theodota* provides an illustration of how a Roman aristocracy
might persist into the period of Arab rule. Theodota could pick and choose
the aristocrats he engaged with, but he did not exclude the possibility of working with all aristocratic patrons. Inscriptions at the monastery of Mar Jacob at

44. *Life of Theodota*, 85–96.
45. *Life of Theodota*, 124. On another occasion, he is unwilling to pray for supplicants because
they were Chalcedonians (86).
46. *Life of Theodota*, 127.
47. *Life of Theodota*, 192–93.
48. *Life of Theodota*, 149–50.
49. *Life of Theodota*, 148.
50. *Life of Theodota*, 156.

Salaḥ in the Tur Abdin reveal that members of elite families with Greek names were among the major donors, which suggests that the report concerning the illustriya of Dara in the *Life of Theodota* is credible and that patronage to charismatic figures and powerful monasteries could cross confessional boundaries.[51]

Theodota is represented as a widely respected figure who was recognized as judge for the Christians of Amida.[52] It is apparent from other sources that the conquerors allowed bishops to retain the judicial authority they had enjoyed under the Roman empire or exercised de facto in the Sasanian world. To John of Phenek, an author of the Church of the East writing in the 690s, this position encouraged bishops to engage in tyranny: 'They argue like princes caught up in public affairs and unlawful dispute'.[53] Although the *Life of Theodota* approves of the saint's personal role, it appears that this role flows from his charisma, rather than his formal rank. At any rate, Theodota is much less keen for the lower clergy to support the regime by functioning as tax collectors, and he punishes a deacon who disobeys his ruling.[54] Clerics' literacy might have made them good candidates for such a role.[55] But the higher clergy would have had a vested interest in preventing their underlings from collecting taxes, both because it would have given the latter access to

51. Palmer 1990: 208–9, inscription A4. This records the burial of one 'Lady Mary' in 760, 'daughter of Lazarus, son of Petruno, and daughter of Patricia, daughter of Candidatus of Dara'. The use of Greek names and the record of descent going back two generations is remarkable for the epigraphy in this region collected by Palmer. In general, he notes that the Jacobites did not normally use funeral epigraphy, which further suggests that this was a Chalcedonian family. However, not all the aristocrats that Theodota encountered were Chalcedonian. For instance, he deliberately lodged with Jacobite nobles rather than with 'schismatics' when he stayed in Edessa: *Life of Theodota*, 185. Palmer 2006: 117 notes a bizarre feature in *Life of Theodota*, 89: the saint calls on 'all the saints of Constantinople' to perform an exorcism, which suggests that the imperial city still retained a reputation for holiness among the Jacobites, even if chiefly as a storehouse of relics.

52. I disagree with the suggestion of Palmer 2006: 129 that Amida had been purged of Chalcedonians because of their absence from the *Life of Theodota*. In this instance, the absence of evidence is not evidence of absence.

53. John of Phenek 148–49 / 176–77.

54. *Life of Theodota*, 154.

55. Wipszycka 1972: 168–72 records Egyptian cases in which deacons were delegated the role of tax collectors by the pagarch or calculated the tax burden of a locality. Schenke 2018 notes Egyptian monks who acted as tax collectors for lands owned by their monastery; the tax seems to have been collected at the same time as rent.

alternative hierarchies of influence that were not related to their bishops and because of the unpleasant reputation of tax collectors, clearly seen in the case of Sergius.

I draw a fourth and final case of the close relationship between aristocrats and the monastic movement from a tale set in northern Iraq later in the Umayyad period and recounted in the hagiographic collection of Thomas of Marga. Thomas describes how one Hugair founded a monastery toward the end of the Marwanid period 'not out of good intentions, but for boasting and pride. Acting as if he were a good man, he named it Hugair-abad, after the manner of the Magians, from whose race he had come'. But nearby monks refused to consecrate the new building or to come to the monastery. It was said that 'the house of Hugair-abad is ruined while it is still new'.[56]

Hugair may have assumed that, like the benefactors of Zoroastrian pious foundations, he would be able to exert considerable control over his religiously dedicated estate through, for example, the disposal of cash crops or prestigious local charity. The monks' rejection of Hugair, and the very dissemination of this narrative, suggest that his approach was not welcomed by some.[57] We can read this story as a declaration by the monks of Marga that they would not accept patronage on just any terms and that, like Theodota, they saw themselves as entitled to pick and choose among potential donors. How often such aristocratic patronage was rejected in reality is impossible to know.

The Changing Role of the Aristocracy

Chris Wickham states that an 'aristocracy' in the period 300–800 is defined by its members' ability to remember their ancestry, their control of land and official positions, their expensive lifestyles, their mutual recognition and their ability to control *Königsnähe* (proximity to royal influence).[58] The hagiographies we have examined here show us an aristocracy that profited from the fall of the old empires by monopolizing the collection of taxes with little interference from the state. On the other hand, the post-Roman and post-Sasanian aristocracy had to adapt to a world without the courtly patronage and honours that they had received in the sixth century.

56. Thomas of Marga II, 43 (136–37 / 282–83).

57. Though not all commentators were so selective: see above for the naming of churches in the Jazira after sponsors.

58. Wickham 2005: 154.

Wickham sees memory as a crucial aspect of aristocracy, and the foundation of monasteries and churches was an important means of preserving the memory of the leaders of a notable family and of legitimating its wealth through the provision of charity. The hagiographic sources we have seen reflect, on the one hand, the tension between holy men's desire to criticize aristocrats' overtaxation of the less powerful and to determine the conditions of donations and, on the other, their wish to garner further aristocratic support.

However, the tightening of the caliphal state's control and tax system[59] and the expansion of Arabic as the language of bureaucracy[60] generated challenges for aristocrats whose wealth was based on the land. The *Chronicle to 1234* reports how the caliph ʿAbd al-Malik's eastern governor al-Hajjaj (d. 714) attacked Christian leaders using trumped-up charges: 'He murdered Mardānshāh son of Zarnōsh, the administrators of Nisibis and Simeon son of Nonnus of Ḥalūghā. The Armenian leaders he herded into a church that he set on fire . . . and he killed Anastasius son of Andrew, the administrator of Edessa, and seized all his possessions. Yet Christians still held office as scribes and administrators in the Arab territories'.[61]

The late Marwanid period also saw the beginnings of Arab settlement outside the amṣār, which meant competition for land.[62] Nevertheless, lower ranks of aristocracy did persist, even into the ninth century. Arietta Papaconstantinou notes that low-level Christian lay elites continued to wield power at the village level in Egypt and Iraq.[63]

---

59. The clearest account of this development for the Jazira is given in the *Chronicle of Zuqnin*, beginning with ʿAbd al-Malik's census and then in great detail in the first decades of Abbasid rule.

60. For the effects of this shift in Egypt and the removal of Christian pagarchs, see Sijpesteijn 2009. For a wider discussion on the relative fates of Greek, Aramaic, Arabic and Coptic, see Hoyland 2004; Papaconstantinou 2012; Wasserstein 2003.

61. MS XI. 16 (IV, 447–48 / II, 475); X1234 (I, 294 / 228–29). Translated in Palmer et al. 1993: 202.

62. See, e.g., Papaconstantinou 2012: 67–68 for Egypt. For Mesopotamia, see *Chronicle of Zuqnin*, 269/237, which describes the government's trying to remove 'Tayyaye' who had settled on the land. Vacca 2016: 169–70 stresses that the beginning of both the Marwanid and the Abbasid periods saw an intensification of government intrusion in the Caucasus.

63. Papaconstantinou 2008: 145–47. Papaconstantinou gives the examples of the lay *archontes* in Jeme in Egypt and the village leaders referred to in the letters of the Nestorian patriarch Henanisho I. She qualifies the conclusions of Morony 2005, which characterizes the caliphate as a communalist society, with different religious groups each led by clerical leaders. I will return

Some aristocrats prospered in this new environment as state functionaries. Wealth could still buy education, and groups that switched to Arabic early, such as the Chalcedonians, were especially well placed to take advantage of the needs of the caliphal government. The tax structures that extracted the wealth of landed magnates needed to be staffed by competent administrators.[64] We cannot make a neat separation between administrators and aristocrats here. The skills required to be an administrator changed over the long eighth century and incentivized the acquisition of Arabic. But initial investments in education still needed to be paid for, and this probably favoured families that were already wealthy. What changed was that landed wealth and political influence became harder and harder to hold without patronage links to government.

Muriel Debié has shown how the Mansur family of Damascus flourished in this environment and used its influence and wealth to undermine its Maronite opponents. Similarly, government employment brought wealth to Athanasius bar Gumaye, the descendant of late Roman elites and the ancestor of Dionysius of Tel-Mahre.[65] Athanasius was a prominent patron of Christian institutions, such as the chapel of Abgar in Edessa.[66] But he also made long-term landed investments to secure his family's position in the future.

[At this time], Athanasius bar Gumaye of the city of Edessa became rich and famous. ʿAbd al-Malik was informed of his reputation as an intelligent man, well trained in the scribal skills, and he summoned him to Damascus, where he made him the guardian of his younger brother ʿAbd al-ʿAziz, whom he had made the emir of Egypt while still a child.[67] He commanded that Athanasius should be not only his scribe but the manager

to this idea below. Papaconstantinou 2020 develops this argument. Drawing on papyrological evidence from Egypt, Papaconstantinou notes that real decision-making powers continued to rest with lay elites (*lashane*), even if clergy did claim influence on the basis of their moral authority.

64. Essid 1995: 15 observes the role of secretaries in supporting land taxation by calculating yields, organizing land registers and surveying. Cf. Campopiano 2012; van Berkel 2013; Wickham 2015.

65. Debié 2016.

66. Cf. Hage 1966: 59 on the restoration of churches in Edessa, Harran and Amida in the same period.

67. The source is wrong to identify ʿAbd al-ʿAziz as a child at this stage: he already had several children of his own. Mabra 2017: 103.

of his affairs and that authority and administrative direction should be his, while ʿAbd al-ʿAziz should have the nominal power. So it came about that the distinguished Athanasius ruled Egypt and assigned taxes throughout the land. His sons were put in charge of the region of Gunada, though he sent his eldest son, Peter, to maintain and manage his possessions in Edessa. It is said that apart from the generous income and privileges that he enjoyed from the caliph, his sons also had a publicly acknowledged right to one denarius every year from each man drawing wages in the army. The strength of this army was 30,000 men and they stayed in Egypt for twenty-one years.

Athanasius himself was not only wise but also strictly orthodox. He had great respect for the hierarchy of the Church, and he built new churches and renovated old ones, as well as distributing alms abundantly to the orphans and the widows. He collected gold and silver like pebbles and he had four thousand slaves, all bought out of his own purse, besides grand houses, villages, various estates and gardens worthy of a king. In Edessa he had three hundred shops and nine inns.[68]

The appointment of the Edessene Athanasius to run the Egyptian *dīwān* was an atypical occurrence: we know about it principally because he was a famous ancestor of Dionysius whom Dionysius was keen to celebrate.[69] Much of Athanasius' wealth was confiscated on the death of ʿAbd al-ʿAziz when ʿAbd al-Malik imposed direct government on Egypt.[70] Nevertheless, we can stress that Athanasius utilized the wealth earnt in government service in landed and commercial investments and as a sponsor of Christian welfare and church foundations, and this may be typical of wider patterns for administrators employed at lower levels of government.

Taxation and the Abbasid Revolution

The two trends we have seen under the Marwanids—an increasingly intrusive tax system and a growing demand for literate labour to man it—are even more starkly visible in the non-Muslim sources after the Abbasid revolution

68. X1234 (I, 294–95 / 229–30). Translated in Palmer et al. 1993: 202. Cf. MS XI. 16 (IV, 447–48 / III, 475).

69. Mabra 2017: 142 argues that ʿAbd al-ʿAziz sought to patronize the Theodosian church in Egypt and recruited Athanasius as part of a wider policy of sponsoring Miaphysites.

70. Mabra 2017: 94–96.

of 750.[71] The Abbasids employed a large professional army, paid in cash.[72] And an important mandate for the revolution was the exemption of converts to Islam from the poll tax (*jizya*).[73] Both changes meant a greater tax burden on non-Muslims.

The *Chronicle of Zuqnin* describes the aftermath of the Abbasid revolution as a period of misery for the rural inhabitants of what had once been Roman Mesopotamia.[74] Though the *Chronicle* records a census under ʿAbd al-Malik,[75] the region had been relatively free of the hand of the state until circa 750, and the sense of shock may reflect the novelty of taxation. The *Chronicle* reports that the governor Musa ibn Musʿab used informers to ascertain people's real wealth, and that tax agents exaggerated the cost of merchandise to line their own pockets.[76] Control of crown property (*ṣawāfī*) was exploited to charge fines on those who crossed waterways or set up markets,[77] and agents were dispatched to track down fugitives who were trying to avoid paying the poll tax.[78]

The chronicler complains bitterly of the agents' lack of mercy toward the elderly and the poor.[79] In some circumstances, the levying of collective taxes on villages prompted villagers to denounce the wealthy (or those presumed to be wealthy). They would say, 'All our production was taken away by this one. Therefore, order him to pay on behalf of the village!' According to the *Chronicle of Zuqnin*,

> The prefect would harass him to the point of making him disappear from the earth. He would confiscate all that he owned and carry away all that he had plundered or not plundered. As a consequence, the wealthy used to run away from the villagers, like goats before wolves, and hide, while renouncing the vineyards and everything that they took away from them.[80]

71. Robinson 2000: 157; Wickham 2011: 210–13. Van Berkel 2013 notes the proliferation of specialized bureaucratic tasks under the early Abbasids.

72. Kennedy 2001: 86–87.

73. Hoyland 2015: 202.

74. Cahen 1954; Robinson 2016.

75. *Chronicle of Zuqnin*, 154/147.

76. *Chronicle of Zuqnin*, 293/255.

77. *Chronicle of Zuqnin*, 266/234.

78. *Chronicle of Zuqnin*, 295/258.

79. *Chronicle of Zuqnin*, 300/261.

80. *Chronicle of Zuqnin*, 330–31 / 285.

The Armenian historian Łewond (wr. c. 790) describes a similarly intrusive tax regime in the Caucasus in circa 750:

> When ʿAbd Allah [the future caliph al-Mansur, r. 754–75] came to the land of the Armenians, he reduced everyone to bankruptcy with many afflictions and torments, to the point that he was demanding taxes from the dead.[81] He made many orphans and widows suffer greatly and tortured priests and servants of the churches mockingly, beating them with sticks to make them reveal the names of the dead and their families. He viciously tormented the inhabitants of our land with bitter tax demands, imposing a tax of many silver *zuze* per capita and placing a lead seal around their necks.[82]

A third example from the mountainous north of the caliphate comes from Thomas of Marga's *Book of Governors*. There had been very little sign in this region of the Arabs or of state structures in the seventh century.[83] Thomas provides a lengthy saint's life, the *Life of Maranemmeh*, which allows us to glimpse the effects of the Abbasid revolution on the local aristocracy, on whom Christian monasteries had relied for their funding.[84]

Maranemmeh seems to have been associated with a particular group of villages in the vicinity of the mountains of Izla. Maranemmeh's villages were apparently dominated by a powerful upper level of aristocrats, the *shahrigan*, who tyrannized both the local peasantry and lower-level elites (*dihqāns*) as property owners and tax collectors on behalf of the Muslim caliphate. These high-level aristocrats seem to have done very well in the immediate aftermath of the conquests. In rural areas in particular, the Arab authorities continued to rely on local elites to raise taxes, and in practice this gave the latter

81. This may refer to the levying of taxes according to the size of the population recorded in the census. Note other examples and discussion in Morony 1984: 113–14. Papaconstantinou 2010: 60 argues that the *Maronite Chronicle* (written in the 680s) describes a collective poll tax negotiated by the patriarch on behalf of his confession, though it was paid to prevent persecution of the Jacobites by the Maronites in Jerusalem, rather than by the Muslims.

82. Łewond §28. On Łewond as a historian of the caliphate focused on a region with a non-Muslim population, see Vacca 2016: 25 and, on this passage in particular, 205–8. Vacca extends the arguments of Robinson 2005b by arguing that sealing was an instrument of public shaming.

83. Wood 2013: 166–69.

84. I previously believed this scene to be set in the Marwanid period (Wood 2018a), but on rereading its context in the *Book of Governors*, I now believe it must date to c. 750, following Robinson 2000: 82.

considerable leeway to exempt their clients from tax and to cream off a profit for themselves.[85]

The agonistic relationship between the weaker dihqāns, who seek Maranemmeh as an ally, and the more powerful shahrigan provides the background to Maranemmeh's condemnation of the latter. Maranemmeh's tour of the region of Salakh is dominated by his denunciations of polygamy and sexual misbehaviour, especially that of the shahrigan. In one such instance, Maranemmeh is moved to intercede on behalf of the wife of the shahrig Armenazwai after he commits adultery with a nun from the convent of Beth Tehunai. The shahrig ignores the saint's chastisement and moves to strike him, whereupon the holy man curses him: 'I trust in our Lord that you and all your village will go down alive into Sheol like Korah, Daithan and Abiram'. Following the saint's curse, the shahrig and his village are swallowed up in the middle of the night.[86]

Similar scenes of destruction are visited on a number of villages on the saint's itinerary in Salakh and Zab. The hagiographer's chief theme is the fleeting nature of the wealth of the shahrigan, sinful men who had opposed God and his agent Maranemmeh. To the shahrig Zadhai, the owner of some seventy-two estates in the region of Nineveh, Maranemmeh announces, 'You shall fall from all this glory, and your estates shall be taken from you and you shall die of hunger'.[87] The disappearance of the Sasanian state had afforded great opportunities for the shahrigan's political and religious independence in the uplands of northern Iraq, but, as we see in Thomas of Marga, this independence was challenged by their monastic neighbours, who continued to assert their own moral leadership of the Christians of the north and the immorality of the shahrigan.

A final scene, in which the saint prophesies the destruction of numerous village-estates dependent on the shahrigan, constitutes a warning to the aristocrats of the north to respect the censure of the monks, but it is also a response to the precipitous decline in the fortunes of these aristocrats after the imposition of a new central authority under the Abbasids. The increase in the

---

85. On the farming out of taxation, see Morony 1984: 112 and Choksy 1997: 118. Karel Nováček et al. (2017: 180–81) have observed that in Adiabene the seventh and eighth centuries witnessed a proliferation of fortified sites without urban planning, and that many of these sites were associated with monasteries. They plausibly link these sites to the shahrigan.

86. Thomas of Marga III, 8 (161 / 324–25).

87. Thomas of Marga III, 8 (163/329).

intensity of government intervention precipitated the fall of the shahrigan and allowed Maranemmeh's hagiographer to parade the saint's victory over the pride of Armenazwai and his fellows. But the lack of political detail in the text is also a deliberate rhetorical strategy: the author avoids mentioning the Arab authorities directly in order to emphasize the power of the holy man. I propose that it was the Abbasids and their agents who drew Armenazwai 'into Sheol' and stripped Zadhai of his many estates.[88]

Aristocrats and Bishops

Michael Morony portrays the Islamic caliphate as a communalist society. He argues that a key shift took place between 500 and 900 from civic identities toward religious ones, as the state recognized the part that religious leaders played in lawmaking, the delivery of justice and taxation.[89] To a substantial extent I concur with this vision. Still, as Arietta Papaconstantinou has argued, I think we do need to recognize that aristocratic landed wealth and influence persisted in many quarters and that the clerical leadership of Christian communities should not be treated as a given.[90] However, the development of middle-class professionals with great political influence at court in ninth- and tenth-century Baghdad[91] can be seen as the fulfilment of a process that is already evident in the case of 'Abd al-Malik and Bar Gumaye: Königsnähe became increasingly important as a source of elite wealth and status, whereas political autonomy based on independent landed wealth became less and less possible or attractive, at least for non-Muslims.

We should also be wary of drawing too neat a distinction between the interests of bishops and those of aristocrats. The sources reviewed in this chapter indicate that, in the seventh century at least, successful bishops were often themselves aristocrats, and that the expansion of monasticism in this period was a by-product of aristocratic ambition. Some Muslim sources do emphasize the significance of bishops as the leaders of Christian communities from the moment of the conquests.[92] And bishops had played a role as social patrons

88. For the dating of this passage, see Robinson 2000: 82.

89. Morony 2005.

90. Papaconstantinou 2020. Note that when Abu Yusuf 70/190 advocates the use of non-Muslim notables to facilitate taxation, he does not mention clerics explicitly.

91. Putman 1975.

92. E.g., Baladhuri 112/172 (Damascus), 273/174 (Edessa).

and judges in the sixth century that they sometimes continued in the Islamic period, as we have seen in the case of Theodota.[93] But the *Life of Theodota* suggests that his position reflected exceptional charisma rather than an institutionalized norm.

The texture of ecclesiastical history produced in the seventh century confirms this impression, at least for the Jacobites and the Church of the East. In Bar Hebraeus and Michael the Syrian, we hear very little of the Jacobite patriarchs between circa 630 and circa 740 compared to the periods before and after. And in the histories of the Church of the East by ʿAmr ibn Matta and Mari ibn Sulayman, there is a similar gulf between the fall of the Sasanians and the Abbasid revolution. ʿAmr covers the entirety of the seventh and eighth centuries in four pages, whereas he gives three pages to the usurper Surin in the year 753. Although modern historians have been able to write rich histories of the seventh century, they have done so using hagiography, not ecclesiastical history. I believe that the dearth of the latter type of material reflects the patriarchs' failure to command significant prestige or resources during the Umayyad period. This may reflect the distance of both Iraq and the Jazira from Umayyad centres of government.[94]

However, in the long term, it was the lay aristocrats who tended to be forgotten. There are certainly indications that they wished to preserve the memory of their houses: we see this wish in the tracing of a lineage for Simeon of the Olives and in Hugair's desire to name a monastery after himself. But such attempts at recollection were ultimately unsuccessful. Thomas of Marga delights in the destruction of Hugair's monastery, and no memory of Mundhar, the father of Simeon, or of Shahrizar of Shirwan endured to the end of the eighth century.

---

93. For bishops' efforts to secure tax remission for their clients, note Rapp 2005: 261 (on Cyrene); Brown 1992: 144 (on Sohag) and 151 (on peasants near Antioch). For their role in social networks that encompassed a variety of lay clients and patrons and their attempts to find employment for their contacts, see Schor 2011; Brown 1992: 106–9. And for their involvement in directing welfare, see Patlagean 1977; Brown 1992.

94. We can make a contrast here with Umayyad policies in Egypt and southern Syria, where intervention in church politics appears with much more regularity. A key example from the *History of the Patriarchs* (PO 10:62–63) is John of Ṣa, who persuaded the emir Qurra ibn Sharik to double the jizya on non-Miaphysites and then toured the Delta rebaptizing monks and laymen (discussion in Mikhail 2016: 44). For Muʿawiya's intervention on behalf of the Maronites against the Jacobites, see the account in the *Maronite Chronicle*, which is unmentioned in Jacobite sources.

The great exceptions to this rule are the noble histories recorded by Michael the Syrian, which derive from the history of Dionysius of Tel-Mahre. Michael devotes several scenes to showcasing the wealth of aristocrats in Edessa. He describes the Rusafaye, a noble family of the late sixth century, and tells the story of how, inspired by their competition with a rival aristocrat, one Marinus, they hosted the exiled shah Khusrau II (r. 591–628) in lavish splendour. However, Iwannis Rusafaya's refusal to allow his wife to serve wine to the shah ultimately led to his undoing: when the shah returned to the city as a conqueror a few years later, he seized Iwannis' wife and took her as a prisoner.[95]

Later on during the Persian occupation, a man named Cyrus acts as Khusrau's tax farmer in Edessa. Other aristocrats complain to Khusrau that Cyrus is overtaxing them. But the complaint only prompts the shah to raise taxes, to confiscate the treasures of the churches and to imprison those suspected of hiding their money, including Iwannis' son Sergius.[96]

The story of Athanasius bar Gumaye and ʿAbd al-Malik comes to us from Dionysius. But Dionysius also reports that the treasures of the Gumaye and Rusafaye were ultimately inherited by his own family, the Tel-Mahraye. Although he claims (probably disingenuously) that all these treasures had been spent by his time, the government of Harun al-Rashid became convinced that the Tel-Mahraye were concealing their wealth and sought to find and confiscate the family's treasures with the help of a Chalcedonian in Edessa. Dionysius describes Harun's despatch of one of his court eunuchs to locate the treasures and gives a detailed list of the items confiscated.[97]

The descriptions of the Rusafaye, Gumaye and Tel-Mahraye correspond well to Wickham's definition of aristocracy. Dionysius celebrates the families' acquisition of wealth and their protection of it from tax collectors, their competition with aristocratic peers and, in the later narratives, the importance of their connections to government. By virtue of these stories' survival, we also see that the aristocrats were concerned with their own memorialization. Dionysius recorded the stories because he was related to all these families and drew on the work of his grandfather Daniel of Tur Abdin to reach back across the six generations that lay between him and the Rusafaye.

---

95. MS X. 23 (IV, 386–87 / II, 371–72).
96. MS XI. 1 and 3 (IV, 404 / II, 402 and IV, 408–9 / II, 411).
97. MS XII. 4 (IV, 485–86 / III, 14). See also X1234 (II, 5/3) and BH Chron 130/167.

Conclusions

Should these Edessene families be considered unusual examples of aristocratic survival? With the caveat that proximity to government became increasingly significant for elites of all kinds, the answer is probably no. For instance, if we read Michael the Syrian's material for the ninth century carefully, we see lay elites wielding considerable influence in cities as different as Cyrrhus in northern Syria and Takrit in Iraq, case studies that I will examine further in chapters 4 and 5. What is unusual about the Rusafaye and the Gumaye is that their private histories were written down and survive because two of their descendants went on to become historians, and one of these was a patriarch. Indeed, Dionysius, according to his own depiction of himself in his history, exhibits several of the aristocratic behaviours that are celebrated in the anecdotes he tells of his ancestors: he is proud of his expensive education and prizes his ability to reduce government taxation or interference.[98] He is appalled by the efforts of a Muslim governor to free slaves, and he displays none of the concern for the poor that so marks the *Chronicle of Zuqnin*. Dionysius' self-fashioning then begs a further question, which I consider in the following chapter: at what point and why did a career in the church become an attractive proposition for an aristocrat such as Dionysius? And why did other bishops want a man like Dionysius to be patriarch?

98. These behaviours are analysed in chapter 2.

2

Patriarchs and Bishops

THE PERIOD CIRCA 740 TO 842 was particularly rich for history writing within the Jacobite church. The resulting material did not entail the naive recollection of events but rather provided a means of charting the lineage of the patriarchs of the Jacobite church and delineating the appropriate behaviour of contemporary patriarchs and bishops using models from the past.

We read about the events of this period in medieval compilations, most notably that of the patriarch Michael the Syrian. But much of what Michael reports he received (and often reformulated or abbreviated) from Dionysius of Tel-Mahre, his predecessor as patriarch.

In the accounts preserved in Michael, the history of the first half of this period, roughly 740–80, is a time of anarchy, and the underlying sources that he uses complain bitterly of the tyrannical rule of a series of anti-patriarchs, especially the notorious Athanasius Sandalaya (d. 758), bishop of Maypherkat. The 740s see a dramatic expansion in the density and complexity of ecclesiastical history writing among the Jacobites. This development is a sign both of the new prosperity of church institutions, which benefited from the same kind of caliphal patronage that Sandalaya received, and of the contentious nature of the events of this decade, particularly innovative practices such as tithing and the use of government troops, which were often condemned by various strands in the historical tradition. By contrast, the material preserved for the period 780–842 is much more at ease with the centralization of church government and the proximity of major churchmen to Muslim rulers.

Dionysius' introduction refers to two of his predecessors who wrote 'narratives resembling ecclesiastical history', Daniel son of Moses of Tur Abdin (Dionysius' grandfather) and John son of Samuel of the western regions. I propose that the multivocality of Michael's *Chronicle* for the period 740–80

likely reflects Dionysius' use of multiple sources, to which Dionysius has occasionally added his own comments.

Dionysius also refers to one Theodosius of Edessa, probably Dionysius'
own brother, who enjoyed a prominent position during the reign of Cyriacus
of Takrit (r. 793–817). The shift in attitudes that I lay out below may reflect the
transition from one source base to another, from peripheral commentators
less connected to major circles of power to a lieutenant of the patriarch who
is able to offer well-informed criticism but is broadly sympathetic to the political necessities of the day.

In this chapter I examine the layered narratives that Dionysius provides
for the period of 'anarchy' and then turn to Dionysius' depiction of his own
generation. Using the contrast between the earlier and the later material, I
argue that two major changes are apparent. The first is the shift in the recruitment of patriarchs from Qartmin, the monastery that had dominated the
patriarchate in the mid-eighth century, to other monasteries, such as Qenneshre, Dionysius' alma mater. The second is the change in the criteria for
patriarchal tyranny between the eighth-century historians and Dionysius.[1]
Whereas the Qartminite patriarchs are often criticized for their proximity
to Muslim rulers, reliance on caliphal support had become much more
common by the time of Dionysius and correlates with the greater security
and central authority of ninth-century patriarchs. Both of these changes
are linked to the questions posed at the end of the first chapter regarding
how an aristocrat such as Dionysius became an attractive appointee as
patriarch.

Athanasius Sandalaya in the *Chronicle* of Michael the Syrian

One of the first instances of a Jacobite churchman receiving patronage from
Muslim rulers occurs in the controversial career of Athanasius Sandalaya ('the
cobbler'), bishop of Maypherkat and monk of Qartmin. Much of the narrative
preserved by Michael the Syrian represents Sandalaya as a villain. But this was
not a universal opinion.[2] The *Chronicle of 819*, written in the monastery of
Qartmin, records the accession of three Qartminite monks to the patriarchate:

---

1. The existence of this contrast suggests that the eighth-century sources have been transmitted reasonably faithfully. Their attraction for Dionysius may have been that they took a critical
position during a period of Qartminite domination of the patriarchate.

2. Cf. Palmer 1990: 170; R. Abramowski 1940: 95 n. 1 and 102 n. 1.

Ishaq of Harran, Athanasius Sandalaya and David of Dara.[3] In the thirteenth-century martyrology of Rabban Sliba, also from Qartmin, Sandalaya is venerated as a saint.[4] The *Chronicle of Zuqnin*, written soon after Sandalaya's death, displays none of the animus of Michael's chronicle. In a note set in the 740s (the reign of Marwan II), he is simply the holy Athanasius, bishop of Maypherkat, 'who later became patriarch'.[5] On Sandalaya's death, the *Chronicle* refers to the existence of a controversy but refuses to say more: '[Like Ishaq] he did not live long, but he died quickly [after entering office]. Other people say other things, but, as for us, we dare not say anything about concealed things, but we leave them to God'.[6]

We get a sense of the complexity of Sandalaya's reputation from the first anecdote that Dionysius gives about him (which is also the first point at which he can give any kind of detailed narrative of events in the Jacobite church since before the Muslim conquest). In a very brief paragraph, Dionysius describes how the bishops came to elect Iwannis of the monastery of Eusebona as patriarch and notes that Athanasius of Maypherkat was present at the election along with the other bishops.

This passage is then followed by an account of the election itself, under the heading 'How *adbē* (lots) first came to be used in the church'. The historian reports that Sandalaya was selected to administer the election because of his age and piety and that he was responsible for writing the names of the candidates on slips of paper before placing them on the altar. Another man then chose one at random. The historian comments that Sandalaya tricked the assembly by writing Iwannis' name on all three slips of paper. A slip was chosen three times, he says, and each time the name of Iwannis came up. A bystander announced, 'This was the finger of God!'[7]

---

3. *Chronicle to 819*, AG 1066 and 1073 (18–19 / 13). The text stresses that all three bishops were also monks of Qartmin. The ecclesiastical history in this chronicle extends up to c. 785; the material after this consists of lists of caliphs (to 813) and patriarchs (to 819).

4. Peeters 1908: 133. BH HE I, 319 also notes the continued veneration of Sandalaya at Qartmin.

5. *Chronicle of Zuqnin*, 190/176.

6. *Chronicle of Zuqnin*, 210/193.

7. MS XI. 21 (IV, 462–63 / II, 503–4). The main biblical precedent for this procedure was the selection of an apostle to replace Judas in Acts 1:23–26. Lot casting was widely used in Near Eastern societies in contexts ranging from inheritance to the division of booty and the manumission of slaves. Although the practice petered out in most late Roman settings, it persisted in sixth-century Petra and in Arabia. The example here coincides with the seventh- and

However, Dionysius makes an editorial comment at this point in the narrative. Dionysius seems to have been unhappy with the ironic, almost blasphemous tone of the earlier story, in which Sandalaya falsely invokes the Holy Spirit. Dionysius argues that Iwannis' election could not have been due to Sandalaya's ruse but rather was the outcome of divine providence. He asks rhetorically, 'If God should know that a sparrow will fall from the sky, how could he allow the fraudulent election of a patriarch?'[8]

Later sections of Michael's *Chronicle* relate the anarchy of Iwannis' reign as patriarch and the lavish presents he gives to the caliph Marwan II to ensure his election. The *Chronicle* reports the strife of Iwannis and Sandalaya against bishop David of Dara over the election of a bishop for the Tur Abdin and the rebellion of bishop Bacchus of Nineveh, who had been consecrated without the consent of his metropolitan (in Takrit).[9] This is followed by a breakdown in relations between Iwannis and Sandalaya when the patriarch is faced with numerous nominations for candidates to the sees of Amida and the Tur Abdin from the new caliph al-Mansur, from the citizens of these sees and from various bishops. As Dionysius puts it, 'This was the start of the divisions between Sandalaya and the patriarch Iwannis. Amid these [events] the patriarch was very confused and turned first to the caliph, then to the bishops, and then to the people. And he was besieged by divisions and discord. This was not because of [matters of] faith, but because of their desire for leadership'.[10]

The following chapter of the *Chronicle* (23) describes Sandalaya's cultivation of his relationship with Marwan II and how he accused Iwannis of receiving money for ordinations and performing magic and unspeakable sexual practices. Iwannis, meanwhile, accuses Sandalaya of gathering a harem of women and bribing the caliph. One consequence was that Iwannis was forced

---

eighth-century data collected by Crone and Silverstein (2016), who plausibly argue that lot casting represented a reassertion of local practices after the Arab conquests. Though there are no other examples of lot casting in books 11 and 12 of Michael, Ibn Jarir (31, 97) refers to it as regular practice in the eleventh century.

8. This passage is also quoted in BH HE I, 307.

9. MS XI. 22 (IV, 465–66 / II, 507–8).

10. MS XI. 22 (IV, 467 / II, 510). I attribute this statement to Dionysius because of the very similar sentiments expressed in MS XII. 14 (IV, 517 / III, 65), which Michael explicitly attributes to Dionysius: 'The Lord did not allow divisions (*sedqē*) to appear among us because of heresy (*erisis*), but He troubled us with the quarrels and plots of dioceses against their bishops and dreadful accusations . . . against their high priests'.

to pay a colossal bribe to Marwan.[11] However, Sandalaya experienced a sudden loss of power when Marwan was toppled in the Abbasid revolution, and we are told that all the bishops, led by David of Dara, stood with Iwannis and condemned Sandalaya at a synod in Harran in 750.[12] However, not long afterward, Sandalaya was able to arrange a reconciliation with Iwannis at a private meeting at Tamarna in Syria and also acquired a new Muslim patron in the form of ʿAbd Allah, the future caliph al-Mansur and brother of the new caliph al-Saffah.[13] Wielding a diploma issued by ʿAbd Allah, Sandalaya was confirmed as metropolitan of Maypherkat at a synod held in Tella in 752.[14] This decision involved the creation of a new metropolitanate in Maypherkat and represented a major reordering of the precedence of the episcopal sees. Iwannis composed a long letter to David of Dara and the bishops at Tella in which he rehabilitates Sandalaya in the interests of harmony, but our historian reads the Tella synod as a major embarrassment, in which 'the work that was demolished at Harran was rebuilt' and where political pressure meant that an earlier, principled opposition to Sandalaya was abandoned. Immediately after his elevation, Sandalaya built an impressive church at Maypherkat.[15]

However, in chapter 24 the historian grimly notes that the protestations of humility that Sandalaya had made to Iwannis did not generate any real change in Sandalaya's behaviour. Sandalaya establishes an alleged 'alchemist', Ishaq, as bishop of Harran in order to gain access to the government.[16] He uses this influence to denounce his opponents, Timothy of Edessa[17] and David of Dara,[18] and to parcel out bishoprics to his clients.[19] The opposition to Sandalaya in this part of the narrative comes from David of Dara rather than the patriarch himself.

Chapter 25 opens with the death of Iwannis. He is swiftly followed as patriarch by the alchemist Ishaq of Harran, Sandalaya's nominee. But Ishaq is soon

---

11. MS XI. 23 (IV, 468 / II, 512).

12. MS XI. 23 (IV, 468 / II, 512). The detail on the fall of Marwan is not mentioned in MS but is present in BH HE I, 311.

13. The fact that he is referred to as ʿAbd Allah, not al-Mansur, may suggest that the narrative was composed very close to the events described.

14. MS XI. 23 (IV, 470 / II, 514–15).

15. MS XI. 23 (IV, 470 / II, 516–17).

16. Alchemy was a well-known interest of the caliph al-Mansur: Gutas 1998: 115.

17. MS XI. 24 (IV, 472 / II, 519).

18. MS XI. 24 (IV, 472 / II, 519–20).

19. MS XI. 24 (IV, 472–73 / II, 520–21).

put to death after the caliph al-Mansur (allegedly) realizes that he cannot transmute lead into gold.[20] Sandalaya is then himself elected patriarch, only to be strangled in the night by the citizens of Harran when he tries to impose his choice of bishop on them.[21] He is succeeded by George of Beltan, a monk of Qenneshre who is selected because of his learning in Greek and Syriac and whose piety had been foretold in visions.[22] However, David of Dara and John of Callinicum raise objections to George's consecration because he is only a deacon, and the bishops eventually consecrate John as patriarch. George then establishes himself as a rival patriarch to John. After John's death, George is imprisoned by the caliph, and David of Dara controversially succeeds him as the sole patriarch.

A Shifting Cast of Villains

The disjointed texture of the narrative we have just reviewed is striking. Most noticeably, its sections have quite different central protagonists: we move from Iwannis and Sandalaya operating together to the conflict between them, to the conflict between Sandalaya and David of Dara, to the reigns of Ishaq and Sandalaya as patriarchs. One possible reason for this lack of cohesion is that the narrative was composed as the events unfolded. The initial section may have been written at a time when Iwannis seemed like a political contender who faced defiance from Sandalaya and did not receive the support he deserved from David of Dara and the other bishops. But chapter 25 adopts Sandalaya as an antihero, suppressing all mention of Iwannis and elevating David of Dara to the role of Sandalaya's chief adversary. Here Sandalaya is identified as the source of the woes of the church, which leads the author to emphasize David as his opponent, whereas later parts of the narrative make David the villain for his opposition to the saintly George of Beltan. Chapter 26 lacks any obvious focus and gives the sense that the author is a prisoner of his genre. The author of this chapter seems to expect that the patriarch and the bishops ought to wield the agency in his history, but here it is the caliph who determines the election and deposition of candidates.

20. MS XI. 25 (IV, 474 / II, 524).
21. MS XI. 25 (IV, 475 / II, 525).
22. For George's composition of poetry and commentaries on the Greek patristics, see Barsoum 2003: 369–70.

If these chapters had been written as a single piece, we would expect the death of Sandalaya to be worked up into a major denouement, given that he is identified as the main source of the anarchy of the preceding years. But instead his death is passed over in a paragraph. It is certainly a shameful event, as the chronicler of Zuqnin observed,[23] and it may reach us through the reports of Sandalaya's opponents, but it is notable that the author of this section makes so little of it. Events had already moved ahead by the time this chapter was composed, and the author was more concerned with the failure of the church to acknowledge George.

A major theme of these narratives is Sandalaya's corruption: he is accused of bribing the caliph and selling offices to gain influence. In particular, the author (or authors) highlights his wish to control the see of Harran. This seat was significant because Harran was the caliphal capital during the 740s and thus a prime site in which to influence the caliph.[24] But it was also a pocket see of the monastery of Qartmin. One of the intentions behind the *Chronicle to 819* was to advertise the Qartminite origins of the bishops of Harran and Dara and the monastery's control of these sees (and occasionally the patriarchate as well).[25] Moreover, as Andrew Palmer has shown, the *Chronicle to 846* can be seen as a continuation of the *Chronicle to 819*, one that was written in Harran itself.[26]

With these links in mind, we can read chapters 22 and 23 as a protest against the worldly behaviour of the monks of Qartmin, who used their influence over the caliph to secure power for their own supporters and to ignore church precedent by dividing sees and raising Maypherkat to a metropolitanate. This anti-Qartmin stance is focused against Sandalaya in particular in chapter 24 and then finds a hero of its own in George of Beltan. George was a monk of Qenneshre, the same monastery that produced Dionysius of Tel-Mahre, and

23. *Chronicle of Zuqnin*, 210/193.

24. Iwannis had been bishop of Harran before becoming patriarch. I discuss the significance of Harran further in chapter 4.

25. Palmer 1990: 153–55 suggests that Qartmin's importance began in the early seventh century, at a time when Chalcedonians dominated the cities but abbot Daniel of Qartmin was made metropolitan of Tella, Mardin, Dara and the Tur Abdin, according to the *Chronicle to 819*, AG 926 (10/7). Similarly, the ten bishops present at the funeral of Gabriel of Qartmin (*Life of Gabriel*, LXXXVII) may suggest that Gabriel held an elevated status as bishop of the Tur Abdin. Also see Honigmann 1954: 140–41.

26. Palmer et al. 1993: 83; Palmer 1990: 8–13.

PATRIARCHS AND BISHOPS 69

it seems likely that the layered source that is repeated here was composed in Qenneshre.

The case of the patriarch Iwannis is slightly more complex. He was a monk of Eusebona near Antioch and does not fit clearly into the networks of any of the great monasteries that tended to produce patriarchs in the eighth and ninth centuries. He also engaged in the kinds of activities that were condemned in Sandalaya's case, namely bribing the caliph and dividing sees to maximize patronage or raise revenue.[27] But he is presented in Michael's *Chronicle* as a victim of Sandalaya rather than an agent of corruption, which raises the question of why the author of this account is so keen to shield him.

If we return to the scene of Iwannis' election, I suspect that the underlying narrative had emphasized Iwannis as the legitimate candidate because of Sandalaya's holiness; the assertion of the latter's preeminence among the bishops contradicts his later depiction as a villain and must form part of a narrative in which the use of lots in an election was defended. A later author then composed the detailed description of Sandalaya's forgery. Palmer persuasively argues that this author was Daniel, Dionysius' own grandfather, who seems to have had a predilection for tales of political deceit and trickery.[28] This second narrative was written with foreknowledge of Sandalaya's villainous reputation, and it reduces Iwannis to the position of a pawn of Sandalaya. There are hints in chapter 22 of a more independent view of Iwannis, which sees him at least as an equal partner and ally of Sandalaya, criticizes the bishops for their jealousy of Iwannis' position and passes over his gifts to Marwan II without comment. It is likely, then, that the story of Sandalaya's rigging of the election of Iwannis reflects the later depiction of Sandalaya as a villain in chapter 24, where Iwannis is reduced to a powerless figurehead and criticism of episcopal corruption becomes a major concern of the text.

However, as we have seen, Dionysius was not happy with his grandfather's sceptical reading of the lot scene. Dionysius lived in a period in which patriarchal elections tended to be relatively straightforward and could command consensus. Furthermore, Dionysius' own legislation in the synods puts great emphasis on the centrality of the Eucharist and on the role of excommunication in punishing Christian wrongdoers.[29] This vision of Christian life depends on the presence of the Holy Spirit and the ability of the clergy to invoke

27. This is discussed in further detail in chapter 3.
28. Palmer 1990: 169.
29. I explore this legislation in chapter 6.

it, and Daniel's cynicism regarding Iwannis' election may thus have challenged his grandson's image of Jacobite society.

The Characteristics of a Patriarch

One way of reading the narrative of these events is as a series of recommendations for the behaviour of patriarchs. The accusations levelled at Sandalaya and Iwannis—of simony and magic in the case of Iwannis and of fornication in that of Sandalaya—are telling indications of the potential pitfalls of the role.[30] Fornication was an obvious accusation to make against a celibate bishop, especially in an environment in which non-episcopal priests could marry. An allegation of magic was a dangerous threat against the product of a bookish monastery, and it could draw the wrath of Muslim rulers as well as fellow Christians.[31] And in spite of Michael's positive presentation of Iwannis, a charge of simony would be credible for a patriarch who paid large sums of money to the caliph.[32] As in any many political systems, the line between bribery and a patron-client relationship may well have been unclear, and one man's gift (as Michael depicts Iwannis' payment to Marwan II) was another man's bribe.[33]

Though simony obviously continued to be a major sin in Dionysius' eyes,[34] it seems likely that by his day, the securing of expensive courtly influence was an important and expected part of the patriarchal office.[35] The authors of chapters 22–26 had seen the close relationships enjoyed by Sandalaya and David of Dara with Muslim governors as evidence of their corruption. But

30. MS XI. 23 (IV, 468 / II, 512).

31. Note, for instance, the warnings against priests performing magic in the *Life of Theodota*, 108, and in the responses of Jacob of Edessa (Tannous 2018: 265). Also compare the cautionary tale in the *Chronicle of Seert* (PO 13:464), which is directed at priests tempted to employ magic, and the accusations of sorcery made against the monks of Mar Mattai (see *Life of Rabban Hormizd*, 22 [95/141], for the saint battling the sorcerer Ignatius). See further Tannous 2018: 228–33.

32. However, the definition of simony changed over time. In the sixth century, unlike in the fourth, charges of simony were in practice restricted to the auctioning of offices to the highest bidder, rather than entailing a complete ban on money changing hands. See Huebner 2009: 177.

33. A point underscored in Kelly 2004, which comments on the moralizing tone of much of the secondary literature on late Roman corruption.

34. See MS XII. 17 (IV, 525 / III, 80) for Dionysius condemning simony in Egypt.

35. See further discussion in chapter 3.

Dionysius is proud of his close relationship with 'Abd Allah ibn Tahir, the governor of Syria and Egypt,[36] and with the caliph al-Ma'mun himself.[37] When David of Dara uses Persian troops to force the people to attend church, he is denounced as a false patriarch.[38] But when patriarch Cyriacus of Takrit uses his governmental connections to force his way into the church of a defiant bishop, Severus of Samosata, it is Cyriacus whom Dionysius deems to be in the right.[39]

The contrast in attitudes toward the use of paid influence and government coercion is partly a matter of perspective. From the historian's point of view, David of Dara and Sandalaya were, of course, anti-patriarchs. But there was also a broader shift that led such activity to be considered natural. For the *Chronicle's* author(s), political connections between the patriarchs and Muslim leaders seem to have been largely uncontroversial, and they saw no need to defend them. In my view, this generational shift in attitudes reflects a break in the sources that Michael draws on through Dionysius, which move from the layered narratives of Sandalaya and his contemporaries to narratives that conceive of George's reign as a precursor to the reigns of Cyriacus and Dionysius, and from the more peripheral perspective of men such as Daniel to the viewpoint of Theodosius of Edessa (Dionysius' brother) and Dionysius.

Perhaps the most striking example of the divergence in attitudes relates to the use of allegations of anti-Islamic blasphemy. Sandalaya is said to have accused Timothy of Edessa of criticizing Sandalaya himself, the caliph al-Mansur and the Prophet Muhammad.[40] Such an accusation, brought to a ruler who had come to power through revolution and was keen to display his Islamic credentials, could have been a canny manipulation of the political situation.[41] The accusation conflates the respective authority of the patriarch, the caliph

36. See MS XII. 12 (IV, 508–9 / III, 56) for Dionysius' meeting with 'Abd Allah ibn Tahir at Raqqa to denounce Abiram of Cyrrhus, and MS XII. 13 (IV, 514 / III, 62) for Dionysius petitioning 'Abd Allah to prevent the persecution of Yaqdan at Edessa.

37. MS XII. 14 (IV, 517ff. / III, 65ff.).

38. MS XI. 26 (IV, 477 / II, 529).

39. MS XII. 3 (IV, 484 / III, 12).

40. MS XI. 24 (IV, 472 / II, 519).

41. For the credentials of the Abbasids as restorers of divine rule in the Muslim world through their blessed regime (*dawla mubāraka*), see, amid a large literature, El-Hibri 1999: 1–3; Tillier 2009: 96; Crone 2004: 88–96; Zaman 1997. For al-Mansur's own bloody role in the Abbasid revolution, see Kennedy 1986: chs. 3–5.

and the Prophet and represents Timothy as a blasphemous opponent of good order in the caliphate.[42]

In a similar vein, David of Dara is said to have accused George of Beltan of saying that the reason he, George, did not carry a caliphal diploma (*sigiliyun*) to confirm his authority was that he would not carry the name of Muhammad on his person.[43] Diplomas were issued to allow a patriarch to act legitimately, especially in collecting tithes from his co-religionists. There is no sense in the narrative preserved in Michael that George really did resent holding a document with the name of Muhammad, or criticize the use of diplomas per se. In this narrative it seems to be an opportunistic accusation by David that plays on Muslim suspicions of what Christians really thought. It seems possible that David's accusation was an invention of his Christian opponents, made after the caliph imprisoned George. [44]

However, the representation of the patriarch's diploma in the *Chronicle to 813* is rather different. Here diplomas are much more prominent: Ishaq is said to ask for a diploma because he knows that his authority would otherwise be ignored,[45] and Athanasius Sandalaya and David of Dara are both said to have been given a diploma and the use of imperial troops, who force the unwilling to accept communion.[46] For this chronicle, George's refusal to carry a diploma is a principled opposition: he tells the caliph, 'It is not my intention to compel anyone to submit to me.'[47] In the *Chronicle to 813* there is a direct connection between the diploma and force, and it is associated with Qartminite anti-patriarchs who are contrasted to the pious George.[48]

42. MS XI. 24 (IV, 472 / II, 519).

43. MS XI. 26 (IV, 476 / II, 527). *Sigiliyun* is the standard term for a diploma to confirm patriarchal authority. It derives from Greek.

44. The *Chronicle of Zuqnin* (249–50 / 220–21) gives a more complex picture in which David is elected unwillingly after the caliph insists that the Jacobites select a leader, and the caliph's men use force in David's name without his command. In this account, the popular hatred for David is widespread but undeserved.

45. *Chronicle to 813* (244/185).

46. *Chronicle to 813* (244/186; 247/187).

47. *Chronicle to 813* (247/187).

48. It may be that there was quite a stark difference in attitudes to the diploma between Dionysius and his sources that was not reconciled in his history, and that the *Chronicle to 813* is an early witness to Dionysius that left this difference intact. In this case it would be Michael or another intermediary who has downplayed the negative associations of the diploma given that Dionysius himself used a caliphal diploma in his dispute with Abiram. Alternatively, the

At any rate, the depiction of Sandalaya or David as being in league with the Muslims may have been a credible allegation, since it extended accusations of worldly corruption by emphasizing the Islamic character of the Abbasid caliphate, the patriarchs' patrons. In these anecdotes, Sandalaya and David appear as power-hungry allies of the new regime who exploit the vulnerability of their own co-religionists, Timothy and George, to accusations of blasphemy. But again, there is a marked contrast to the attitudes conveyed in accounts of Dionysius' own reign. Whereas the truth of David's reported willingness to cooperate with the Muslim authorities is unknown, Dionysius tells us quite matter-of-factly of his own attempts to win over al-Maʾmun by presenting patriarchal authority in Islamic terms.[49] There was thus a shift in the way in which the profile of a legitimate patriarch was constructed. In the earlier narratives, alignment with Muslim rulers was an illegitimate act that could be used to undermine the anti-patriarchs of the era. But to a later generation, Cyriacus' and Dionysius' collusion with the government was not controversial. In Dionysius' description of his actions, there is no sense that he felt a need to cover them up as inappropriate or unchristian.

George of Beltan and Joseph of Gubba Barraya

In the earlier narratives, David of Dara and Athanasius Sandalaya are antiheroes who embody inverted images of patriarchal legitimacy. We encounter a very different presentation of George of Beltan and Cyriacus of Takrit, who were Dionysius' immediate predecessors.

George is presented in Michael's *Chronicle* as a learned ascetic who is unfairly imprisoned and replaced by David. Those who remain loyal to him are characterized in the terms used by sixth-century Jacobite historians for the great missionaries Jacob Baradeus and John of Tella: they are forced to wear ragged clothes and travel in secret out of fear of a persecuting state.[50] Conversely, David of Dara and his Muslim allies are portrayed in the negative terms

---

Chronicle to 813 may not draw on Dionysius himself and instead uses similar sources. It is hard to draw a conclusion here because the *Chronicle to 813* is an acephalous fragment.

49. MS XII. 14 (IV, 517ff. / III, 65ff.)

50. For these figures, see Menze 2008; Wood 2010: 167–69; Bundy 1978; Saint-Laurent 2015. The hagiographic texts are Elias, *Life of John of Tella*; John of Ephesus, *Lives of the Eastern Saints*, PO 18 and PO 19; and the spurious *Life of Jacob Baradeus* (included in Brooks' edition and translation of John's *Lives of the Eastern Saints*, PO 19). John of Tella was long commemorated as a victim of Chalcedonian persecution: Peeters 1908: 175.

used for earlier Chalcedonian persecutors in the works of sixth-century hagiographers.

George was widely considered the legitimate patriarch by the time of his death, and his purging of bishops ordained by David meant that his successors had an obvious motivation to uphold his memory over that of David.[51] Though skilled in Greek and Syriac, George had been consecrated patriarch while only a deacon, and this had been a point of criticism at the time. David of Dara and John of Callinicum are said to have objected to the elevation of 'a man in white garments' to the patriarchal throne and organized a rival faction, which consecrated John as an anti-patriarch.[52] But the subsequent histories of John and David, as told in Michael's *Chronicle*, invalidate the objections raised against George: readers are meant to conclude that George's learning and piety made him a suitable patriarch. This conclusion would be especially pointed if Dionysius was the author or transmitter of this section, since he, like George, was a monk of Qenneshre, famous for its educational programme in Greek and Syriac, and like George he was selected as patriarch without being ordained.[53]

However, in spite of George's pious reputation, the two depictions of George's encounters with Muslim authority in Michael's history can be read as tacit criticisms of the patriarch for his lack of political acumen and his lack of ability in Arabic. As we have seen, David reportedly accused George of re-fusing to carry the caliph's diploma because it bore the name of the Prophet. George is brought before the caliph and swears in Greek, *Theotokou boēthē*, 'Mother of God, help me!' His enemies seize on the words to accuse him of blaspheming the name of the Prophet, and the guards strike him. Although our source claims that George was able to pacify the situation, the scene none-theless ends in George's imprisonment and David's elevation.[54]

In the second scene, which takes place after al-Mansur's death, George is released from prison and appears before 'Ali, governor of the Jazira, who brings him to Callinicum. George is able to convince 'Ali that the accusations made against him were false only through the assistance of one Theodosius, who translates George's statements into Arabic.[55]

51. MS XII. 1 (IV, 478 / III, 3).
52. MS XI. 25 (IV, 475 / II, 525).
53. MS XII. 10 (IV, 502 / III, 41).
54. MS XI. 26 (IV, 476–77 / II, 527–28).
55. MS XII. 2 (IV, 479 / III, 3–4).

The point that comes across from these reports, without ever being stated explicitly, is that proficiency in Arabic is a necessary component of the diplomatic competency of a patriarch. By a similar token, although the mastery of Greek is an important intellectual skill, Greek is also the language of the caliph's Byzantine enemies and thus not one to use in the caliph's court, where George's innocent exclamation is taken as blasphemy.[56] A possible reason for Dionysius' repeating of this anecdote was to emphasize the importance of his own linguistic skills.

A similar point about the importance of patriarchal eloquence is made in the *Chronicle*'s comments on George's short-lived successor, Joseph of Gubba Barraya: 'When the bishops saw his beautiful face they rejoiced in him, but when they heard his barbarous tongue they wanted to send him back to his convent.'[57] The issue may have been Joseph's use of Syriac rather than his lack of proficiency in Arabic, and the subtext may be that Gubba Barraya did not have Qenneshre's educational reputation.[58] Especially since both Cyriacus and Dionysius experienced considerable problems with the Gubbite monks, it may be that this barbed comment also served to highlight the poor cultural capital of the Gubbites when compared to men who hailed from the elite families of Edessa and Takrit or were equipped with an education from Qenneshre or Mar Zakkai.

Cyriacus of Takrit

If the comments on George and Joseph betray desiderata for the linguistic capabilities of a patriarch, no such criticism is made of Cyriacus. He is described as 'an eloquent man, holy in his body and in his soul', who is received 'like an angel' by the people of Edessa. However, Cyriacus' reign was filled with strife with the monks of Gubba Barraya and Mar Mattai, and much of this strife, our author implies, was his own fault.

Cyriacus was the product of an intellectual complex: he was a member of an elite family in Takrit, a city that produced the lion's share of the Jacobite

56. The period of instability around the Abbasid revolution allowed a number of Byzantine military victories, which the Greek historian Theophanes (AM 6249) implies prompted increased suspicion of Christians within the caliphate and a curtailment of their political rights. Fiey 1980: 27 suggests that this phenomenon was restricted to border regions.

57. MS XII. 3 (IV, 483 / III, 10).

58. For the significance of Qenneshre as an educational centre in both Greek and Syriac, see Tannous 2013.

theologians of the ninth century. Unlike his predecessors, he also produced works of theology himself, including a voluminous work on divine providence and an Arabic *Life of Severus of Antioch*.[59] It was his interest in theology that led him to attempt a reform of the liturgy employed among the Jacobites of Syria and the Jazira, which I discuss in detail in chapter 4.[60]

Cyriacus' proposed liturgical intervention prompted a strong reaction from the Gubbite monks, who saw it as an unprecedented innovation that flew in the face of established custom, and this schism persisted into Dionysius' reign. Dionysius' own approach was markedly different from that of Cyriacus. He assured the Gubbites that although Cyriacus had been theologically correct, he, Dionysius, would not make any attempt to enforce Cyriacus' plan, and each priest could follow his own conscience.[61] In his history, Dionysius notes that George had taken a similarly agnostic stance on this issue, which makes Cyriacus' actions look like an outlier.[62] Dionysius thus compares Cyriacus' exacting theological attitude unfavourably with his own pragmatism.

A second, slightly different, criticism of Cyriacus emerges if one reads between the lines of Dionysius' account, namely that he was a poor judge of character. Cyriacus relies on faulty advice and appoints a man named Solomon to the see of Cyrrhus, which was historically always held by a monk of Gubba Barraya; the appointment contributes to the Gubbite schism.[63] Even in his hometown of Takrit, Cyriacus seems to mismanage matters when the citizens of Takrit complain about their bishop, Simeon. Cyriacus attempts, unsuccessfully, to reconcile Simeon to the Takritians, and Dionysius, probably relying on Theodosius, gives the impression that Cyriacus is spared further conflict only by Simeon's early death.[64] In each of these cases, Cyriacus seems reluctant to allow extra-episcopal forces to determine the fate of a bishop. By contrast, yet again, Dionysius seems to advocate a pragmatic course that acknowledges

59. Oez 2012 summarizes Cyriacus' oeuvre.

60. MS XII. 2 (481–82 / 5–7) (for the theological issues) and XII. 3 (484/11) (for the implementation).

61. This decision was reached during the interregnum synod that followed Cyriacus' death; MS XII. 9 (IV, 498–501 / III, 37–41). For its introduction by Dionysius in his discussions with the Gubbites, see XII. 11 (IV, 504 / III, 44). I examine these events in greater detail in chapter 4.

62. MS XII. 2 (IV, 481 / III, 5). Cf. BH HE I, 331.

63. MS XII. 6 (IV, 488 / III, 19).

64. MS XII. 8 (IV, 493–94 / III, 28). For further discussion, see chapter 5.

the practical control exerted by certain cities and monasteries over their pocket bishoprics.

Conclusions

I have argued in this chapter that Dionysius was heir to a historical tradition rooted in the monastery of Qenneshre that vilified Athanasius Sandalaya as a scion of the rival monastery of Qartmin and as an innovator of 'tyrannical' methods of church governance, such as the collection of tithes. The sources that Dionysius preserves reveal evolving attitudes to a rapidly changing political landscape at the time of the Abbasid revolution.

The irony is that Dionysius himself views such practices as the gathering of tithes as quite unexceptional. His condemnation of Sandalaya involves two kinds of amnesia: in the first, the patriarchs produced by the monastery of Qartmin are labelled anti-patriarchs, and in the second, the perceived tyrannies of one generation are accepted as normal practice in another. However, Dionysius is unable to simply alter the memory of his immediate predecessors, George and Cyriacus. Accordingly, his approach in discussing these figures is more nuanced, and he carefully sets out his own pragmatism and competence without making his criticisms explicit.

Through the shifting representation of Dionysius' predecessors, we see the changing forms of cultural capital required of a patriarch with close links to the caliphal government and the growing capacity of church authorities to intervene in the affairs of Christians, in particular their new ability to raise large revenues. I believe that these developments help to explain Dionysius' attractiveness as a patriarch on the one hand and the attractiveness of the position for Dionysius himself on the other: by his time, the patriarchate had become a highly influential institution, but patriarchs also required a greater range of political skills than had hitherto been the case. In terms of both the rewards of the office and the necessary qualifications for it, established aristocratic families now perceived a good fit between their interests and the position of the patriarch.

3

Tithes, Authority and Hierarchy, 740–840

THE PRECEDING CHAPTER examined the narrative in books 11 and 12 of Michael the Syrian's *Chronicle* for evidence of the changing motivations of historians in representing the patriarchate. But we can also use the same narrative to describe the patriarchs' governance of the church in greater detail. Here I identify three areas in which the infrastructure of church governance changed in this period: the involvement of the caliphal government in the promotion of bishops, the ratification of patriarchal rights through official diplomas and patriarchs' use of their ties to the caliph to protect the rights of Christians. In particular, I demonstrate what the greater proximity between the patriarch and the caliph meant for the Jacobite hierarchy, and how the threat of Muslim populations encouraged the Jacobite leadership to act as a service elite for the caliph.

Monopoly of Access and the Clerical Hierarchy

In the church of the sixth century, it had been the emperor who convened the great councils of the church to agree on orthodox doctrine and the excommunication of dissenters.[1] But after the Arab conquests, churches within the caliphate could be left uncertain about who could legitimately convene a council, especially when there were multiple claimants to the patriarchate or no sitting patriarch at all. The history of the Jacobite church as an

1. Drake 2000 (on councils under Constantine); Gaddis 2005: ch. 8 and Graumann 2013 (on the councils of Ephesus I in 431 and Chalcedon in 451); Price and Whitby 2010 (on Chalcedon and the councils of the sixth and seventh centuries).

organization whose episcopal structure had developed during rural exile also meant that the seats of this development were closely connected to the patriarchate: monasteries such as Qenneshre, Qartmin and Gubba Barraya had traditionally been nurseries of future patriarchs, and they constituted hotbeds of opposition to patriarchs who did not come from this background.[2]

The relatively decentralized, rural composition of the Jacobite church meant that bishops could find it hard to maintain their prerogatives according to church canons. Canonists had to condemn the practice of laypeople going to individuals other than bishops for judgement, whether these were monks[3] or powerful laymen.[4] The laymen in question may have been Christian magnates or local Muslim leaders. Other canons denounced those who form factions and appeal to laymen to intervene in theological quarrels,[5] and they excommunicated members of the lower clergy who ask Muslim leaders to overturn decisions.[6] I will return to these issues in chapter 6, but it is worth stressing here that the concern of these canons was not only to insulate Christians from Muslim jurisdiction but also to assert the rights of the clergy over lay and monastic rivals.

The shrill condemnations of perceived usurpations of authority indicate the church's reliance on symbolic power: bishops could impose bans on communion or acts of penance, such as chastity, but their ability to enforce these penalties was normally limited to excommunication and calls for ostracism.[7] Bishops were empowered to act as judges, but even then the authority of a given bishop relied on the acquiescence of other Christians to his decisions.[8] The patriarchs Cyriacus and Dionysius were given the support of the caliph's

2. See Frend 1972: 294–95 and 320; Wood 2010: 170 on the rural displacement of the sixth century. The appendix to MS gives the training and places of ordination for all the Jacobite patriarchs, which makes the dominance of these monasteries in the sixth to ninth centuries very clear. See also *Chronicle of Zuqnin*, 244–45 / 217–18, for comments on the arrogance of bishops drawn from 'famous monasteries'. Cf. the comments of Oez 2012: I, 38.

3. Synod of Dionysius II, canons 8 and 10 (Vööbus 1975–76: 60–61 / 64–65).

4. Synod of Ignatius, canon 4 (Vööbus 1975–76: 53/57).

5. Synod of Cyriacus, canon 14 (Vööbus 1975–76: 21/23).

6. Synod of Dionysius, canon 4 (Vööbus 1975–76: 29/32).

7. Simonsohn 2010; Simonsohn 2011: 154–55.

8. Simonsohn 2011. Edelby 1950–51 remains important and useful. Note, for instance, the scene in the *Life of Theodota*, §156, discussed in chapter 1, in which the saint is made responsible for 'the laws of the city of Amida' after being elected bishop. There is no sense, however, that this is an automatic function of his office, and in the *Life* as a whole, the norm is for laymen bearing Greek names to hold offices on behalf of the caliph.

troops to force open the churches of their opponents or imprison dissidents, and this was a major escalation of the powers of the patriarch.[9] Nevertheless, a patriarch who regularly required coercive backup from the state would not have been seen as an effective manager of his co-religionists. Such powers would be granted only to incumbents who did not need the state's support too frequently.

If we conceive of Muslim and Christian governance structures as independent hierarchies, it was in the interests of a patriarch to monopolize interactions between the two hierarchies and to ensure that it was he and he alone who spoke on behalf of the caliphal government to Christians. Whenever his subordinates were able to secure the support of a local emir or, worse still, the caliph, his ability to guarantee his judgements and to secure patronage was diluted.

As we have seen, a good example of the chaos—from the perspective of Dionysius, at least—that might follow when a patriarch loses his monopoly of access to Muslim authority is the decade of the 740s. But this was also a decade dominated by Athanasius Sandalaya, and it is characterized by the deployment of royal influence by figures other than the patriarch. For instance, one Cyriacus of Segestan, together with a doctor, a Bar Salta of Reshaina, composed an apocalypse that foretells the rule of the descendants of Marwan II (who was, in fact, the last Umayyad to rule as caliph in the Middle East).[10] Marwan rewarded Cyriacus' and Bar Salta's sycophancy by proclaiming Cyriacus bishop of the Tur Abdin, an appointment that contravened the rules against the transfer of episcopal sees and the right of the higher bishops to fill the see.[11] It was not possible to excommunicate Cyriacus until 'after the tyrant who protected him had died',[12] and even then the historian can express his condemnation of Marwan and Cyriacus in such stark terms only because of the collapse of the Umayyad dynasty with the Abbasid revolution; in other circumstances, historians would have had to be more circumspect.

---

9. E.g., MS XII. 12 (IV, 512 / III, 58) for the arrest of Gubbite monks; MS XII. 7 (IV, 491 / III, 24) for the arrest of John of Kokta. This threat of force may also have been implicit when the patriarch showed the caliph's diploma, e.g., MS XII. 3 (IV, 4844 / III, 12). Also note the discussion of the *Chronicle to 813* in chapter 2.

10. MS XI. 22 (IV, 464 / II, 507).

11. Hage 1966: 35.

12. MS XI. 22 (IV, 466 / II, 507).

The control of courtly influence is even more apparent in the case of San-dalaya himself. He accuses the patriarch Iwannis II of simony to Marwan II and is accused in turn of paying massive bribes to the caliph. Sandalaya and six other bishops are excommunicated at a synod at Harran organized by the metropolitan David of Dara in 750, but it is striking that neither David nor the patriarch feels able to convince the other bishops; instead, they appeal to the caliph to send a neutral bishop to act as an arbitrator.[13]

According to the sources used by Michael, probably via Dionysius, Sanda-laya is temporarily humiliated at Harran in 750, but he manages to restore his dominance by obtaining the intercession of 'Abd Allah, the brother of the caliph (and the future caliph al-Mansur), at a later synod at Tella (752). 'Abd Allah secures Sandalaya's promotion as metropolitan of Maypherkat.[14] In canonical terms, this is especially unusual because Maypherkat had not previously been a metropolitanate: the city's prestige thus increased at the same time as Sandalaya's own. It may be that Sandalaya took this route be-cause Maypherkat was his personal power base (for unstated reasons of family background or influence).[15] At any rate, Sandalaya's promotion is fol-lowed by his endowment of a major church at Maypherkat and a monastery at Tell-Bashmai.[16]

When a patriarch failed to inspire confidence in his bishops or to mo-nopolize access to higher authorities, the door was opened for bishops such as Cyriacus of Segestan and Athanasius Sandalaya to use contacts with Muslim leaders to achieve their own promotion. By circumventing the patriarch, how-ever, they damaged established conventions for church governance and un-dermined the authority of the office of the patriarch.

Established Churches

If the patriarch aspired to monopolize contacts with the caliph and his agents, we should also remember that the caliph in turn benefited from Christian governmental structures that could be used to bolster the regime's legitimacy in the eyes of its Christian population (which probably constituted a majority in many regions, including the Jazira). Individual caliphs also relied on

---

13. MS XI. 23 (IV, 468 / II, 512).
14. MS XI. 23 (IV, 469 / II, 514).
15. Hage 1966: 32.
16. MS XI. 23 (IV, 469 / II, 514); *Chronicle of Zuqnin*, 210/192.

distinctive skills possessed by higher clergy: their diplomatic connections to Christian states such as Byzantium[17] and Nubia,[18] their ability to intervene in the governance of Christian populations in other provinces[19] and their mastery of arcane knowledge (such as alchemy).[20] In addition, the presence of the patriarch at court also served to legitimize the caliph by providing a sign of the universal reach of his empire.[21]

Caliphal attitudes toward the Jacobite patriarchs never incorporated an interventionist stance on points of theology, perhaps because Jacobite theology never had the political salience of Chalcedonianism, the state religion of the Byzantine empire.[22] However, as I observed in the introduction, the period covered here does witness the disappearance of many confessional groups and the dominance of three Christian confessions—the Church of the East, Chalcedonianism and Jacobitism—as the orthodox Christianities of the Islamicate world, to the exclusion of others. For instance, when the Church of the East patriarch Timothy I issued a general statement on the unity of the faith, he stressed the common belief of his own confession, the Melkites and the Jacobites in the resurrection and in the saving power of Christ, but he passed in silence over other groups that might have also called themselves Christian, such as the Marcionites and the Julianists.[23]

17. MS XII. 5 (IV, 487 / III, 18). The patriarch Cyriacus of Takrit was accused of being a Roman collaborator because he had funded the building of a church across the border. These kinds of contact might have been diplomatically advantageous to the caliph in some circumstances, so the allegation may have been accurate. Also note MS XII. 9 (IV, 500 / III, 36) for the rebel Nasr's use of a Christian secretary to write to the Byzantines.

18. See MS XII. 19 (IV, 530–31 / III, 90–91) for the Nubian embassy to Raqqa that met Dionysius. For Sasanian precedents for the use of Christian bishops as diplomats, see Sako 1986.

19. See MS XII. 13 (IV, 516 / III, 63) for Dionysius' visit to Egypt. Caliphs also employed Christians from the Church of the East to destroy the churches of other confessions in Egypt and Palestine: Meinardus 1967.

20. See MS XI. 25 (IV, 523 / II, 473) for the election of Ishaq of Harran because of his presumed knowledge of alchemy on the recommendation of 'Akhi' (al-'Akkī), emir of the Jazira. For the wider appeal of Christians as specialists in medicine, philosophy and the translation of the Greek classics, see Fattal 1958; Putman 1975; Gutas 1998; Watt 2014.

21. Compare the cosmopolitan self-fashioning of Sasanian shahs: Payne 2016.

22. Contrast Marwan II's intervention in favour of the Chalcedonian patriarch Theophylact bar Qanbara and his actions against supporters of the Trisagion prayer (probably Maronites in this context), see MS XI. 22 (IV, 467 / II, 511). Also note Signes-Codoñer 2014: 396–97 for the extent of the communication between Byzantium and the Melkite patriarchates of the east.

23. On this letter, see Briquel-Chatonnet et al. 2000.

The relations between the Julianists and the Jacobites offer a good example of the trend toward the consolidation of Christians into three main confessions. Julian of Halicarnassus had been a Miaphysite theologian who had disagreed with Severus, the Miaphysite patriarch of Antioch, in the 520s.[24] Julian's followers had persisted as a distinct group and had launched missions from Syria and Egypt into Armenia, South Arabia and Iraq. They subscribed to an alternative version of Miaphysite theology that was distinct from the theology of the Jacobites, and they formed an independent church (though we do not know anything of its internal administrative details).[25]

René Draguet has argued that the Julianist church in Syria and the Jazira was dominated by a single monastery, Beth Mar Ishaq de Gabbula.[26] This seems plausible, since it mirrors the dominance of the Jacobites by a small number of monasteries. It is also comparable to the preeminence of the monastery of Beth Mar Maron among the Maronites. The Julianists were criticized for (allegedly) relying on a single bishop to consecrate another, which was thought to imperil the apostolic succession. This practice may pertain to periods in which the Julianist leadership was relatively small. Nevertheless, by the end of the eighth century the Julianists were able to muster four bishops, including their patriarch, to attend a synod of reconciliation in September 797 with some seven Jacobites. These seven represented only a small fraction of the total number of Jacobite bishops, and it is likely that the Julianists, too, sent only some of their bishops to these negotiations and that their representation here did not reflect their total numbers.[27]

Though various attempts at reconciliation had been made in the seventh and eighth centuries, the meeting of 797 was the highest in profile. Gabriel, the Julianist leader, 'recognized the stupidity of the doctrine of Julian and

24. Menze 2008: 152.

25. Moss 2016c; Possekel 2013; Grillmeier and Hainthaler 1996: 45–52; Jugie 1937. The Julianists in Egypt were known as Gaianites, after an early sixth-century leader, whom Julian had consecrated as patriarch of Alexandria.

26. Draguet 1941: 93. He identifies this monastery, which was very significant in the sixth century, with the 'monastery of the tombs' mentioned in the eighth-century document. On this monastery, see further Possekel 2013: 439, 447.

27. I draw my data here from Draguet 1941 and his comments on the document of reconciliation drawn up in BL Add 17145. The Julianist bishops represented Callinicum, Qinnasrin (Chalcis) and Harran. I read the formula 'bishop of the district of x' in the list at 109 to refer to Julianist bishops, whereas the Jacobites are simply 'bishop of x', which would fit with the Jacobite predominance in these negotiations.

agreed to follow the things that we confess'. Dionysius reports that Gabriel agreed to include Severus in the diptychs and even to accept his anti-Julianist writings, though he would not anathematize Julian himself. Cyriacus and Gabriel then agreed that the names of both men would be proclaimed in the churches and that whoever outlived the other would reign as sole patriarch. Following this agreement, Cyriacus and Gabriel received communion from one another.[28]

The agreement seems to have been a magnanimous arrangement by Cyriacus to resolve a long-standing separation. However, he faced considerable problems from his own intransigent bishops, who demanded that Gabriel anathematize Julian. Gabriel responded that although he was willing to do so, he did not feel that his followers were prepared to accept such a move. The Jacobite bishops pressed the point, which ultimately prompted Gabriel to break off negotiations.[29]

One reason for the opposition to reconciliation with Gabriel was likely Cyriacus' own position as an outsider (he was the first 'easterner' to reign as Jacobite patriarch) and a sense on the part of the Jacobite bishops that Gabriel's succession would further remove power from the monasteries that had traditionally produced patriarchs.[30] But even though the reconciliation with the Julianists failed, the fact that Gabriel was so receptive to Cyriacus' overtures may also point to changes within the Jacobite church during Cyriacus' tenure that made union seem attractive. [31]

Collecting Taxes and Tithes

As we have seen, church officials were periodically employed as tax collectors by the state. The jurist Abu Yusuf even recommends that trusted Jews and Christians be employed to collect taxes from their co-religionists.[32] Yet

28. MS XII. 4 (IV, 485 / III, 13). See also BH HE I, 335, which stresses that the proposed union was Gabriel's initiative. Cyriacus and Gabriel also composed a creed together: Barsoum 2003: 358.

29. MS XII. 4 (IV, 486–87 / III, 14–15). One long-term consequence of the negotiations for Cyriacus was periodic suspicion that he was himself a Julianist: MS XII. 6 (IV, 492 / III, 25).

30. For the dominance of Mesopotamia in patriarchal elections, see Hage 1966: 11.

31. Mikhail 2016: 63, commenting on the *History of the Patriarchs* (PO 10:415), observes a similar pattern in Egypt, where smaller groups such as the Barsanuphians sought union with the Theodosian church during the early Abbasid period.

32. Abu Yusuf 70/190.

Dionysius is extremely critical of this practice. He represents the collection of taxes (*madātā*/*gzitā*)[33] as characteristic of Jews and Zoroastrians, whose authority is based on their lineage and their appointment by the caliph.[34] And he views clerics who collect taxes like his opponent, Job, bishop of Mopsuestia (an ally of Dionysius' opponents in Gubba Barraya), as engaged in a corrupt activity that does not befit a priest.[35]

A key example of Dionysius' suspicion of clerics engaging in tax gathering comes in the case of Basil of Balad, a former lay administrator whom Cyriacus had nominated as bishop of Takrit. Dionysius describes how Basil, who 'kept the company of princes', was appointed as tax collector over both Christians and Muslims in Takrit, which triggered an anti-Christian riot from the Muslims who resented a Christian being placed in authority over them. This situation escalated when first Basil and then his Muslim opponents complained to the government in Baghdad. Ultimately a Christian notable, ʿAbdun, was put to death and Basil was permanently exiled from Takrit.[36]

Acting as a tax agent was thus deemed both improper for priests and dangerous, because it could trigger the response of the Muslim crowd. But excluding clerics from tax collection was also a means for Dionysius to maintain a monopoly on Königsnähe: He criticizes Basil for keeping the company of princes and neglecting his proper duties in the church, but, of course, he himself kept the company of the governor ʿAbd Allah ibn Tahir. Furthermore, an ability to allocate the tax burden would give bishops or lesser clergy considerable influence with both Muslim and Christian lay elites. The implication that underlies the cautionary tale of Basil is that it is only the patriarch who should be making contacts within the government. And this was because government connections played such an important role in legitimating the authority of patriarchs.

However, Dionysius draws a key distinction between taxes and tithes. The first time his history reports tithing is when David of Dara accuses George of Beltan of raising tithes without holding a document from the

33. Sokoloff 2009: 225 notes that *gzitā* was first thought to be a loan word derived from the Arabic *jizya* (Payne-Smith 1903: 67 renders it 'poll tax'), but it appears already in the Talmud and is more likely to be a loan from Aramaic to Arabic. Thus we need not assume that it translates *jizya*. Here, at least, the word refers to a tax on property rather than a poll tax.

34. See Brody 1998: 69–73; Gil 2004: 89–94 for the Jewish exilarchs raising taxes from their co-religionists; and Choksy 1997: 118 for Zoroastrian clergy.

35. MS XII. 6 (IV, 491 / III, 24).

36. MS XII. 11 (IV, 506 / III, 48–49). For further analysis of this scene, see Sahner 2018: 227.

caliph to legitimate him as patriarch.[37] The second occasion is when the Gubbite monks complain to Harun al-Rashid that Cyriacus has oppressed them with heavy exactions (*tab ʿātē*) (though they do acknowledge that he holds a diploma from the caliph).[38] The canons first mention the practice of tithing (*gebyātā*) in Cyriacus' synod of Beth Botin (canon 30), and Cyriacus is also much concerned that Jacobites should pay tithes to a Jacobite church and no other (canons 14 and 30) and that the payments of tithes should be properly recorded. It seems, then, that tithing was considered a legitimate practice, even by enemies of the patriarch, but that the sum raised through tithes was increasing, and more of this revenue was being accounted for (and probably sent to the patriarchate rather than being dispersed locally).[39] The word *gbitā* implies that tithes were represented as voluntary in theory, but the complaints about excessive tithing also suggest that they were, in practice, obligatory.[40]

In addition to tithes the patriarch also received revenues from the patrimonies that were held by each church, which were probably mostly made up of land, but may have also included rent from shops or other amenities. Cyriacus (canon 26) forbade individuals from stealing, usurping or giving away such church lands. Cyriacus' canons show a marked concern for financial oversight in general. This included accounting for church income, inventories of church property and the proper recording of debts owed to the church (canons 41 and 45). A later patriarch would insist that wills be kept in church archives and that properties donated to the church be managed by church officials rather than the testator's kin (Dionysius II, canons 8 and 13). Presumably this was a response to testators' kin trying to alter wills that bequeathed property to the church or creaming off the income of donated properties.

We could explain the appearance of such financial clauses in patriarchal legislation through the accession of a Takritian patriarch who had knowledge

37. MS XI. 26 (IV, 476 / II, 527). The text uses the term *šqonē*, which normally means 'taxes', but George's accusers seem to imagine that he intends to keep this money for himself, rather than give it to the government.

38. MS XII. 5 (IV, 488 / III, 19).

39. Eva Wipszycka (1972: 90–95) observes that in Egypt the practice is first noted for private churches at a local level in the 730s (as a *demosion*) and then appears in the *History of the Patriarchs* for the whole church under Shenute I in the 860s (as a *diyariyya*). Shenute's predecessor Alexander I is also said to have tried and failed to raise a diyariyya.

40. There are already indications from the early sixth century that church tithes, while voluntary in theory, were being treated as obligatory: Jones 1964: 895.

of mercantile systems of accounting and who prized subordinates skilled in administration. But we should also situate it against the growing capacity of the Abbasid state to collect taxes (including the *ṣadaqa/zakāt*, the religious taxes paid by Muslims on their income and assets).[41] The ability of multiple community leaders, such as the Husaynid imams or the Jewish exilarchs,[42] to collect tithes of their own in this period may indicate, on the one hand, a dissemination of practices of accounting, surveying and census taking between the state administration and different confessional groups and, on the other, a populace that was increasingly accustomed to paying taxes in cash and hence planning future sales and expenditures to take account of regular taxation, both by the state and by other institutions. I have found no direct evidence of whether the Jacobite *gebyātā* were paid in cash or kind, but I think that the concern for accounting points to a more monetized environment where central institutions might more reasonably expect tithes to be forwarded to them for redistribution rather than being spent locally.

How this money was spent is unclear in the case of the Jacobites, but the experience of other communities may offer possible models. The Catholic Church in the West divided its revenue between the upkeep of property, the welfare of the poor and the salaries of priests and bishops.[43] And the Church of the East specifically designated tithes for the salaries of those who served the church (with 40 percent reserved for the patriarch).[44]

An indication of the improved financial situation of the Jacobite patriarchate is the capacity to organize synods to deal with disciplinary issues and reform church administration, as well as to regulate the provision of sacraments. It may be no coincidence that the first Jacobite patriarch to issue and disseminate canons was George of Beltan, who was also the first to be mentioned as raising tithes. Cyriacus was able to organize five synods and issue over sixty canons. The end of the eighth century also witnesses the detailed recording of episcopal ordinations. Cyriacus is the first patriarch for whom Michael gives a full list of bishops consecrated (eighty-six in total).[45]

---

41. Sijpesteijn 2007; Sourdel 1999: 48; Daniel 1979: 197. The *Samaritan Chronicle*, 53 and 57, and part 4 of the *Chronicle of Zuqnin* also chart the increasingly systematic raising of poll taxes, which must have provided an incentive for all sections of the population to enter a monetized economy.

42. Hayes 2017; Gil 2004: 89.

43. Jones 1964: 902; Bingham 1722: I, 192.

44. Weitz 2016: 93 n. 86.

45. MS appendix III: 450–53.

The Use of Diplomas

A major mechanism used by caliphs to promote the authority of their Christian appointees and sometimes to give them independence from local emirs was the issuing of royal diplomas. These pertained to the right to hold office as patriarch, the right to build new churches and the right to tax exemptions for a given city or monastery.

The first example of such diplomas being used is the entrance of the patriarch Elias into Antioch to consecrate the first Jacobite church in the city thanks to a diploma granted by Yazid II in 723. The construction of this church was a major coup: Antioch was the titular see of the Jacobite patriarch, but there had not been a Miaphysite incumbent in the city itself since Severus in the early sixth century.[46] It is one of the first signs of (implied) public recognition of the Jacobites by the Arab authorities. Other diplomas issued in this period for the building of churches permitted, for example, the restoration of churches in Edessa, Harran and Amida and the construction of new churches in Takrit, Mosul, Edessa and Maypherkat.[47]

The construction of new Christian religious buildings was, in theory, forbidden by many Muslim jurists. However, rulings on this subject varied markedly in this period, with jurists responding in different ways to the growing proximity of Muslims and non-Muslims. Some banned the building of new churches outright; others prohibited it only in places conquered without a treaty or inhabited by large numbers of Muslims.[48] On several occasions in Dionysius' history, Muslim emirs destroy churches built after the Arab conquests, which may indicate that restrictive rules were promoted by some sections of the Muslim population (and that the destruction of churches could be a source of revenue or building materials).[49]

---

46. MS XI. 19 (IV, 456 / II, 491).

47. Hage 1966: 59–61. Cf. Timothy I's intercession with the caliph al-Hadi to get churches rebuilt: Fiey 1980: 49. There is no contestation of the government's right to permit or forbid church building in any of these examples.

48. Levy-Rubin 2011: 62–87. She sees the early Abbasid period as a time of juristic experimentation, when jurists attempted to generate normative rules for the dhimmīs to replace the mass of treaties between individual communities and their conquerors. It was only under al-Mutawakkil, just after Dionysius' death, that the markedly intolerant *shurūṭ 'Umar* were adopted as the official norm for dhimmī rights in the caliphate (Levy-Rubin 2011: 99–112).

49. See X1234 (II, 10/6) and MS XII. 11 (IV, 505 / III, 47) for Ibrahim, emir of Harran, being informed about the building of new churches in Edessa by the pagan population of Harran; MS

In an environment in which Christian authorities felt threatened by local Muslims' wish to destroy churches and in which the destruction of new churches was seen as legitimate, caliphal intervention constituted a suspension of normal rules of behaviour. As has been observed for several authoritarian societies, the primacy of the caliph was underscored by his ability to overturn expected law or custom and to respond to pleas for intercession from patriarchs or bishops.[50] By doing so the caliph confirmed the importance of the patriarch for his flock and, more importantly, the caliph's own primacy in both Muslim and Christian hierarchies.

The use of diplomas to mark the patriarchal office is first mentioned in the reign of Iwannis, who is said to have received such a diploma after his election by his fellow bishops by offering a bribe to Marwan II. His controversial successors David of Dara, John of Callinicum, Ishaq of Harran and Athanasius Sandalaya also held patriarchal diplomas from Marwan II or from al-Mansur.[51] But it is clear that possession of a diploma did not necessarily guarantee a patriarch the obedience of his flock. For instance, Iwannis was unable to force his metropolitans to accept the popular election of one Dionysius as bishop of the Tur Abdin and was then placed in an embarrassing position when his patron, Marwan, tried to impose his own creature, Cyriacus of Segestan, as bishop.[52] Likewise, Sandalaya may have presumed that his possession of a diploma would give him the ability to impose his own bishop, Abdani, on the independent-minded see of Harran, but Sandalaya was strangled by the town's citizens.[53]

One reason for the large number of patriarchs between 740 and 760 is that this was still a transitional period. At this point, bishops and Christian notables had not yet become accustomed to the intervention of the state in elections or the state's endorsement of the right of the patriarch to raise tithes. The author of the *Chronicle to 813* made it explicit that the state's guarantee of patriarchal authority was backed by the use of force, and he was critical of the use of diplomas. But when caliphs sought to impose particular bishops

---

XII. 1 (IV, 478 / III, 3) for the *muḥtasib's* destruction of new churches; MS XII. 13 (IV, 513 / III, 60–61) for Yaqdan's destruction of churches in Takrit and Edessa, especially targeting new buildings; Azdi's description of a Muslim mob in Mosul destroying a church that had taken over a piece of land owned by a mosque (cited in Fiey 1959: 20–21); MS XII. 6 (IV, 490 / III, 21) for the lucrative destruction of ancient churches in Jerusalem and Aleppo.

50. Brown 1992: 3; Kelly 2004. I am grateful to Miles Pattenden for discussion of this point.

51. Hage 1966: 20, 67.

52. MS XI. 14 (IV, 464–65 / II, 506–7).

53. MS XI. 25 (IV, 473 / II, 523).

(Cyriacus of Segestan) or patriarchs (the 'alchemist' Ishaq of Harran) on the Jacobites, they enjoyed little long-term success.[54] Al-Ma'mun expressed a more laissez-faire attitude when he ordered that a diploma be given to 'whoever the Jacobites agree upon'; this statement may reflect a recognition of the fact that the patriarch's effectiveness would be compromised if the caliph interfered unnecessarily with the structures of church governance (the elections of Cyriacus of Takrit and Dionysius as patriarch seem to have been much smoother than were those of their predecessors).[55]

The Emirs, Urban Muslims and the Bishops

Muslim elites, whether government appointees or local aristocracies, did not always share the attitude of the caliph toward his Christian subjects. We first hear of an emir of the Jazira in the *Chronicle* of Michael the Syrian when a man named Muhammad crucifies local Christian notables in the 690s. As seen in chapter 1, the government sought to increase its tax revenues, and it used harsh methods to make examples of elites who resisted tax demands.[56] Later governors continued to collect taxes effectively and were much resented for it. Dionysius complains about the agents sent by Harun al-Rashid to find the fabled wealth of the Gumaye family,[57] and he narrates the zealous acts of governors closer to his own day.

According to Dionysius, the ability of the state to gather information about the wealthy and to extract taxes reached a new peak during the reign of al-Ma'mun's successor al-Mu'tasim:

> More than at any other time during the rule of the Arabs, the suffering of the people increased at this time because of the greed of the prefects (ʾamanē). Each of them took for himself what he charged in taxes (qbiltē)[58]

---

54. The frequent interventions of al-Mansur in episcopal and patriarchal elections have a parallel in his interventions in the centralized appointment of qāḍīs: Tillier 2009: 103. At the same time, however, al-Mansur was quite prepared to appoint qāḍīs, governors and bishops who, like Sandalaya, had enjoyed close connections to the Umayyads: Tillier 2009: 98; Robinson 2000: 157. Al-Mansur's willingness to intervene may be linked to the relative instability of the first generation of Abbasid rule, which is explored in Lassner 1980.

55. MS XII. 12 (IV, 511 / III, 57).

56. MS XI. 16 (IV, 447 / II, 473).

57. MS XII. 4 (IV, 485 / III, 13).

58. From Arabic *qabāla* (Sokoloff 2009: 1312).

and added whatever he wished. They designated and established functionaries for each category, and they consumed and devoured the poor in all
ways. They established at Callinicum a judge, called a *qāḍī*, and a governor
to collect taxes and a prefect to be in charge of crimes and another to su-
pervise the post (*barīd*) to write to the caliph about the news of the land
and another to oversee the produce of the *ṣawāfī* [state land] and another
to deal with injustice towards the people (and he was the worst of the lot!).
And thus it was in every city.[59]

This kind of 'injustice' was not limited to Callinicum. In Damascus, Dionysius reports, ʿAli, the governor, abused his position by investigating the deaths
of wealthy men and accusing their sons of having murdered them. The charge
allowed him to confiscate the sons' inheritances and to execute them.[60] And
in Cyrrhus, he claims that if two men wanted to contest a lawsuit, the governor
simply imprisoned both men until he had ruined them, presumably by extracting bribes from their families.[61]

Quite how novel this infrastructure of taxation really was, is hard to determine. Much of it can also be attested for the Marwanid period or the
reign of al-Mansur.[62] And complaints of corrupt officials who cream off
additional income are endemic to most preindustrial societies.[63] Dionysius'
complaints here may reflect the reestablishment of a tax infrastructure after
a period of fitna.[64]

At points where tax collection became increasingly effective, it came to alter
elite behaviour. Firstly, the government's appetite for information to facilitate

59. MS XII. 21 (IV, 538 / III, 104–5).

60. MS XII. 21 (IV, 539 / III, 105); X1234 (II, 36/26).

61. MS XII. 21 (IV, 539–40 / III, 106); X1234 (II, 37/26). The *Chronicle to 1234* dates the anecdotes on Cyrrhus and Damascus to the reign of al-Wathiq (842–47).

62. Cobb 2001: 243; Sijpesteijn 2013: 90; Silverstein 2007: 85–86; Robinson 2016. These in-
stitutions/practices are also all recorded in the *Chronicle of Zuqnin*: see 154/147 for the census
under ʿAbd al-Malik, 266/235 for the registration of crown properties and 290/235 for the use
of informers under al-Mansur. The *Samaritan Chronicle*, 57, reports a doubling of the land tax
and an increase in the poll tax (which it calls *jāliya*) immediately after the Abbasid revolution.

63. Gibb 1955 for Umar II. Ruling V stipulates that ṣadaqa go to the poor rather than to the
powerful, ruling XV prevents government agents from trading in the area in which they are
employed, and ruling XX orders that inheritance be permitted without interference. Katbi 2010:
144–47 for Abu Yusuf's comments on the late eighth century.

64. Dionysius' personal antipathy to al-Muʿtasim may also lead him to attribute oppressive
innovations to him rather than al-Maʾmun.

effective tax collection may have made elite families more vulnerable to informants. In other words, because of the intrusive state, local elites now had an
interest in social solidarity that they might not have had a generation earlier.
Secondly, higher levels of taxation placed a greater premium on different forms
of influence with Muslim elites. The caliph himself was the most important,
but so too were his governors and Muslim notables such as the Alid family.

An example of the first of these responses, in which distrust between social
classes threatened Christian aristocrats, is provided by a scene that occurred
just after the Abbasid revolution, when a Persian who had been denied lodging
by the Gumaye accused them of Manichaeism in Baghdad. Manichaeism was
a banned religion in the caliphate, as it had been in the Roman empire, and
this accusation was thus a grave one to make against any intellectual or cultural
elite.[65] But the fact that the accusation posed a serious threat is also an indication of the ease with which information could flow between the capital and
the Jazira, which in turn may point to the interlinking of Muslim social networks between provinces in the aftermath of the revolution, as well as the
improvement of the physical infrastructure.

An increasingly common route for information to reach governors to the
detriment of the Christian population was through the Christians' Muslim
and pagan neighbours. Muslims in Edessa are said to have encouraged looting
by invading armies during the fourth fitna.[66] Pagans in Harran (who possibly
constituted a local majority) allegedly encouraged the emir Ibrahim to destroy
churches and synagogues.[67] And Harranian Muslims raided Christian properties during Yaqdan's actions against Christian slave owners in Edessa, when he
freed slaves 'in order to make them Muslims'.[68] In these cases local

65. Cf. Arjomand 1994; Chokr 1993. For the accusations of human sacrifice made against
Manichaeans in Harran, see *Chronicle of Zuqnin*, 224–25 / 203.

66. MS XII. 6 (IV, 492 / III, 22).

67. MS XII. 11 (IV, 505 / III, 47).

68. MS XII. 13 (IV, 514 / III, 62). Slaves owned by Christians were also freed during the reign
of al-Mahdi (MS XII. 1 [IV, 478 / III, 3]). According to Muslim jurists, Christians were forbidden from owning Muslim slaves and were technically obliged to free or sell any slaves who
converted to Islam (Lewis 1992: 8; Fattal 1958: 149), but the initiative in these instances seems
to have come from local Muslim notables rather than the caliph. Dionysius himself was probably
a slave owner, and he lists four thousand slaves as part of the estate of Athanasius bar Gumaye:
MS XI. 16 (IV, 448 / II, 475). Also note prayers for the return of escaped slaves made in the
Palestinian *Life of Stephen the Sabaite*, 39.1 (written circa 800). We should not think of church
or monastic institutions as insulated from or critical of slave owning.

non-Christian populations may have provided information to emirs who were outside appointees as well as given physical support to any emir who wanted to penalize the Christian population. Likewise, a newly appointed emir might view Christians who hoarded wealth, built new churches or owned slaves as soft targets, who might be 'shaken down' for funds while also cementing their own Islamic legitimacy and changing the local demographic balance.

The flow of information to the capital was a negative development for elites whose status and interests were not at that time sustained by service to the state. Consequently, as the Abbasid revolution facilitated the involvement of Muslims of diverse origins in the state, giving them resources and influence, it also altered the priorities of Christian elite families. It encouraged aristocrats to refashion themselves as a service elite (whether as administrators or as clerics), whose links to the court could protect them from the envious. In other words, one way of protecting landed wealth was to maximize contacts with the Muslim protectors.

Dionysius advertises how he himself provided this kind of intercession during the reign of al-Ma'mun, when he appealed above the head of the local emir to a higher-ranking governor or to the caliph. For instance, when Yaqdan was demolishing Jacobite churches in Edessa and freeing the slaves of the Christians, Dionysius successfully appealed to 'Abd Allah ibn Tahir, the governor of Syria and Egypt, to put a stop to Yaqdan's campaign.[69] As a result of Dionysius' request, al-Ma'mun visited Edessa and agreed to spare inns and shops owned by the church from taxation, 'since so much of the church's wealth was absorbed in tax (*gzitā*)'.[70] Here Dionysius is primarily acting to defend church property, but he is also, secondarily, defending the interests of a landed elite who might have owned slaves or founded private churches.

Dionysius was thus able to use his influence at court to prevent the demolitions of churches and the seizure of slaves, but he could not do so by appealing to Yaqdan directly. This case demonstrates that sponsorship and employment by the caliph did not alter the vulnerability of the Jacobites of Edessa to a local governor who was opposed to them. To the contrary, their vulnerability heightened Dionysius' dependency on the caliph and on the Abbasid family. The need for protection gave Dionysius and others a strong incentive to remain connected to and continue their support of the central government.

---

69. MS XII. 13 (IV, 513–14 / III, 61).
70. MS XII. 16 (IV, 522–23 / III, 74).

Migration

An important illustration of the limitation of Dionysius' capacity to inter-
cede comes in cases where 'oppression' was caused by recent migrants who
remained attached to seminomadic tribal groupings. The Jazira was an attractive site for nomads because it combined year-round pasturage with
close proximity to urban centres where pastoral products could be exchanged for weapons and wheat.[71] Settled-nomad symbiosis was fragile,
however, and the periods of flooding and harsh winters that Dionysius reports for the 830s may have pushed nomads to seize land and food from
surrounding settled populations.[72]

Dionysius singles out several Bedouin groups for their theft of property and
their arrogance toward the settled Christian population during the fourth fitna
and afterward.[73] He reports that members of the Banu ʿIyad seized Christians
labouring in their fields and forced them to work on and harvest the crops of
the land of the ʿIyad. But complaints fell on deaf ears, since the governor at
the time, Ahmad bar Abu Dawud, was himself a member of the tribe. Another
member of the ʿIyad charged taxes at such a high level that a landowner was
forced to sell his property, and the ʿIyadi bought it himself. 'In this manner
Ahmad seized many villages; the people were persecuted by the ʿIyad and by
the prefects'.[74]

The scene illustrates how the state could use prominent tribesmen in order
to govern effectively. Tribal connections may have secured the availability of
manpower to collect taxes and enforce order without draining the capital's
resources, while ensuring that tribesmen did not interfere with the business
of government.[75]

71. Posner 1985: 87–90. For the significance of the leather trade for pre-Islamic Arabia, see
Crone 2007. For examples of sites of exchange between nomadic and settled populations, see
Lewin 1985 (Shivta in the Negev); B. de Vries 1998 (Umm el-Jimal in the Hauran) and Sartre
1985 (Bostra).

72. E.g., MS XII. 18 (IV, 528 / III, 86) for flooding in Iraq.

73. E.g., MS XII. 7 (IV, 492 / III, 27) and MS XII. 9 (IV, 499 / III, 35).

74. MS XII. 21 (IV, 540–41 / III, 107). See also X1234 (II, 37–38 / 27). 'Tayyaye' here seems
to refer to previously settled Muslim Arabs.

75. Al-Maʾmun seems to have preferred to co-opt, rather than fight, Bedouin rebels at the
conclusion of the fourth fitna: MS XII. 12 (IV, 511–12 / III, 54–55). For the caliphate's earlier
management of nomads during the period of conquest, see Donner 1981.

The downside to this arrangement was often felt by settled populations, which were subjected to corvées and overtaxation.[76] The case demonstrates the vulnerability of the Abbasid state to takeover by tribal groups such as the Banu 'Iyad, who could co-opt institutions for their own collective interest and block the accountability of their members for transgressions. That well-connected individuals might help their allies and clients escape justice or derive personal profit from government positions comes as no surprise, but when such an individual was embedded in a tribe, he was both expected to provide substantial patronage to fellow tribe members and better able to resist attempts by the central government to remove him from office. I suggest that tribal groups that had recently acquired roles on behalf of the state were especially difficult for Christian leaders to negotiate with. Incidentally, the inability of Dionysius to protect Christians from the 'Iyad in the way he had from Yaqdan also points to a wider vulnerability of the Abbasid state, whereby tribal groupings could circumvent the normal systems of reward and censure.

Conclusions

The growing capacity of government in the Abbasid period was mirrored by the capacities of the Jacobite patriarchs. In this period we see the patriarchs begin to use caliphal diplomas to legitimate the construction of churches, the use of state troops against their opponents and the levying of tithes. Tithing in particular seems to have occurred at higher levels than before, and this allowed a more sophisticated church governance with regular synods, something that had not existed since the Roman period. Church leadership was becoming both more powerful and more lucrative. This initially prompted the simony and bribery of the period 740–60, but it was eventually followed by the recruitment of experienced administrators and aristocrats into the church leadership, men such as Cyriacus of Takrit, Basil of Balad, Theodosius of Edessa and Dionysius himself.

However, Jacobite institutions and populations also appear increasingly vulnerable to the violence of Muslim urban populations and to Muslim governors who were ill disposed toward Christians. Appeals to the caliph or other ties to the Muslim elite offered some protection, and Dionysius emphasizes

76. This practice had been banned by Umar II: Gibb 1955: ruling XVIII.

his political links in this regard. Like late Roman bishops such as Ambrose of Milan and Synesius of Cyrene, Dionysius possessed training and connections as an aristocrat that had become very useful to the church.[77] But the powers of the Abbasid government had their limits, and no intervention was possible when government officials were also members of the nomadic groups that inhabited the edges of the Jazira at this time.

However, we should also make certain caveats to the picture that Dionysius presents, in which it is his good influence with the caliph that protects his flock. First, Dionysius was very vulnerable to changes in the composition of government: we shall see in chapter 7 how the death of al-Ma'mun left Dionysius without an effective patron. Second, the moral tales of Dionysius' history against tax-gathering clerics are self-serving, and he aims to create a patriarchal monopoly on access to Muslim elites. But, at the same time, the narrative illustrates a reality in which Basil of Balad, and possibly less famous bishops too, could, in fact, develop their own political ties independent of Dionysius.

77. For the qualifications for the episcopate in the late Roman period and the ease with which aristocrats could meet them, see Rapp 2000: 385–87. Gregory of Nyssa's exhortation to citizens to ignore 'trappings of outward show, powerful friends, long list of offices, large revenues or noble ancestry' (cited in Norton 2007: 63) was probably highly (and disingenuously) unrealistic.

4

Changing Centres of Power

HARRAN, KAKUSHTA AND CYRRHUS

WE HAVE OBSERVED that the eighth and ninth centuries saw an intensification of the tax regime of the caliphate that increased pressure on non-Muslim landed aristocracies. At the same time, the institutions of the Jacobite church were able to mirror the government's growing ability to raise revenue, in part because the caliph began to recognize the patriarch and sometimes enforce his authority over the patriarch's Christian opponents.

Neither of these trends occurred in a uniform fashion across the whole caliphate. In this chapter and the next we examine how pre-Islamic elites survived into the ninth century and how ancient claims to ecclesiastical authority came into conflict with the new settlements (amṣār) created by the Arab conquerors of the Middle East.

The most famous such settlements were Kufa and Basra in southern Iraq and Fustat in Egypt, which were later joined by smaller centres such as Wasit, Merv, Shiraz and Mosul.[1] In the amṣār, the conquerors were paid cash stipends from the revenue generated by taxes,[2] and it was here that Islamic justice and governance were organized.[3] In time, the concentration of the new political power holders in a small number of cities attracted settlers from non-Muslim backgrounds, who were drawn in by the creation of employment, patronage and business opportunities by those with money to spend.[4]

1. Kennedy 2006; Kennedy 2002: 156.
2. Kennedy 2015: 393–94; Kennedy 2002: 157.
3. Tillier 2009.
4. Kennedy 2011; Kennedy 2015: 393–95.

However, the changes experienced in the Levant were more muted than those in Iraq. In Syria, immigration was probably lower, and undertaken mainly by people who already had links to the region.[5] And in the Jazira we find relatively low-status tribes that converted to Islam fairly late and that were not settled in amṣār but remained seminomadic.[6]

We can identify three trends in the changing geography of power in the first three centuries of Arab rule in the Middle East. The first is the shift toward a small number of significant cities, many of them new foundations. The second is the growing centralization of government, culminating in the Abbasid regime and its high capacity for interventions that made imperial service so rewarding and defiance by preexisting aristocracies so difficult. The third is the movement of the centre of power: first to southern Syria and Palestine under the Umayyads; then, very briefly, to the Jazira when Marwan II moved his capital to Harran; and finally to Iraq under the Abbasids, where the new capital of Baghdad provided massive patronage.[7] Al-Rashid's foundation at Raqqa also substantially changed the landscape of patronage and trade by linking the Jazira more closely to the economy of Iraq and stimulating settlement along the Balikh valley.[8] Previous chapters examined institutional changes within the Jacobite church in response to government patronage and intervention. Now we turn to the ways in which Arab rule and settlement affected the geographical distribution of power and influence, and how this shaped church structures that had evolved in very different, pre-Islamic conditions.

5. Donner 1981: 249.

6. Robinson 1996; Shaban 1971: 145. Later geographers' identification of Amida, Raqqa and Mosul as the 'capitals' of the three regions (e.g., Hamadhani 155) should be seen as a retrojection, which imagines the Jaziran provinces to have been like those of Syria or Iraq. See the comments of Wheatley 2001: 103; Robinson 1996: 430; Forand 1969: 102.

7. Kennedy 2011; Webb 2016: 271. Zaman 1997: 161 and Tillier 2009: 478–79 discuss the 'brain drain' to Baghdad from Kufa and Basra. For the transfer of the institutions of the Church of the East to Baghdad, see Wood 2013: ch. 8 and Fiey 1980: 20, and for the transfer of the gaonic academies, see Sklare 1996: 2. For elite patronage in Baghdad more broadly, see Osti 2010.

8. Heidemann 2011: 48–49; Eger 2014: 154–57; Berthier 2001: 166–67. Heidemann 2015: 36 identifies the construction of large population centres as a stimulus to regional agriculture. Heidemann 2015: 51 and Heidemann 2006 observe that the shift in glass technology from natron to the use of a flux derived from plant material allowed the development of hitherto marginal sites as industrial centres. He stresses the migration of skilled craftsmen from Iraqi cities such as Hira and Basra to sites further north in response to these developments.

Survivals

Muslim Arabic narratives purport to tell us a great deal about the urban foundations of the early caliphate, in cities like Kufa and Basra. The distribution of political favour probably followed the steep rank-size distribution of cities observed in other young empires of conquest, with a small number of substantial cities, where wealth and patronage are concentrated, and a much larger number of smaller sites, many of whom had been of importance in the past.[9] But sixth-century Syria and Iraq were densely settled lands, studded with sites of every size, many of which saw no settlement by the conquerors.[10]

It has become increasingly apparent that settlement in much of late Roman Syria persisted into the Umayyad and early Abbasid periods without substantial interruption. Clive Foss comments that in central and northern Syria, 'the Arabs found a densely populated countryside to which they brought few changes' and that outside hubs of Arab settlement, 'the life of late Roman city and countryside continued as it [had been]'.[11] This impression of continuous habitation is consonant with hagiographical literature set in the seventh to ninth centuries: Syria, the Jazira and northern Iraq appear in them as worlds of Christian villages and monasteries, in which Arabs or Muslims are only occasional interlopers.

This is not to imply that the places left unsettled by Muslims all retained their earlier prosperity. Two cases in point are the cities of Antioch and Apamea. In the sixth century they were the capitals of the Roman provinces of Syria I and II, respectively, and the former was also the capital of the entire diocese of Oriens. Both cities remained settled during the early Abbasid period, but they underwent a loss of population and a degradation of their infrastructure. Antioch's Hippodrome and the massive aristocratic mansions of Apamea were subdivided into smaller dwellings. At this time, Apamea had one small mosque, but it nonetheless remained 'an overwhelmingly Christian city'.[12]

9. Woolf 1997. Kennedy 2008 discusses the 'inheritance' of pre-Islamic cities by Muslims in general terms.

10. Adams 1965; Decker 2009: esp. ch. 6.

11. Foss 1997: 237 and 267. A recent summary of the archaeological literature on Syria's Limestone Massif, between Aleppo and Antioch, is Zerbini 2013: 95–100, which draws on Tchalenko 1953–58, Tate 1992 and Magness 2003. Zerbini stresses that Tate overlooked eighth-century inscriptions in the region, which led him to argue for a decline in population in the late sixth century. Also note Eger 2014: esp. 204–6, which emphasizes the function of Christian monasteries as economic actors.

12. Foss 1997: 265.

The changes in Antioch and Apamea were generated not by new settlement but by higher-order shifts in economic and political power. One such shift was the flight of the interregional aristocracy, whose fate was tied to the Roman empire and the establishment of new imperial centres in Damascus and Jerusalem.[13] And another was the drift of trade routes away from the Mediterranean littoral, which had now become part of the frontier with Byzantium, and toward Iraq.[14] This was a trend that benefited cities such as Homs, Hama and Aleppo to the detriment of cities that had been more closely embedded into late Roman political and economic systems.

However, against the backdrop of the changing political and economic fortunes of cities under the new regime, it is worth emphasizing that the Christian populations of the Middle East inherited the episcopal structures of the later Roman empire, which had been moulded to the civic geography of the fourth to sixth centuries.[15] In the Roman east, bishops were state functionaries with the formal capacity to act as adjudicators in courts of law, and the existence of a large Christian majority meant that the episcopate was widely distributed. Indeed, Fergus Millar has called it the most widespread and longest-lasting Roman civic institution.[16]

In a situation in which Muslim settlers and converts might use a new, Arabic name for a city and bishops might relocate to accommodate shifts in political power, the fact that sees continued to be known by their sixth-century names meant that Christian claims to antiquity and priority were not forgotten. For instance, the leaders of the Jacobite church remained patriarchs of Antioch, even though they lived in Harran or Raqqa. Bishops resident in Raqqa continued to use the pre-Islamic name of Callinicum, now part of a much larger conurbation.[17] And bishops resident in Mosul styled themselves 'bishops of Nineveh'.

13. Foss 1997: 224. Donner 1981: 246 surveys the textual evidence to suggest a flight of the 'Rūm' from Damascus. Eger 2014: 65 situates Antioch's 'decline' within the spread of wetlands in the Amuq plain.

14. Wickham 2005: 620–21. Nevertheless, Antioch's decline was far from total: Eger 2014: 66.

15. Fedalto 1988.

16. Millar 2015b: 184.

17. Heidemann 2003: 25 stresses that for Arab Muslim administrators and geographers, the conurbation consisted of two cities, al-Raqqa and al-Rafiqa, each with its own Friday mosque, which lay adjacent to the older Roman settlement. But in Michael's *Chronicle*, the whole conurbation is referred to interchangeably as Callinicum and Raqqa (though the former is more frequent). The only Christian see here continued to be known as Callinicum.

Episcopal institutions asserted an alternative past for the region in which the innovations of the Islamic period were passed over in silence. One aspect of this preservation of pre-Islamic history is that episcopal lists preserve an older hierarchy of cities. For instance, the ordination lists contained in the *Chronicle* of Michael the Syrian show that Apamea remained a metropolitanate in spite of the city's relative unimportance in the ninth century.[18] This status does not necessarily mean that the bishop was resident in the city, but it shows that the Jacobite church preserved the memory of the city's importance, even though the region had been altered by Muslim rule and Chalcedonian opposition.

However, if we wish to underscore the importance of episcopal structures in preserving ancient claims, we should also recognize the potential downsides of this long memory. Long-standing sees that were attached to cities that had become relatively insignificant could formally outrank sees that were attached to up-and-coming regional rivals. Conflict between sees could easily result from changes in the distribution of political power among the cities of the caliphate that had consequences for the Königsnähe of Christian elites.

In what follows I examine such tensions in the Jazira, in Syria proper and in Iraq. I demonstrate that the adoption of preexisting cities as capitals challenged long-standing regional hierarchies and strained relations between sees and between different levels of the church hierarchy.

The Jazira

Chapter 2 revealed the extent to which our narrative of the period circa 740–60 is dominated by the struggles between the monastery of Qartmin and that of Qenneshre. The *Chronicle to 819* is, as already observed, a mouthpiece of Qartmin. It celebrates the monastery's members who held the office of patriarch (Ishaq of Harran, David of Dara and Athanasius Sandalaya) and passes over the substantial disagreements among these men. Further, it lists the monks of Qartmin who were appointed to two nearby bishoprics, Harran and the Tur Abdin, and takes an interest in their attendance at councils. One purpose of the *Chronicle to 819* seems to be to advertise the status of these bishoprics as the monastery's pocket sees and to trace the actions of their bishops as representatives of Qartmin.[19]

18. Apamea ceased to hold a bishopric in c. 985: Honigmann 1954: 114.

19. A similar argument can be made for the representation of Simeon of the Olives. Simeon was a bishop of Harran, consecrated c. 700, and a monk of Qartmin (*Life of Gabriel of Qartmin*, LXXXIX). Tannous 2016: 326 notes that the attribution of churches to Simeon may have been

A striking feature of patriarchal elections in the 740s and 750s is their domination by monks of Qartmin. Though we cannot reconstruct their careers in much detail, their predecessors had largely come from other famous monasteries, notably Gubba Barraya near Cyrrhus and, to a lesser extent, Qenneshre. The primacy of Qartmin in this period coincides with the flourishing of building inscriptions in the Tur Abdin, which occur in great numbers around the middle of the eighth century.[20]

I propose that the shift in the fortunes of Qartmin is related to the sudden elevation of Harran as the chosen capital of Marwan II. Before 740, Michael's *Chronicle* mentions Harran and its bishops only very occasionally. But from the 740s onward, following Marwan's transfer of the capital, Harran appears as a major site of politics in its own right. Dionysius recounts how the patriarch Iwannis greeted Marwan with camels laden with treasure.[21] He does not depict this meeting as an exaction by the caliph; rather, he frames it as an opportunity for the patriarch to demonstrate his loyalty. Marwan's reign offered the patriarch a measure of public support that none of his predecessors had enjoyed, in the shape of an official diploma.

Iwannis had been bishop of Harran before his elevation to the patriarchate, and it is possible that he was selected for office by his peers because of his links to local notables in a city that had suddenly (and unexpectedly) become a locus of power and influence. Bar Hebraeus describes him as 'Iwannis of Harran'.[22] We do not know when he was made bishop of Harran, but that appointment seems to have taken place at a time when the see did not yet provide a stepping stone to the office of patriarch or an avenue to influence with the caliph. However, the following decades saw bitter competition for the sees of Harran and the Tur Abdin that had not been seen before. As we have seen, the conflict over appointments to these sees was a major source of strife

---

an attempt to protect these foundations from expropriation, but it also served the secondary purpose of associating these churches with Qartmin.

20. Keser-Kayaalp 2018: 200–203.

21. MS XI. 22 (IV, 464 / II, 506).

22. BH HE I, 305. Note, however, that the appellation may be an interpolation by Bar Hebraeus, rather than Dionysius' own wording. Iwannis was probably a monk of Eusebona (MS XI. 21 [IV, 462 / II, 503]), a monastery that had not often produced patriarchs. The monastery was located on the outskirts of Antioch and was a famous centre of Syriac scholarship (Brock 2007: 299–300). Bar Hebraeus states that Ishaq was a monk of Zuqnin.

between Iwannis and Athanasius Sandalaya. And the possibilities offered by appointment to Harran attracted Cyriacus of Segestan to make a personal appeal to Marwan.

In this era, the see of Harran provided an obvious ladder to high office. Sandalaya's client Ishaq was made patriarch with seemingly no other qualifications (if we disbelieve the incredible stories of alchemy and murder). The Melkite patriarch Theophylact bar Qanbara, who was responsible for a significant persecution of the Maronites, was similarly a former bishop of Harran.[23] In both cases, attachment to Harran seems to have allowed the patriarchs to break the older rules of engagement in order to enforce controversial changes to the liturgy (in the case of Theophylact) or to condemn powerful bishops and parcel out sees to clients (in the case of Ishaq and Sandalaya).

However, Harran seems to have rapidly lost its political influence in the wake of the Abbasid revolution and the end of the city's brief status as the imperial capital. Dionysius attributes Ishaq's execution to al-Mansur's discovery that he could not perform alchemy, but it seems possible that the caliph in fact removed the patriarch because he was unqualified for the role and because strong links to Harran no longer ensured influence at court after the transfer of the capital.

The subsequent fifty years confirmed the city's loss of importance. During the reign of al-Mahdi, 'Ali, governor of Mesopotamia, summoned the patriarch George from his residence at Harran to Raqqa to face charges from his opponents. Harran had been stripped of its governorate and mint in the 770s, and the accusations against George may reflect his distance from the new centre of power and the foolishness of attempting to maintain the patriarchate in the old Marwanid capital.[24] George's successor, Cyriacus, was elected at Harran and issued canons at a synod at Beth Botin, just outside the city, and in Harran itself.[25] But these actions should be read as attempts to build bridges with older sees that were now far from political influence. Cyriacus must have owed his appointment in part to the fact that, as a monk of the monastery of the Pillars in Raqqa, he was well connected to the Abbasid authorities in a city that would soon be made al-Rashid's capital.

23. MS XI. 22 (IV, 467 / II, 511).

24. MS XII. 1 (IV, 479 / II, 3–4). Heidemann 2011: 47–48 observes that Harran remained the seat of the governor of the Jazira and a mint site until the 770s.

25. Mounayer 1963: 43–44, 59.

Harran's brief political prominence must have seemed rather surprising to any audience familiar with Syriac literature. Harran was a long-standing pagan centre that had provided an antitype to Christian Edessa in Syriac writing, in the writings of Ephrem and in the sixth-century *Julian Romance*. This history is never mentioned explicitly by the sources quoted by Dionysius. But they do express shock at the eclipse of Edessa in this period,[26] when they report Sandalaya's claiming of the title of metropolitan of Mesopotamia for Maypherkat. This title had traditionally fallen to Edessa as the apostolic foundation of Addai, who was said to have brought Christianity to Abgar the Black, king of Edessa, soon after the death of Christ.[27] Dionysius of Tel-Mahre describes how Sandalaya set out to slander Timothy of Edessa to reduce the latter's legitimacy and to boost his own claim to the metropolitanate.[28]

In the longer term, however, Harran's large pagan population and the presence of Muslim Arab settlers meant that the city fared much worse than Edessa did, at least as a Christian centre. Harranian Christians had benefited from the persecution of pagans at the end of Maurice's reign around 600. Dionysius reports that a Christian secretary named Iyarios had denounced the pagan aristocrats, and his descendants, the Beth Iyar, had dominated the politics of the city.[29] But after the city lost its political significance, the pagans were able to reassert themselves. The governor Ibrahim permitted public pagan worship at Harran and was receptive to pagan denunciations of Christians.[30] The restoration of the pagans' fortunes coincided with their recognition as 'Sabians', a monotheistic group mentioned in the Quran, and with the acquisition of fame by several Harranian intellectuals in Baghdad.[31] Though Dionysius' narrative gives no sense of this wider context, it is likely that the Harranians' success at inserting themselves into Islamic categories of religion

26. Cf. Honigmann 1954: 123.

27. For this story and its variants, see Griffith 2003; Wood 2010: ch. 4, citing earlier literature.

28. MS XI. 24 (IV, 472 / II, 519–20). Judging by his presence in the signatory lists at MS IV, 468 / II, 512 and IV, 470 / II, 516, Timothy was an ally of Sandalaya's opponent David of Dara. In Sandalaya's hands, the title of metropolitan may have corresponded to a much greater area than the Roman province of Mesopotamia and embraced the entire Jazira.

29. MS X. 24 (388 / 375–76). I ascribe this passage to Dionysius on the basis of his interest in familial histories stretching back to the reign of Maurice.

30. MS XII. 9 (IV, 35 / II, 499) and MS XII. 11 (IV, 505 / III, 47).

31. Roberts 2017. For Harranian ('Sabian') ideas more broadly, see van Bladel 2009.

allowed them to develop good relations with Ibrahim and to oppose local Christian elites.

Though Harran was important as a centre of Christian scholarship[32] and pilgrimage,[33] it also had great religious diversity: in addition to Jacobites, Melkites and the Church of the East, it also hosted Manichaeans[34] and Quqites,[35] as well as pagans and Muslims. Harran's physical setting next to an open plain with readily available grazing had made it a prime choice for Marwan's Qaysi Arab troops and prompted him to make Harran his capital.[36] But if this coincidence had made Harran a site of influence for Christians in the 740s, it made life much harder for local Christians a century later, when Muslim Arab settlers and their descendants attacked Christians and demolished churches.[37] Further, it may be that the religious diversity of the city meant that it was harder for individual confessions to fund welfare programs or to secure political influence. Certainly, the mass conversions from Christianity to Islam that the *Chronicle of Zuqnin* reports for the city may be explained by these demographic factors: the settlement of Muslim Arabs occurred in a city with large numbers of competing religious groups that were each quite small in size.[38]

32. Many of the manuscripts collected in the Wadi Natrun in Egypt were commissioned at Harran or were owned at some point by Harranians (Blanchard 1995: 22; S. Johnson 2015: 50). For the Melkite intellectuals Constantine of Harran, Leo of Harran and Theodore Abu Qurra (who was an Edessene but served as bishop of Harran), see Possekel 2015, with references to further literature.

33. The Piacenza pilgrim (§47) visited Harran and believed it to be the birthplace of Abraham. For the extensive church buildings identified at the site, including a large three-aisled basilica and baptistery, see Lloyd and Brice 1951: 107–8.

34. *Chronicle of Zuqnin*, 224–25 / 202–4.

35. Bar Koni §77 (333–34 / 249–50). This sect originated in Edessa in the second century. It was accused of altering the New Testament, of practicing astrology, of refusing to touch the corpses of the dead and of approving of fornication. Drijvers 1967 suggests that the group combined 'pagan', Jewish and Christian ideas.

36. Katbi 2010: 443–45. Harran also offered easy access to two distinct routes between the Jazira and Iraq: toward Mosul and the Tigris and toward Ana and the Euphrates (Lloyd and Brice 1951: 80–81).

37. See MS XII. 18 (IV, 529 / III, 86) for the destruction of the church of Ahudemmeh in Harran in 826.

38. *Chronicle of Zuqnin*, 395ff. / 331ff., on the martyrdom of Cyrus of Harran (with discussion in Harrak 2003).

Syria: The Limestone Massif

In the Jazira, the inauguration of Marwan's new capital inverted the traditional hierarchy among the cities of the region. Harran and, later, Raqqa became major Christian centres, which brought power and influence first to Qartmin and then to Mar Zakkai and the monastery of the Pillars. Ninth-century Syria, by contrast, experienced a marked, wholescale loss of significance. This was obviously true for the region's Arab Muslim elite, who had once been at the centre of the Umayyad regime but who saw their influence dwindle under the Abbasids.[39] But it was, perhaps, even more true for Christian populations in Antiocheia, a territory that had once hosted a Roman imperial capital, a prosperous hinterland and an extremely wealthy elite with international connections. The transformation of Antiocheia into a frontier province, the flight of the Roman elite and the marshification of its hinterland undermined the territory's importance. Yet, as we have seen above, the villages of the Limestone Massif, on the road between Antioch and Aleppo, seem to have retained their prosperity. The life of a Melkite saint, the *Life of Timothy of Kakushta*, written in Arabic and set in the late eighth century, describes a world of affluent villages, well connected to one another but with limited interregional links.[40]

The *Life of Timothy* is especially interesting for our purposes because of its witness to the tense relationship between the holy man Timothy (and the rural society that he claimed to lead) and Theodoret, the Melkite patriarch of Antioch. Timothy appears in the *Life* as a wonder-working charismatic, able to heal the sick and to perceive the hidden sins of the villagers. Timothy's fame means that the two villages associated with him, Kakushta and Kfar Zuma, receive pilgrims from as far afield as Antioch,[41] Aleppo[42] and Homs,[43] and even a Muslim from Fars.[44] Such far-flung connections do not seem to have been typical for the region, and Timothy himself was exceptional among

39. Cobb 2001: 130–31. Cobb sees the reign of al-Mu'tasim as the key turning point for the loss of influence of the Syrian *ashrāf*.

40. Published in PO 48. I cite the earlier Paris manuscript (P), except in cases of lacunae, when I use the Seidnaya manuscript (S). The Seidnaya manuscript dates to the eleventh century, i.e., to the period after the Byzantine conquest of Antiocheia. P is older, but its date is unclear. Lamoureaux and Cairala 2001: 453.

41. P 28.1.

42. S 46.1.

43. P 34.1.

44. P 36.

his contemporaries for his visits to the great Melkite shrines in Jerusalem and Sinai.[45]

The *Life* makes little reference to a formal parish system or to the presence of local cenobitic monasteries. Both surely existed, however, and their omission probably reflects a decision by the hagiographer to focus the account on Timothy himself. The main occasion on which the clergy are mentioned at all is in Timothy's conflict with Theodoret, patriarch of Antioch, which forms the work's centrepiece.[46] We do not need to place any faith in the hagiographer's depiction of real events or individuals to see the *Life of Timothy* as an important criticism of the patriarch of Antioch and his claim to represent the Melkite community at Baghdad.

We first encounter the patriarch in a scene in which Timothy has criticized a rich local notable from the nearby village of D-q-s who has committed adultery. Timothy curses the man, whereupon he implores Timothy to forgive him. Timothy refuses, so the man goes to Antioch to ask the patriarch Theodoret to intercede for him. Theodoret writes to Timothy, 'Father, I ask you to have mercy on this wretch. This request is both mine and God's'. But Timothy replies, 'Behold! We bind and we release. . . . We nullify the laws of God!' Instead of lifting the curse, Timothy delays, until a messenger comes one week later to announce that the man's wife has died. At the news, 'the saint gave thanks to God, who desires the salvation of people and did not allow a man to have two wives in the same family'.[47] Part of Timothy's importance throughout the *Life* stems from his unique role as arbiter of human moral behaviour, and the hagiographer has chosen to represent the patriarch's request for leniency as a challenge both to divine justice and to Timothy's own legitimacy as its sole interpreter for his petitioners.

This tension between the respective roles of Timothy and the patriarch serves as a prelude to the second scene involving Theodoret, which follows shortly afterward. Here the patriarch travels to see the saint to receive a blessing. The hagiographer describes him arriving 'in a beautifully adorned carriage wearing fine clothes that were not worn by the disciples'. During the meeting, the patriarch offers Timothy any assistance the saint may desire, but Timothy

45. P 3 and P 26.

46. Theodoret was a historical figure. The dates of his tenure are uncertain, but they did lie in the last decades of the eighth century, and possibly the first decade of the ninth, which makes him a contemporary of Harun al-Rashid. Lamoureaux and Cairala 2001: 457.

47. P 22.1–2.

replies by telling him about a vision he has experienced: 'I asked God how he receives this riding and this finery that you wear, and he showed me the apostles and all those who served Him in poverty. I saw them all wearing crowns of glory, while you stood in their midst wearing lowly clothes and with the face of an Indian'. Therefore, Timothy continues, the patriarch must give up his present luxury, give money to the poor and orphans and take care in the visitation of churches and monasteries.[48]

In response, the patriarch initially agrees to follow Timothy's advice, but after a few days he relapses into his old ways. During Lent, Timothy warns him that if he continues his bad behaviour, he will be unable to consecrate the *myron* (the holy oil used in baptism) on Maundy Thursday. Theodoret dismisses Timothy's warning and goes to consecrate the myron, but his enemies have already slandered him to the caliph, Harun al-Rashid, and horsemen arrive to arrest him just before he can enter the church. They lead him away on a mule, weighed down with irons, but he manages to bribe them to take him to Timothy first before continuing to Baghdad. In this second meeting, Timothy chastises the patriarch again but gives him a final chance, instructing him on how to behave once he has been taken to al-Rashid. Timothy promises to use his *parrhēsia* (his powers of intercession) with God to ensure Theodoret's safety and tells him not to accept any rewards from the caliph. Instead, Timothy tells him that he should ask the caliph to consider the hardship faced by the poor with regard to the jizya and to provide him with written confirmation 'about the freedom to follow the laws of the churches and that they be built and repaired and that no monk be accosted in any way, in accordance with what is enjoined on them [the Muslims] in the pact drawn up by their master [Muhammad]'.[49]

In Baghdad, Timothy's promises come true. Theodoret is condemned to death, but the executioner is unable to kill him because his hand miraculously withers up. Next, the caliph's concubine asks the caliph to make Theodoret his doorkeeper instead of killing him. While serving the caliph in this capacity, Theodoret finds his opportunity when the caliph's son falls sick and cannot be cured by any of the doctors of Baghdad: Theodoret anoints the boy with holy oil that has been blessed by Timothy, and he recovers. The caliph rejoices in the words of Luke's Gospel—'Today I have great joy for my son, for he was dead, but

48. P 27.1–2.

49. S 33.3–5 (the parallel passages must have been present in P also, but the relevant folio is missing).

now he lives'[50]—and grants to all Christians all the remissions that Timothy had suggested to Theodoret for monks, churches and the poor.[51] On his return to Kakushta, the patriarch meets again with Timothy, who informs him that he knew of Theodoret's tribulations throughout and prayed to God to allow him to heal the caliph's son. 'From that time on', the hagiographer concludes, 'he promised God that he would not ride out with his finery, and he freed slaves and began to ride a donkey, following the example of the apostles.'[52]

The obvious crux of this miracle is to demonstrate the superiority of Timothy's Christian life, its effect on his parrhēsia with God, and his consequent success as a miracle worker. The contrast to the patriarch is built around their different attitudes to asceticism: Timothy, by implication, walks in the path of the apostles, whereas Theodoret is pejoratively identified as 'an Indian' in God's eyes.[53] Such comparisons between ascetics and more worldly leaders have a history that stretches back into the patristic period: the sixth-century hagiographer John of Ephesus describes Miaphysite saints choosing to flee into exile rather than accept the bribes and promotions of the Chalcedonian authorities.[54] But they may have had special resonance in a political context in which the patriarch represented Christians before a Muslim government and some may have resented this collaboration and the wealth that the higher clergy accumulated. In this example, the Melkite Chalcedonian community of Antiocheia is represented by Timothy and his asceticism is juxtaposed with the worldly behaviour of the higher clergy. In this respect, the tension between Timothy and the patriarch is a symptom of the adaptation of Levantine Chalcedonians to the shift from a system in which they were a favoured community toward a new order in which they were just one dhimmī group among many.

That riding a horse is singled out as a sign of luxury is noteworthy, since it was also identified as an undesirable feature of Christian social mobility in Baghdad by ninth-century Muslim legal scholars, who periodically attempted to curtail this kind of self-promotion at court by newly prominent Christian

50. Luke 15:24.

51. P 27.5–11 and S 33.6–11.

52. P 27.13.

53. For the representation of the Devil as an 'Ethiopian' or an 'Indian' in late antique hagiography, see Mayerson 1978 and, more generally, Byron 2002. Cf. *Life of Stephen the Sabaite*, 30.7.

54. John of Ephesus, *Lives of the Eastern Saints*, PO 18:127. Note comments in Wood 2010: 189–90 on John of Ephesus' *Life of Harfat*.

elites.[55] I believe that this shared complaint of a Christian saint's life and Muslim sumptuary law reflects the new opportunities available in Baghdad for people whose political influence transcended individual provinces of the caliphate. We can see the 'extravagance' of men such as Theodoret both as an attempt to maximize their stature as recognized leaders of a dhimmī group and as an effort to play according to the rules of the Abbasid court by engaging in the kind of display that would distinguish them above rival dhimmī groups in Baghdad—a display that indicates the broader reappearance of Sasanian court culture under the Abbasids.[56]

Therefore, the resentment shown by the author of the *Life of Timothy* can also be situated in the context of changes in the display and loci of power that followed the Abbasid revolution and the foundation of Baghdad. The relationship between the caliph and dhimmīs privileged certain appointed spokesmen and granted them special access to the court and to patronage. However, we should remember that the position of Christian leaders in Baghdad was also legitimated by their role as defenders of their flock. In addition to defending the faith in staged debates before the caliph and contributing to the intellectual life of the court, Christian patriarchs played an important role in defending the property and tax rights of Christians in matters such as the poll tax, church construction and monastic property, which are brought up in the *Life of Timothy*.

In the hagiography's portrayal, the Muslim rulers who protected Christians were acting justly according to their own quranic criteria. Timothy reminds the patriarch that Muhammad had guaranteed the protection of dhimmīs, and the backing of the Quran and Muhammad's precedent are invoked again in Theodoret's request to the caliph.[57] In my view, the hagiographer's aim here is to participate in the discourse about the rights of the dhimmīs but simultaneously to subvert the patriarch's attempt to claim control of the relationship with the caliph and to criticize the economic advantages associated with the position of patriarch. Timothy not only demonstrates his importance as a

55. Fiey 1980: 46 and Levy-Rubin 2011: chs. 3 and 5.

56. For neo-Sasanian elements in Abbasid court culture, see Latham 1990: 55; Marsham 2009: 200, 300, 313. Brody 1998: 73–74 notes the emphasis placed by Jewish exilarchs on their ability to present themselves in high style before the caliph in order to act as effective representatives of the Jews, exactly the approach that the *Life of Timothy* contests or subverts in a Christian context. Sasanian iconographic and administrative practices are already visible under the late Marwanids (Marsham 2009: 161–64).

57. P 27.11.

miracle worker and an ascetic but also uses his abilities to make Theodoret's success at court possible. Timothy rarely takes the opportunity to criticize individual Muslims or Islam in the *Life*,[58] with the result that the hagiographer's disapproval is largely directed not at a tyrannical caliph or his advisers but at powerful Christians such as Theodoret and those who fail to respect Timothy's authority. It is Timothy who, in this telling, constitutes the ultimate source of Christian influence over the caliph.

The hagiographer's depiction of Theodoret and the corrupting effect of wealth is contextualized by the historical attenuation of Antioch's influence on its hinterland. If my reading of the narrative is correct, the patriarch claimed preeminence as the spokesman of the Melkite community, but his claim was not accepted by all members of his flock. Some of them may have had to pay tithes to the patriarch or to tolerate the use of clergy as tax collectors on the state's behalf, practices attested in other Christian contexts.[59] It may be that one goal of the hagiography was to redirect locals' sympathies and donations to places and institutions associated with Timothy. At any rate, whereas Greek texts of the fourth and fifth centuries drew close connections between Antioch and its hinterland through urban patronage of villages and the interest of Antiochenes in the holy men and monasteries of the countryside,[60] the *Life of Timothy* suggests a different kind of relationship, in which Kakushta and Kfar Zuma are almost as distant from Antioch as they are from Baghdad.

Cyrrhus and Gubba Barraya under Cyriacus

If the *Life of Timothy* gives us a case of intraregional networks being disrupted when Antioch lost importance and influence, the case of Cyrrhus and the famous monastery of Gubba Barraya, which lay between Cyrrhus and Diocle, reveals a slightly different symptom of Syria's broader loss of importance. In Dionysius' account of Cyriacus' and Dionysius' quarrels with the Gubbite

58. The omission is especially pointed in P 27.9, where the doctors of Baghdad fail to cure the caliph's son. See also P 36, where Timothy assures a Persian that he will not have to convert for his son to be healed.

59. See chapter 1.

60. I am referring particularly to Libanius of Antioch and Theodoret of Cyrrhus; see the analysis of Liebeschuetz 1972: 64–70, 199–208 and Millar 2015c for links of patronage, credit and rent between elites in the city of Antioch and its hinterland. Schor 2011: 138–40 points to the city-dwelling elites of Cyrrhus whose wealth was drawn from scattered rural estates.

monks, we find indicators that Cyrrhus retained an independent local aristocracy that backed the monks in their struggle against Cyriacus and his centralizing reforms.

Gubba Barraya was a very famous Jacobite centre. Though it has not attracted much attention from modern scholars,[61] it was the residence of the patriarch Paul of Callinicum during his famous dispute with Damian of Alexandria in the 580s. It was here that Paul denounced the 'heretical' philosopher Probus and attempted to convene a synod to iron out his differences with Damian, pointing to the ease with which the monastery could be reached from Antioch, Aleppo and Mabbug.[62] The monastery retained its importance into the eighth century, and it was the residence and place of ordination of three further patriarchs, who were themselves Gubbite monks. These were John Sedra (631–48), Elias (709–23) (the first Jacobite patriarch to enter the city of Antioch since Severus) and Athanasius III (724–40).

The monastery is not mentioned in Dionysius' narrative of the period between 740 and 760, which is focused on the Jazira, but it and its monks appear again as a major actors during the famous dispute over the heavenly bread during the reign of Cyriacus. The narrative is complex, but it has rarely been discussed in the secondary literature, so it is worth setting out in detail.

The dispute arose from the practice of breaking the consecrated host at the Eucharist in the name of the Father, the Son and the Holy Spirit. This practice had become traditional in the Jacobite church, but the patriarch George already observes that the phrase cannot be found in patristic writings and was not used by Egyptian Miaphysites.[63] He points out that the phrase in effect introduces a second Son into the Trinity: since God the Son is already present in the consecrated host, it is necessary to invoke God only as Father and as Holy Spirit. George suggests that the tripartite phrase is an innovation introduced by the Dyophysite Diodore of Tarsus, 'the enemy of truth and the opponent of Christ'—in other words, that the introduction of two Christs into the liturgy was prompted by a 'heretical' Christology that had already divided Christ by giving him two natures.[64]

61. An exception is Ebied, Van Roey and Wickham 1981: 40–41.
62. MS X. 22 (IV, 382 / II, 366).
63. MS XII. 2 (IV, 481 / III, 6).
64. MS XII. 2 (IV, 482 / III, 7). Diodore (d. 394) was the teacher of Theodore of Mopsuestia and a major early Dyophysite theologian. He remained an important church father for the Church of the East (L. Abramowski 1960).

George's accusation of Diodoran influence seems unlikely to be accurate,[65] but we should note that he does not accuse Jacobites who use the formula of doing so wilfully; rather, he says, they use it out of 'rustic ignorance'. Indeed, George finishes his letter on the subject by stating that he will not seek to ban the formula for fear of dividing the church. Dionysius notes at the start of this chapter that George's tolerant position on the issue was not widely known, and he may have included George's letter in his history to legitimate his own position, which was similarly tolerant but not theologically agnostic.

George is succeeded as patriarch by the short-lived Joseph of Gubba Barraya (whom Dionysius mocks for his 'barbaric' language, presumably his poor Syriac). After Joseph's sudden death, the bishops elect Cyriacus. This unexpected turn of events must have dashed the Gubbites' expectations of continued influence. Soon after his election Cyriacus alters the official position on the heavenly bread formula at the synod of Beth Botin. Dionysius reports: 'Seeing that the affairs [of the church] prospered . . . he wished to suppress the formula *We break the heavenly bread*. This is why he forbade the priests he ordained from reciting it. He did not consider the fact that George had tolerated it and refrained from banning it to avoid dividing the church.'[66]

Cyriacus' unilateral move prompts an objection from the Gubbites. Subsequently, their bishop Bacchus, 'who was also the bishop of the Cyrrhesticans', is excommunicated and removed from office for unnamed faults. Dionysius tells us that Bacchus harboured great resentment against Cyriacus and encouraged priests to use the heavenly bread formula to annoy the patriarch. On his deathbed, Bacchus exhorts the notables of Cyrrhus and the Gubbites never to give up the formula or to accept bishops who are not from Gubba Barraya. 'Nothing afflicts me [causes my death] except for this little Garamean [Cyriacus] who has divided the land into two principalities (*rišnūtē*) and abolished the formula of the heavenly bread.'[67]

After the death of Bacchus, his disciple Philoxenus goes to Cyriacus with a delegation of Gubbites and asks to be ordained as bishop. But Cyriacus replies, 'It is not just for this land to be held as the patrimony of one monastery. We will ordain you for another see and someone from somewhere else for this see'.

---

65. Contra Palmer 1990: 179 and R. Abramowski 1940: 98.

66. MS XII. 3 (IV, 484 / III, 11). For the affair of Cyriacus and the heavenly bread, see further Oez 2012: I, 43–57. The account in Nabe-von Schönberg 1977: 89–92 cleaves very closely to the sources.

67. MS XII. 5 (IV, 487 / III, 17–18).

In response, Philoxenus and the Gubbites encourage the Cyrrhesticans to revolt against the patriarch. 'Because of their riches', they follow the monks' advice and refuse 'to allow their country to be divided in two'.[68]

After Philoxenus and Cyriacus fail to reach an agreement, Cyriacus decides to proceed with the despatch of bishops. Cyriacus appoints Solomon from the monastery of Jacob of Cyrrhus, but he is received in only two villages, Gubrin and Tamarna, and the people of Cyrrhus stop acknowledging Cyriacus as patriarch.[69] The rebels then seek out the caliph al-Rashid at Dabiq and complain that Cyriacus was ordained as patriarch without the consent of the church, that he oppresses the people with heavy tithes and that he has committed treason against the caliph. We are told that the caliph reacts by ordering the churches of Tagra to be destroyed and by summoning Cyriacus. Appearing before the caliph, Cyriacus is forced to defend himself against the accusation that he had arranged the assassination of one Simeon, a monk of Gubba Barraya who had been killed by brigands while serving as bishop of the Arab tribes.[70]

After confirming his rank with the caliph, Cyriacus attempts to win over the Gubbites with a personal meeting in the diocese of Cyrrhus. But crowds of monks stone Cyriacus and his bishops, and he is forced to retreat. Using his contacts with the emir, Cyriacus has forty monks arrested and arranges an independent meeting with the notables of Cyrrhus. Here he finds more success: the nobles receive the patriarch's blessing and promise that the monks will keep their peace.[71]

Cyriacus releases the monks from prison and leaves the area, but the Gubbites begin to defy his authority and illegally call on two deposed bishops, John of Kokta and Job of Mopsuestia, to consecrate Gubbite monks for the rural dioceses of Goulia and Kumit (the see of the Banu Tanukh). In response, Cyriacus asks the emir to arrest one of the Gubbite bishops, John of Kokta,

68. MS XII. 5 (IV, 487 / III, 18). The link between Cyrrhus and Gubba Barraya has a parallel in the link of Qartmin and the Tur Abdin: Palmer 1990: 180.

69. Cyriacus may have been attempting to build up the monastery of Jacob of Cyrrhus as an alternative to Gubba Barraya. He ordained Timothy, another monk of this monastery, as metropolitan of Jerusalem (MS appendix III: XVII, 28). For Solomon, see MS appendix III: XVII, 49. The monastery of Mar Jacob was not insignificant, and it had been the seat of the patriarch Julian II (BH HE I, 295; X1234 [I, 232/175]). Hage 1966: 15 n. 90.

70. MS XII. 5 (IV, 488–89 / III, 19–21). Cf. BH HE I, 339 on the link between the Gubbite accusations and the destruction of churches.

71. MS XII. 6 (IV, 490 / III, 23).

and convenes a synod at Gubrin to excommunicate John and seven others, including Philoxenus.[72]

However, Cyriacus' decisive response fails to solve the controversy. One Abraham, a brother of one of the Gubbites condemned at Gubrin and a monk of Qartmin, enters into an alliance with the Gubbite leaders, and they start to ordain peripatetic bishops without dioceses. Dionysius refers to this Abraham as Abiram (the name of the man who conspired against Moses and Aaron in Numbers 16). Abiram calls Cyriacus a heretic linked to the Julianists and justifies his opposition as defence of the heavenly bread formula.[73] He even claims the rank of patriarch. Dionysius accuses him of accepting all manner of murderers, robbers and bigamists as priests and deacons.[74]

Cyriacus himself dies shortly afterward, and his death promises to put an end to the schism. Dionysius reports that 'the Cyrrhesticans and the Gubbites' tell Abiram that they can stop living under anathemas from Syria and Egypt now that the man who wished to abandon the heavenly bread formula is dead. Abiram promises to renounce his position as anti-patriarch if the other bishops agree to elect someone who will say the formula just once. Dionysius adds that Abiram said these things in the expectation that it would be he himself who would be elected.[75]

The bishops assemble at Callinicum and, before electing a new patriarch, promise to allow a plurality of positions on the heavenly bread formula, but they order that anyone who anathematizes anyone else over the issue would himself be anathematized by his fellows.[76] When Dionysius is elected, Abiram is furious and refuses to step down as anti-patriarch. 'See!' he tells his followers, 'they have chosen a leader from a monastery and a city that condemn the formula of the heavenly bread'. Abiram and his followers depart from Callinicum for Cyrrhus.

Like Cyriacus, Dionysius makes overtures to reconcile the schismatics. One of his first episcopal ordinations is the appointment of a Gubbite monk named Habib as bishop of Beth Balash.[77] Though the Gubbite monks

---

72. MS XII. 6 (IV, 491 / III, 23–24).
73. MS XII. 6 (IV, 492 / III, 25).
74. MS XII. 8 (IV, 495 / III, 32).
75. MS XII. 9 (IV, 498–99 / III, 37).
76. MS XII. 10 (IV, 500–501 / III, 39–40).
77. MS appendix III: XVIII, 2.

themselves remain obdurate, Dionysius is able to win over the Cyrrhesticans by assuring them that they will be allowed to continue using the formula.[78]

The denouement to the affair comes when Abiram seeks an audience with the governor of the whole of the western caliphate, ʿAbd Allah ibn Tahir. Using his connections at court, Abiram seeks to denounce Dionysius as a false patriarch. But Dionysius' good relations with the authorities carry the day, and Abiram is forbidden from wearing the kūšītā, the headdress of a patriarch. Abiram and his companions depart secretly to the region of Cyrrhus, but Dionysius pursues them and uses Persian troops to have them arrested and imprisoned in Aleppo.[79] Abiram himself remains an anti-patriarch, but the movement he headed does not survive his death. Although his brother Simeon is ordained as his successor, Simeon does not seem able to command support. Dionysius concludes: 'The wings of Abiram's party were scorched, and, like the idols of the Gentiles, they could no longer do good or bad.'[80]

The Gubbite Rebellion: An Analysis

On one level, the Gubbite rebellion was triggered by a liturgical issue. Bacchus, Philoxenus and then Abiram presented themselves as defenders of an ancient formula against Cyriacus' intervention. That first George and then Cyriacus identified the formula as a problem is indicative of a growing interest in theological reasoning (and the growing centrality of the liturgy within this) on the part of the church's leaders. This trend, in turn, may be linked to the development of scholarly centres such as Takrit, which produced a number of Jacobite intellectuals over the following century.[81]

On the other hand, that the issue prompted such an emotional reaction suggests that the trends toward greater scholarly engagement and international connections were not widespread. The stance of the Gubbites often seems to reduce Abiram's defence of the heavenly bread formula to an appeal to ancient tradition, whereas George provides a reasoned theological argument. It is also telling that George explains people's adherence to the formula as a result of 'rustic ignorance'. Obviously, the narrative concerning Abiram cannot simply be read as fact, as it must also reflect Dionysius' own animus. But Dionysius'

---

78. MS XII. 11 (IV, 504 / III, 44).
79. MS XII. 12 (IV, 508–12 / III, 56–59).
80. MS XII. 19 (IV, 531–32 / III, 92–93).
81. Nabe-von Schönberg 1977: 101ff.

mockery of Joseph of Gubba Barraya for his poor education and Abiram's comment that Qenneshre and Edessa, where Dionysius was trained, consistently opposed the formula might suggest a difference in intellectual culture between Gubba Barraya, Cyrrhus and Qartmin, on the one hand, and Qenneshre, Mar Zakkai in Raqqa, Edessa and Takrit, on the other.[82] Although Gubba Barraya was an ancient Jacobite centre, there is little indication in Dionysius' narrative that Cyrrhus enjoyed close links to other urban sees except for Bostra and Mopsuestia, neither of which was significant or centrally located. The rebel bishops who were consecrated in defiance of Cyriacus are said to have been peripatetic, without fixed sees.[83]

Cyrrhus' relative isolation is visible already in the late Roman period. Part of the province of Euphratensia, it formed a western outlier (together with Germanicia) in a province in which most urban centres were strung out along the Euphrates.[84] It was certainly a significant see, and it was endowed with hundreds of churches in the fifth century, but it was an autocephalous metropolitanate (and continued to hold this status into the Abbasid period), so its bishops did not automatically have links to any subordinate bishops.[85] Edmond Frézouls, who conducted a survey of the city in the 1950s, commented that although Cyrrhus itself was well endowed with civic infrastructure, it was a 'peripheral and isolated district', accessible only during the summer.[86]

Nor does Cyrrhus seem to have been well integrated into Muslim patronage networks. For instance, when al-Walid I wanted to seize columns for a new mosque in Aleppo, he took them not from the churches of Aleppo but rather from Cyrrhus, from a church once renowned as a wonder of the world.[87] This

82. Note also that Cyriacus composed his work *On Divine Providence* in response to requests from a certain Walid and Yeshu' of Tirminaz, near Cyrrhus, so it would be wrong to suppose that Cyriacus lacked connections to the region or that its inhabitants had no interest in speculative theology (Oez 2012: I, 9). R. Abramowski 1940: 97 suggests that the formula was an issue only for certain provinces, but he does not develop this point.

83. BH HE I, 341.

84. Millar 2015b: 184–86. Also cf. Millar 2015a on late Roman Cyrrhus.

85. Vailhé 1908; Honigmann 1954: 103, 120.

86. Frézouls 1954–55: esp. 114. Perhaps the comments about Gubba Barraya being accessible from Aleppo and Antioch at MS X. 22 (IV, 382 / II, 366) reflect summer conditions or are simply an exaggeration, made to criticize Damian of Alexandria, who had refused to hold a synod in such 'a distant and barbaric place'.

87. Ibn Shaddad 31 describes the beauty and cost of the pillars taken from Cyrrhus. Cf. Straughn 2006: 211.

choice does not mean that the latter city had been denuded of its aristocracy, as has been proposed in the case of the multiprovincial Roman aristocrats resident in Antioch and Apamea.[88] Rather, I interpret it as a sign of the difference that influence at court could make: the Christians of Aleppo may have seemed more significant or more useful because of their greater visibility to Muslim power. Another indication of Cyrrhus' low profile is the fact that it was settled at the government's behest by Slavs who had defected from the Byzantine army in the 690s. This policy suggests that the city was seen as a tabula rasa by Muslim authorities, who did not want to place the settlers near established Arab populations.[89] So when we read that the Gubbites were unable to undermine 'Abd Allah ibn Tahir's support for Dionysius, or that Dionysius could harness government troops to imprison recalcitrant monks in Aleppo, the Gubbites' relative powerlessness reinforces the impression of a city and a monastery that lacked the influence enjoyed by some other centres.

Envisioning Cyrrhus as a relatively self-contained world helps to make sense of the Gubbites' expectation that they should be able to monopolize appointments to the nearby see (in the way that Qartmin did for the Tur Abdin). Cyriacus' plan, by contrast, was to appoint monks to bishoprics away from their home monasteries, probably with the hope that this would promote their dependence on the patriarch who appointed them rather than on local backers, and thus reduce the likelihood of schism. But Cyriacus' policy seems to have fanned the flames of opposition to the patriarch's theological reforms, perhaps because it was seen as a centralizing initiative that removed the traditional privileges of Gubba Barraya and threatened the Gubbites' relationship with Cyrrhus.

In the long term, however, the pattern of episcopal appointments in Cyrrhus shows that the capacity to choose their own bishops was taken out of the hands of the Gubbite monks; their fears had thus been justified. Early in his patriarchate, Dionysius ordained a Gubbite monk named Sergius as metropolitan of Cyrrhus.[90] This event is unmentioned in the narrative, and Dionysius may have simply been prepared to make pragmatic concessions to the Gubbites to keep the channels of communication open. But at the same time he also ordained a number of bishops from the monastery of Jacob of Cyrrhus,

88. Bonner 1996: 137.
89. MS XI. 15 (IV, 446 / II, 470). See the analysis in Straughn 2006: 219–20.
90. MS appendix III: XVIII, 23.

which Cyriacus had supported as an alternative to Gubba Barraya.[91] Overall, Dionysius' ordinations reveal a stark decline in the importance of Gubba Barraya over time: after Sergius, only one Gubbite monk received a bishopric,[92] in marked contrast to the many monks from Qartmin or from the vicinity of Edessa and Amida who were ordained in the same period.[93] Cyrrhus itself was given over to outsiders, chiefly from Mesopotamia, though no one monastery was allowed a monopoly over the see.[94]

Conclusions

This chapter has examined three areas—Harran, Antiocheia and Cyrrhus—that were left behind by administrative and political changes in the ninth century. These changes were sometimes slow in coming. Cyrrhus' elites might have been outflanked by those of other cities that were closer to the new centres of power by the eighth century, but they could continue to expect to control episcopal elections and to engage in controversial church politics. In Harran, by contrast, we find a city that was suddenly thrust into the political limelight by Marwan II's inauguration of it as the capital, only to lose its influence within a generation. And in the countryside near Antioch, we see how the social contract between Christians and their higher clergy could be broken when bishops and patriarchs chose to model themselves after the courtiers of far-off Baghdad.

All these case studies illustrate the significance of Königsnähe. Proximity to Marwan made the patriarchate a lucrative office, which was worth initial

91. MS appendix III: XVIII, 6 (Habib, bishop of Marash); XVIII, 24 (Michael of Anazarbus).

92. MS appendix III: XVIII, 94 (George, bishop of Hadeth).

93. It is noteworthy that Abiram is so rarely associated with his home monastery of Qartmin in the historical narrative. It may be that obscuring the connection was a deliberate strategy by Dionysius or his peers, who sought to stress Abiram's rebellion as a Gubbite affair to deter any potential alliance with other Qartminites. The large number of Qartminite ordinations may also represent an attempt to compensate Qartmin for the lack of a Qartminite patriarch and to forestall any sympathy for Abiram.

94. The bishops of Cyrrhus were Abraham, from the monastery of the Arabs (MS appendix III: XVIII, 72); Elias, from the monastery of the easterners in Amida (XIX, 7); Aaron, from the monastery of Jacob of Cyrrhus (XIX, 25); Isaac, from the monastery of the mountain of Edessa (XIX, 70); and Sergius, from the monastery of Lazarus in Harran (XX, 3). BH HE I, 337 claims that all the people of Cyrrhus became Muslims, but I think this is more likely to be an editorial intervention by Bar Hebraeus in the thirteenth century than a comment by Dionysius.

major investment. And the period when Harran was the capital also coincided with Qartmin's dominance, when Qartminite patriarchs controlled a number of high-profile bishoprics. Historians associated with other monasteries might have condemned these patriarchs as tyrants, but Dionysius outdid them in their use of government patronage. Though the patriarchs' ability to strong-arm their rivals was temporarily interrupted by the fourth fitna, in the long run their ties to government allowed them to use troops to arrest recalcitrant monks and bishops in Gubba Barraya. The *Life of Timothy* illustrates how the Melkite patriarchs, like their Jacobite counterparts, used their ability to inter-cede with the government on behalf of their co-religionists to legitimate their own close links with the Muslim authorities and the wealth they drew from them. But the *Life* shows that these claims did not always go uncontested, especially in places that were far removed from the centres of power.

Finally, we should note that there were parts of the Jacobite church that were ignored entirely in the Syriac narratives as well as the Muslim Arabic texts. We are aware of the Jacobite church in Palestine and southern Syria almost solely from episcopal lists, and we hear once or twice of a Jacobite community in Central Asia (and then only because it was so difficult to ap-point bishops there).[95] Similarly, there is a marked contrast between the inter-est that eighth-century Syriac historians took in the Christian Arabs, as inter-locutors with the Muslims or as the objects of persecution, and Dionysius' lack of interest in contemporary Christian Arabs.[96] Harran and Cyrrhus were both displaced from the key political circles of the Jacobite church in or near the time when Dionysius wrote, but Palestine or Central Asia never provided a route to the patriarchate and are mostly left unmentioned.

95. Bishops in Central Asia: MS XI. 22 (IV, 465 / II, 507) and MS XII. 17 (IV, 525 / III, 79). For the distribution of Jacobite sees, as well as those of the other confessions, in Central Asia, see Fiey 1973 and Fiey 1993.

96. Christian Arab interlocutors and Bible translators: MS XI. 9 (IV, 422 / II, 432); persecu-tion: MS XI. 17 (IV, 451–52 / II, 481) and MS XII. 1 (IV, 479 / III, 1). There continued to be bishops of the Christian Arabs in the ninth century (Honigmann 1954: 148). For the persecution of Christian Arabs in general, see Friedmann 2003: 62–68; Gilliot 1991–92. Dionysius' lack of interest may reflect genuine demographic change, in which Christian Arabs converted to Islam, but it might also be linked to their support for the Abiramites (e.g. MS XII, 8 [IV, 495 / III, 32]).

5

Takrit and Mosul

THE JACOBITE EAST

THE ABBASID CALIPHATE WAS probably one of the largest economies in the world in the ninth century. Political boundaries between the great population centres of Iraq and Egypt were removed by the Arab conquests. By the end of the century, traders regularly sailed from ports in Iraq, Iran and the Arabian Peninsula to purchase finished goods, raw materials and slaves from East Africa and South Asia. Industry and agriculture thrived in Iraq in particular, where the building of huge new cities such as Baghdad and Samarra stimulated the economy by creating new markets and fostering innovation in industrial production. Hugh Kennedy has argued that the caliphal government played a major role in encouraging agricultural development by allowing deserted land (*mawāt*) to be claimed by private investors, as well as by guaranteeing security, creating an infrastructure for trade and regulating weights and measures.[1]

The increasingly dominant role of southern Iraq in these economic transformations may provide a context for the ecclesiastical politics of the ninth century, in which the city of Takrit in central Iraq increasingly overtook its rivals within the Jacobite east and became the hub of a trading network with a strong sense of its own distinctive identity.

1. Kennedy 2011; Bessard 2020.

Mosul and Takrit

The Jacobite church had enjoyed a presence in Iraq since the sixth century. This was partly a consequence of missionary activity and migration from the Roman empire.[2] But we should remember that Miaphysites in the east claimed to be indigenous communities that had preserved orthodoxy after the 'heretic' Barsauma of Nisibis (d. 491) spread Dyophysite 'Nestorianism' with the support of the Sasanian shah.[3] Thus in Bar Hebraeus' list of the leaders of the Jacobite east (in his day called 'maphrians'), he reproduces the biographies of the catholicoi of the Church of the East at Ctesiphon until the fifth century but continues this list with the Miaphysite leaders Ahudemmeh and Marutha in the late sixth and early seventh centuries.[4] For some eastern Jacobites, their leader was a catholicos, a figure entitled to ordain all the other bishops of the east and to convene councils (a role that was otherwise reserved for the patriarch).[5]

Leadership of the Jacobite east oscillated between two sees: Mosul in the north, whose bishop resided in the famous monastery of Mar Mattai, and

2. John of Ephesus, *Lives of the Eastern Saints*, PO 17:137ff.; *Chronicle of Seert*, PO 7:142–44, for Miaphysites at al-Hira, some of whom were expelled to Najran. Many or all of these Hiran Miaphysites were Julianists. *Chronicle of Seert*, PO 7:142, states that Jacobite doctrine was received in Takrit and the nearby towns of Karme and Hassassa in the early sixth century, but this may be an anachronism. In general, see Fiey 1970a: 127–32 and Fisher et al. 2015: 357–63.

3. This story appears in three different versions in Michael's *Chronicle*. A brief story in Michael describes Athanasius Gamala's rapprochement with Christopher of Mar Mattai (MS IX. 5 [IV, 413 / II, 417]), emphasizing the east as an autocephalous catholicosate and the preservation of episcopal succession at Mar Mattai. A much longer account is placed in the correspondence between Marutha and John Sedra in MS X. 9. This focuses on the history of Nestorius and Barsauma's violent propagation of Nestorian ideas. A third account appears briefly in the course of an account of negotiations between Takrit and Mar Mattai during the reign of Dionysius: MS XII. 7 (IV, 494 / III, 29). For discussion of the legendary claims that Mar Mattai had led resistance to the persecutions of Barsauma of Nisibis, see Gero 1982: esp 118 and Fiey 1970a: 114–16.

4. BH HE II, 99.

5. Hage 1966: 25 notes the different terminologies used to refer to the bishops of Takrit: 'bishops and metropolitans of Persia' (MS XI. 7 [IV, 433 / II, 423]), 'metropolitan of Takrit and the whole orient' (*Life of Marutha*, PO 3:61) and 'catholicos' (MS XI. 14 [IV, 503 / II, 462]). The title 'maphrian' used by Bar Hebraeus is a later invention that he retrojects onto his sources (Fiey 1970a: 141; Honigmann 1954: 96 n. 4). The significance of the term 'catholicos' is discussed in Leclerq 1928; Gero 1982; van Esbroeck 1991.

Takrit in the south.[6] The city of Takrit was created as a Roman army base during the Roman occupation of Sasanian Iraq in the years immediately before the Arab conquests.[7] It was promoted by the Romans as the chief see of the Jacobite east, and its first bishop, Marutha, was an appointee of the Jacobite patriarch of Antioch, Athanasius Gamala, whose actions were probably sanctioned by the emperor Heraclius.[8]

Nevertheless, in spite of Takrit's official importance, a number of Mattean monks reigned as bishops of Takrit after the Arab conquests: Brisho (669–83), John Saba (686–88) and John Kiunaya (759–85). Another bishop of Takrit, Paul (727–58), was a monk of Kinushya in Sinjar, a region that was part of Mar Mattai's traditional zone of influence. Mosul became an administrative hub under the Marwanids, when it enjoyed political authority over central Iraq, including Takrit.[9] It was this political influence that seems to have allowed Mar Mattai to consistently secure high-profile appointments under the Umayyads.

The Era of Cyriacus

However, the city of Takrit became suddenly more prominent in the age of Cyriacus and Dionysius. On one level, the reason for the city's sudden rise was the election of Cyriacus as the first Jacobite patriarch to come from Iraq, and his reign was characterized by a new concern with the reception of patriarchal policies in the east. But his election was also a symptom of the much closer links of easterners, and Takritians in particular, to the social and economic networks of the wider caliphate. These links, in turn, reflect the growing importance of southern Iraq in this period for trade and industrial production, as well as the investments that were taking place in translation, scholarship and book production.

Manuscript production and art history offer a useful lens for tracking the growing networks of Takritians in the ninth century. Accidents of manuscript

6. Mar Mattai was probably acquired from the Church of the East only at the start of the seventh century. This is described in *Life of Rabban Bar ʿIdta*, 158/239.

7. Fiey 1963; Posner 1985: 89–90.

8. See the extracts from Michael above as well as Elias of Nisibis 127/61. There is a detailed discussion in Fiey 1992. Also note Jankowiak 2009: 59, who stresses that it was Roman intervention that underpinned Athanasius' activities in the east and his promotion of Takrit.

9. See Robinson 2000: 69–84 for patronage in Mosul itself; Forand 1969: 102, with Hamadhani 156, for Mosul's administrative remit. Also note *Life of Rabban Hormizd*, esp. 70–71 / 104–5, for the influence of the Matteans over local Arab governors in the seventh century.

survival mean that we can see the strong relationship that existed between Takrit and Egypt in the ninth century, and this may have been mirrored in other Takritian colonies as well.

'Suryaye' are first mentioned in a manuscript colophon located at the monastery of Deir es-Surian in the Wadi Natrun in Egypt; the colophon carries the year 816, just after Cyriacus' death.[10] Another colophon, dated 820, mentions the patriarchs of Alexandria and Antioch as well as the metropolitan of Takrit.[11] The monastery is known as the monastery of 'Suriani', but it is important to remember that, at least initially, many of the leaders of this community, and its major donors, were specifically Takritians. Some of the earliest graffiti recorded in the monastery come from the pen of two Takritian 'brothers', Mattai and Yaqoub, who describe in 819 how the monastery was consecrated.[12] And another inscription, probably dating to 817 and reproduced with an elaborate mirror image, recounts the dedication of the church of the Virgin in the time of the patriarch Cyriacus.[13] Murals in the central nave of the church include dedications by two monks named Marutha and Papas of Takrit, possibly dating to the late ninth century.[14] An abbot, Maqari (d. 888), is described as a Takritian in his Syriac epitaph.[15] A book manuscript includes an illustration of the patriarch Cyriacus with a nimbus, implying that he was venerated as a saint in this community.[16] Eastern links are also attested in the employment of Samarran craftsmen, who decorated the sanctuary with

10. The monastery was founded in the late sixth century by Egyptian opponents of the Julianist Gaianus; it was originally known as Deir Anba Bishoi. It may have been abandoned for a period before being resettled by both Egyptians and speakers of Syriac. This resettlement is sometimes dated to the 710s, but this is likely to be a later forgery. Innemée and Van Rompay 1998: 192.

11. Innemée and Van Rompay 1998: 182. The reference to both patriarchs is an important indication that this monastery was embedded in a pan-Miaphysite network, in which Antioch and Alexandria recognized and guaranteed each other's orthodoxy. This pattern continued in the tenth century, when the double dedication is found on two sets of doors dedicated in the tenth century under the abbacy of Moses of Nisibis: White 1932–33: III, 187 and 197. Ancient patriarchs of both sees (Ignatius of Antioch and Mark of Alexandria) are depicted in frescos in the sanctuary: Innemée 2015: 214.

12. Innemée and Van Rompay 1998: 179–80.

13. Innemée and Van Rompay 1998: 200.

14. Innemée and Van Rompay 1998: 185; Van Rompay 1999: 196.

15. Innemée, Ochała and Van Rompay 2015: 164. However, there is no mention of his home city in the Coptic epitaph for the same abbot (167–68).

16. Oez 2012: I, 38.

stucco, and the use of cedar and padauk wood for the doors of the sanctuary, which were not made locally.[17]

Through the ninth century, Takritians donated a variety of patristic and ascetic writings to the monastery, including collections of Ephrem's writings, Eusebius' *Ecclesiastical History*, the *Pleriphories* of John Rufus and the *Hymns* of Severus—major texts that evoked shared membership in a Syrophone Miaphysite tradition.[18] In the following century, Deir es-Surian benefited from the connoisseurship of Moses of Nisibis. Moses was instrumental in facilitating the donation of a rare sixth-century manuscript to the monastery by a Takritian family in 907. And in 932, Moses gathered some 250 manuscripts, including several rare, early manuscripts from Baghdad, Edessa and Reshaina, and commissioned new ones from Edessa, Harran and Takrit for the monastery's library. It is worth emphasizing that the cost of manuscripts was very high at the time. Hundreds of animal skins were required to make a single book, so a donation like Moses' was substantial.[19]

Takrit's status as a place where one might commission manuscripts or solicit donations exemplifies the city's significance as an intellectual and cultural centre. Indeed, Takrit produced the lion's share of Jacobite intellectuals in the ninth century, including the apologist Abu Ra'ita,[20] the theological disputant Nonnus of Nisibis,[21] the liturgical commentator and theologian Moses bar Kepha[22] and the philosophers Yahya ibn 'Adi[23] and Anton of Takrit.[24] Abu Ra'ita and Yahya wrote in Arabic and engaged with the ideas of Muslim theology and Islamicate philosophy, and the eastern Jacobite world shows a much earlier use of Arabic as a Christian language than does the western one, which may have helped the easterners' ability to cultivate powerful allies as well as to

17. Immerzeel 2008. Immerzeel 2004 situates these Samarran craftsmen in the context of the broader use of easterners in Egypt in Tulunid foundations in Cairo.

18. White 1932–33: II, 440. The index of names in Brock and Van Rompay 2014 reveals some ten colophons that are specifically ascribed to Takritians in manuscripts still at Deir es-Surian.

19. On Moses and his collection of manuscripts, cf. White 1932–33: II, 444; Blanchard 1995; Brock 2004.

20. Keating 2006.

21. Griffith 2002d.

22. Rickards 1974.

23. Griffith 2002h; Platti 2015.

24. Watt 2011. A manuscript of Anton of Takrit was deposited at Deir es-Surian (number 32 in the list of Brock and Van Rompay 2014: 4).

engage in theological discussions. Though they remained important scribal centres, the older heartlands of Syriac culture, such as Edessa and Amida, were relatively backward in this regard.

The provision of education and the production of manuscripts were, of course, expensive activities, and Takrit's intellectual significance was likely linked to its importance as a centre of trade. Takrit was the hub of a series of expatriate communities in other cities, often centred around a distinctive church dedicated to an Iraqi saint.[25] Scattered across the chronicles of Michael and Bar Hebraeus we find mention of Takritians in Mosul, Harran, Edessa, Callinicum (Raqqa), Reshaina, Damascus, Nisibis, Amida, Maypherkat and Arzun, as well as in Deir es-Surian.[26]

We get a good sense of Takrit's mercantile identity from the anonymous *madrashe* composed on the death of Cyriacus. The author fashions Cyriacus after the wise servant of the parable who invests his master's money and is thanked on the latter's return: 'The high priest made him treasurer and he multiplied his talents by thousands and tens of thousands / he abandoned families, races and possessions and gained heavenly riches'.[27]

We are told that Cyriacus 'broke the yoke of pride', which is possibly a reference to his struggles with the citizens of Takrit, a point that is left discreetly ambiguous.[28] In general, the poet characterizes him as a proponent of compromise (which is not always the impression we gain from Dionysius): 'At all times he summoned peace and comforted all people with his love'.[29]

Cyriacus is described as immune to bribery, which may be a defence of Takrit's reputation for fair and honest dealing.[30] The author even depicts Cyriacus himself an object of merchandise: 'The merchandise of Antioch in Syria has been snatched away by the land of the Arabs, the splendid treasure of Mesopotamia has been removed by the land of the Arabs, and the prize and wealth of Syria has been plundered and gathered in by Takrit'.[31] Cyriacus is a

---

25. Fiey 1959: 25. The church in Mosul, known as the church of the Takritians, was in modern times renamed the mosque of the Takritians. For the destruction of churches belonging to the Takritians in Harran, see X1234 (II, 30/21).

26. Nabe-von Schönberg 1977: 63; Fiey 1959: 27 n. 2.

27. Madrasha 1, stanza 5 (Oez 2012: II, 526–27).

28. Madrasha 1, stanza 5 (Oez 2012: II, 526–27).

29. Madrasha 2, stanza 2 (Oez 2012: II, 528–29).

30. Madrasha 2, stanza 3 (Oez 2012: II, 528–29).

31. Madrasha 2, stanza 12 (Oez 2012: II, 534–35).

second saintly defender for Takrit after its first bishop, Marutha: 'Blessed are you, city of Cyriacus, for behold, your citadel has returned to you! The money which you lent to Syria, behold, it has been repaid, by thousands and tens of thousands.'[32]

The madrashe dwell explicitly on trade and investment to characterize the Takritian patriarch. The mercantile culture that they evoke appears as a distinctive feature of Takrit that has allowed the city, and its broader region of Beth Arabaye, to outcompete other parts of the Jacobite world in Syria and the Jazira. This characterization of Cyriacus in the madrashe is an assertion of the mercantile values of a whole city.

A manuscript found in the Wadi Natrun provides a further illustration of the distinctiveness of the Takritian network beyond Iraq. The manuscript is a lectionary commissioned by a Takritian, one Mihr-Shapur son of Elias, in Harran in 824, from where it found its way to Egypt. Although it was composed in the western part of the church, the festivals it contains have a markedly eastern flavour. In addition to celebrating common Miaphysite saints such as Severus, it also commemorates the fast of the Ninevites and the martyrdoms of the bishops of Ctesiphon in the fourth century.[33]

The fast of the Ninevites has its roots in the penitence of the people of Nineveh after the prophet Jonah called on them to repent (Jonah 3:5–9). It was established as a fast in the Church of the East in response to an outbreak of plague in the late sixth century. Similarly, the martyrs of Ctesiphon, of whom Simeon bar Sabba'e is the most famous, provided archetypes for many of the later saints of the Church of the East.[34] Their commemoration in this lectionary illustrates how festivals might cross confessional boundaries. The fast of the Ninevites is a response to the proto-Christian past of ancient Iraq as well as a way of asserting Mosul's links to the Old Testament.[35] These connections made it attractive to Jacobites, even though the fast originated in the Church of the East.[36] Likewise, the eastern Jacobites' willingness to commemorate the martyrs of Ctesiphon reminds us that they saw themselves as successors to the ancient, pre-Dyophysite Church of the East. Many bishops

32. Madrasha 2, stanza 15 (Oez 2012: II, 536–37).

33. Heiming 1970. The lectionary is described in Wright 1870: I, 146–49.

34. Wood 2013: ch. 2.

35. Becker 2008: 404; Fiey 1966–68: II, 20.

36. The Ninevites are also mentioned in Ibn Jarir 31, 14; Ibn Jarir was also an eastern Jacobite.

of Takrit, like their predecessors at Ctesiphon, styled themselves as catholicoi, which implied an enhanced level of autonomy from the patriarch of
Antioch.

There are signs, therefore, that Takrit's diaspora enjoyed a distinctive religious identity that was linked to a slightly different festal calendar and a different set of saintly patrons compared to western Jacobites. There are no parallels
to this network of diaspora churches among other Jacobite populations, and
the phenomenon thus seems to have been unique to Takrit.

One of the most substantive benefits that accrued to Takrit as a result of its
network was the capture of the patriarchate itself under Cyriacus. The madrashe on Cyriacus' funeral clearly see his election as a coup on the part of the
whole of the east over Syria and Mesopotamia. Dionysius tells us very little
about Cyriacus' election or about his background more broadly. But it seems
likely that his appointment was connected to his membership of the monastery of the Pillars (Bizona) at Raqqa. As seen in earlier chapters, the city had
been the recipient of major caliphal patronage since the 770s, before its elevation to al-Rashid's capital from 796 to 806. Cyriacus' affiliation with a monastery located in a growing caliphal centre may have allowed him to develop the
good connections to the court that won him his election.

Cyriacus and Simeon

By the ninth century, therefore, Takrit was the hub of a significant commercial
and intellectual network that stretched into Syria, Egypt and Mesopotamia.
But Cyriacus' election did not benefit all Takritians in the way that they expected. Dionysius reports that some Takritians opposed the patriarch because
he 'did not acknowledge the honour of the see'. In particular, the Takritians
complained about Cyriacus' appointee as metropolitan, one Simeon, whom,
some felt, Cyriacus had imposed on them without consultation. Cyriacus responded by telling Simeon to leave the city and withdraw to his convent, but
Simeon refused and attempted to align himself with the townspeople. This
prompted Cyriacus to threaten to excommunicate him. This threat resulted in
the division of the townspeople into two factions, one of which opposed both
Simeon and Cyriacus whereas the other opposed only Cyriacus himself.[37]

Five eastern bishops then sought out Cyriacus and attempted to resolve the
affair. They assembled a synod, which heard a range of scandalous accusations

37. MS XII. 7 (IV, 493 / III, 27).

against Simeon; Dionysius refuses to record them precisely, but they included murder. The bishops found against Simeon, but Cyriacus was reluctant to depose him outright and instead attempted to reconcile him to the bishops and make him repent. However, during this diplomatic impasse Simeon died.[38]

Dionysius' brother, Theodosius of Edessa, acted as a go-between for Cyriacus during these events, and it seems likely that Dionysius has relied on Theodosius as his source here and that Dionysius, in turn, is Michael's source.[39] The account describes Cyriacus vacillating over whether to depose Simeon, but it also implies that Simeon was clearly guilty and had been deemed so through due process. Cyriacus' refusal to remove him is thus depicted as foolish, because it goes against the findings of the bishops, because Simeon's presence continues to cause disruption in Takrit and because Simeon has proven disloyal. The source implies that given his earlier mismanagement of affairs, Cyriacus was lucky that Simeon died at such a convenient juncture.

Basil of Balad

Simeon was replaced as the metropolitan of Takrit in about 813 by Basil of Balad, whom we have already encountered in chapter 3, who had worked as a lay judge and as a customs official.[40] Cyriacus' legislation was concerned with ensuring that church revenues were correctly paid and accounts properly kept, so it may be that he selected Basil for the second most important Jacobite see to implement the kind of administrative reforms that he desired for the whole church.[41] However, Dionysius reports that Basil's reign was troubled, and this depiction may again imply tacit criticism of the patriarch and his credentials as a judge of character. For Basil caused serious altercations with Mar Mattai through his attempts to impose his own choice as bishop of Mosul:

> Basil suffered from the disease of pride: he stirred up difficulties with the people of Mosul because they proclaimed the metropolitan Daniel as their bishop, according to their custom. At this the monks of Mar Mattai and all the bishops [attached to the monastery] went into schism with (*estadaq*) him [Basil], and with the patriarch at the same time, because he was

---

38. MS XII. 7 (IV, 494 / III, 28).
39. MS XII. 7 (IV, 494 / III, 28).
40. MS XII. 7 (IV, 494 / III, 29). On this affair, note also Fiey 1959: 25–28.
41. See the discussion in chapter 6.

assisting Basil and sought to suppress the honour of their monastery. Mosul was divided into two parties: one of these supported the Matteans and Daniel, while the other rejected them and advanced horrible accusations against Daniel and demanded that they be examined. The result was that they made mutual accusations and were imprisoned and fined by the governor. The patriarch Cyriacus anathematized the Matteans and their bishops, and the Matteans and bishops from their monastery had the audacity to anathematize the patriarch and Basil.[42]

Basil's objection to the installation of Daniel as metropolitan of Mosul contravened the customary rights of Mar Mattai and triggered a revolt by the Matteans, supported by a portion of Mosul's Jacobite citizenry. But there was also a faction that supported Basil against Daniel. A later passage identifies these two groups as Mosulis and Takritians resident in Mosul, respectively. The latter group seems to have consisted of the members of a trading colony, who wielded considerable political power. It is impossible to judge the substance of their accusations against Daniel, but their presence seems to have enabled Basil's interference in Mosul. Nothing like this fracas is reported for earlier periods, and it may be that the see of Takrit enjoyed newly enhanced political reach at this time because of the existence of colonies allied to its interests.

Cyriacus' response to these developments was to gather the loyal eastern bishops at a synod in Mosul. He refused to hear the complaints made against Daniel, perhaps remembering the negative effects on the church's reputation of the accusations made against Simeon. Instead, Cyriacus drew up a series of rulings to prevent the Takritians from engaging in forms of political interference that would disturb order, while still assuring Takrit of its primacy. Cyriacus ordered that the bishop of Takrit would not be able to ordain bishops 'without the consent of Mar Mattai and the other bishops' and could not interfere in the sees of the other eastern bishops without permission. The other bishops should come together when summoned by the bishop of Takrit, and the latter would enjoy primacy among them. As a condition of his reinstallation, Daniel agreed not to pursue his Takritian opponents in Mosul for alleged breaches of the canons during the schism. All these things, Cyriacus concluded, 'have been done for the peace of God and the dignity of the throne of Peter [i.e., the patriarchate of Antioch]:[43]

---

42. MS XII. 7 (IV, 494 / III, 29).

43. MS XII. 8 (IV, 495–97 / III, 32–34). The text given here is that promulgated by Cyriacus to end the schism.

However, Basil and the citizens of Takrit continued to harbour resentment against the patriarchate for this offence against the honour of their see. Cyriacus died shortly after issuing the proclamation quoted above, and he was buried in Takrit, where he was commemorated as a saint.[44] His successor, Dionysius, faced considerable opposition from Basil. According to Dionysius, Basil

> sought to make himself catholicos, on the example of the cursed Barsauma of Nisibis. Though he had not been able to do so in the reign of Cyriacus, because he [Cyriacus] was from Takrit himself, in our days he actually dared to do so and hoped to realize his project through the help of the Takritians. He began to spread hatred against me, saying to the Takritians, 'This patriarch is your enemy'. And to the bishops he said, 'Since when were we subject to the westerners, who give us orders and take the money that we collect? Why don't they honour us and our see like that of Egypt, since we are equal to it in dignity?'[45]

Basil ended his life in ignominy, exiled from Takrit and afflicted by a wasting disease.[46] But Dionysius continued to experience problems caused by the competition between Takrit and Mosul. Toward the end of his patriarchate, the people of Mosul elected one Cyriacus of Mar Mattai as metropolitan, but his election was rejected by the Takritians. When Dionysius went to Takrit to ordain a metropolitan for the city, he issued a ruling before an assembly of seven eastern bishops to solve the continued struggle over primacy. He noted that the Matteans would customarily ordain the 'bishop of Nineveh' (i.e., Mosul) and argued that this bishop should be proclaimed metropolitan in the Takritian church in Mosul. But the Takritians objected to this and asserted that he should simply be proclaimed bishop, rather than metropolitan. Dionysius asserts that he 'reunited the priests, deacons, monks and notables of Takrit' and secured a solution to this disagreement.[47]

Here, Dionysius observes that the honour of Takrit is not lessened if the bishop of Mosul is a metropolitan; rather, it is increased, since submission to a metropolitan is more honourable than is submission to a mere bishop. Dionysius allows for the metropolitan of Mosul to be proclaimed twice a year in

---

44. MS XII. 8 (IV, 497 / III, 35).
45. MS XII. 11 (IV, 505–6 / III, 47–48).
46. MX XII. 11 (IV, 507 / III, 49).
47. MS XII. 18 (IV, 528–29 / III, 85–86).

the church of the Takritians, but he specifies that the Takritians can proclaim whomever they like in their church for the rest of the year.[48] He quotes the conclusion of the patriarch Cyriacus that the metropolitan of Mosul should be proclaimed in the Takritian church of Mosul, but that he in turn should submit to the metropolitan of Takrit.[49]

Takrit, Mosul and Antioch: An Analysis

Takrit's political significance appears to have grown after circa 800, when the city's diaspora engaged in the conspicuous sponsorship of monasteries outside Iraq. These interregional links brought political dividends. In particular, the foundation of Raqqa, a political centre with strong political and economic links to Iraq, provided the opportunity for easterners to influence affairs in the Jacobite heartlands of the Jazira, culminating in the election of Cyriacus as patriarch.[50]

The accounts of church politics in the ninth century pay only lip service to Mar Mattai's claims to ancient precedence, and they do not seem to have been especially influential in practice at this stage. Nevertheless, Takritian expectations of being able to intrude on Mar Mattai's traditional zone of influence were not realized. The Takritian push for expanded influence appears to have come not from the bishops of Takrit but from the city's population, which threatened to undermine bishop Simeon as well as the patriarch Cyriacus. The attempts of Simeon's successor, Basil, to promote the honour of his see and the ambitions of Takrit's colony in Mosul triggered a confrontation with both Mar Mattai and the patriarch.

Cyriacus was, in my reading, keen to maintain the status quo. His ruling to keep the peace in Iraq is indeed concerned with the public prestige of Christians before their Muslim co-citizens and with preserving his personal authority. But by laying out a democratic structure for the bishop of Takrit he was effectively downgrading the see's authority: the metropolitan of Takrit could not run a patriarchate in miniature if he had to be invited before he could intervene in eastern sees and if he required the consent of Mar Mattai and the

---

48. These two occasions are Palm Sunday, when all Mosul gathered in the church of the Takritians for the blessing of the olive branches, and the blessing of the myron by the bishop (which was often done on Maundy Thursday).

49. MS XII. 18 (IV, 529–30 / III, 87).

50. For Raqqa's economic links to the east, see Heidemann 2011: 48–49; Heidemann 2006.

other eastern bishops to perform consecrations. Although Cyriacus' solution to the schism left Mosul with an empty position of honour, it also shackled the metropolitan of Takrit with democratic constraints that the patriarch of Antioch was not subject to.

Basil's fury at Takrit's demotion is therefore understandable. The patriarch Cyriacus had enjoyed considerable influence in his home city, but his death freed Basil to attempt to reverse Cyriacus' policies. In his appeal to the eastern bishops Basil observed that the Jacobite east ought to be the equal of Egypt, that is, independent from Antioch. In other words, Takrit ought to be treated as a patriarchate in all but name. Of course, his statement ignored ecclesiological theory, according to which Antioch and Alexandria were both ancient patriarchates. But it did reflect the ninth-century reality in which Takrit's wealth and learning were substantial, equalling or exceeding those of any other part of the Jacobite world, and the city was located close to caliphal centres of power at a time when Egypt was seen as intellectually moribund and lacking in political connections (according to Dionysius at least).[51]

Dionysius draws on the fifth-century legends of the 'Nestorianization' of the east to liken Basil to Barsauma of Nisibis. The accusation is extremely polemical: Barsauma was (allegedly) a persecutor, famous for killing the monks of Mar Mattai in order to spread a Dyophysite (i.e., 'Nestorian') Christology in Iraq. Dionysius' analogy may be intended to allude to the squabbles between Mar Mattai and Basil and to Basil's attempt to deny the Matteans' right to select a bishop. He also says that Basil, like Barsauma, wanted to make himself a catholicos. But we should remember that the bishops of Takrit did indeed consider themselves catholicoi with some justification, and that this term was used without qualification in sections of Michael's *Chronicle* that describe the eighth century. Dionysius depicts Basil as engaging in an arrogant power grab, but he underplays the fact that the bishops of Takrit had quite recently claimed to be the successors of the ancient bishops of Ctesiphon.

Dionysius presents himself as having laid these quarrels to rest, but in reality the matter required further legislation from his successors after his death. In the middle of the ninth century, the patriarch Yohannan (846–73) agreed that he would not intervene in the eastern sees without the permission of the

---

51. MS XII. 17 (IV, 525–26 / III, 80). Dionysius' accusations of simony may have had some truth: Wipszycka 2011: 250–59 notes that one consequence of the heavy poll tax burden on Egyptian monasteries was the drive to recruit wealthy abbots who could pay the tax on the monastery's behalf.

bishop of Takrit, that the bishop of Takrit would consecrate the new patriarch and that the patriarch would in turn consecrate the bishop of Takrit.[52] It is hard to know whether the bishops of Takrit did in fact consult their eastern counterparts before selecting new candidates for consecration, but the laws created after Dionysius' death suggest an arrangement in which Takrit was explicitly seen as a near equal to the patriarchate.

Finally, we should note that like Cyrrhus, both Mosul and Takrit featured vibrant, and occasionally violent, urban politics that involved monks, laymen and secular clergy. Dionysius makes a point of appealing to all these groups when he attempts his reconciliation of the Matteans and the Takritians. The case of Simeon also suggests that, in the case of Takrit, it is the townsmen themselves who call the tune, pressuring the bishop to revolt against the patriarch. This capacity, too, may be a function of the Takritians' wealth and of the existence of a diaspora that could generate political favours or provide the casus belli for conflict.

Conclusions

I have argued in this chapter that the city of Takrit benefited most from the economic development of Baghdad and southern Iraq by cultivating a widespread trading diaspora and by seeing one of its sons become the first eastern patriarch. Evidence from Deir es-Surian testifies to these western links and the channelling of Takrit's wealth into education and the collection of manuscripts. Moreover, the Takritian diaspora sponsored its own churches, often revering Iraqi saints and festivals. In the case of Mosul, the Takritians' growing assertiveness led the community into conflict when they refused to acknowledge the metropolitan of Mosul, and this provides a good example of how Mosul's earlier preeminence, rooted in Umayyad-era patronage as well as stories of martyrdom, was challenged by the new economic and political prominence of Takrit.

We saw in the previous chapter how important the lay elites of Cyrrhus were for sustaining the rebellion of Gubba Barraya against the patriarch. A key moment in Dionysius' campaign against Abiram was persuading these aristocrats

---

52. Mounayer 1963: 73–75. The one exception to this policy of noninterference seems to have been the bishopric of Baghdad. Because of the political sensitivity of the position, the patriarchs of Antioch regularly consecrated (and presumably selected) this bishop themselves, even though it formally lay in the east.

to abandon their support for the Gubbite monks. But Cyrrhus had become relatively peripheral within the caliphate. Takrit, by contrast, was more centrally located and prosperous. That Dionysius had to appeal to the Takritians, rather than act against them using physical force as he did in Cyrrhus, is an indication both of Dionysius' reliance on ʿAbd Allah's patronage, which was relevant in the Jazira, Syria and Egypt but not in Iraq, and of the political ties enjoyed by the easterners themselves.

6

Worldviews and Communal Boundaries

THE HISTORY OF Dionysius of Tel-Mahre, and the earlier sources that it draws on, have so far been investigated for what they reveal about the institutional and structural changes in the Jacobite church, some of which were stimulated by the changing priorities of the caliphs who oversaw them. However, these shifts in politics and economics were underpinned by significant cultural and social continuities that are best illustrated by other sources. For there to be any Jacobite community that could generate tithes or elect bishops, there had to be a coherent worldview that individual Jacobites found attractive and convincing (or at least more attractive and convincing than the alternatives), as well as social boundaries that encouraged Jacobites to defer to their clerical rulers, marry their co-religionists and bequeath property to fellow Jacobites or to Jacobite institutions.

The sources I examine in this chapter—legal rulings issued at Jacobite synods between 780 and 896 and ninth-century Jacobite commentaries on the liturgy—provide glimpses into how this continuity was managed. After all, the celebration of the liturgy and the provision of legal rulings occupied a great part of any bishop's time, and they are far more typical of a bishop's activities than is writing history. And liturgy was the chief means by which laypeople were exposed to Christian history and cosmology.

Nevertheless, we should bear in mind a major caveat. We have seen in previous chapters that there were several different powerful groups within the Jacobite community: not just the patriarch and the higher clergy, but also powerful monasteries that expected to control nearby bishoprics and lay elites who continued to play a role in ecclesiastical politics. Both of these groups might seek their own connections with Muslim patrons, in spite of the patriarchs' objections. Why should the monasteries or the lay elites accept the right of the patriarch to raise tithes or to generate law? Why should laymen tolerate the tax exemptions that the patriarch claimed for church property or attend the Eucharist at all?

The legal sources illustrate patriarchal ambitions, but their real effect is hard to gauge. There were certainly moments when the Christian peasantry seem to have challenged the idea that church institutions existed to serve a wider community rather than simply being repositories of wealth. For instance, the *Chronicle of Zuqnin* records how Christian laymen seized the property of churches and monasteries when told to pay the jizya. They said, 'What is the church suffering, after all? We are in need because we have to pay the poll tax and we have children'.[1]

The legal canons that I examine here are (allegedly) products of the consensus of councils convened by the Jacobite patriarchs George of Beltan (758–66 and 775–90), Cyriacus (793–817),[2] Dionysius of Tel-Mahre (817–45), Yohannan (846–73), Ignatius (878–83) and Dionysius II (897–909), often on the occasion of their election.[3] The last three patriarchs are not well covered in the chronicles, but they seem to have suffered similar kinds of threats to their authority as did Dionysius of Tel-Mahre, including poor relations between the patriarch and the bishop of Takrit and problems of clerical discipline. The canons concern the orchestration of the liturgy and the behaviour of priests, the behaviour of monks and powerful laymen, the financing of the church and the maintenance of proper boundaries between Jacobites and non-Jacobites.

1. *Chronicle of Zuqnin*, 261/230. Note here Sarris 2011a: 223, 'the . . . involvement of the Church and its personnel in agrarian social relations is likely to have had marked implications for how elements of the peasantry viewed their ecclesiastical masters'. Cf. Sarris 2011b.

2. Cyriacus issued canons at two synods, Beth Botin and Harran. I cite the Beth Botin canons unless otherwise indicated.

3. See the survey of material in Kitchen 2017. Selb 1989: 92–153 provides details on the collection of the legal material across different manuscripts. Kaufhold 2012: 238–54 has a useful summary of all West Syriac canon law, including the reception of Roman law and Greek canon law. Some of the rulings seem to have been issued in response to quite precise complaints, which does suggest a role for bishops in supplying the patriarch with information. The patriarch might have been faced with legislative problems similar to those confronting the Roman emperor, who was forced to rely on interested parties to acquire information (Kelly 2004: 204–8; Heather 2005: 103–10). Harries 2001: 28–30 discusses the development of general laws out of petitions relating to specific circumstances (imperial rescripts) in the fifth century.

The moral concerns of this legislation are presaged in the writings of earlier authors. The alien customs of the Arab invaders prompted complaints and censure from the famous Jacobite intellectual Jacob of Edessa at the turn of the eighth century.[4] But we should remember that Jacob famously burned the canons in front of the patriarch's monastery because of his frustration at the patriarch's lack of interest.[5] What had changed by the late eighth century was that the patriarchs had acquired the inclination and the means to issue canons themselves, and Jacob's concern with moral behaviour, clerical discipline and contacts with non-Jacobites had been adopted at the highest levels of the church.[6]

The People and the Liturgy

To write about the liturgy may seem rather unnecessary to many readers, because its content is so obvious and familiar (as it has been to many historians of the past two centuries). Nevertheless, it demands attention because it is what set Christians apart from their neighbours, especially in an environment in which being a Christian could not be taken for granted.[7] We can emphasize the contribution of the liturgy to a group's self-understanding without either focusing only on novel developments or ignoring theology as an arcane irrelevance.[8]

Jan Assmann has argued that religious diasporas are made possible by sacred texts. Texts that are seen as belonging to closed canons can offer prescriptions

---

4. Tannous 2018: 85–106; Hoyland 1997: 601–11. Simonsohn 2013b: 364 and Weitz 2018: 49 stress that Jacob's ideas about the reintegration of apostates are themselves rooted in the Nicene canons or Roman tradition more broadly. Also note Haldon 1992 and Papaconstantinou 2011 on Anastasius of Sinai, who likewise discusses problems surrounding the maintenance of boundaries with religious outsiders and proper Christian religious practice.

5. MS XI. 15 (IV, 446 / II, 472).

6. Similar legislation was undertaken in Byzantium; see M. Humphreys 2014 and Haldon 2016 on the Qinisext council of 690/91 and Leo III's *Ekloga*. Simonsohn 2016b frames the Christian legislation of this period as a response to Muslim assumptions that scripture should generate law and the professed embarrassment of Christians at the multitude of legal systems. On this presumption, see further Morony 1984: 364–67; Simonsohn 2011: 99–116; and Weitz 2018: 100–101. For the coincidence of attempts by the Church of the East and the Jacobites to produce systematic, centralized legislation and their Abbasid context, see Weitz 2018: 89–90.

7. Tannous 2018: 134–46. As Taft 2000: 45 observes, the sheer amount of ink spilled on liturgical commentary in the late Roman empire and Byzantium indicates the liturgy's importance there.

8. Cf. Carlson 2018: 115.

for behaviour and communal preservation that set a population apart from others. And because they are rendered holy by constant repetition, reflection and exegesis, they are shielded from the criticism of outsiders who do not share the same 'proper' approach to the sacred texts.[9] The scriptural canon provides a narrative that gives the community its identity, that prescribes rituals recalling this narrative and the believers' place within it and that endorses the social practices keeping the community separate from other communities. Assmann, discussing the Israelites of the Exodus, describes these virtual barriers as creating a 'portable homeland'.[10]

Much of what Assmann says about the Jewish canon can also be applied to the case of the Christians. The latter, too, saw themselves as possessing a special relationship with God—indeed, as inheriting the same relationship that had hitherto been the particular preserve of the Jews. And Christians, too, celebrated this relationship through both texts and rituals, the rituals commemorating the events described in scripture and the texts explaining and interpreting the rituals for the wider community.

Baptism provides a major communal recognition of birth, a ceremony in which the growth of the community is celebrated and the social alliances of parents acknowledged by the church through the selection of godparents. The water of baptism symbolizes purification and the washing away of sins. Baptism was the sacrament that defined the Christian community at its broadest, including those who were not taking communion or did not attend church, as well as members of other confessions who would (in theory) be excluded from communion. As such, it was a key boundary marker against people who had not been purified of their sins in this way; it may also have been recognized as a form of protection against the material and spiritual attacks of the demons who lived all around.[11]

9. Halbertal 1997; J. Smith 1982: ch. 3; Fowden 2014: 165–66. Fowden comments that 'it is in the everyday socialization of ideas and scholarly techniques, in the repercussions for example of scriptural exegesis on financial dealings or the marriage bed, that we come fully to appreciate the role of ideas in non-elite history as well'.

10. Assmann 2011: 192–200 (a discussion of the book of Deuteronomy). For the 'portable homeland'—'fatherland' in the published translation—which is a quotation from Heinrich Heine, see 90 and 196. Cf. Assmann 2006: chs. 3 and 5 and G. Stroumsa 2015: 108 for Judaism and Christianity as 'religions based on books'.

11. Cf. Moses bar Kepha, *On Baptism*, 18, for baptism as protection against demons. Note that some Muslims still asked for their children to receive baptism: Taylor 2015.

The Eucharistic liturgy was of even greater significance. It entailed the regular celebration of God's incarnation as man in Christ and His sacrifice of Himself on the Cross. It was an act of communication by God but also 'the expression of the faith of the church, expressed, celebrated, renewed and continually constituted in liturgical assembly'.[12] It was in the Eucharist that a mostly illiterate congregation was presented with the narrative that made them a Christian people and showed them, through the story of Christ's deeds and its prefiguration in the Old Testament, how their salvation had been achieved and how they had inherited the promises made by God to the Jews. And it was here that the Last Supper was commemorated by the priest and the deacons, where a shared meal of bread and wine became the body and blood of Christ, and the members of the congregation played their own parts as disciples at the Last Supper before a priest who repeated the words spoken by Christ.[13]

We cannot know exactly how the congregation understood this activity. But we can speculate that a sense of a single, unified community was articulated through the peace and the shared witnessing of communion (even though not all would have taken communion). The lectionary cycle marked out the church's year by mapping biblical events onto contemporary time.[14] Prayers that recalled the deceased and the diptychs that evoked chains of orthodox authority extended the imagined community not only to other parishes in which the same liturgy was simultaneously being celebrated but also to the orthodox dead and to the angels.[15] Even in environments in which Christians felt embattled or outnumbered, communal services might have reminded them that they were, in fact, part of a great host, immortal and innumerable.[16]

Chronicles provided a way for Christian communities to fashion themselves in reaction to the threats of schism, heresy and persecution. But we

12. M. Johnson 2013: xiii.

13. The liturgical works used in the Jacobite context are usefully summarized in Barsoum 2003: 55–100.

14. Cf. Krueger 2014: ch. 3, esp. 73–76; Varghese 2004: ch. 8; Taft 1991: 191.

15. Er 2016 discusses the attitudes toward prayers for the deceased among Syriac theologians and their attempts to confine such prayers to church, rather than the graveside. The patriarchs regularly show concern about excessive lamentation over the dead, which presumably contributed to the effort to situate their memorial in the liturgy.

16. Florovsky 1972: 61 calls the Eucharist a 'fellowship in holy things' and 'a fellowship with the saints'; Varghese 2004: 95 calls it 'a communion of prayer with the saints' and a 'celebration of the interrelatedness of God, man and the world' (172); Markus 1990: 22 observes that 'to be a Christian meant being part of a group that straddled earth and heaven'.

should keep in mind that this form of self-fashioning took place in the context of another form of history making in the liturgy itself, which was far more widespread and probably much more effective, too, than chronicles were. In the liturgy of the word and the liturgy of the Eucharist, priest and congregation were engaged in an act of communal history telling that placed the Last Supper and the Gospels at the centre. A secondary role was given to the Old Testament, which was much longer and so repeated much less frequently. As for the 'Christian era' that lay between Christ and the present day, this was represented only in the prayers for the deceased and in the names read out in the diptychs.[17] These names included the great theologians whose disputes against 'heresy' constituted the distinctiveness of Miaphysite theology, the orthodox bishops through whom each diocese traced its link back to the apostles and the patriarchs who provided mutual assurance of one another's orthodoxy. Nevertheless, the history that mattered most in the liturgy was the events with the greatest soteriological significance, namely the Gospels' account of the Holy Week and the run-up to the Crucifixion. These events stood at the core of the Eucharist and of the bonding memory of late antique Christian communities.[18] As the Russian Orthodox theologian George Florovsky put it, 'worship comes first, doctrine and dogma [and, we might add, ecclesiastical history or canon law] second'.[19]

In Dionysius' testimony, the clearest proof of Florovsky's statement is the potential of liturgical reform to sustain the Gubbite rebellion against Cyriacus and Dionysius. As much as the rebellion was motivated by the personal ambitions of Philoxenus and Abiram, lay support for the rebellion was significant, and Dionysius' major coup consisted of convincing the lay elites that the heavenly bread formula would be retained. Much of the power of the liturgy lay not in the exposition of coherent theology and the examination of erudite

17. A seventh-century Theodosian diptych in Greek from Egypt, the Moir Bryce diptych, is in the British Museum: Crum 1908. I thank Phil Booth for this reference. For diptychs in general, see Menze 2008: 78–85.

18. It was probably in seventh-century Chalcedonian circles that the tension between a sense of history focused on the Eusebian vision of empire and one focused on the liturgy and the Gospels became most exposed. Booth 2013b: 26 comments that Maximus the confessor and Sophronius of Jerusalem 'located the effective past not in the ephemeral triumphs of the Christian Roman empire, but in the inevitable progression of God's chosen people from creation through revelation to redemption, a progression re-created and guaranteed in the eucharistic rites of the orthodox Church'.

19. Cited and discussed in Ware 1990: 27.

texts but in the repetition of familiar words. For the citizens of Cyrrhus, as for many others, orthodoxy was whatever one's fathers had done.

Laws on the Priesthood

The legislation of the Jacobite patriarchs demonstrates that they held the clergy to high standards of behaviour. This stringency was due to the soteriological role of the actions that the clergy performed within the church as well as the fact that their conduct was very visible to the congregation, and may have been judged in comparison with other sects.[20] And congregations probably expected the actions in the liturgy to be completed in exactly the same way each time and saw the legitimacy of the patriarch and the bishops reflected in the priests and deacons they appointed.

Much of the legislation of George of Beltan deals with scandalous behaviour among the clergy. His was the first set of canons issued by a Jacobite patriarch, and this was his primary concern. Priests were prohibited from taking a second wife after the divorce or death of the first wife (canons 2–4), from marrying their godmothers and from marrying widows or adulteresses (canon 7). Nor should they baptize members of the opposite sex or join in drunken parties (canon 5). It is noteworthy that in George's day, priests were held to higher standards than the laity were. At this time, laity were permitted to divorce for reasons of adultery (canon 9).[21]

Cyriacus, in his canons, shared many of George's concerns but also added a number of issues that concern bishops' oversight of priests' characters and the behaviour of priests in the liturgy.[22] Priests and deacons could serve in the liturgy outside their dioceses only if they were known to the bishop (canons 2–3). Priests should be ordained only after the age of thirty and deacons after the age of twenty (canon 4).

Monks should not exercise the functions of priests without ordination (Dionysius II canon 5), and they were banned from using bribery to obtain

20. Yohannan (canon 7) warns against the sacred mysteries being mocked 'both by the orthodox and by heretics' because of laxity in enforcing the canons.

21. Divorce is also permitted in the *Laws of the Christian Kings*, 80–86 (Vööbus 1975–76: 130–33 / 134–36). These laws are attributed to the emperors Constantine, Theodosius and Leo and circulated in a West Syriac context. For the persistence of divorce in Roman law in general, in spite of the objections of the clergy, see Giardina 2000: 396–97 and Weitz 2018: 25–27.

22. Beyond his legislation, Cyriacus also addresses liturgical issues in his answers to the questions posed by the priests Walid and Yeshuʿ of Cyrrhus: Oez 2012: I, 9.

ordination (Cyriacus canon 19) or becoming ordained without the proper education (Dionysius canon 9). Likewise, abbots were banned from pronouncing anathemas or omitting the name of the patriarch from the diptych (Cyriacus canons 17 and 18). The reduction of the independence of action of overmighty monasteries may have been an especially live concern in the context of the patriarchs' disputes with Gubba Barraya.

Yohannan's legislation on the liturgy was particularly extensive. He ruled that, when at the altar, priests and deacons should be tonsured and clothed in a tunic (canon 5). Clergy should not play a role in the liturgy that is inappropriate to their rank, and in particular a subdeacon should not give the peace (Cyriacus, Harran canon 3) nor a priest give out the myron (Yohannan canon 8).

Yohannan issued several detailed canons concerning the correct use of liturgical objects: he admonished priests to use a consecrated altar (*tabula*) to celebrate the Eucharist, rather than just a piece of cloth or leather, and to take care that the altar stone has not been damaged or consecrated by heretics (canon 4). Similarly, he instructed priests to cover the consecrated elements with a veil that bears a cross and to leave a light in a church that contains the consecrated elements (canon 5).

Yohannan also seems to have been particularly concerned about the use of the correct formulas by priests: he censured those who fail to say the (inaudible) prayers of inclining at the start of baptism, and he demanded that deacons be tested on their knowledge of the liturgical text, so that those who recite by heart do so accurately and those who use a book speak with understanding (canon 6). Baptism should be sealed with myron by all priests, 'according to ancient custom', and the bishop should ensure that the myron has been properly consecrated (canon 8). Misconduct also afflicted the provision of the Eucharist in Yohannan's view: 'This Christ-loving synod was informed that some priests, out of ignorance or contempt, sometimes offer a drink made from raisins [instead of wine]. . . . The bishops again shall admonish the priests that they should not give the offering without the cup, for the word of the Gospels teaches us to "eat my body and drink my blood". Thus we have decided, not only because it is canonical, but because it has scandalized many and is scandalizing those who have knowledge of the mysteries of the church' (canon 10).

Liturgical matters had always preoccupied church legislators. Their pronouncements convey a sense that in matters of clerical discipline, there is little new under the sun. Nevertheless, some matters seem to have troubled some patriarchs more than others, and the types of disciplinary problems that the legislation tackles vary.[23] George's principal concern was the propriety of the priesthood, which may reflect the relative weakness of church governance in the eighth century. Cyriacus' main interest lay in the areas of proper hierarchy and oversight. Like his efforts to appoint bishops far from sees where they might have established networks, his moves to regulate the promotion of the clergy and to get bishops to vouchsafe for the lower clergy suggest a desire to depersonalize the activities of the church to reduce the potential for feuds and to ensure that church functions were actually carried out. By contrast, Dionysius made no mention of these issues in the canons he proclaimed at Raqqa in 818. His avoidance of liturgical issues proper might be explained by the controversies that raged over Cyriacus' intervention in the matter of the heavenly bread formula: Dionysius may have preferred to let sleeping dogs lie. But Yohannan's detailed instructions on proper liturgy suggest that he had greater aspirations for the oversight of the clergy, which extended into the micromanagement of the liturgy.

It is difficult to determine whether this legislation had any real effect, and the repetition of canons on clerical marriage suggests that some ideals were very hard to enforce. That said, I believe that we can trace an escalation of ambition across the ninth century, which might imply that earlier goals had indeed been achieved.

The patriarchs' second form of engagement with the Eucharist in their canonical legislation was to use the threat of excommunication and penitential fasting (*nzirutā*) against the laity. George prohibited laymen from using the need to harvest or thresh wheat as an excuse to avoid the Sunday service (canon 20). Under Cyriacus, believers were banned from trading or travelling on Sundays (canon 23) and from hosting guests who do not keep the Sunday feast (canon 28). Conversely, people who abuse priests (canon 16) and believers who fail to fast or who drink alcohol during Lent were suspended from the Eucharist (canon 29). Attendance at the Eucharist was asserted as a norm for all lay Christians except for those who had been excluded because of misdemeanours.

The penalties applied by Cyriacus were widely used by his successors. Patriarchs and bishops rarely had access to coercive force, and the fact that excommunication could serve as a penalty suggests that attendance at

23. For concerns over sacramental validity in the sixth century, see Alpi 2009: 145–47 (on baptism); Menze 2008: 145–48, 158–65, 175–86.

communion offered important advantages even to the lax or the belligerent. The power of the promise of salvation and the fear of damnation should not be underestimated, but communion was also a public sign of inclusion, of harmonious coexistence with one's proper community and of acceptance by its spiritual leaders.

Exegesis of the Liturgy

The concern that Yohannan showed for the minutiae of the liturgy and the ability of the patriarchs to influence the laity through exclusion from communion are good indications of the liturgy's importance. It was not mere verbiage that could be altered at will. Two Jacobite intellectuals, Moses bar Kepha and John of Dara, both near contemporaries of Dionysius, wrote extensively on the liturgy and on its relationship to scripture and to Christian society.[24] Their commentaries provide illuminative insights into why the conduct of the liturgy was of such importance. It goes without saying that their commentaries do not reflect what the laity thought about the liturgy, though some ideas might have been disseminated more broadly through sermons or informal discussion. Rather, their writings sketch a social and theological ideal and tell us how one section of the Jacobite higher clergy conceived of their own roles vis-à-vis one another, the laity and God.

Moses bar Kepha wrote three commentaries on the liturgy, in which he dealt with the three sacraments of the Eucharist,[25] baptism and the consecration of the myron, respectively. John of Dara was a friend of Dionysius of Tel-Mahre and is mentioned in the dedication of the latter's history. Like Moses, John wrote a general commentary on the Eucharist, *On Oblation*, and a quartet of works of symbolic theology.[26] Both of these authors tend to accumulate typologies that describe the significance of liturgical objects and rituals.[27] Thus oil is used in baptism because the baptized person is like a

---

24. On these men and their writings, see Barsoum 2003: 391 and 398–404.

25. This was the first full-scale commentary on the liturgy, though it drew on the writings of Jacob of Serug, George of the Arabs and Jacob of Edessa. It was intended as a guide to correct practice as well as a commentary. Varghese 2004: 27–28.

26. John's work took a more allegorical approach than that of Moses to interpreting ritual and scripture and was less widely consulted in later centuries. Varghese 2004: 30–32.

27. Cf. Varghese 2004: 17–19. Rickards 1974: 139ff. notes that liturgical practice often drives Moses' exegesis.

wrestler, venturing out to fight Satan in life.[28] The altar is the Tree of Life, which had been withheld from Adam in the garden of Eden but is now given to humankind in the form of Christ and His sacrifice.[29] The myron is composed of two different oils, balsam and olive oil, because it stands for the union of God the word with the flesh.[30] It is this kind of symbolic reasoning that may drive the focus on minutiae in the canons. To insist on a veil embroidered with a cross, as Yohannan does, is understandable if the veil symbolizes the veiling of the meaning of scripture (and therefore justifies allegorical exegesis).[31]

A key theme that runs through the legislation is the importance of priesthood and the need to maintain its propriety by avoiding quarrelling, maintaining educational standards and punishing laymen who insult priests. The significance of priests as representatives of God, acting in His place before the congregation, is also threaded through the commentaries. Accordingly, in baptism the priest breathes on the water 'like God breathed on Adam', and he lays his hands on the head of the baptized 'like God laid His hands upon Adam'.[32] Here the priest and the new Christian stand for God and all people.[33] And in consecrating the myron, 'the high priest stands in the place of God' and is surrounded by the priests and deacons, who represent the seraphim and the apostles.[34]

Of Men and Angels

The analogy between the clergy on the one hand and God and the angels on the other is especially pronounced in the mystical works of John of Dara. These are essentially an explanation (and recapitulation) of the works of the early sixth-century mystic (Pseudo-)Dionysius the Areopagite, whose works

28. Moses bar Kepha, *On Baptism*, 10.
29. Moses bar Kepha, *On the Eucharist*, 34 (here he is citing Pseudo-Dionysius the Areopagite); cf. Moses bar Kepha, *On Myron*, 24.
30. Moses bar Kepha, *On Myron*, 7.
31. John of Dara, *On Oblation*, II, 30.
32. Moses bar Kepha, *On Baptism*, 12 and 15. In his *Hexaemeron*, Moses reads Adam as denoting 'all men' rather than referring to a specific individual (Rickards 1974: 126).
33. If the baptized person was an infant, as would have been common in this period, the sacrament might have further symbolized God's fatherly relationship to humankind.
34. Moses bar Kepha, *On Myron*, 9 and 20. See similar imagery in John of Dara, *On Oblation*, II, 9. The eleventh-century theologian Ibn Jarir (31, 9) also stresses that the priestly hierarchy imitates the angelic hierarchy, probably also drawing on Pseudo-Dionysius the Areopagite.

had been translated into Syriac twice and were popular among and influential for exegetes.[35] Pseudo-Dionysius applied a strongly allegorical approach to scripture and emphasized the experience of the Eucharist as a means of accessing God.[36] For him, creation consisted of a hierarchy of beings in which each level, thanks to God's grace, was able to act in a way that was more similar to the divine than were the actions of the level below and to radiate this grace to others.[37] In other words, for Pseudo-Dionysius, salvation and grace were not individual concerns but rather communal activities.[38] The Eucharist and the sacraments of baptism and consecration of the myron are crucial means through which divine grace is radiated to others, and the clergy play the central role in this process. Their efficacy is not just a feature of the office but also a product of their moral and intellectual qualities, since a sacred man renders other things sacred.[39] Averil Cameron has described this cohesive, hierarchical vision as 'a handbook to the truth, not a guide to rational discourse', an example of hegemonic thought that takes the practice of the church for granted.[40] Its refusal to engage in speculative Christology makes it reassuring to individual believers.[41]

John of Dara adapts Pseudo-Dionysius the Areopagite by addressing the origins of the priesthood and incorporating the ideas of Syriac theologians such as Ephrem into a Pseudo-Dionysian framework.[42] For John, there are three levels of access to the divine: the angels, the ecclesiastical priesthood (the Christian church) and the legal priesthood (the Jewish priesthood of the Old Testament). Like Pseudo-Dionysius, John sees the sacraments as central to access to God: 'All things have some resemblance to God, but they can

35. Brock 1972: 21; Barsoum 2003: 123–29; Grillmeier and Hainthaler 2013: 623–24. See Fiori 2014 for the translation of Dionysius into Syriac by Sergius of Reshaina in the sixth century and its adaptation in the seventh by one Photius. For a consideration of Dionysius from the point of view of sixth-century Christological debates, see Grillmeier and Hainthaler 2013: 298–342.

36. Louth 1989: 23–24; Golitzin 1994: 194–203.

37. Louth 1989: 39; Roques 1954: 92–94; Golitzin 1994: 141–60.

38. Louth 1989: 42; Roques 1954: 258–59, 269, 299.

39. Louth 1989: 60–67; Roques 1954: 192–94, 244–77, 297; Golitzin 1994: 185–208. For the importance of the imagery of light in Dionysius, see Mortley 1986: 232, 238.

40. Cameron 1991: 217–20. For Dionysius' use of Neoplatonic political ideas, see O'Meara 2005: 159–71. Golitzin 1994: 414 notes the 'centripetal thrust' of Dionysius' ideas, which reinforce a political and social status quo by emphasizing the eternal nature of hierarchies.

41. Mortley 1986: 252–54 comments on Dionysius' characterization of the divine as unintelligible, which avoids contentious definitions of God.

42. I draw deeply on Anderson 2016 in my comments on John of Dara.

perfect this resemblance only through priesthood'; 'Union with God is possible only through the gifts that come from Him. The greatest gift is priesthood, through which we are divinized'.[43] And like Pseudo-Dionysius, John holds that priesthood reflects inner moral qualities: 'Priesthood infuses those who desire it purely, as fire infuses iron'.[44] This is important because priests act as types of God 'because they bear the divine image',[45] and through priests, the whole church 'perceives the being of God'.[46]

John draws a number of parallels between priests and angels. For him, priests are 'angels' in the sense that they announce God's words. Like the seraphim, they dispense light; like the cherubim, they possess wisdom in abundance; like thrones, they are the lawgivers of God; like dominions, they possess a liberating power; like authorities, they embody wisdom without confusion; like principalities, they are suited to leadership; and like angels, they are sent to minister to the people.[47] These parallels establish priests (and perhaps bishops in particular) as legitimate holders of social authority as judges and leaders in addition to their function in the liturgy, but they also assert the priests' role in transmitting grace to the people and enabling the latter to be divinized. Nevertheless, John stresses that angels themselves would be unsuited to the office of priests for humankind because they would have no sympathy with humanity's imperfections. Priests' recognition of their own sins is an important part of their ministry. They are married men, enmeshed in society: 'Christ did not entrust his priesthood to the celibate John but to the married Simon, who erred'.[48]

The priests' engagement with the laity is an important feature of John's thought. John composed a work, *On Demons*, that suggests that even fallen angels could repent and be saved. The implication, I presume, is that if redemption was possible for demons, all people could potentially be saved.[49] According to

43. John of Dara, *On Priesthood*, I, 1; *On Priesthood*, II, 1. Cf. *On the Celestial Priesthood*, 2–3.
44. John of Dara, *On Priesthood*, II, 1.
45. John of Dara, *On Priesthood*, II, 11.
46. John of Dara, *On Priesthood*, II, 12.
47. See the discussion in Anderson 2016: 65–67. John gives a detailed account of the angelic ranks in *On the Celestial Priesthood*, 7–9, which expands the ideas of Dionysius the Areopagite.
48. John of Dara, *On Priesthood*, II, 6.
49. Similar ideas had been propounded in the sixth century by Stephen bar Sudaili, whose ideas are often associated with the Syriac *Book of the Holy Hierotheos*. Cyriacus condemned Stephen as a heretic, which implies that his thought remained attractive (Oez 2012: II, 410–11). Stephen had already been condemned in the early sixth century by Philoxenus of Mabbug (Reinink

his writings on the priestly hierarchy, catechumens and the possessed can be saved by witnessing the sacraments, even without receiving them.[50] On the other hand, John is anxious that the laity be appropriately prepared for the Eucharist and have 'set sinful deeds to one side' through confession.[51]

As Liza Anderson remarks, John's writings are remarkable for what they omit. There is no indication of Christological divisions. And although John is very interested in the Old Testament prototypes for Christ and the church (which he calls the legal priesthood), nothing indicates that he had any real Jewish interlocutors.[52] Whereas Christian apologetic texts from this period sometimes conceal their attitudes to Muslims behind discussion of Jews, such a strategy does not seem to be in play here.[53] John writes as if there were no competing religious narratives, and reading his works one would not guess that John was part of a Jacobite religious minority. He conveys a totalizing worldview in which humans and angels are united in the practice of the sacraments through the ministration of priests and bishops. He entirely ignores the existence of Muslims, Julianists and Chalcedonians. John's argument constitutes what Berger and Luckmann call the 'highest form of legitimation', through which individuals can rest assured that they are living correctly even in a lived environment that is unclear or contradictory.[54]

Lower Clergy and Laymen: Abiram and Uzziah

One of John of Dara's priorities for the ecclesiastical hierarchy is that it should be ordered.[55] Just as cherubim cannot fulfil the role of seraphim, he argues, it is not appropriate for priests to fill the roles of bishops in ordination or the

---

1999: 237). This precedent may explain why John of Dara approaches similar themes rather allusively. For the relationships between Pseudo-Dionysius, Stephen, Philoxenus and the *Book of Hierotheos*, see Fiori 2011. For Bar Hebraeus' complex attitude to the *Book*, see Reinink 1999.

50. Anderson 2016: 69. For the significance of witnessing sacraments as a form of participation in the liturgy in Pseudo-Dionysius, see Roques 1954: 269.

51. John of Dara, *On Priesthood*, I, 6. One of John's criticisms of the 'legal priesthood' of the Old Testament is that its purification concerned only the sins of evil actions rather than the states of conscience that led to those actions: *On Priesthood*, II, 13.

52. Anderson 2016: 108–11.

53. Anderson 2016: 129ff.; Griffith 1988 (for Muslims as 'new Jews').

54. Berger and Luckmann 1966: 111–17.

55. See John of Dara, *On Priesthood*, II, 9 for the divine origin of the orders of deacons, priests and bishops.

consecration of the myron.[56] Pseudo-Dionysius the Areopagite had stressed the importance of bishops as successors to the apostles, who had known Christ directly, and as direct appointees of God.[57] But John goes much further than Dionysius by making numerous references to three scenes in the Old Testament to justify this structure: Numbers 16, Leviticus 10, and 2 Chronicles 26:16–19. These scenes concern the 'insolence' of the Levites Korah, Dathan and Abiram against Moses' leadership, the death of Aaron's sons Nadab and Abihu when they place incense in the censers without permission and the leprosy that afflicts King Uzziah of Judah when he uses the censers in the Temple. John's choice of examples may reflect his opinion of the sources of disorder in the church. Dionysius of Tel-Mahre often calls his opponent Abraham of Qartmin 'Abiram', after Moses' enemy, and John may be tacitly making the same reference here, representing Abiram as an unconsecrated and illegitimate opponent of proper hierarchy. The reference to Uzziah may also indicate that he objected to improper lay intervention in the church. Given the example, he may be thinking of Christian lay elites, such as the Cyrrhestican aristocrats who supported the Gubbite rebellion, rather than of Muslims.[58]

Much of the patriarchal legislation targets the unwarranted roles of priests in the sacraments. I interpret this focus as reflecting the same concern with hierarchy and order that we see in John of Dara. Priests and monks are prohibited from consecrating or distributing the myron (George canons 18 and 19; Cyriacus canon 8); priests are warned not to usurp the administration of the church from their bishops (Cyriacus canon 13). Bishops are banned from encroaching on one another's territory by performing sacraments outside their dioceses (Dionysius canons 1 and 3; Yohannan canons 1 and 26).[59] It is possible that the escalation of the target of the patriarchs' interest from priests to

56. John of Dara, *On the Celestial Priesthood*, 3.

57. Roques 1954: 180, 327.

58. Niketas Stethatos, the eleventh-century Byzantine commentator on Pseudo-Dionysius the Areopagite, 'tidied up' the Dionysian hierarchy by adding a 'triad' of archbishops, metropolitans and patriarchs above bishops (Louth 2009: 64). Whether or not Pseudo-Dionysius' omission of the patriarchate was deliberate, I think it is unlikely that John of Dara was criticizing the patriarchate as a non-apostolic institution, given that he was a close friend of Dionysius of Tel-Mahre and the dedicatee of his history. I thank Phil Booth for discussion of this point.

59. In Yohannan's case, this rule seems to have been prompted by political disruption in Persia that caused eastern bishops to flee to Syria.

bishops indicates that Cyriacus was relatively successful in asserting episcopal monopoly over the myron.[60]

But the patriarchal legislation is also worried about new Uzziahs who seek to intervene in church affairs. Accordingly, canons forbid laymen to seize control of church administration (Cyriacus canon 13) or to speak with priests of ecclesiastical affairs (Cyriacus canon 27). Nor are laymen to sit higher than priests at banquets for the departed 'or to talk about the affairs [of the clergy] or support them against one another in their quarrels' (Cyriacus canon 42). The fear of lay-clerical alliances that might oppose patriarchal authority remains an issue for Dionysius (canon 11), who legislates against people (both clerics and laymen) who make oaths for 'stirring up trouble'.

As in the legislation on monks, the patriarchs' intention in these canons seems to have been to dilute the 'horizontal' connections between different bodies of Christians (monks, the lower clergy and the laity) to render all of them dependent on the patriarch and to prevent them from making common cause in a given region to oppose the patriarch's writ. One aspect of this assertion of a certain kind of Christian hierarchy was the denigration of anyone who sought justice from laymen.[61] Cyriacus condemns those who abandon their bishops to 'take refuge with worldly rulers' (canon 25). Likewise, people who flee to 'dignitaries of the Christians whose force is hard' after being anathematized by their bishops shall not be pardoned by the Son of God 'either in this world or in the one which is prepared' (Yohannan canon 18). Dionysius similarly threatens transgressors with exclusion from mingling with other Christians, from participation in the holy mysteries and from the giving and receiving of greetings (canon 4). Dionysius' fear in such a scenario is that exiles may try to use force to get the bishop to change his mind, and he thus promises that even if the bishop reverses the sinner's judgement, 'the Son of God will not pardon him, either in this world or in the next, because he has become a traitor to the piety and law of the Christians'.

---

60. For a comparative discussion of Jacobite usage of the myron, see Varghese 1989; cf. Moses bar Kepha's *On Myron*. The significance of the patriarch's role in consecrating the myron on Maundy Thursday is a clear feature of the *Life of Timothy of Kakushta*. Indeed, the sacrament is portrayed almost as an epitome of the role of the patriarch. This monopoly was certainly breached at some points: note the account of myron being used extracanonically to heal a sick child in the *Life of Samuel of Qartmin*, XI. My thanks to Sebastian Brock for discussion of this point.

61. For this phenomenon, see Simonsohn 2010.

The patriarchs' threats against people who defy their authority are especially dramatic: they invoke the full consequences of their own position in the divine hierarchy to guarantee the damnation of anyone who disobeys them. And in this life, they urge their co-religionists to ostracize anyone who tries to circumvent their own power as judges. On the one hand, these threats may be directed at Christians who sought the help of Muslim elites to challenge rulings issued by Christian clergy. But the phrasing of Yohannan's canon 18 suggests that the patriarchs were also disturbed by the provision of alternative judgements by Christian aristocrats (who, after all, had commonly played a judicial role in the Roman world).[62] Notably, Dionysius does not contest such aristocrats' ability to act as judges; he only prohibits their intervention in matters that bishops have already decided.

Communities and Boundaries

The legal sources of the long ninth century portray a Jacobite patriarchate that was becoming increasingly ambitious, though they also show that the patriarchs coexisted with other powerful Christian elites, including the abbots of powerful monasteries and lay aristocrats. Another important aspect of the legislation is the assertion of strong social boundaries against non-Christian and non-Jacobite outsiders. This, I argue, is a crucial reason for the acceptance by the patriarch's co-religionists of his authority. The imagination of a self-contained Christian society in the law codes and the liturgical commentaries took place within a social context in which men and women are likely to have found their spouses within their own 'groups', as defined by ethnicity, tribe, village and extended family as well as higher-order categories such as religion. Endogamy was commonplace and occurred on many levels.

The anthropologist Jack Goody has remarked that in much of Eurasia, unlike in Africa, land is a scarce resource that must thus be retained in the family. This fact, in turn, has meant that in environments where women might inherit property, female marriage choices need to be carefully policed to ensure that a family's land does not pass to rivals who might oppose the family's interests. Arranged marriages (within groups, especially within extended families),

62. For the importance of various classes of aristocrats in arbitration as well as in the formal implementation of justice in late Roman Egypt, see Gagos and van Minnen 1994. On the episcopal desire for 'judicial exclusiveness', see further Simonsohn 2015, which notes parallels to the Church of the East.

respect for premarital virginity and control over the socialization of young women within a wider culture of honour and shame can all be seen as responses to this economic imperative (though it manifests many regional variations).[63]

The Jacobite legislation deals with marriage and inheritance in three domains. These are restrictions on marriage to outsiders and sharing their customs, the ability of heads of households to arrange the marriages of their children and the definition of incest and illegal marriage.

Marriage to religious outsiders was restricted first at a local level in the writings of Jacob of Edessa. This was then followed by patriarchal legislation which banned Muslims, pagans and 'Nestorians' and then Zoroastrians and Jews as potential marriage partners for Christians.[64] Christians before Constantine had adopted a variety of marriage strategies toward their pagan co-citizens,[65] but the eighth- and ninth-century context generated a much stronger stance on the part of church leaders that demanded intraconfessional endogamy. The disappearance of a Christian Roman empire and the reality of life alongside other religious groups coincided with new legislation by Christian leaders to prohibit marriage to outsiders.

In addition, the regulation of dress and diet might often be linked, implicitly or explicitly, to the breakdown of the segregation of women from contact with outsiders. Ignatius' condemnation of Christians who adopt the fashions of the 'Gentiles', presumably Muslims, in hairstyles and clothing (canon 8) provides one example. In Ignatius' view, by abandoning Christian norms of display and adopting those common to Muslim society, Christians would lose the signs that differentiated them from outsiders and would join a larger social world in which their identity would be threatened. In particular, Ignatius

---

63. Goody 1976: 13–20; Goody 1983; Weitz 2018: 59. Marriage between cousins was widespread in the sixth-century Roman East: CJ (the Code of Justinian) 5.4.19. Lee 1988 and Sarris 2017 discuss attempts to regulate other forms of close-kin marriage (probably nephew-niece marriage and/or levirate marriage) in Justinian's Novels.

64. George canons 12–13 and Yohannan canon 23. Note discussion in Selb 1989: 253–63 and the parallels in East Syriac contexts collected and discussed in Weitz 2016 and Simonsohn 2016b. Penn 2015a: 151–54 reads the bans on marriage to outsiders as evidence that such marriages were common. But I find it hard to imagine the survival of minority religious communities if intermarriage was commonplace over a long period of time.

65. New Testament attitudes toward exogamy are ambiguous. Marriage between Christians and pagans was commonplace in Augustine's North Africa: Giardina 2000: 398. Stark 1996 argues that, in practice, Christian exogamy was used as a tool for expansion.

feared that the expansion of social networks would lead to sexual activity: 'Those who are of this sort [i.e., wear 'Gentile' clothing] readily deviate licentiously to obscene acts. Consequently, by that, they are a cause of their own perdition and appear as a bad example to others'.

We can make a similar point about Athanasius of Balad's sermonizing against Christians mixing with 'pagans' over a century earlier, where he links the keeping of dietary taboos with the separation of Christian women from improper contact with outsiders:

> A terrible report about dissipated Christians has come to the hearing of our humble self. Greedy men, who are slaves of the belly, are heedlessly and senselessly taking part with the pagans in feasts together, wretched women mingle anyhow with the pagans unlawfully and indecently, and all at times eat without distinction from their sacrifices. They are going astray in their neglect of the prescriptions and exhortations of the apostles who often would cry out about this to those who believe in Christ, that they should distance themselves from fornication, from what is strangled and from blood, and from the food of pagan sacrifices, lest they be by this associates of the demons and of their unclean table.[66]

It is worth laying out the social context in which this change in attitude toward marriage boundaries occurred. It should be remembered that Dionysius and his fellow patriarchs were legislating some years after Arabs had begun to settle in the countryside as agriculturalists and landowners.[67] The settlement of powerful outsiders must have been a threatening event for local non-Muslims. Wealthy foreign soldiers billeted in a village would always have posed a danger to local families, since they threatened to attract girls into unsuitable matches that would take the girls and their property away from their families.[68]

---

66. See the discussion and translation in Penn 2015b: 79–84. Compare the attempted restrictions on Christian feasting in late Sasanian Iran: Debié 2010: 350–53; Payne 2015: 117–22. Who these 'pagans' are is unclear. If they are Muslims (rather than polytheists or Zoroastrians) then Athanasius seems to have been misinformed about their dietary laws when he presumes that they consumed animals that had been killed by strangulation.

67. Sijpesteijn 2009 dates this process to the 720s in Egypt. Numerous Arabic narratives describe the conversion of slaves and prisoners of war, many of them women (Simonsohn 2016a).

68. Note the comparable case of Gothic soldiers billeted in Mesopotamia in the fifth century: Wood 2010: 95–98. There is likely to have been tension wherever endogamous communities coexisted in the same geographical space, especially when some groups were more

The anthropologist Julian Pitt-Rivers has characterized marriage strategy as a key aspect of the preservation of communal resources and the consolidation of conquest. One way of reading the quranic prohibition on female Muslims marrying non-Muslims and the ability of male Muslims to marry Jews and Christians and to contract polygamous marriages (Q 5:5) is to see them as an aggressive strategy 'aiming to deny [one's own] women to outsiders and take their women' in order to maximize the property and population growth of the dominant community. Conversely, the development of Christian endogamy after the conquest can be understood as a defensive reaction on the part of the clerical leadership, aimed at 'reserving its women within the group and [avoiding] outsiders'.[69] The Quran's injunction may also imply that greater care needs to be taken in safeguarding the virtue of Muslim women compared to that of non-Muslim women. This is certainly the implication of later laws that impose lower penalties for a Muslim man's fornication with a female dhimmī than for fornication with a female Muslim,[70] and that inflict the death penalty on a dhimmī convicted of fornication with a Muslim woman.[71]

One of Cyriacus' canons evokes this situation especially well. Canon 38 insists that a believing woman should not go out on the street unless 'her head is covered and clothed in another cloak above it'. Though the precise meaning of this command is opaque, Cyriacus' concern with women's appearance in public seems to be motivated by their (perceived) vulnerability to outsiders, as well as the notion that the Jacobite community as a whole is judged by the appearance of its women: to be visible is to be without protection and hence without value.[72]

In the Abbasid Jazira, marriage to Muslims also meant the loss of family land, and of children born in that marriage, to a different religious community.[73] Here the economic and political interests of family and clergy were aligned

---

powerful than others and might seize women by force or persuasion. A good example of this from Adiabene, involving a Zoroastrian lord threatening to carry off an unmarried girl, is found in the *Life of Rabban Bar 'Idta*, 185/280.

69. Julian Pitt-Rivers, cited in Barton 2015: 39. For the effects of these prohibitions on conversion, see Tritton 1930: 12 and Fattal 1958: 129–34.

70. Tritton 1930: 189.

71. Levy-Rubin 2011: 80.

72. Compare the Talmud's concern with Jewish women's head covering in mixed society, which signalled their Jewishness and their respectability and hence also their sexual nonavailability. Lapin 2012: 136–38.

73. Simonsohn 2016a: 261.

(except in cases where the whole extended family converted to Islam). This alignment may explain the willingness of the wider Jacobite community—the laity, the monks and the lower clergy—to tolerate the claims of the patriarch. These community members held a peripheral political and cultural position and were consequently prepared to make concessions to leaders who could help protect their property from loss through out-marriage and provide welfare.

Patterns of marriage and socialization and the differential practices that mark them are themselves justified through acts of legislation by governments and communities. As Morony notes, all the religious communities of the late Sasanian world and the early caliphate attempted to do this.[74] We can also see the writing of 'communal' history, the teaching and exegesis of theology and the celebration of prayers and liturgy as means of emphasizing communal boundaries, since they focus on what unites the community against outsiders to the exclusion of other possible narratives that might foreground commonalities instead and thus encourage political or sexual collaboration across group boundaries. In addition, a community that can provide advantageous legal rights or economic welfare to its members incentivizes its members to remain within the fold (and attracts new recruits).[75] Elite members of minority populations provided incentives for group membership by funding educational and welfare institutions, by providing patronage and by paying tax debts.[76] Theological arguments between communities often attract the attention of modern scholars, and patristic florilegia did provide ammunition for the kinds of debates that might occur between lay members of different communities.[77] But the ability of a community's leadership to organize marriage

74. Morony 2005. For examples from Islamic jurisprudence, see Marlow 1997: 31–32 and Friedmann 2003: esp. ch. 5. These encompassed restrictions on marriage between Arabs and *mawālī* and between Quraysh and non-Quraysh as well as between Muslims and non-Muslims.

75. Wimmer 2013.

76. Mazza 2011: 278; Wipszycka 1972: 111–14. Non-Muslims were banned from receiving charity from the state's ṣadaqa/zakāt revenues (Salaymeh 2016: 343). Choksy 1987: 98–99 sees the inadequate provision of charity for the poor and the weakening upkeep of buildings as key factors in the decline of Zoroastrianism. By contrast, Goitein 1963 identifies Jews' ability to pay the jizya on behalf of the poor and to support refugees as important reasons for the community's cohesion.

77. Miaphysite florilegia in various languages are surveyed in Grillmeier 1987: 63–70. For an example of anti-Julianist florilegia, see Moss 2016a: 217–18, though many others exist. Sergey Minov informs me that he is editing a collection of anti-Jewish florilegia collected in BL Add 12154.

strategies and to control socialization and economic welfare is likely to have been just as important, if not more so, in determining the community's intergenerational survival.

In addition to regulating marriage to religious outsiders, many of the patriarchal canons are concerned with marriages among Christians. These laws give considerable powers to the heads of households to betroth their sons and daughters in order to secure advantageous matches. As Goody has noted, marriage was much too important for the political and economic fate of a household for its leaders to allow it to be left to romantic chance.[78] Legislation demanded that betrothal be confirmed in a church with witnesses, and it threatened men who broke their betrothals or had premarital sex with excommunication and ostracism.[79] Such official endorsement of betrothals meant that marriages could be planned and arranged when the betrothed parties themselves were still dependent on their parents.[80] On the other hand, the insistence that betrothals be conducted in church is another example of how lay customs that had formerly been conducted independently of the church might be co-opted by the church, indirectly supporting the authority of the clergy.[81]

But the patriarchs did not simply endorse the ability of heads of households to create marriage alliances as they wished. They also legislated in some detail on the limits of incest. There was never a ban on marriage between cousins among the Jacobites, as there was in Catholic Europe.[82] But patriarchal

78. Goody 1976.

79. However, it was not able to inflict the economic penalties that had been possible under Roman civil law (Giardina 2000: 400).

80. Cyriacus canons 31 and 32. Yohannan added a further caveat that required the agreement of the betrothed parties (canon 15). For the canons of the Church of the East on Christian betrothal and the importance of marriage within the church in the seventh century, see Weitz 2018: 42, 54. Note, however, that these laws in the Church of the East were issued for Qatar, which would have experienced an influx of Muslim conquerors long before the Jazira.

81. Compare to similar trends in ninth- and tenth-century Byzantium (Rapp 2016: 213).

82. Goody 1983: 36–42 and 134–46. Goody argues that the prohibition of cousin marriage, coupled with bans on divorce and adoption, made it harder for lay lineages to concentrate their wealth or to prevent their extinction because of a lack of male heirs. In Goody 2000: 44 and 53 he argues that the Catholic Church's enforcement of voluntary marriage and of female property rights may also have weakened aristocratic lineages. We do not see the ban on cousin marriage in the Jacobite case. Though the patriarch Timothy I (780–823) did attempt such a ban in the Church of the East, it was reversed by his successor Ishobarnun (823–28). See Weitz 2018: 145–72.

legislation did restrict the ability of families to make multiple marriage alliances with one another. Yohannan's detailed list[83] of forbidden degrees of union includes two brothers marrying a woman and her daughter, a man and his son marrying two sisters or a man giving his daughter to his father-in-law.[84] Dionysius II also included godparents in his marriage ban, so that 'no Christian has the right to take a wife who is related to himself, his brothers or his parents by sponsorship for five generations' (canon 14).[85] The economic and political effect of this legislation may have been to make it difficult to concentrate wealth and influence in the hands of individual families while at the same time ensuring that marriages, and hence inheritances, remained inside Jacobite circles.

The main mechanisms for policing the marriage boundaries approved by the patriarchs were excommunication and ostracism.[86] The legislators envisaged that defaulters would be penalized through their social capital, with friends and allies turning against anyone who dared to cross religious boundaries. Direct bans on exogamy were complemented by bans on seeking sacraments at non-Jacobite churches and on accepting non-Jacobites into Jacobite congregations.[87] Restricting attendance at the services of other confessions and asserting intraconfessional endogamy were ways of preventing the blurring of identity boundaries, which might have provided a stepping-stone toward full apostasy or the loss of future children to another Christian

83. Yohannan devoted a separate legal text to this subject, *On Illegitimate Marriages*.

84. This would include, I presume, the father of a second wife, not related to his daughter by blood.

85. For parallels in Byzantium, see Rapp 2016: 10, 213–16 (banning the marriage of uncles and nieces that might consolidate family landholdings and defining links of *synketnia* [godparenthood] as family relations for the purposes of incest legislation). Rapp sees *adelphopoiesis* (brother making) as a strategy to avoid the limitation of inheritance by the state.

86. Note the discussion of ostracism in Simonsohn 2013a. The effects of ostracism are likely to have been keenly felt in preindustrial rural contexts in which individuals were highly reliant on their neighbours for help in times of dearth (for loans of food, money, tools or labour). I have found the comments of Anigbo 1978 on the failure of ostracism in colonial Nigeria useful on this point.

87. These were Cyriacus canon 9 against baptizing the children of heretics and canon 14 against making donations to heretical institutions. Note parallels in the Church of the East, where Ishobarnun banned church members from receiving Melkite communion while away from home. See the discussion in Weitz 2016: 89.

confession.[88] The legislators imagined a Jacobite-only social world, with sacraments administered by the clergy at its centre.

Conclusions

The liturgy was presented to Christians as the reenactment of the only history that mattered, a history in which the temporal fate of Christian polities was peripheral. Commentators imagined an all-encompassing world of men and angels, in which the priests' celebration of the sacraments transmitted grace between heaven and earth.

The liturgy and its commentaries are also important for what they exclude. They ignore the existence of non-Christians, whose growing power was clearly disturbing to many, in order to position the liturgy as the consummation of human existence. And they disregard the financial and social apparatus that made clerical leadership possible.

But, as we have seen, the higher clergy did make material claims on their flock. These claims were tolerated in part because of the authority given to the clergy by the Abbasid government that allowed them to use force against dissenters and to legitimate the collection of tithes. Another aspect, illustrated in patriarchal legislation, is the stress on endogamous marriage and the clerical monopoly over lawmaking. These attempted acts of boundary creation were not simply intended to undermine Christian landholders: in several ways they endorsed the latter's ability to arrange marriages to suit their purposes and, in so doing, sustained vested interests in the preservation of church institutions and the patriarch's right to produce legislation.

Nevertheless, we cannot read this legislation as evidence for the successful creation of boundaries, but as attempts to bring such boundaries into being. In a recent study of the Cairo Geniza, Eve Krakowski observes that Judaism is a primary identity, but not a totalizing one: the Geniza Jews were linked to their Muslim and Christian neighbours by ties of cohabitation, friendship, debt and labour, even if their access to welfare, their use of law and their participation in ritual differed.[89] And in spite of the declarations of the geonim, Jewish women often exercised considerable agency in their marriage choices.[90] We

---

88. For the complex situation of the children of mixed marriages, who were sometimes represented in the hagiographies as secret Christians, see Sahner 2016.

89. Krakowski 2017: 18

90. Krakowski 2017: 210.

do not possess such detailed evidence here, but the kind of material that Jack Tannous has assembled from the questions and answers of Jacob of Edessa and the *Life of Theodota of Amida* point to regular mundane links across notional communal boundaries, where a Jacobite monastery might employ a travelling carpenter even though he was a 'Nestorian', where members of different confessions regularly share meals or close friendship and where Jacobite scribes might write out books for 'heretics'.[91] The social world described in the texts examined in this chapter was a messy one, and social boundaries were often unclear; what the Jacobite patriarchs were attempting to do in their law codes was create boundaries and modes of behaviour that, they hoped, would preserve a Jacobite community that respected episcopal authority.

91. Tannous 2018: 93–97.

7

Dionysius and al-Ma'mun

DIONYSIUS CLAIMED TO WIELD considerable political influence in court at Baghdad. He attributed his ability to overcome rivals such as Abiram and Basil of Balad to the protection granted to him by the caliph al-Ma'mun and his general 'Abd Allah ibn Tahir. Dionysius used his chronicle to demonstrate his own suitability for the patriarchate as a man familiar with Arabic and with the internal politics of the Muslim elite. One of the purposes of Dionysius' history is to lead its readers to conclude that Dionysius' relationship with the ruling authorities allowed Dionysius to protect his co-religionists from predatory Muslim outsiders. This legitimation of the relationship between the higher clergy and the Muslim elite was, as we have seen, a relatively recent feature of church politics. It relied on two different images of Muslim rule: on one hand, it validated caliphal government as fair and just, vindicating Dionysius' own contacts with al-Ma'mun and 'Abd Allah ibn Tahir. On the other, it maintained an image of many Muslims, including servants of the government, as predators against Jacobite collective interest. The threat of men like the rebel Nasr ibn Shabath (fl. 811–25) or the governor Yaqdan showed that influence with the government was necessary.

The influence that Dionysius claims in his history is closely tied to his personal relationship with al-Ma'mun and his servants. We should remember, however, that al-Ma'mun himself was, to some extent, an idiosyncratic outsider within Abbasid politics. In this chapter, I set out the context for al-Ma'mun's controversial rise to power, in which Syria and the Jazira was wracked by banditry. I argue that al-Ma'mun's reign restored and strengthened links between Iraq and Syria, which once more allowed clerics with access to the caliph to coerce their opponents into submission. In addition, al-Ma'mun was the first (and only) Abbasid caliph to visit Egypt. Dionysius visited Egypt twice, once at the request of the caliph, and this gave him a political prominence that none of his predecessors had enjoyed. Al-Ma'mun's victory over his various opponents was a prerequisite for the stability of the patriarch's authority and for the development of interregional links by the Jacobite church.

Al-Ma'mun's Rise to Power

The caliph Harun al-Rashid divided the caliphate between his two sons, al-Amin (809–13) and al-Ma'mun. The two reigned as caliphs simultaneously, one in Baghdad, the Abbasid capital since 762, and the other in Merv in Khurasan. Merv held a special position in Abbasid politics because it had been the flashpoint of the revolution of 750 that had toppled the Umayyads and because it was the original home of many of the troops settled in Baghdad at the city's foundation. Khurasan was also home to an influential Muslim population that was conscious of its rights and importance. Al-Rashid's decision to place al-Ma'mun in Merv was a recognition of Khurasan's continued significance for the regime and of the eastward shift in the demographic weight of the caliphate's Muslim population.[1] But it also sowed the seeds of future tension between the brothers.[2]

Arabic accounts of the civil war between al-Amin and al-Ma'mun, known as the fourth fitna, are coloured by retrospective attempts to legitimize or criticize al-Ma'mun.[3] Modern historians have represented the war as an ethnic squabble or as a personal conflict between the brothers or their ministers.[4] Andrew Marsham plausibly argues that there was a systemic tension in the management of the Abbasid succession, which involved designated heirs holding important frontier posts with large armies to safeguard themselves against the ruling caliph and to distribute military patronage to elites outside Iraq.[5] The immediate casus belli in this case is said to have been al-Amin's demands

---

1. For al-Rashid's succession documents, see Marsham 2009: 221–27, with discussion of earlier literature. Azdi, *Tarikh al-Mawsil*, 318, is uncertain whether or not al-Ma'mun ever took the *bay'a* (oath of allegiance) to al-Amin; this uncertainty may reflect later Ma'munid propaganda.

2. Crone 1980: 75.

3. Cooperson 2005: 40–43; Cooperson 2000: ch. 2; El-Hibri 1999: chs. 1–3.

4. Daniel 1979: 175; Kennedy 1986: 135–36. The conflict between the viziers of the two brothers is probably the most significant factor for Tabari, whose emphasis has often been followed by modern historians. The letters between the brothers are allegedly preserved in Tabari III, 777–93 / XXXI, 22–42.

5. Marsham 2009: 190, 210–11.

that al-Ma'mun surrender territory and station a Baghdadi 'officer of the post' in Khurasan, followed by the dropping of al-Ma'mun's name from the coinage and from the *khuṭba* (the Friday sermon) in 810.[6]

In Khurasan, al-Ma'mun represented himself as a liberator from Baghdad's tyrannical rule. He increased military stipends and lowered taxes on the populace; he cultivated support from local *fuqahā'* (jurists) and honoured the magnates of eastern Khurasan, who had long been sidelined by the caliphal administration. At the same time, he appealed to Arab tribal groups in Khurasan using the language of the *da'wa*, a term that denotes both an invitation to Islam and the call to participate in the Abbasid revolution of 750.[7] Al-Amin was cast as an impious ruler in the mould of the Umayyads[8] and variously charged with personal immorality and incompetence, reliance on low-born advisers' alleged failure to 'rule by the sunna', and overtaxation.[9] In a letter to his Khurasanian forces, al-Ma'mun stated that the caliph was chosen by God, not by men, and that al-Amin had forfeited his right to rule.[10]

Battles at Rayy and Hamadan defeated two of al-Amin's forces, opening the way for al-Ma'mun's troops under Tahir (d. 822) and Harthama (d. 816) to seize Baghdad and capture al-Amin himself in 813.[11] In controversial circumstances, Tahir ordered the execution of al-Amin, who had been caught at night

6. Daniel 1979: 177. For the quranic resonances of the language in the mutual accusations of al-Amin and al-Ma'mun, see De Gifis 2014: 47–75.

7. Daniel 1979: 177–79. For al-Ma'mun's tax relief in Khurasan, see Azdi, *Tarikh al-Mawsil*, 318. For the emphasis on eastern Khurasan, see de la Vaissière 2007.

8. See Arazi and Elad 1987: 34 for a comparison between of al-Amin and Abu Sufyan, the opponent of the Prophet and the father of the Umayyad caliph Mu'awiya. Al-Amin is further described as engaged in apostasy (*ridda*) (Arazi and Elad 1988: 59), in contrast to al-Ma'mun who is portrayed as a rightly guided (*rāshid*) imam on the model of Abu Bakr (Elad 1988: 62). These comparisons render the fourth fitna a reenactment of both the Prophet's wars against Mecca and the Ridda wars that united the Arabian Peninsula under Medinan rule.

9. Daniel 1979: 177–79; Katbi 2010: 184; El-Hibri 1999: 60. Contrast with the concerns of earlier Abbasid officials about overtaxation: Katbi 2010: 144–47 on Abu Yusuf. The *Samaritan Chronicle*, 68, notes al-Amin's alleged penchant for transvestite boys. See Tabari III, 803 / XXXI, 56 for the story that al-Amin was more interested in catching fish during the siege of Baghdad than he was in dealing with political issues; Tabari III, 805 / XXXI, 58 for his alleged homosexual relationship with his vizier.

10. Cooperson 2005: 41, citing Arazi and Elad 1988: 56. The letter is preserved in a compilation of historical documents made by Ibn Abi Tahir Tayfur (d. 893). Arazi and Elad 1987 provides an extensive discussion.

11. Daniel 1979: 178; Cooperson 2005: 50; Marsham 2009: 261.

in a warehouse by the Tigris. There are many contradictory accounts of al-Amin's death, and they vary greatly in how they apportion blame. Some see his execution as the justifiable death of a tyrant,[12] others present al-Amin as a lamentable figure deserving of our pity,[13] and still others represent his execution as an overhasty act by Tahir, acting on his own initiative against a repentant prisoner.[14] Tayeb El-Hibri is surely correct that these scenes are as much Shakespearean observations on the quandaries of power as they are factual accounts.[15] At any rate, the diversity of these narratives and the interest that some narrators show in displacing blame from al-Ma'mun illustrate the key issue: that al-Amin's death dealt a serious blow to the inviolability of the office of caliph.[16]

This crisis in Abbasid legitimacy was compounded by al-Ma'mun's decision to rule the empire as sole caliph from Merv, instead of relocating to Baghdad.[17] He faced revolts from Arab tribal groups in Egypt, the Levant and the Jazira; Abbasid pretenders in Baghdad; and Alid claimants in Yemen and Iraq. All these challenges may have been encouraged by his apparent lack of legitimacy and the difficulties that the government experienced in subduing its rivals from its capital in Merv.[18] Al-Ma'mun's response was to recognize 'Ali 'al-Rida', a descendant of 'Ali by his son Husayn, as his successor in 817.[19] He even altered the colour of his livery from black, the traditional colour of the Abbasids, to the green of the Alids.[20] This act was, on one level, aimed at broadening al-Ma'mun's support base among supporters of the house of 'Ali and at threatening disobedient members of the Abbasid family.[21] But it prompted a fierce reaction from Abbasid loyalists in Baghdad, who feared

12. Arazi and Elad 1987: 41; Mas'udi, Muruj, VI, 262; Dinawari, 383. Ya'qubi's very brief treatment (II, 536 / III, 1202) may also fall in this category.

13. Tabari III, 923 / XXXI, 193.

14. Mas'udi, Muruj, VI, 269. A tradition in defence of Tahir also emerged, which imagined al-Amin trying to double-cross the general by attempting to retain the caliphal insignia after his surrender: Tabari III, 929 / XXXI, 200.

15. El-Hibri 1999: 61–85. I draw many of the references above from El-Hibri.

16. Kennedy 1986: 148; Daniel 1979: 180; El-Hibri 1999: 75.

17. Kennedy 1986: 151.

18. Kennedy 1986: 151–57.

19. Cooperson 2005: 58; Kennedy 1986: 158–60 gives the initiative here to al-Ma'mun's vizier al-Fadl ibn Sahl.

20. Tabari III, 1012–13 / XXXII, 31; Ya'qubi II, 545 / III, 1211.

21. Marsham 2009: 262–65.

total exclusion from the new regime. The new caliph was accused of wanting to restore the Sasanians and even of leading a 'Zoroastrian rebellion'.[22] Al-Maʾmun faced a further rebellion from his uncle Ibrahim, who enjoyed the support of these factions in Baghdad and proclaimed himself a rival caliph in 817.[23] After defeating Ibrahim, al-Maʾmun reversed his earlier decision and returned the capital to Baghdad.[24] He also restored the palace livery to black in 819 after the death of al-Rida in the previous year (whether he died of conveniently timed natural causes or poisoning is unknown).[25]

Al-Maʾmun's victory over Ibrahim was followed by the consolidation of his rule in the Levant. Tahir's son ʿAbd Allah was instrumental in defeating rebels in Syria, such as the famous Nasr ibn Shabath, and in Egypt.[26] Dionysius describes the period from the start of the fitna to the arrival in the Jazira of ʿAbd Allah ibn Tahir as 'the time of anarchy' and treats it in a discrete section of his secular history (810–24). In the following examination of Dionysius' representation of these events, my primary focus is not on the reconstruction of the military history of this period but on what the narrative can tell us about Dionysius' depiction of his own relationship with the Muslim elite.

The Fourth Fitna in Michael the Syrian

The material preserved in books 10–12 of Michael the Syrian's *Chronicle* includes substantial accounts of military and political history. Until the death of Harun al-Rashid, they focus primarily on the border warfare between the Byzantines and the Arabs, picking out the foundations of cities and the creation and destruction of fortifications, with occasional excursuses into political history.

But when it comes to the fourth fitna, Michael's *Chronicle* shifts quite suddenly from military and political history to a description of events in the Jazira,

22. Cooperson 2005: 66, citing Yaʿqubi II, 546 / III, 1212 for Harthama's accusation; see also Crone 1980: 77 n. 604. Cooperson 2016 discusses the prejudice against the Iranian background of the Sahlid viziers. Webb 2016: 271–73 observes that the fourth fitna was seen as a threshold for the end of Arab influence and ʿasabiyya (tribal politics). Nevertheless, the court retained distinctions between Arabs and non-Arabs until the 860s (Sourdel 1999: 142), and the abnāʾ persisted as a potential military counterweight to the Turks (Crone 1980: 76).

23. Cooperson 2005: 31.

24. Kennedy 1986: 161–62.

25. Tabari III, 1038 / XXXII, 96; Yaʿqubi II, 551 / III, 1218.

26. Kennedy 1998: 80; Kennedy 1986: 168. Bosworth 1992 summarizes the Muslim sources on Nasr.

though he retains a broader context and tries to situate these events within the conflict between the brothers in Iraq and Khurasan. The scope of this account, which emphasizes eyewitness accounts of events near Edessa and Raqqa that are peripheral to the main events of the war, makes it likely to be a composition by Dionysius himself and/or a précis of his work by later hand(s).

The Iraqi material in this account follows a similar outline to the narratives of Tabari or Ya'qubi concerning the fourth fitna and probably reflects 'public knowledge' of the war that was available in the Jazira. Dionysius tells us that al-Amin transported the treasure of al-Rashid and al-Ma'mun to Baghdad and was infamous for his debauchery and his neglect of the affairs of state. Al-Ma'mun, by contrast, was renowned for his knowledge of 'the book and the law', which seems to be a Syriac translation of 'the Quran and the sunna', the phrase used by al-Ma'mun in his appeal to his Khurasanian armies.[27]

Dionysius identifies the casus belli as al-Amin's refusal to give up the treasure. Most of his narrative from this point on deals with events in the Jazira, but it does identify a number of red-letter days that correspond roughly to the narrative found in Tabari and Ya'qubi:

- Tahir's defeat of al-Amin's general 'Ali (XII. 6 [IV, 491 / III, 22]);
- The killing of al-Amin while he was hiding in the house of a cloth merchant after trying to escape by swimming across the Tigris (XII. 8 [IV, 497 / III, 30]);[28]
- Harthama's criticism of the murder of al-Amin, his subsequent killing, his companions' killing of his killers and the companions' crucifixion by al-Ma'mun (XII. 8 [IV, 497/ III, 31]);
- Ibrahim's election by the people of Baghdad, who feared that power would leave the 'Hashemites' (XII. 9 [IV, 498 / III, 35]);
- Al-Ma'mun's transfer of his capital to Baghdad after hearing that his troops were holed up in Rafiqa and Kufa (XII. 11 [IV, 505 / III, 45]).

27. MS XII. 6 (IV, 490 / III, 20). Crone and Hinds 1986: 60 and Marsham 2009: 183 note that this was a recurrent slogan used by rebels to condemn 'tyrants' with whom they disagreed. Marsham 2009: 72 questions whether the slogan might have a pre-Marwanid history and (at 315) discusses the changing meaning of sunna.

28. Compare the moving account by al-Amin's companion Ibn Sallam in Tabari III, 920 / XXXI, 190.

There are several differences between the Syriac account and that of Tabari, which reflect the fact that Dionysius, though probably a contemporary of the events, sometimes misunderstands their significance. Thus he refers to the Baghdadis' fear that the Hashemites will lose out through al-Ma'mun's nomination of 'Ali al-Rida as his successor, without realizing that the Alids are also Hashemites. To our author, 'Hashemites' seems to mean simply the Abbasid family.[29]

Dionysius' understanding of Harthama's execution is also quite different from Tabari's. According to Tabari, Harthama was killed as the result of a ruse by al-Ma'mun's vizier al-Fadl ibn Sahl (d. 818), who wanted to remove him from the scene after the occupation of Baghdad.[30] The Syriac narrative shares Tabari's impression that Harthama was more sympathetic to al-Amin than Tahir was and wanted to protect his person, if not his empire.[31] But Dionysius goes further than Tabari does by making this desire the reason for Harthama's execution. One reason that his explanation is different may be that he seems to have no sense of the vizierate as a feature of caliphal politics: he never mentions al-Fadl ibn Sahl, al-Ma'mun's vizier, to whom Tabari ascribes many of the key decisions of the first phase of the civil war.[32] And while Dionysius is aware of al-Fadl's son, al-Hasan ibn Sahl (d. 850/51), he says nothing of his lineage.[33] Instead, al-Hasan is simply one general among many. This narrative illustrates the difficulty that Dionysius faced in acquiring accurate information about events in the east or about the details of Muslim political ideas, which he may not have always fully understood. These gaps in knowledge, in turn, indicate that we should not exaggerate Dionysius' personal connections to the caliph or to the court in Baghdad, which were probably mediated through his patron, 'Abd Allah ibn Tahir.[34]

29. There is a similar elision between Abbasids and Hashemites in the description of al-Mu'tasim's entry into Baghdad in X1234 (II, 29/20), which probably also comes from Dionysius.

30. Tabari III, 1026 / XXXII, 79, with Kennedy 1986: 154.

31. MS XII. 8 (IV, 496–97 / III, 30).

32. Sourdel 1959–60: 200.

33. For the role of the Sahlids as viziers, see Sourdel 1959–60: 196–216. The Sahlids were an Iranian family of Zoroastrian origin who had been clients of the Barmakid viziers and had survived the latter's fall. Al-Hasan, unlike his father, was never known as *wazīr* (minister) to Muslim historians; rather, he is referred to as *amīr* (commander).

34. The misunderstandings in the accounts of Iraqi history preserved in Michael make them more likely to be derived from Dionysius rather than from a later Muslim source that might be closer to the account given by Tabari.

Nasr ibn Shabath and the Fortification of the Jazira

The majority of the Syriac narrative on the fourth fitna is dedicated to the re-bellion in the Jazira. Our author describes how a man named 'Amr escaped from prison in Samosata and went on to raid Palestine, and he reports that 'Amr was later accompanied by one Nasr, an Arab soldier stationed in Arme-nia who took the opportunity to seize Samosata, Serug and Kaishum in 811.[35] These two are the most prominent of a series of warlords who take control of the Jazira and northern Syria, while others take Harran, Tella, Reshaina, Mar-din, Cyrrhus, Qinnasrin, Antioch and Apamea.[36] The narrative is tightly fo-cused on the Jazira, and much of the action is set in otherwise unknown vil-lages. This feature, together with the confusion of the military narrative, suggests a close contemporary eyewitness.[37]

The Syriac narrative charts the actions of the rebels against the regime forces sent to fight them and frames the conflict in terms of a contest between Arabs (Tayyaye) and Persians.[38] The activities of the Arab rebels devastate the local Christian population. 'Amr constructs new walls at Samosata using a corvée of Christian peasants.[39] The Gannawaye Arabs billet their families

35. MS XII. 6 (IV, 491 / III, 21–22). Serug and Kaishum were small towns that had not been previously significant. The prominence they enjoy in this narrative is solely a function of their use as rebel capitals. Dionysius' coverage of the rebellion is also summarized in X1234 (II, 11–15 / 7–10) and in BH Chron 137 / 175ff.

36. MS XII. 7 (IV, 493 / III, 25 and IV, 484 / III, 27). Cf. the list of new warlords in this period in Ya'qubi II, 540–41 / III, 1207.

37. Dionysius' personal account of Nasr's siege of Edessa is given at MS XII. 9 (IV, 499 / III, 38). The detailed list of articles that Nasr was allowed to take with him after his surrender also sug-gests either an eyewitness or access to documentary evidence: MS XII. 12 (IV, 511 / III, 53).

38. In book 12 of Michael, 'Tayyaye' is normally used to mean Syrian/Jaziran Arabs rather than Muslims in general. It is usually contrasted with Christians or with Persians (see IV, 498 / III, 31 for Tahir's Persians' massacre of Arabs; IV, 499 / III, 38 for hopes for the Persians' victory over the Arabs; IV, 510 / III, 53 for Nasr's forces' killing of Persians and Christians) but some-times also with other specific groups, such as the Banu Tanukh near Aleppo (IV, 497 / III, 31, where the contrast is between Muslim and Christians) or the Kufans who held Callinicum against Nasr (IV, 497 / III, 30, where the contrast is between Kufans and the Syrian Arab rebels). But, confusingly, 'Tayyaye' can also be used to refer to the caliph's Muslim subjects in general, and both al-Amin and al-Ma'mun are called 'kings of the Tayyaye' (IV, 500 / III, 36 and IV, 505 / III, 45).

39. MS XII. 7 (IV, 492 / III, 27).

on Edessa and raise tribute from the population to build new walls.[40] Later
they seize the village of Mariba near Harran and confiscate the property of the
poor, and after they are driven off by Nasr, he does the same in 813.[41] When
'Abd Allah ibn Tahir besieges Nasr in the fortress of Balash near Serug, Nasr
uses Christian women and children as human shields to deter 'Abd Allah from
bombarding the walls.[42] And the rebels regularly pillage monasteries, including the famous monastery of Qenneshre, where Dionysius was trained.[43]

A particularly noteworthy feature of the narrative is the author's interest in,
and his ambivalence toward, the construction of walls around cities. His hesi-
tation is striking because late antique Syriac literature often takes pride in the
fact that the great cities of the region were walled. The fifth-century *Doctrina
Addai* boasts of Edessa's impregnable walls, protected by the promises of Jesus
himself.[44] And the sixth-century *History of Karka de Beth Slouq* records how
the kings of the distant past had transported various aristocratic families to the
city and built its walls and towers.[45] In both cases, I believe that this attitude
of pride in the cities' walls reflects the degree to which local elites were embedded in the empires in which their cities lay, as well as celebration of their ability
to resist foreign invaders or rebels. Such ideas certainly persisted in the caliphate: conquest treaties negotiated between the Arabs and the Christians of Syria
often stipulated that city walls not be torn down.[46]

However, these sentiments were complicated by the Abbasid period. Hugh
Kennedy has observed that the caliphate underwent a process of *decastellamento*: rural elites increasingly abandoned fortified dwellings and were drawn
to the great cities.[47] One explanation for this phenomenon may lie in the

40. MS XII. 7 (IV, 492 / III, 27).

41. MS XII. 8 (IV, 497 / III, 31).

42. MS XII. 12 (IV, 510 / III, 53).

43. MS XII. 6 (IV, 492 / III, 22) on the ravaging of villages and monasteries near Edessa; MS
XII. 11 (IV, 507 / III, 47) for the monastery of Borim. See also XII. 12 (IV, 508 / III, 50ff.) for a
Khurramite attack on the monastery of Qartmin. On this movement, see further Crone 2012:
22–27 and 46–72.

44. *Doctrina Addai*. See further Wood 2010: ch. 4.

45. See the *History of Karka de Beth Slouq*, 509–11, for construction by the Assyrians, Seleu-
cids and Persians.

46. Donner 1981: 246.

47. Kennedy 2006: 30. Kennedy is here adapting the term *incastellamento* used by Toubert
1973 to describe the creation of fortified hilltop villages by independent lords in early medieval
Italy.

attraction of potential employment in new cities such as Baghdad, Raqqa and Mosul, where the caliphate's massive wealth offered great incentives and opportunities. Another may be that the discrepancy between the military force of the caliph and that of the landed elite was now great enough to tip the balance against any lord who tried to defy the caliph, except in times of political instability or in the most inaccessible territories. It seems possible that the Abbasid caliphs took advantage of changes in the composition of the elite to demolish fortified sites. A Byzantine resurgence seemed ever less likely, whereas the use of fortifications by rebels rather than by the caliph's own forces was more likely. Dionysius' narrative suggests that this last potential factor was true in the Jazira, where al-Mansur and al-Ma'mun both razed fortresses after their respective victories in civil wars.[48]

From the point of view of local Christian and Muslim populations, the downside of this caliphal policy was that although it discouraged revolts by local elites, it also left cities open to attack by mobile forces based in the steppe, as Nasr's forces seem to have been. Chase Robinson notes that the historian Azdi identified the demolition of Mosul's walls as the point at which the city's elites lost their independence, which allowed Mosul's integration into the governing structures of the empire but also caused its vulnerability to the Bedouin armies of the Jaziran steppe.[49] The rapidity with which the cities of the Levant fell into rebel hands may be linked to their lack of walls.[50] In this region, at least, earlier Abbasid decastellamento may have been premature.

The rebel rulers soon took steps to fortify their new possessions, and this move was a significant source of misfortune for local Christian populations who had to build and pay for the walls. Dionysius embeds his account of the new fortification into a broader description of extortion and ruin. This period of anarchy was a period of 'Arab' rule and of fortification:

> They began to take captives, to pillage and to oppress the lands. 'Amr rebuilt the wall of Samosata with an army of poor Christians. Abu Šok Gannawaya rebuilt the walls of Edessa with money he had taken from the

48. Al-Mansur destroys the walls of Edessa: MS XII. 3 (IV, 482 / III, 8) and Theophanes AM 6241; al-Ma'mun destroys walls in Cyrrhus and 'many other places in Syria and Palestine': MS XII. 16 (IV, 524 / III, 75). Also note Ya'qubi II, 560 / III, 1225.

49. Robinson 2000: 163.

50. This point is made explicitly in the case of Aleppo (MS XII. 8 [IV, 497 / III, 31]), but it is also implicit in the fact that most of the rebel rulers sought to fortify their cities soon after capturing them.

Edessenes. . . . Nasr seized Resh-Kepha, Serug and Kaishum and built
three walls around Kaishum. The reconstruction of the walls of Edessa,
Samosata and Kaishum, in the time of the Arabs, took place in the year
AG 1125 [815]. And soon afterwards the walls of Kaishum and Samosata
were razed.[51]

The protection of these walls allowed the rebels to resist several of the Abbasid armies sent against them. Occasionally, Dionysius is able to tell a story in
which would-be pillagers are defied from behind fortifications, as at Nasr's siege
of Edessa, whose walls had been built by the Gannawaye Arabs. But in general,
the fortification of the region is a sign of its lawlessness and of the limitations
of the rule of the government. Unlike authors writing in Syriac in the fifth and
sixth centuries, Dionysius does not see walls as symbols of civic pride for a local
elite, but as memorials to past oppression and as portents of future injustice.
His stance is much more passive than that taken by Joshua the Stylite, writing
of the Persian siege of Edessa in the early sixth century: for Joshua, the defence
of his city is a joint enterprise between Roman armies and government and the
local population. By contrast, for Dionysius all military forces, whether Arab or
Persian, are untrustworthy and dangerous, and the end of the conflict is
achieved only through the deus ex machina of 'Abd Allah ibn Tahir, who is
responsible for forcing Nasr and the other warlords into submission.[52]

Dionysius and 'Abd Allah ibn Tahir

Dionysius' representation of 'Abd Allah sets him apart from both the rebels
and the other agents of the government.[53] For instance, when 'Abd Allah's
father, Tahir, is sent to the Jazira, the Christians hope that he will prove a just

51. MS XII. 7 (IV, 494 / III, 27). The last sentence quoted here is written in red ink in the
manuscript.
52. The exultation at al-Ma'mun's victory is especially clear in the X1234 (II, 15/10). 'Abd
Allah's preference seems to have been to co-opt rebels of all sorts rather than fight and punish
them: Ya'qubi II, 560–61 / III, 1225–26.
53. The *Samaritan Chronicle* (75) gives a similar depiction of 'Abd Allah as a man who can
restore order and prevent the oppression of non-Muslims by warlords. Unlike other governors,
'Abd Allah is not depicted as being focused solely on extracting high taxes: 'He came against
the rebels with an army the like of which had never been seen. When he went forth from Baghdad he conquered the lands before him; God gave him victory and worked good deeds through
him, and he crushed all the tyrants of the land'.

ruler, but instead he increases taxes and mistreats the people of Edessa and Serug.[54] ʿAbd Allah, by contrast, is merciful and fair, even in his battle with Nasr.[55] He protects Christians in Mesopotamia from the demands of local Arabs that their churches be destroyed.[56] And his piety is described favourably in an account of his praying in Jerusalem after his campaign in Palestine.[57]

Assuming that the author of these sections is Dionysius, the positive characterization is probably explained by ʿAbd Allah's role as Dionysius' patron and as the person who facilitated Dionysius' defence of his claim to the patriarchate against his Gubbite rivals and represented al-Maʾmun in resolving the dispute between the Jacobites.[58] Dionysius gives a detailed account of the stage-managing of his encounter with the Gubbites in 825:

> At this time, the emir ʿAbd Allah came to Callinicum. Abiram and his band of rebels arrived and came to find him to obtain a diploma (*sigiliyun*). The patriarch Dionysius also came to the same place.
>
> The patriarch entered first, and the emir asked him about Abiram and his band. The patriarch told him about his rebellion against the patriarch Cyriacus and the rest of his actions and how he [Abiram] wanted to obtain a diploma to trouble the land, because no one would accept him. Then the emir ordered the wretch to be brought in and asked him, 'Who are you?' He replied, 'I am the patriarch. He over there is not the real [patriarch], and I am opposed to him', and he explained the question of the formula (*bart qānā*) [of the heavenly bread].[59]

According to Dionysius, the formula was a pretext for Abiram's seizure of power, which was causing dissension in the church. Dionysius complains to ʿAbd Allah:

> When the one who is called an 'imam' stands to pray before the masses (*sagiʾē*),[60] he takes the part of the Books that he wants and recites it at the start of his prayer, and none of the people who are praying behind him

---

54. MS XII. 9 (IV, 502 / III, 32).
55. MS XII. 12 (IV, 510–12 / III, 53–55).
56. X1234 (II, 16/11).
57. MS XII. 13 (IV, 513 / III, 61).
58. MS XII. 13 (IV, 509–12 / III, 55–58).
59. MS XII. 12 (IV, 508 / III, 55–56).
60. Dionysius' choice of word for the congregation is interesting, since it seems to emphasize the patriarch/imam's role as a guarantor of order, as well as stressing the common role of

should say, 'Do not recite that passage but rather recite another', as these bold men have dared to do and stirred up trouble in the church.

'Abd Allah orders the officer of the guard to go out and establish whom the Christians want as their leader. When the officer returns, he proclaims their reply in a loud voice: 'Abiram is not our chief; he is not even a Christian'. Then, when 'Abd Allah sees Dionysius' diploma, signed by his father, Tahir, he strips Abiram of his *birunā* (the patriarchal insignia) and expels him with a threat: 'If I hear that you have been roaming around the cities [presenting yourself as patriarch], your blood will be on your head [i.e., any punishment you suffer will be your own fault]'.[61]

However, the Abiramites decide to escalate the situation by appealing to connections in Baghdad. They use a document allegedly signed by 'Ali ibn Abi Talib that was in the possession of Gubba Barraya to acquire a fresh diploma for Abiram with the help of the Alids of Baghdad.[62] Presumably the Alids had acquired this diploma directly from al-Ma'mun. 'Abd Allah then summons both Dionysius and Abiram to Raqqa, where he writes to al-Ma'mun to investigate the matter. After twenty days, 'Abd Allah receives a letter from al-Ma'mun telling him that the Christians have petitioned him to proclaim Abiram patriarch, though their incumbent patriarch is Dionysius. The letter concludes: 'Convoke the Jacobites of the region and confirm the authority of whomever they accept'. 'Abd Allah responds by giving Dionysius a diploma to annul Abiram's claims. He tells his chamberlain to take Dionysius by the hand and proclaim him patriarch outside the palace. The chamberlain does so, 'before all the Christians and Muslims'. He informs the rebels that the patriarch now has the right to judge them, excommunicate them and expel them.[63]

Dionysius' depiction of the fourth fitna in the Jazira cannot be separated from his political links to 'Abd Allah. Dionysius' legitimacy over Abiram rests on 'Abd Allah's intervention, and this fact probably motivates his portrayal of the general as a just restorer of order. By displaying Tahir's diploma and warning

---

Dionysius and al-Ma'mun as imams in the sense of prayer leaders. *Kenušāyā* is perhaps a more usual word for a Christian congregation.

61. MS XII. 12 (IV, 509–10 / III, 56). The involvement of the urban population in the election of a bishop has good late Roman precedents: see Van Nuffelen 2011 and Norton 2007: 240–41.

62. Who these Alids were is unclear. Bernheimer 2013: 3 observes that the family of 'Ali could be defined much more broadly than simply as the descendants of Hasan and Husayn.

63. MS XII. 12 (IV, 510–11 / III, 57–58). See the brief discussion in Nabe-von Schönberg 1977: 63.

of religious innovation and dissent, Dionysius is able to present himself as standing for consistency and order. Throughout the narrative, Dionysius signals his special access to ʿAbd Allah, who speaks to Dionysius before speaking to Abiram and excludes Abiram from his audience until he has consulted with Dionysius. Thus there is always the sense that Abiram is the interloper and Dionysius the rightful patriarch. In Dionysius' view, al-Maʾmun's attitude toward the Christians is primarily pragmatic, and any decisions to be made on the spot are delegated to ʿAbd Allah. There is a notion that the patriarch should be established by consensus, but in practice, it is ʿAbd Allah who decides where that consensus lies and backs up the rights of the patriarch with force.

However, the Gubbites also have their own allies in the form of the Alids of Baghdad. The fact that they are able to petition these allies to get a diploma of their own even after ʿAbd Allah's ruling demonstrates that the caliphate was, in practice, a multicentred network rather than a simple hierarchy running straight from the provinces to the caliph via the governors. In Dionysius' account, it is thus possible for the Gubbites to appeal over ʿAbd Allah's head directly to Baghdad using their contacts with the Alids.

That their appeal was possible may reflect the reconfiguration of the hierarchies of Maʾmunid administration after the civil war. Even though Raqqa had been a centre of government for the Jazira since al-Rashid, it may not have been clear to actors on the ground just how far al-Maʾmun would be able or willing to back up his general ʿAbd Allah, especially since he had only recently established his capital at Baghdad. Additionally, the Gubbites' use of a letter from ʿAli points to the particular significance of the Alids under al-Maʾmun after his acknowledgement of ʿAli al-Rida as his successor and the caliph's adoption of Alid slogans and language. ʿAli al-Rida's death should not necessarily be seen as a turning point for the Alids: al-Maʾmun always presented the death as an accident, and the relationship between the Abbasids and the Alids seems to have remained ambiguous for the rest of al-Maʾmun's reign. In this context, the Gubbites' appeal, though ultimately unsuccessful, does not seem an unreasonable reading of politics in Baghdad at this time.

Dionysius in Egypt

The account of the fourth fitna in Michael's *Chronicle* continues with the arrival of al-Maʾmun's forces in Egypt. Once more, Michael is likely to be reliant on Dionysius, who was a contemporary of these events. Here we are told that the time of anarchy in the Jazira found a parallel in the continuous warfare of two local warlords, Sari and Gauri, who seized all of Egypt's wealth for them-selves. After their deaths, their sons continued their struggle, but, like Nasr in the Jazira, they were ultimately pacified by a combination of offers of employ-ment and an overwhelming show of force from 'Abd Allah ibn Tahir in 826. A group of Andalusian Arab refugees resisted 'Abd Allah more strenuously, hav-ing taken over the city of Alexandria and dispossessed many of its Christian inhabitants. These Andalusians were eventually defeated and expelled.[64] Here, too, 'Abd Allah ibn Tahir appears as the restorer of order and the guarantor of justice for the Christians against local Arab Muslim forces.

However, Dionysius inserts himself into the narrative just after 'Abd Allah's victory, leading to a scene that is unprecedented in earlier ecclesiastical history: the author provides personal information in the manner of the excursuses of classical historians such as Herodotus or Ammianus Marcel-linus. Dionysius describes how the confiscation of churches in Edessa prompts him to seek out 'Abd Allah in Egypt to ask him to intervene against his subordinates.[65] Soon after, he is personally summoned to Egypt to act as a negotiator with Christian rebels (the Bashmurites, or Biamaye) in the Egyptian Delta.

In a series of rich accounts, Dionysius takes the opportunity to describe not only his meeting with 'Abd Allah but also his meetings with the officials of the Theodosian (Miaphysite) church in Egypt, as well as his reflections on the antiquities of ancient Egypt such as the Pyramids and the Nilometer. Diony-sius' visit to Egypt is especially important for his own self-fashioning as an orthodox patriarch. He stresses that he was recognized as patriarch in person by his Alexandrian counterparts and that he was the first patriarch of Antioch to visit Egypt since the start of the seventh century.[66] The mutual recognition of Alexandria and Antioch had been an important source of legitimacy for

64. MS XII. 13 (IV, 513–15 / III, 59–60). For these events more broadly, see Dunn 1975: 70–75. After their expulsion, the Andalusians conquered Byzantine Crete (Canard 1971), a fact that is not mentioned in the Syriac compilations. A long account of these disruptions can also be found in the *History of the Patriarchs*, PO 10:428ff., and in Tabari III, 1086ff. / XXXII, 159ff. The narra-tives in the *History of the Patriarchs* that deal with Dionysius are part of the so-called fourth cycle, written by the scribe John, which runs c. 767–880. Den Heijer 1991 and den Heijer 1989.

65. MS XII. 13 (IV, 513–15 / III, 61–62). See also X1234 (II, 17–21 / 12–14) and BH HE II, 359 on Dionysius' first visit to Egypt. His second visit is treated in BH HE II, 373–91 and X1234 (II, 266–68 / 200–202).

66. MS XII. 13 (IV, 516 / III, 63) and MS XII. 17 (IV, 525 / III, 80). Karel Innemée notes that the patriarchs of both 'Syria' and 'Egypt' (Dionysius and Jacob) were mentioned in frescos and

both of the Severan Miaphysite patriarchs, but this had normally been under-taken through synodal letters.[67] In visiting Egypt personally, and advertising his Egyptian journey through his history, Dionysius emphasizes an achieve-ment that had been equalled by few of his predecessors, an achievement ren-dered possible by his close relations to ʿAbd Allah and al-Maʾmun.[68] The nar-ratives of his Egyptian visits repay analysis as examples of Dionysius' depiction of good and bad Muslim rulers and their effects on Christians.

In the first of these narratives, Dionysius recounts his journey from Joppa to the island of Tanis in the Delta in 826 to ask ʿAbd Allah for help in preventing the destruction of churches in Edessa. Delayed by storms at sea, he is preceded by Theodosius, bishop of Edessa. In a section that claims to reproduce Diony-sius' words verbatim, Dionysius explains his delay to ʿAbd Allah ibn Tahir:

> When I entered the camp of the Persians, he [ʿAbd Allah] criticized me for travelling by sea. . . . He said, 'What obliged you to come to Egypt when you could have informed me by letter of what you desired, especially since your brother, who was the chief interested party [lit. the master of the thing], has come in person?' I replied to him, 'He is a metropolitan, O great one, who has come on his own account because it is his city, Edessa, that suffers; but it is I who am the most afflicted and oppressed because our churches are being destroyed and our laws are being abolished, and because my interest extends to all lands'.[69]

ʿAbd Allah asks why Dionysius cannot simply communicate by letter, prob-ably the question in many readers' minds, as well. But by travelling to see ʿAbd Allah in person, Dionysius tells us, he shows his commitment to his flock.

---

manuscript colophons at the monastery of Deir es-Surian in the Wadi Natrun, which was heavily patronized by monks from Takrit. Innemée 2016: 41; Innemée and Van Rompay 1998: 182.

67. Synodal letters are mentioned in MS XI. 3 (IV, 408 / II, 411) and XI. 5 (IV, 414 / II, 419), as well as in the *History of the Patriarchs* (PO 10:382, 393–95; 409). Cyriacus also received back-ing from his Alexandrian counterpart, Marcus, during the dispute over the heavenly bread for-mula: MS XII. 6 (IV, 492 / III, 25).

68. There had also been a breach in correspondence immediately before Dionysius' visit due to the fitna: *History of the Patriarchs* (PO 10:455). Egypt also features prominently in the earliest part of Dionysius' history, which opens with an account of the philosopher Probus in Egypt: Van Nuffelen forthcoming. In MS XII. 17 (IV, 525 / III, 80) Dionysius refers to the meeting of Athana-sius Gamala, patriarch of Antioch, with Andronicus of Alexandria to proclaim a union in 616, so Dionysius is likely to be Michael's source for the letters preserved in MS X. 26 (IV, 399 / II, 392).

69. MS XII. 13 (IV, 515–16 / III, 63).

Undertaking the trip also allows Dionysius to demonstrate his superiority over his brother Theodosius of Edessa: he is at pains to explain to ʿAbd Allah that he is not Theodosius' equal and that, as patriarch, he owns all the churches of the land and is responsible for all the Christians. On a practical level, Dionysius needs to make clear that patriarchal authority extends to all dioceses and that Theodosius is neither the ultimate master of these churches nor capable of making his own independent representations to ʿAbd Allah. I doubt that Dionysius actually viewed Theodosius as a threat, but he does seem to use his meeting with ʿAbd Allah to clarify the superiority of patriarchs over bishops for his Muslim patron. Though he does not say so explicitly, in making this trip, Dionysius may have also been underlining his own potential usefulness to ʿAbd Allah in dealing with Egyptian Christians in this newly acquired territory.

After asking ʿAbd Allah to censure his deputies in the Jazira, Dionysius makes a second deputation on behalf of the citizens of Tanis. He has learned during his visit that the Tanisiotes are suffering greatly because they are overcharged by the mainlanders for fresh water. In addition, they are unable to pay the jizya (poll tax), which has been set at an excessive level. To raise the money, the Tanisiotes report that they have been forced to sell their children into temporary servitude, and their daughters are often made pregnant by their masters.[70] ʿAbd Allah listens to Dionysius' request and orders that the jizya for Tanis be set at the level that was normal in the Jazira—forty-eight dirhams for the wealthy, twenty-four for those of middling wealth and twelve for the poor.[71]

The subtext of this account is that although order is restored by ʿAbd Allah, the achievement of good governance for Christians still requires the intercession of a well-placed patriarch such as Dionysius. The local clergy are incapable of resolving the oppression of the Tanisiotes, but Dionysius is able to 'export' the kind of entente enjoyed by the Christians of the Jazira to Egypt. One implication of this scene, therefore, is that Islamic law prescribes a fair and manageable level of taxation on Christians, but that it must be implemented properly. Unjust practice is the fault of wicked officials on the ground, not of the caliph. And proper administration requires both good Muslim officials (like ʿAbd Allah) and Christians who can provide them with effective information.

---

70. This use of labour to compensate for debt is part of a wider pattern in Egypt that Papaconstantinou 2016 has described as central to the dominance of towns over the countryside.

71. MS XII. 13 (IV, 516 / III, 63–64).

The Second Visit to Egypt

Similar themes are apparent in Dionysius' account of his second visit to Egypt in 830. This visit took place as a consequence of Dionysius' meeting with al-Ma'mun at Kaishum in the Jazira, where the caliph was conducting the war against the Byzantines. Al-Ma'mun engaged Dionysius to travel to Egypt to act as his intermediary in negotiations with the Biamaye rebels in order to avoid further bloodshed.[72] Al-Ma'mun and Dionysius travelled together to Damascus and then to Pelusium on the Egyptian coast, from where the caliph dispatched Dionysius to the Biamaye 'together with the bishops you have with you and the Egyptian bishops', including the Egyptian patriarch Joseph.[73]

The Biamaye lived in a region of marshes and tiny islands from which they had resisted efforts at taxation both during the period of anarchy and before it.[74] They had already experienced one major caliphal campaign to put down their rebellion, which had culminated in the occupation of several of their villages by the caliph's forces.

According to his account of the events, when Dionysius meets the leaders of the Biamaye, they lay the blame for the conflict on the oppressive occupation of their land by the general Abu al-Wazir, who has charged them heavy tribute, imprisoned their people and allowed his soldiers to commit rape. They also claim that Abu al-Wazir has pushed the caliph's commander, Afshin (d. 841), to try to exterminate the men of the Biamaye. They report that the second revolt was sparked by an incident in which the Biamaye interrupted soldiers trying to rape a woman, prompting the Biamaye to rise up and kill the occupying forces.[75]

---

72. 'Biamaye' means 'sons of the forty' in Coptic. The (probably false) etymology of the name casts the Biamaye as the descendants of forty Roman soldiers who remained in the Delta after the land was seized by the Arabs. As Mikhail 2016: 189–91 observes, this etymology may imply a sense of ethnic difference from other 'Coptic' populations and possibly helps to explain the tension between the Biamaye and the patriarch of Alexandria.

73. MS XII. 16 (IV, 522–23 / III, 76–77).

74. Dunn 1975: 80–87; Kennedy 1998: 80–82; Sijpesteijn 2017: 63–70; Mikhail 2016: 75–76, 121, 125, 189–91; Wissa 2016. Lev 2012 rebuts speculation in earlier scholarship (e.g., Lapidus 1972) that the Biamaye rebellions constituted key moments in the conversion of Egypt to Islam.

75. MS XII. 16 (IV, 523–24 / III, 77–78). The *History of the Patriarchs* lays the blame much more squarely on Afshin himself (PO 10:488): 'He made no attempt to differentiate between the innocent and the guilty'. For Afshin's initial difficulties in entering the marshes of the Delta, see PO 10:494.

Dionysius tells Afshin that the Biamaye are willing to make peace, but Afshin replies that the peace has been broken and that Dionysius should tell the caliph that peace is not possible. He then orders his soldiers to set fire to the Biamaye's houses. Many Persians are killed by the Biamaye, but ultimately the whole Biamaye population is taken into captivity.[76] When he arrives on the scene, al-Maʾmun puts a stop to the fighting.

Because the livelihoods of the Biamaye are based on fishing and making papyrus, al-Maʾmun suggests that the captives be relocated to Baghdad. The entire population is deported by sea via Antioch, with many dying en route. However, those taken captive in war are sold as slaves in Damascus. Dionysius comments: 'Such a thing had never been seen before in the empire of the Tayyaye—selling people who paid the jizya.'[77]

Dionysius' exclamation points to the contract that, he asserts, existed between the Muslim conquerors on the one hand and Christians and Jews as dhimmīs on the other. Individual cities were believed to have concluded their own treaties with the conquerors that laid down rates of tribute and religious freedoms in exchange for promises to accept Muslim rule and to refrain from aiding the enemies of the Muslims. Such treaties were made only with 'peoples of the book' (which often meant only Jews or Christians) and were dependent on continued peaceful behaviour. By the Abbasid period, the treaties of individual cities were increasingly replaced by uniform agreements for all dhimmīs, in which rates of taxation were set at consistent (high) levels.[78]

Dhimmīs were subject to a number of social liabilities, including the payment of the jizya by adult males, the receipt of only half of the diya (blood money) owed to Muslims for equivalent injuries and being accorded half the

76. MS XII. 16 (IV, 525 / III, 79). The History of the Patriarchs simply reports that the patriarchs were unsuccessful in persuading the Biamaye (PO 10:493). In general, the History is less sympathetic to the rebels: it acknowledges the injustice of the occupying forces but views rebellion as an act of 'self-destruction' (PO 10:487).

77. MS XII. 16 (IV, 527 / III, 83). Another account of al-Maʾmun's visit is given in Tabari III, 1107 / XXXII, 191. The History of the Patriarchs (PO 10:494) says simply that the captives were sold as slaves in Baghdad, and it does not differentiate between individuals seized in war and those taken by treaty.

78. Calder 1993: 132. Note that the debate over the tax rate of Edessa hinges on different accounts of the conquest treaty. Zaman 1997: 92–96 persuasively rebuts Calder's arguments for a tenth-century date for Abu Yusuf's Kitab al-kharaj, which is probably a product of the late eighth century.

testamentary weight of Muslim witnesses in criminal courts. Nor could the dhimmīs bear arms at this time. These disabilities were deemed justified because the dhimmīs were both conquered and protected: it was the duty of the Muslims to fight on their behalf if they were threatened. Indeed, in one story relating to the early conquests, money taken in jizya is repaid to the Christians when the Muslims find themselves unable to defend the Christians' city against a Byzantine raid. We ought to read the story not as an account of a historical event but rather as an item of case law, a statement that the Christians' legal disabilities were part of a contract that could be violated by Christian rebellion or by Muslim failure to guarantee order.[79]

Dionysius presents the enslavement of the vanquished Biamaye as a gross violation of the treaty between Muslims and Christians. For him, it is an example of the abuse of the caliph's authority by his supposed servants: they treat the Christians that they are obliged to protect in an oppressive manner. The revolt is a forced reaction to this oppression, and it is brought to an end by the order-restoring presence of the caliph himself.

Dionysius' criticisms here echo the criticisms of contemporary Muslim commentators. Edward Zychowicz-Coghill, in his study of the Egyptian Arab author Ibn ʿAbd al-Hakam, notes that the he practically equates 'the Copts' with the population that did not resist the conquest (in contrast to 'the Romans', who rejected the treaty and fought the Arabs). On one hand, Ibn ʿAbd al-Hakam uses this device to stress the subservience of the native Egyptians, whose only function is to toil on the land and generate tax revenue for their rulers (first the Romans and later the Arabs). But within his wider imperial apology, Ibn ʿAbd al-Hakam also stresses the duty owed by the Muslims to peoples who did not resist them and who therefore deserve the protections of dhimma.

A passage in Yaʿqubi's history makes a similar point more explicitly. Yaʿqubi reports that al-Maʾmun consulted an Egyptian jurist (faqīh), al-Harith ibn al-Miskin, about how he should treat the Biamaye. Ibn al-Miskin replied, 'If they were to rebel because of some wrong done to them, their lives or property may not be harmed'. According to Yaʿqubi,

> Al-Maʾmun replied, 'You are a jackass and Malik [ibn Anas, the founder of Ibn al-Miskin's legal school] is even more of a jackass. These are kuffār (unbelievers) who have a right to protection. When they are wronged, they appeal to the imams; they do not have a right to seek support by [their

79. Levy-Rubin 2011: 171–72; Friedmann 2003: 48–50.

swords/themselves]⁸⁰ or to shed the blood of Muslims in their own homes'.
Al-Ma'mun seized their leaders and had them transported to Baghdad.⁸¹

Zychowicz-Coghill reads these passages as reflecting criticism of the caliphal regime's mistreatment of Egyptian dhimmīs at a time when new
Khurasanian and Central Asian elites, such as 'Abd Allah ibn Tahir and Afshin,
were displacing Arab elite families (like that of Ibn 'Abd al-Hakam) who
claimed descent from the seventh-century conquerors. The disorder of the
Biamaye revolts was then cast as a consequence of the regime's failure to heed
the original agreements between the conquerors and the conquered. If
Zychowicz-Coghill is correct, Dionysius' argument about the rights of the
Biamaye as dhimmīs illustrates a use of Islamic history as a means of criticism
that transcended boundaries between Muslims and Christians.⁸² Nevertheless, Dionysius does not give the caliph himself a role in demanding the punishment of the Biamaye as Ya'qubi does. In laying the blame on Afshin, and in
describing his own failed intercession on behalf of the Biamaye, Dionysius is
attacking a personal opponent, but he is also legitimating his own links to al-
Ma'mun: it is not the caliph himself who acts tyrannically but his overmighty
Central Asian servant.

Dionysius Pleads with the Caliph

Even though his discussion of dhimmīs may constitute criticism of those in
power, Dionysius is careful to exempt his own patrons from this criticism.
According to the material preserved in Michael, Dionysius plays his part in the
defence of Christian rights by denouncing the oppression of Abu al-Wazir in
a brave act of free speech, in spite of the scepticism of the caliph's brother Abu
Ishaq (later the caliph al-Mu'tasim). But al-Ma'mun himself is exonerated in
this narrative, which quotes him as saying: 'My representatives were not acting
according to my will. . . . If I have pity on the Romans, who are my enemies,
how much more should I have pity on my subjects? If God wills it, I will re-
dress all these things'.⁸³

---

80. There is a lacuna here in the manuscripts. These are emendations suggested by the editor:
III, 1234 n. 3494.
81. Ya'qubi II, 569 / III, 1233–34.
82. Zychowicz-Coghill 2017: 47–52. Cf. H. Omar 2013; Mikhail 2016: 21.
83. MS XII. 17 (IV, 525 / III, 80).

This passage depicts al-Ma'mun as making a clear difference between his Roman enemies in times of war and his Christian subjects; Dionysius undermines any notion that all Christians should simply be lumped together. Al-Ma'mun's subsequent actions toward the Biamaye fit the image of a just monarch restoring order: he remits half of the taxes of Egypt and orders his officers to avoid force in administering the law (both of these steps are credible responses to rebellion to restore stability and prosperity).[84] His deportation of the Biamaye to Baghdad is represented by Dionysius as an agreement for the benefit of both parties, rather than as the punishment it seems to be in Ya'qubi. Later on, the Biamaye fight on behalf of the caliph to put down the Zanj revolt in the marshes of Iraq.[85] On the other hand, Dionysius concludes this chapter by decrying 'the calamities that multiplied in Egypt after the caliph left', when 'the Persians entered the villages and chained those who rested ten by ten and twenty by twenty, without finding out who was guilty and who was innocent. . . . The roads were filled with those who had been unjustly killed. The sword, captivity, famine and pestilence reigned over the land of Egypt at this time'.[86]

The *History of the Patriarchs of Alexandria* gives a rather different account of Dionysius' audience with al-Ma'mun. Here, too, Dionysius blames the tax collectors for the rebellion, but his criticism results in the caliph telling him to leave Egypt. Al-Ma'mun warns him: 'If this statement is reported to my brother Ibrahim [Abu Ishaq, the future al-Mu'tasim], he will put you to death, because the tax collectors are his followers'.[87] Dionysius departs 'sadly', narrowly escaping an enraged Abu Ishaq.[88] Dionysius seems to have suppressed this scene to make his intervention seem more effective and al-Ma'mun more sympathetic and powerful.

Dionysius' ability to intervene on behalf of the Tanisiotes and the Biamaye stems, in part, from the reorganization of the administration of Egypt under al-Ma'mun, who placed it within a supergovernate that included the Jazira, Syria and Palestine and that was governed first by 'Abd Allah ibn Tahir and then by Abu Ishaq. Al-Ma'mun's victory in the fitna gave him a mandate to establish new governmental structures, and this meant that individuals in the

84. MS XII. 17 (IV, 527 / III, 83).
85. MS XII. 18 (IV, 529 / III, 84).
86. MS XII. 17 (IV, 527 / III, 83).
87. *History of the Patriarchs*, PO 10:495.
88. *History of the Patriarchs*, PO 10:496.

Jazira who had enjoyed early access to 'Abd Allah in Raqqa could maintain their ties to him as 'Abd Allah's power grew.

Dionysius' narrative reinforces a positive impression of al-Ma'mun as a ruler who restrains his own troublesome servants. Caliphal rule, which Dionysius endorses through his negotiations with the Biamaye, is based on just principles that ought to protect Christians. Nevertheless, there are several silences in Dionysius' narrative that indicate points of weakness in his own position. Abu al-Wazir, whom Dionysius blames for the oppression of the Biamaye, is never brought to task by the caliph. It is possible that Dionysius is also being economical with the truth when he tells us that the Biamaye were willing to make peace and that it was Afshin who insisted on further warfare, or that the decision to deport the Biamaye was the product of an agreement between them and al-Ma'mun, rather than something imposed by force. Without external corroborating evidence, we should obviously be wary of taking these details at face value, since they dovetail rather neatly with Dionysius' agenda, which places himself and al-Ma'mun at centre stage and presents al-Ma'mun's rule as relatively benevolent.

This presentation of the justice of al-Ma'mun's government takes place against an understated context in which Christians were forbidden to bear arms against the government. Dionysius' depiction of the rebellion is complicated by the fact that he wishes to emphasize his own prestigious intercession, but the *History of the Patriarchs of Alexandria* is much more explicit in condemning the rebels for their foolish act of 'self-destruction'.[89] But the Biamaye revolt was a sensitive issue for Dionysius precisely because there were also other Christians who continued traditions of arms bearing and were sometimes willing to use these to oppose the caliph's agents or aid his opponents.[90] This ability to threaten the government could act as an important guarantee of rights in a preindustrial society, especially for people who lived in difficult terrain such as highlands, deserts or marshland. But it was a model that Dionysius, who relied on official support for his own rank and sought to monopolize

---

89. *History of the Patriarchs*, PO 10:487.

90. Cobb 2001: 114–16 discusses the revolt of Theodore at Baalbek and his subsequent flight to the Byzantines. Thomas of Marga V, 13 (294 /524–26) describes the warlike villagers of Zarn, who killed the caliph's tax collector and then were co-opted into government as 'poachers turned gamekeepers'. *Chronicle of Zuqnin*, 196–207 / 181–89 describes the rebellion of John of Pheison during the Abbasid revolution, his conflict with the Arabs of Qulab and his eventual recognition by the Abbasid governor 'Abd Allah.

Christian influence with the caliph, was keen to criticize or downplay. In Edessa, Dionysius criticized the aristocrat Shmuna for helping the Romans during the border conflicts of the 830s and prompting an anti-Christian back-lash, so Dionysius' condemnation of a right to resistance was an important corollary of the rights he claimed that were based on the (alleged) treaties of the seventh century.[91]

Finally, Dionysius' praise for al-Ma'mun in this scene may also be intended to underscore the difference between the caliph and his brother (and succes-sor) al-Mu'tasim.[92] As he relates in the Egyptian episodes, Dionysius had a poor relationship with al-Mu'tasim, which deteriorated even further after his accession. Indeed, the History of the Patriarchs of Alexandria states that Diony-sius was in terror of being killed by the future caliph and that he would appear for an audience only on the promise that his life would be spared.[93] Dionysius depicts the new caliph as a warmonger who hated the Christians and terror-ized his own citizens.[94] The numerous natural disasters that Dionysius reports for al-Mu'tasim's reign may be interpreted as divine judgements on the rule of a tyrant.[95]

Read in the light of the last chapters of book 12 of Michael's Chronicle, Dio-nysius' defence of his close relationship with al-Ma'mun appears like a golden age of relations between caliph and patriarch. It is contrasted to the sufferings of al-Mu'tasim's reign, when Christians were subject to the exactions of his governors and there was no recourse to protection from the caliph. Dionysius and his fellow clergy were especially vulnerable to the new caliph's suspicions because there were indeed Christian elites who were willing to collaborate with the Byzantines during this period of renewed frontier warfare.[96] By this time, the fair dealing of Islamic government under al-Ma'mun, which legiti-mated Dionysius' own proximity to the court, seems to have withered away.

---

91. For Shmuna: MS XII. 19 (IV, 531 / III, 89). Also note the earlier accusations of espionage against Cyriacus and the destruction of a church MS XII. 5 (IV, 488 / III, 20).

92. For al-Mu'tasim's succession, see Nawas 2010; Marsham 2009: 265–68.

93. History of the Patriarchs, PO 10:495–96.

94. Hatred of the Christians on account of his war with the Byzantines: MS XII. 19 (IV, 532 / III, 89); his war with Nubia: MS XII. 19 (IV, 531 / III, 91); his raids in Anatolia: MS XII. 20 (IV, 535 / III, 95); treating Mesopotamia 'like enemy territory': MS XII. 19 (IV, 532 / III, 89). In actual fact, it was probably al-Ma'mun who restored the policy of aggression against the Byzantines: J. Turner 2013: 129. For the pattern of warfare on the Anatolian frontier, see Brooks 1923.

95. MS XII. 18 (IV, 528 / III, 86) for the flooding of Baghdad.

96. MS XII. 19 (IV, 531 / III, 89).

Conclusions

The aftermath of al-Ma'mun's victory saw new Khurasanian and Central Asian elites installed at high levels of government in the western caliphate. Petra Sijpesteijn has observed that their presence is clearly visible in Egyptian papyri from the 820s and 830s, where we find the introduction of new scribal practices such as authenticating seals that had long been used in the eastern caliphate. She notes that the administrative papyri increasingly treat the government as an abstract entity (the *sulṭān*) instead of referring to individual members of the elite who served (or claimed to serve) the government.[97]

Dionysius benefited from these centralizing processes in several ways. The administrative union of the Jazira, Syria and Egypt allowed him to project his influence much further than any of his predecessors had done, empowered by his role as a servant of the caliph. As we will see in the next chapter, he felt able to oppose other powerful figures in the caliph's entourage and to advocate for many different Christian populations, claiming uniform rights for the Christians of the caliphate. And Dionysius' own authority vis-à-vis his opponents within the church was cemented by the support of 'Abd Allah ibn Tahir. It is no wonder that he celebrated the caliph as a source of order and justice.

Nevertheless, we should keep in mind that Dionysius (and Christian institutions in general) was only a temporary beneficiary of the eastward shift in the caliphate's ruling elite. It is difficult, of course, to generalize from a small number of individuals, but Dionysius does not seem to have enjoyed with Afshin the kind of close relationship that he did with 'Abd Allah, nor could he approach al-Mu'tasim in the way he had al-Ma'mun. It may be that as the new elites brought to power in the 820s and 830s grew in number, less and less leverage was available for men on the ground, such as Dionysius.

97. Sijpesteijn 2017.

8

Patriarchate and Imamate

DIONYSIUS' USE OF MUSLIM POLITICAL THOUGHT

AL-MA'MUN'S COURT in Baghdad was famous for its ability to attract intellectuals and religious leaders from a wide variety of backgrounds. From al-Ma'mun's perspective, this cosmopolitan culture might have represented the resurrection of a late Sasanian tradition, in which the monarch demonstrated his claim to universal authority by patronizing knowledge from all sources.[1] But al-Ma'mun's *majlis* also encouraged interaction among the leaders of different religious communities and facilitated direct contact between the caliph himself and the representatives of the various confessions, such as Dionysius.

We have already seen that Dionysius used the discourse of dhimma to criticize the treatment of the Biamaye in Egypt. The dhimma placed obligations on the caliphal government that allowed Dionysius to present a positive image of Muslim rule in general while criticizing many of al-Ma'mun's Muslim servants. Dionysius' Königsnähe was crucial to his ability to maintain his authority over his rivals, and one way that he legitimated this was to present himself as a successful intercessor to a regime that was fundamentally just.

In this chapter I examine Dionysius' handling of the caliph's decision in 829 to multiply the number of representatives of dhimmī groups as another example of Dionysius' adaptation of the caliph's political discourse for the protection of his own position. In a time of political discord, when he faced a

---

1. See Payne 2016 for interreligious dialogue as a demonstration of the Sasanian monarch's universal power. For the sponsorship of scholarship in general, see Cooperson 2005: 81–106. For al-Ma'mun's patronage of astrology, see Janos 2014; for medicine, see Pradines 1975: 175–220, and for translation, see Gutas 1998, with the correctives of Watt 2014 and Brock 2007.

number of opponents within his own church, Dionysius reimagined the patriarchate as an imamate to create an analogy between himself and the caliph and
to deny the analogy that al-Ma'mun had attempted to draw between Christian
and Jewish religious leaders. As in his appeal to the discourse of the dhimma,
Dionysius employed Islamic history in his discussion with the caliph to define
what just Islamic practice ought to be.

Lazarus of Baghdad

Chapters 4 and 5 showed that Dionysius faced substantial opposition from the
Gubbite monks and from the bishops of Takrit. But he also faced other opponents, especially one Lazarus, bishop of Baghdad, whom Dionysius endeav-
oured to remove from his see after complaints were made against him.[2] Lazarus' misconduct was embarrassing because it took place in the imperial capital,
where Dionysius himself (and the Jacobites in general) enjoyed relatively little
representation. Baghdad had, of course, been cut off from easy contact with
the Levant during the military conflict at the beginning of al-Ma'mun's reign.

Lazarus had faced several accusations from his parishioners, but Dionysius
initially hoped that these would dissipate. Dionysius passes over the substance
of these allegations, possibly because they included sexual impropriety. However, as the accusations continued to accumulate, he felt compelled to intervene, with the result that news of the Jacobites' disunity came to the attention
of the caliph in Baghdad. The affair of Lazarus may have been especially prob-
lematic because of the patriarch's need to be in frequent communication with
the caliph's court. Opposition from figures in Baghdad could have made it hard
for Dionysius to gain the caliph's ear or could simply have given the impression
that Dionysius did not command the respect of his flock. As we have seen, a
good relationship with the caliph was crucial for a patriarch, both to acquire
advantages for his co-religionists (such as tax remissions and the protection
of churches) and to ensure that the caliphal government endorsed his authority as patriarch, through force if necessary.

Strife between the patriarch and other claimants to authority had been a
recurrent feature of the preceding century and a half of Jacobite history, and
in his account of the Lazarus affair Dionysius compares his opponents

---

2. For Lazarus' theological writings on providence, known through citations in Bar Hebraeus,
see Poirier 1987. Dionysius' deposition of Lazarus and Dionysius' meeting with al-Ma'mun is
discussed in Harrak 2015: 216–20.

explicitly to earlier rebels against patriarchal authority: Sergius Zakunaya (fl. c. 680), Denha II of Takrit (688–728), Athanasius Sandalaya, John of Callinicum and David of Dara.[3] What made this affair particularly troubling for Dionysius was that it coincided with a wider redefinition of the caliph's relationship with the dhimmīs of his empire. In a recent declaration, the caliph al-Maʾmun had stated that any group of ten men belonging to the same confession could, if they wished, select their own leader, who could presumably collect tithes from the group members and administer justice among them. This innovation had been a response to a quarrel for control over the exilarchate between David, leader of the Jews in Tiberias in Palestine, and Daniel 'the Ananian', who led a group of Jews who 'desecrated the Sabbath and celebrated it on a Wednesday'.[4] From Dionysius' perspective, however, the new arrangement threatened to undermine the authority of the Jacobite patriarchate, since it removed the patriarch's ability to call on the caliph's powers of coercion and made it easy for priests and laymen to reject his judgements and his right to gather tribute. Dionysius summarizes his objection by quoting a proverb: 'When we have many leaders, we are weakened and they [our enemies] are strengthened against us'.

The Ananian Revolution

Dionysius himself does not provide any further details on the internal quarrel of the Jews. But before we turn to Dionysius' meeting with al-Maʾmun, it is worth considering this conflict to highlight parallels to and differences from the Christian situation. To my knowledge, the quarrel is not reported in other sources, but I think it unlikely that Dionysius would have invented it entirely, though he may have got details wrong and imposed his own interpretation. After all, the division of Jewish authority at this time had dangerous implications for Christians, as Dionysius realized. In particular, the split between the Ananians and other Jews illustrates a broader ninth-century controversy about how dhimmī religions were defined in terms of their scriptural basis and their authorized interpreters, and who should represent their adherents before the caliph.

The Jews of Babylonia were led by an exilarch (rišā d-gālutā), a man allegedly descended from the house of King David who presided over a court,

3. MS XII. 14 (IV, 516–17 / III, 65). The Lazarus affair can also be followed in BH HE II, 365–71.

4. MS XII. 14 (IV, 517 / III, 65).

raised taxes from the Jews and represented the Jews before the caliph.[5] However, the exilarch was not primarily a scholar, and the training of the Jewish scholarly elite, who dominated the interpretation of the Talmud, was concentrated in the academies of Sura and Pumbedita in southern Babylonia.[6] Their priority, Talmudic interpretation, became increasingly significant in the Islamic period as the Talmud was treated more and more as a legal text rather than as a literary one, a 'carbonized constitution' that preserved rulings on everyday Jewish life in Sasanian Babylonia as norms for subsequent behaviour.[7]

Anan, the grandfather of the Daniel mentioned here, had been a failed candidate for the exilarchate around the time of the Abbasid revolution. The ninth-century gaon Natronai of Sura (d. 860) accused him of creating a new Talmud of his own and authorizing new prayers.[8] Medieval stories reported that Anan was thrown into prison with the Muslim jurist Abu Hanifa and there plotted to create a new religion in order to acquire power for himself after his exclusion from the exilarchate.[9] Both claims are polemical. Their purpose is to accuse Anan of undermining the Jewish scriptures and of seeking to use his connections with Muslims to organize a new religion outside the authority of the exilarch. Yet the latter claim, in particular, coincides with Dionysius' description of al-Ma'mun's acknowledgement of a separate dhimma for Anan's followers. From the point of view of the caliph, there were now two distinct Jewish communities (though how widely this view was actually applied in government is unclear).

Anan's own writings, as reproduced in other sources, are not particularly radical: he seems to have proposed slightly more stringent obedience of the Sabbath restrictions and slightly more lenient following of the dietary laws (*kashrut*).[10] Nothing suggests that he proposed a new Sabbath, as Dionysius claims he did. It may be that Dionysius is repeating the polemic of Babylonian rabbis against Anan and that he was motivated by the belief that the division

---

5. Brody 1998: 73–74. For Sasanian precedents, see Herman 2012 (esp. ch. 6 on relations between the exilarchs and the rabbis) and Morony 1984: 316–28. For the gaonic courts and their jurisdiction, see Brody 1998: 58–62.

6. Gil 2004: 84.

7. Astren 2003a: 147; Brody 1998: 333; Krakowski 2017: 84–85.

8. Gil 2003: 75–84.

9. Hughes 2015: 69.

10. Gil 2003: 78–80.

of authority would be a dangerous innovation.[11] Indeed, Dionysius refers to the 'heresy' of Anan, which may imply a sympathy for the 'traditional' religion against the innovations of a schismatic.[12]

However, though Anan's own interpretations were not extreme, his lineage would eventually provide figureheads for the Karaite movement in later centuries.[13] The Karaites were famous for their rejection of the Talmud and their insistence on direct exegetical engagement with the Torah, without any intermediary.[14] They were strongly associated with the employment of kalām, theology based on first principles rather than any specific tradition.[15] Both characterizations are exaggerations: Rabbanite figures such as Saadia Gaon also used kalām to supplement other forms of theology, and the Karaites differed over the proper use of kalām.[16] Furthermore, Karaites often followed local traditions, especially those of Palestine, that were not endorsed by the Babylonian academies.[17]

Fred Astren has proposed that the Karaite movement can be interpreted as a reaction against the centralization of Jewish thought under the caliphate.[18] The government's endorsement of the exilarchate and of the use of the Talmud as a law code triggered a reaction from the defenders of provincial traditions.[19]

11. Gil 2004: 108. The accusation that Anan abolished the Sabbath could reflect confusion with another Jewish leader, Yughdan, who was also accused of doing so. Gil 2003: 85.

12. MS XII. 14 (IV, 517 / III, 65).

13. Anan was celebrated by later Karaites as a figure who stood up to the authority of the exilarch and geonim, but his followers initially constituted a distinct movement (Polliack 2006: 77). Statements attributed to Anan in which he encourages multiple interpretations of scriptural passages ('Search diligently in the Torah, and do not rely on my opinion') are likely to be later inventions that respond to the diversity of tenth-century Karaism and the Karaites' advocacy of the direct application of kalām to the Torah (Brody 1998: 87). Qirqisani listed the differences in interpretation between Anan and the early Karaite leader Benjamin al-Nihavandi (Nemoy 1930: 384–87).

14. Brody 1998: 86.

15. Fowden 2014: 179; Nemoy 1930. Gil 2003: 88 notes that Mas'udi calls the Karaites 'Jewish Mu'tazilites'.

16. Fowden 2014: 180; Hughes 2015: 95.

17. Polliack 2006 (though here it is David who is said to have been supported by the Palestinians; this may be a slip of the pen on Dionysius' part).

18. Astren 2003b: 29. For the wider competition between Babylonia and Palestine, see Brody 1998: 113ff. For the development of rabbinic academies in Palestine on the Babylonian model in c. 800, see Lapin 2012: 62.

19. The Talmud's interpretation as law is far from self-evident and demanded a great deal of effort from the geonim: Brody 1998: 165–67.

The dispute over Anan's election provided a useful opportunity for these provincial Jewish centres to assert their views without immediately seeking to impose an alternative orthodoxy. Indeed, a notable feature of early Karaism is its diversity, due to both its incorporation of a range of traditions and its adherents' interest in kalām.[20]

It is perhaps no coincidence that the dispute over Anan's election took place during a period of political upheaval in the Abbasid world. Like Cyriacus' inability to quell the revolt of the Gubbite monks and the instability that Dionysius faced early in his reign, the Ananians' revolt may have been encouraged by the (temporary) absence of government authority during the fourth fitna. The outcome of the schism was a marked reduction in the power of the exilarchs, who, in al-Ma'mun's reign, were stripped of their rights over Jewish property taxes.[21] Around the same time, the geonim of Pumbedita stopped visiting the exilarch for confirmation of their status.[22] A twelfth-century source, Samuel ben Eli, claims that the exilarchs became inferior to the gaonic academies at this point: 'They were dismissed from the service of the sultan and joined the sages and the yeshivot. However, they were only received if they accepted the conditions of the yeshiva, which gave them certificates to serve as exilarchs'.[23] If we conceive of the exilarchs as analogous to Christian patriarchs, any division of their authority threatened an immediate loss of power. The question that arises, therefore, is how the Jacobite patriarch managed to avoid the loss of status experienced by the exilarch.

Dionysius' Performance

In his history, Dionysius describes how he became aware of intractable and persistent accusations against Lazarus of Baghdad and attempted to try the case in Takrit to avoid any members of the church being exposed to public humiliation. But Lazarus' partisans appealed directly to the caliph, which forced Dionysius to seek a personal audience with al-Ma'mun.[24] In the context of the caliph's earlier decision regarding the Jews there was a wider issue at stake for Dionysius, who needed to protest his right to judge any member of

20. Brody 1998: 87.
21. Brody 1998: 73.
22. Gil 2004: 104.
23. Gil 2004: 105.
24. MS XII. 14 (IV, 517 / III, 66).

the Jacobite community, rather than allowing dissenters to splinter off and be subject directly to the caliph in matters of law, without the patriarch as an intermediary.

Dionysius claims to provide a blow-by-blow account of his meeting with al-Maʾmun. The narrative is intended as a showpiece for his ability to negotiate the politics of the court successfully. At the beginning of the meeting, Dionysius seeks to assuage the caliph's 'anger' at the divisions in the church by offering presents. The caliph ('the peace-bringing king', *malkā mšaynānā*) summons Dionysius to his side, leaving the other bishops at the back of the room, and asks him about his affairs. Dionysius replies, 'We live in a long period of peace thanks to you, as Paul said to Felix,[25] and our people have received many advantages (*teqyātā*) thanks to your government (*šulṭānek*)'.[26]

Dionysius seeks to impress the reader with his Königsnähe—his unique access to the caliph over the other bishops. A recurrent problem for the previous generation of Jacobite church leadership, known in part through Dionysius' own reports, was the ability of minor clergy to circumvent church procedure and to use connections with Muslim elites to obtain lucrative high offices within the church. Dionysius thus highlights his own knowledge of court procedure and his special access to al-Maʾmun. He also stresses his ability to speak for the Christians as a whole in a virtuoso performance that eclipses potential rivals (though of course his presentation of the encounter is likely to be highly idealized).

After praising the caliph, Dionysius goes on to explain the Lazarus affair. He tells the caliph that he investigated and deposed Lazarus in response to complaints that had been made against him, but that Lazarus resisted the deposition, quoting the caliph's decree that any ten men could elect their own chief in matters of religion. Dionysius proclaims his belief that the alleged decree is inauthentic and that Lazarus must have falsely attributed it to the caliph.

When the caliph declares that he has indeed issued the order, Dionysius protests:

O just king (*malkā kinā*)! Where is the righteousness of your judgements? . . . Your wisdom knows that there are promises and covenants (*qyamē*) between us [the Christians] and you [the Muslims] and writings

25. Acts 14:2.
26. MS XII. 14 (IV, 66 / III, 517).

confirmed by the seals and signatures of the kings who seized (*ptaḥ*)[27] the cities, under which we submitted to you. If you ignore the covenants that have been established and do not permit the laws and leadership that we have preserved [among ourselves], we are defrauded by you, . . . since we will be reduced to fighting with one another and you will not be our judge [i.e., it will not be fair for you to hold us responsible for what happens].[28]

Dionysius' strategy here is to remind the caliph that his right to rule over the Christians rests on treaties concluded by the Arab conquerors of the Near East and endorsed by the *rāshidūn* caliphs.[29] Therefore, just rule as a caliph is dependent on following earlier caliphal example. Dionysius appeals to this imagined history of the seventh century to make his objection to the caliph's 'innovation', namely the threat to divide church authority. Dionysius' reference to sealed documents may indicate that he had access to actual specimens in an archive. Certainly, there are reports in the following century of the 'discovery' by historians of the Church of the East of ancient documents that describe a treaty between the Prophet and the Christians and support an eirenic vision of the relationship between the caliph and his Christian subjects.[30]

After Dionysius' speech, the caliph complains about being troubled by the divisions among the Christians and promises to consult Dionysius about the matter in the future. Dionysius comments at this point that all the bishops and soldiers present were amazed that Dionysius could speak to the caliph so freely. In part, Dionysius inserts this observation to emphasize his unique access to the caliph, which is a sign of his effectiveness as patriarch. But Dionysius also places his speech within the tradition of parrhēsia, free speech before a king or a tyrant, whose antecedents go back to the example of Jesus and even earlier to the democratic traditions of classical Athens.[31] Here Dionysius may be positioning himself within the lineage of the holy men who spoke out

27. The choice of word here may reflect Arabic usage, where the root f-t-ḥ refers to the divinely ordained conquests of the first generation of Muslims.

28. MS XII. 14 (IV, 518 / III, 66–67). Also see the translation by Harrak 2015: 219.

29. A number of monasteries and towns preserved alleged treaty documents from the Islamic conquest (see, e.g., Cheikho 1909), and historical narratives circulated that described such conquest treaties, which set out the rights and obligations of conquerors and conquered (Conrad 1991).

30. *Chronicle of Seert*, PO 13:601ff.

31. Brown 1992: ch. 2; Foucault 2001; Bartelink 1970.

before Justinian in the sixth century in the hagiography of John of Ephesus; their virtue and orthodoxy are rewarded with the courage to say the truth.[32]

The Second Audience

Ten days after his meeting with al-Maʾmun, Dionysius uses his influence with a Christian at court, Lazarus of Mardin, to gain another audience with the caliph.[33] The fact that the caliph himself does not summon Dionysius again is a detail that rings true of other authoritarian, court-based societies. In Abbasid Baghdad, as in imperial Rome, the ruler's freedom to behave unpredictably and to alter the rules to suit his circumstances was an illustration of the centrality of royal patronage. In other words, royal unpredictability ensured that contacts with the monarch, rather than with any other figure, were the stuff that influence was made of.

This time, Dionysius reports, the caliph meets him accompanied by his judges and learned men (*ḥakimē*), 'each seated according to his rank', including the 'judge of judges' Yahya ibn Aktham. Al-Maʾmun addresses Dionysius: 'O patriarch, you have wrongly accused me of injustice (*ṭlumyā*) because of the order I issued regarding you. Therefore, I have gathered the jurists (*fuqahā*ʾ) to talk to you in front of them'. Then he says to the assembled scholars:

> Tell me, . . . should I confirm the rulers (*šaliṭānē*) of the Christians, as long as I have authority (*malkutā*) over them, or should I treat them according to the law I proclaimed with regard to them and the Jews, so that they should be at peace and maintain the submission they have given to us and enjoy the peace that they have because of our power? No one prevents them from altering their beliefs and customs and we will be their judge if they do something bad [according to our law].[34]

The caliph presents his arrangement with the Jews as a laissez-faire agreement that grants the dhimmīs freedom of religion while giving them access to

---

32. Wood 2018b; cf. Wood 2010: 191–98. The word *parrhēsia* is not used in this scene in Michael, but Dionysius does use it when he describes his discussions with ʿAbd Allah (X1234 [II, 147/204]), so it is unlikely that it carried negative or critical connotations for him. My thanks to Marianna Mazzola for this observation.
33. MS XII. 14 (IV, 518 / III, 67).
34. MS XII. 14 (IV, 518 / III, 67).

the same justice as that enjoyed by all other citizens of the caliphate. The novelty of the arrangement lies not just in the division of the Jews into two populations but in the erosion of the exilarch's role as an intermediary between 'the Jews' as a whole. The language of tradition and innovation was often invoked in appeals to the caliph aimed at protecting established religious practice, and al-Ma'mun seems aware that the exilarch might intervene to change beliefs and customs in the name of centralization.[35] The caliph's comparison between the two possible ways of relating to the dhimmīs is stacked in favour of the laissez-faire position. It may that Dionysius is accurately reporting the caliph's words here, but he may also be putting the opinions of his own Christian critics into the caliph's mouth. Either way, the caliph's decision poses a threat to the patriarch's position.

Unsurprisingly, the judges agree with the caliph's ruling, but Dionysius asks to be allowed to make an exposition of the Christian faith ('the mysteries [rāzē] of the Christians').[36] This apparent non sequitur allows Dionysius to present the clerical hierarchy as a fundamental part of Christianity. He states that Christ's apostles divided the world into four patriarchates, Rome, Antioch, Constantinople and Alexandria, each of which should ordain ten metropolitans and beneath them bishops, priests and deacons. According to Dionysius, the apostles preached that no one bar the other three patriarchs should resist a patriarch's orders or judgements. Dionysius adds that no king has altered this custom, especially not a king of the Muslims. Indeed, he asserts, the caliph's ancestors 'recognized our authority and gave us a diploma', and al-Ma'mun himself issued such a diploma at the start of his reign. Thus there should be no innovation in the law. As for the accusations brought against Dionysius by Lazarus, Dionysius dismisses these as mere reactions to Lazarus' deposition by the patriarch, comparable to attacks seen in the past, as when George and Cyriacus were accused of being 'enemies of the Muslims' and uttering 'blasphemies against your prophet and other things meriting death'.[37]

35. Cf. Goitein 1970, where the caliph is involved as a defender of ancient Jewish custom in order to prevent changes to the observance of the Sabbath among the Jews of Fatimid Cairo.

36. MS XII. 14 (IV, 519 / III, 68).

37. At the end of the discussion, Dionysius refers specifically to a treaty drawn up between the Christians of Mosul and their Muslim conquerors as part of his claim that the Christians ought to preserve their native laws, which guarantee Dionysius' right to censure Lazarus. MS XII. 14 (IV, 520 / III, 69).

Dionysius' strategy in this speech is to present ecclesiastical structure as part of the apostolic foundation of Christianity, closely linked to Christ's own appointment of apostles. In the ecclesiological model Dionysius sets out, the patriarch is effectively above censure, since two of the four patriarchs resided beyond the frontiers of the caliphate and would not, in practice, judge one of their fellows. Indeed, Dionysius did not recognize the Chalcedonian incumbents of Rome and Constantinople and saw only the Miaphysite patriarch of Alexandria as his peer. Jerusalem, which was the seat of a major Chalcedonian patriarchate that enjoyed links to Byzantium and the Frankish west, is excluded here because it had been raised to the patriarchate only in 451, and its elevation had never been recognized by the Miaphysite churches or the Church of the East.[38] Rome held a theoretical precedence, as it continued to do for many ecclesiologies written in the caliphate. But its primacy has no practical significance for Dionysius.[39] Dionysius entirely omits the claims of the Armenians to an independent catholicosate as well as the powerful patriarchate of the Church of the East in Baghdad.[40] And there is likewise no mention of the Jacobite bishop of Takrit, who claimed to be the successor of the catholicoi of the east and who could often challenge the authority of the Jacobite patriarch of Antioch.[41] Dionysius' ecclesiological theory of a world divided into four patriarchates pays lip service to church history, but in practice its function is to assert his own superiority over other bishops within the caliphate.[42]

Dionysius presents this apostolic arrangement as something that has been defended by all earlier kings 'of the Muslims'. He portrays the preservation of Christian hierarchy as a facet of their just rule, implying that their status as good Muslim kings entails the confirmation of Christian practices. Thus the

38. Van Esbroeck 1991. For Jerusalem's wider links, see Herrin 1987: 244. For Jerusalem's significance for the Melkites, see Griffith 2008b.

39. W. de Vries 1957. Antioch was normally placed after Rome, Constantinople and Alexandria in lists of precedence, reflecting the regular intervention of Constantinople and Alexandria into Antioch's sphere of influence, but these lists could differ considerably depending on the author (Blaudeau 2006: 498–526).

40. For the development of the ecclesiology of the Church of the East, see Fiey 1967; Gero 1982; Wood 2013: ch. 5.

41. See the discussion in chapter 5. Also see Hage 1966: 25–31 and Selb 1989: 222–27.

42. Mas'udi, *Muruj*, III, 406, and *Tanbih*, 201–2, report a four-patriarch Christian ecclesiology and recognize that Jerusalem was added as a patriarchate only later. This information may indicate that Mas'udi relied on Jacobite or Church of the East informants.

status quo, in which the patriarch rules over the clergy, is cast as the product of a deliberate decision by earlier caliphs to respect established custom in accord with agreements made with the Christians at the time of the conquests. Dionysius concludes by warning the caliph that it is the custom of evil Christians who have been deposed (like Lazarus) to slander their superiors in the manner of David of Dara against George or of Abiram against Cyriacus.[43]

An Apostolic Tradition

Dionysius' claim that contemporary ecclesiology had been endorsed by the apostles deserves some attention because it was obviously an invention.[44] This use of the past to justify present organization is not surprising in itself, and it provided a way to silence critics who argued for more egalitarian church structures.

But the assertion of apostolic origins also responded to the peculiar requirements imposed by an Islamic context in which Christianity was represented as a pure and praiseworthy religion in the Quran but contemporary Christians were criticized for their false beliefs (in the Trinity and in the resurrection of Jesus) and for the corruption of their priests. Furthermore, the Quran established the expectation that Jesus was a lawgiver on the model of Moses and that it was the possession of a proto-Muslim sunna that made Christian dhimmī communities respectable and entitled to legal autonomy.[45]

This expectation that Jesus was a lawgiver and that the Christians possess a distinctive law offered, in a sense, an opportunity for would-be clerical lawmakers. One of the first and most extensive legal texts composed in the Islamic period among the Jacobites was the so-called *Testament of Our Lord*, an anonymous composition attributed to Jesus himself. This text imagined Jesus as a lawgiver, using the threat of imminent apocalypse as an additional incentive to obey the church canons.[46]

43. MS XII. 14 (IV, 519 / III, 68). For the accusations of blasphemy or treason against George and Cyriacus, see MS XI. 26 (IV, 476 / II, 528) and MS XII. 5 (IV, 488 / II, 20).

44. Also note Ibn Jarir 31, 72.

45. Edelby 1950–51. Note, however, that some Muslims believed that most Christians had long since corrupted their religion (G. Reynolds 2004: 86, 111–12, 171–74; El-Cheikh 2004: 108; Fowden 2014: 152–53). Griffith (2002 a–g) describes the efforts of theologians from different Christian confessions to defend themselves against charges of innovation and the alteration of Scripture (taḥrīf).

46. Drijvers 1994.

The Jacobite synods of the Islamic period also give a strong emphasis to apostolic authority in general terms and to the authority lent to councils by the Holy Spirit.[47] Thus George of Beltan told his bishops that his legislation drew on 'apostolic and unanimous foundations.'[48] And Cyriacus of Takrit reminded his clergy that since Eden, God had provided laws to regulate his creation and that both Moses and Christ had been lawgivers. Cyriacus represented his own laws as an attempt to restore the divine law and to ameliorate the suffering inflicted by 'barbarian nations.'[49] Dionysius himself emphasized that a council is a place in which the bishops not only hold the dignity of sitting together with one another but also enjoy the fellowship of God the Father and the Holy Spirit and follow the ancient practices of the church. [50] This image of the council as a moment of fellowship with God as well as men is what underpins Dionysius' description to the caliph of episcopal and patriarchal leadership of the Christian community. For Dionysius the council is both a form of government that has apostolic sanction and a means of keeping Christians in line with ancient practice.

'We Do Not Resemble the Gentiles'

In the exchange recorded by Dionysius, the caliph acknowledges the patriarch's statement of precedent, but he remains puzzled: 'Why should the Christians be discontented with an arrangement that suits the other confessions?' Dionysius retorts that the others are also dissatisfied with the law and agree with the Christians. We are meant to infer that unlike Dionysius, these others do not have the courage to speak plainly to the caliph; only Dionysius among all the dhimmī leaders is empowered to tell the truth to al-Ma'mun. (At the end of the meeting the judges will tell the assembled audience that the Christians have rarely had as proficient an advocate as Dionysius.)[51] However, Dionysius goes further and argues that the distinctive nature of Christian authority makes the imposition of the new regime particularly unjust for the Christians:

47. The most detailed defence of councils as a biblically warranted in this period occurs in the ninth-century Melkite Theodore Abu Qurrah: Griffith 2002f.

48. Vööbus 1975–76: 2/3.

49. Vööbus 1975–76: 7–8 / 8–10.

50. Vööbus 1975–76: 26/29.

51. MS XII. 14 (IV, 520 / III, 70).

Our authority is different from that of the Zoroastrians and the Jews, who call their leaders 'kings' and whose authority is transmitted by inheritance. They pay tribute to their kings, something that is never found among us. For, I tell you, there are three kinds of authority in the world: natural (*kyānāytā*) . . . constrained (*qeṭrāytā*) and voluntary (*ṣebyānāytā*). Natural authority is that of a father over his children or a husband over his wife: in these matters, all men are equal. Constrained authority is ordained by God or established by fear of the sword, such as the temporal rule that you have in reality. But as for those who levy taxes (*šqonē*) and tribute (*madātē*), who submit to you and receive their leadership from you, it is because of their avarice that they are raised to authority. . . . By contrast, for us [Christians] authority comes from choice (*gbitā*) and voluntary consent (*šalmutā d-ṣebyānā*) in choosing a leader, and we hold this [authority] as a priesthood, not as [secular] leadership. This is what you call 'imamate'. Just as the imam stands first in prayer and exhorts the people [to good deeds], the patriarch and the bishops stand at our head and pray and exhort us to obey the law and impose the punishment on those who break it: not by putting [the culprit] to death, as you do . . . but by stripping him of the priestly office, if he is a bishop or a priest, or by excommunicating him from the church. Thus, O king, we do not resemble the Gentiles (*ʿammē*), and the damage that is caused by the removal of our authority is not just [a matter of] the loss of riches but touches our faith itself and separates us from God.[52]

The first strand of Dionysius' argument here is that Christian authority is consensual rather than inherited.[53] For the caliph to draw a legal analogy between Jews and Christians as fellow dhimmīs is to fail to recognize that the Christians' distinctive structures of authority are a part of their religion. In Dionysius' schema, Jewish and Magian authority amounts to inherited kingship. Their leaders are not freely chosen but are unthinkingly crowned according to tradition. This accusation may reflect the fact that the Jewish exilarch claimed descent from the house of David, and the Zoroastrian Magi were, in

---

52. MS XII. 14 (IV, 519 / III, 68–69).

53. Dionysius may be drawing here on the divisions of forms of rulership found in Aristotle's *Politics*. The *Politics* is not extant in Syriac, though two translations were made in the sixth century by Sergius of Reshaina and Paul the Persian: Joosse 2011. Joosse argues (at 99) that Arab Muslim authors had knowledge of the first book of *Politics*, probably via Syriac intermediaries. Marianna Mazzola informs me that she is preparing a study of Dionysius' use of Aristotle in this passage; I am grateful to her for this point.

theory at least, descended from the Sasanian priestly caste.[54] The charge of unthinking inheritance reflects Christian polemical descriptions of the Jewish and Zoroastrian religions, which (it is claimed) are based on the uncomprehending repetition of ritual rather than on the use of God-given reason to reflect on creation or scripture.

But there is also a second aspect to Dionysius' argument that is highly original and deserves emphasis. Dionysius presents kingship as alien to Christian consensual authority. In Abbasid political thought, kingship (*mulk*) was a manmade form of authority, inferior to the caliphate granted by God. The Umayyads, for instance, had been mere kings, with no divine mandate.[55] Dionysius seems to draw on this distinction to present Jewish and Zoroastrian leaders as lacking in the kind of divine sanction that the caliph might claim for himself. They are subordinate rulers whose rule is sustained by the constrained authority granted to them by the caliph.[56]

The reference to leaders with constrained authority gathering money through taxes and presenting it to the caliph may suggest that this is a distinctive feature of Jewish and Zoroastrian leaders that Christian leaders do not share. Christian bishops did, of course, receive tithes through church structures, but Dionysius may be differentiating here between the 'taxes and tribute' of leaders with constrained authority, who gather funds on the caliph's behalf, and the tithe-gathering of the church, which he conveniently ignores.

Dionysius' denigration of those who collect tribute for the caliph may also have two further targets. The first is Muslim governors: Dionysius stresses that their authority is a secondary derivative of the authority of the caliph, who holds his authority 'in reality'. Implicitly, this argument legitimates Dionysius' attempts to appeal over governors' heads directly to the caliph. The second target is likely to be Christians who serve the caliph as tax collectors. The eighth-century chief qāḍī Abu Yusuf had recommended employing members of dhimmī communities to collect revenue from their co-religionists, presumably on the assumption that taxation would be most efficient when carried out

---

54. Vevaina 2015: 229; Brody 1998: 70, 75.

55. Crone 2004: 7.

56. We should note that Dionysius may not be using the Syriac word for king (*malkā*) in the sense of the Arabic *malik*: he used *malkā* not only for independent rulers but also for servants of the caliph such as ʿAbd Allah ibn Tahir (R. Abramowski 1940: 103; cf. Harrak 1998: 471 on the usage of the *Chronicle of Zuqnin*). Thus Dionysius' reference to Jewish and Zoroastrian leaders as *malkē* is probably not meant as an accusation of political insubordination but does stress their dependence on the caliph.

by men who knew the community well.[57] But Dionysius was opposed to the involvement of Christians and especially of clergy in caliphal tax collection. Christian tax collectors, he feared, might inadvertently provoke violence against the Christian community, and they posed a threat to the patriarch's authority and to the monopoly on ties to government that he aspired to. In his comment to al-Ma'mun, Dionysius thus stresses that the patriarchate is a form of voluntary authority that is an intrinsic form of Christianity, in contrast to the (inferior) derived, constrained authority of governors and tax collectors.

Dionysius presents his own authority as analogous to but not challenging the authority of the caliph. He does not, he stresses, claim any right to impose the death penalty. But he does claim a resemblance to the caliph as an imam, as a figure who leads prayers and delivers the Friday sermon (khuṭba). He had employed the same analogy earlier when warning 'Abd Allah ibn Tahir of the danger of the Gubbites' quarrelling with the formulas he used when leading prayers as 'imam'.[58] By drawing this analogy between patriarch and imam, Dionysius may be claiming a role for himself in preaching obedience to 'the law' in support of the beneficial role of a 'peace-bringing' caliph.[59]

The specific significance of Dionysius' appeal to 'the law' in this context is to establish that his condemnation of Lazarus of Baghdad was legitimate and constituted an exercise of the patriarch's right to censure bishops for poor behaviour. Indeed, Lazarus had been punished only after criticism from his flock and an investigation by the patriarch and other bishops, and Dionysius may have felt that this recent history further justified his presentation of his authority as consensual rather than merely arbitrary.

Caliph as Imam

Dionysius employs the term *imām* in the passage quoted above to emphasize the shared characteristics of the patriarch and the caliph as leaders of prayers and as holders of consensual authority.[60] But we can fully appreciate the significance

---

57. Abu Yusuf 70/190.

58. See chapter 3.

59. Ibn Jarir 31.16–17 also represents priests as imams, but for him the primary function of the imam is to preserve the dictates of a prophet without alteration, to publicly obey these dictates himself and to encourage others to obey them.

60. Samaritans also described their leader as an imam, though Dionysius does not seem aware of this: *Samaritan Chronicle*, 83.

of this turn in Dionysius' self-fashioning only if we set it against the use of the term in Muslim thought, and in particular in al-Maʾmun's own self-fashioning.

The term *imam* is a common term of reference for the Abbasid rulers. For Abu Yusuf it is a near synonym for the term 'caliph'. However, the usage of the term is also complicated by its use by different Alid groups, who might use it in the sense of the 'rightful' caliph, at a time when the de facto caliph was considered unqualified in the eyes of the writer.

Some argued that the imamate was particular to a pious lineage that excluded all other possible claimants. Only following a true imam of this lineage would bring a believer to salvation.[61] This view generally granted precedence to the Alids (the lineage of Hasan and Husayn, the sons of ʿAli ibn Abi Talib by Fatima, daughter of Muhammad).[62] Some Abbasids also believed that only their own family constituted a pious lineage with a legitimate claim to the caliphate. This tendency, the so-called Rawandiyya, held that Muhammad's uncle Abu al-Abbas should have become caliph, that the senior members of the Abbasid house had been imams and that all reigning caliphs had been illegitimate.[63] Although al-Maʾmun's declaration that he was an imam was unusually prominent, earlier Abbasids had also styled themselves both imams and caliphs.[64]

Some Alids sought to make good their claim to the caliphate through revolution, such as the widely supported rebellion of the Hasanid imam Muhammad 'al-Nafs al-Zakiyya' ('the pure soul'), who was killed by the Abbasids in 762.[65] By contrast, some later Husaynids, such as Jafar al-Sadiq and his followers, adopted a more quietist approach, in which the devotees paid religious taxes to their imam and tried to avoid paying them to the reigning caliph but did not attempt to achieve regime change.[66] These Husaynid imams claimed to be able to purify the sins of their devotees and to possess esoteric knowledge, in particular knowledge of how to interpret the Quran.

Others had less restricted views on proper succession. Some believed that the imamate could be inherited by designation (*naṣṣ*) rather than descent. The

61. Crone 2004: 17–22; Crone and Hinds 1986: 33, 82.

62. Crone 2004: 83. The Imami Shia would eventually posit a complete disconnect between the salvific role of the imam and the political role of the caliph (Crone 2004: 112).

63. Crone 2004: 88–91; Cooperson 2005: 41; Zaman 1997: 45.

64. Nawas 1992: 45.

65. *Hasanid* and *Husaynid* refer to the descendants of Hasan and Husayn, respectively.

66. Crone 2004: 83; Hayes 2017. However, other Alid groups (such as the Zaydis in Tabaristan and the Ismailis in North Africa and Arabia) would continue to provide armed resistance to the Abbasids: Marsham 2009: 255.

Abbasids claimed that they had been designated the heirs to the imamate in the line of Muhammad ibn al-Hanafiyya (the son of ʿAli by a concubine), whose supporters in Kufa had given clandestine help to the Abbasids before the revolutionaries seized power in Khurasan.[67] Others believed that any male member of the Banu Hashim, the Prophet's extended family, could be the imam as long as he took up arms against a tyrant. This doctrine came to mark Zaydism, named after Zayd ibn ʿAli, a Husaynid rebel against the Umayyads who was killed in 740.[68]

Finally, the designation of an imam might be a matter not just of qualifications or actions but also of process. The early caliphs, many believed, had been elected by *shūrā*, a consultation of the Muslims who had been designated the leaders of the *umma*. Narratives vary regarding how many people made up this shūrā, but its precedent gave rise to a persistent, if utopian, strand in Muslim political thought that demanded that the caliph be elected. Patricia Crone has persuasively argued that the wish for shūrā was an important feature of the revolution of 750. She notes that the slogan *riḍā min āl Muḥammad*, 'a chosen man from the family of Muhammad', was a means of concealing the leader of the revolution as well as of asserting the legitimacy of a leader chosen by prominent Muslims. This definition of leadership focused attention on the procedure by which the caliph was chosen, not only on the qualifications of the incumbent.[69]

Though earlier Abbasids had also employed the title of imam,[70] al-Maʾmun was unusual in proclaiming himself imam *during* the period of his joint rule with al-Amin. Kennedy calls this 'a deliberately ambiguous gesture, to announce his defiance of his brother without providing an excuse for an attack'.[71] However, I would read his use of the title as primarily a presentation of himself as caliph-in-waiting. By this reading, al-Maʾmun was modelling himself after Ibrahim al-Imam, official leader of the Abbasid revolution until he was killed by the Umayyads.[72] I would thus stress the specifically Abbasid connotations of al-Maʾmun's imamate, which cast al-Amin as a latter-day Umayyad.[73]

67. Sharon 1983: esp. ch. 5.

68. For Zayd himself, see Blankinship 1994: 225.

69. Crone 1989a.

70. Crone and Hinds 1986: 80.

71. Kennedy 1986: 136.

72. F. Omar 2012.

73. Al-Maʾmun's vizier al-Fadl ibn Sahl had cast al-Maʾmun's rebellion as a reenactment of the Abbasid revolution. Kennedy 1986: 138.

This sense of al-Maʾmun's denigration of al-Amin appears in al-Maʾmun's letter to his army on the eve of the fourth fitna (the *risālat al-khamīs*). In the letter, al-Maʾmun argues that humans are not competent to select an imam themselves, so God has made the Abbasid family, starting with Abu al-Abbas, the vehicle of the imamate. The leaders of the family were driven underground by the descendants of Abu Sufyan (i.e., the Umayyads), and they were known as *imām al-hudā* (the imam of right guidance). But now, al-Maʾmun claims, al-Amin has relinquished his right to rule by his lack of piety and by mistreating the people in the manner of the Umayyads, and his failure has made it necessary for al-Maʾmun to take action against his impious rule. Al-Maʾmun's superior claim to piety is confirmed by the notables and ʿulamāʾ of Khurasan, who testify to al-Maʾmun's qualifications.[74]

The supremacy of the Abbasid house appears very strongly in this letter, partly because al-Maʾmun must have been aware that his rebellion undermined the Abbasids' claim to legitimacy. He stresses that the Abbasids' possession of the imamate is a matter of divine wisdom, not of human choice. At the same time, the language concerning a concealed imam has a specifically Alid ring to it, and there may be a Zaydi strand in al-Maʾmun's thinking: an imam is defined not merely by descent (like al-Amin), piety, or designation by a predecessor, but also by his willingness to take action.

Al-Maʾmun's later management of theological affairs in the caliphate may also indicate his belief in his own particular knowledge of the divine. In the so-called inquisition (*miḥna*) he obliged the ʿulamāʾ to acknowledge that the Quran was created by God instead of existing prior to creation.[75] It was for his refusal to subscribe to the caliph's dictate that the famous traditionist Ahmad ibn Hanbal was flogged and imprisoned, an event that contributed greatly to his future fame.[76]

It is unclear from al-Maʾmun's declaration how far he took the claim to a peculiar knowledge of the divine will. Muhammad Qasim Zaman has observed that al-Maʾmun was a major patron of the ʿulamāʾ, including traditionists (*ahl al-ḥadīth*), and he may simply have been putting forward his own opinion and expecting the ʿulamāʾ to toe the line.[77] El-Hibri suggests that he may have

74. Arazi and Elad 1987; Arazi and Elad 1988.

75. J. Turner 2013; Nawas 1992.

76. For Ibn Hanbal, see Melchert 2006 and Hurvitz 2002, and for the trial of Ibn Hanbal, J. Turner 2013: 86–104.

77. Zaman 1997: 102–12.

become wary of men such as Ibn Hanbal because they had developed a mass following and, following Sasanian precedent, al-Ma'mun found such movements intrinsically dangerous.[78] Alternatively, we may be dealing with a deliberate claim to the authority of the imam over attempts to constrain that authority by reference to the hadith. We might situate this claim to special knowledge either within a continuous tradition going back to the Umayyads[79] or in the context of Alid traditions that emphasized the esoteric knowledge of the imam.[80]

The primary evidence for al-Ma'mun's self-fashioning as imam comes from these two conflicts: the military one with al-Amin and the theological one with Ahmad ibn Hanbal. Dionysius' use of the term 'imam' mirrors the language of the state at the time, and it shows how an aspect of the state's propaganda had filtered down to the provinces. It was, after all, a term that was now found on coinage, where al-Ma'mun was called *imām al-hudā*.[81] Indeed, Dionysius endorses al-Ma'mun's claim to superior piety by describing his knowledge of 'the Quran and the sunna.'[82]

Dionysius' statement focuses on the imam's legitimacy through consent and his role as a force for order; there is little notion of al-Ma'mun's membership in a pious family or of a right to rule based on feats of arms. The latter ideas were, of course, rather unsuitable for Dionysius' argument, given that he was trying to draw an analogy between al-Ma'mun and himself. But his notion of the imam as a source of order fits the political model of the 'mirrors for princes' that circulated in Arabic in the ninth century but claimed to be translations of Middle Persian originals. One classic example of this genre is the *'Ahd Ardashir*, supposedly containing the third-century shah Ardashir's advice to his

---

78. Cf. El-Hibri 1994: 129.

79. El-Hibri 1994: 121–25; Crone and Hinds 1986. Nawas 1992: 75 understands al-Ma'mun to be asserting the fundamental rights of the caliph in deliberately shutting down the claims of the 'ulamā'. See also Fowden 2014: 157.

80. However, as Nawas 1992: 46 notes, most Alid leaders did not believe in the createdness of the Quran, the key issue in the miḥna.

81. See El-Hibri 1994: 119.

82. MS XII. 6 (IV, 490 / III, 20). This slogan was often invoked by Umayyad- and Abbasid-era rebels, though its content is very vague and seems limited to a call for just government in areas such as keeping troops in the field and the distribution of revenues (Crone and Hinds 1986: 64). Lapidus 1975: 379 sees the miḥna as a deliberate attempt to downgrade the significance of 'Quran and sunna' (and therefore the importance of the 'ulamā' who decided what constituted sunna). But I imagine that al-Ma'mun believed himself capable of determining what sunna was: he was not opposed to the 'ulamā' per se, only to 'ulamā' like Ibn Hanbal who seemed to encroach on the caliph's rights.

son Shapur about the dangers of social mobility, which allows inferiors to criticize their natural superiors and ultimately to undermine the hierarchy on which society is based.[83] If this kind of thinking underpinned al-Ma'mun's attitudes in the miḥna, it is natural that he would have seen it as necessary to identify and suppress dissenters such as Ahmad ibn Hanbal because they threatened to undermine societal order.[84]

However, it is interesting that Dionysius sought to draw a parallel between his own imamate and that of al-Ma'mun by emphasizing election as the defining feature of imamate. Shūrā had indeed played a major role in the political thought of the revolution of 750 and in the succession arrangements of later caliphs, including al-Ma'mun's father, al-Rashid. But while al-Ma'mun generally modelled himself on his Abbasid predecessors, shūrā was not a significant part of his own claim to authority, and he specifically denied the ability of the people to select the imam.[85] It may be that Dionysius was drawing on the political language that had been used by al-Ma'mun's Abbasid predecessors and was not fully abreast of the self-representation of the new caliph. Alternatively, Dionysius may have simply ignored the inconvenient military realities of the fourth fitna in order to make his parallel between himself and al-Ma'mun possible.

Conclusions

According to Dionysius' report, the caliph was sufficiently impressed by his performance to grudgingly confirm his right to divest Lazarus of the administration of his churches.[86] It goes without saying that we need not take

---

83. Marlow 1997: 72–74; Marsham 2009: 161–64.

84. Ibn Hanbal and his followers were distinctive for their attempts to avoid the state and its institutions: Hurvitz 2002: 85. Cooperson 2000: 37 suggests that Ibn Hanbal's claim that ordinary Muslims could enforce ḥudūd punishments (punishments for specific misdeeds such as fornication that were considered to have a divine mandate) made him and his followers especially threatening to al-Ma'mun.

85. The early ninth century did indeed see claims to rule by sunna or to select the riḍā min āl Muḥammad, but although both of these slogans had carried implications of the consensual election of leaders in the mid-eighth century (Crone and Hinds 1986: 63–68) and in the designation of Abbasid succession (Marsham 2009: 188), they do not seem to have done so for al-Ma'mun, something he shared with Alid rebels who used these slogans. For these rebels, see Lapidus 1975: 370. For scepticism about the capacity of ijmāʿ (consensus) to determine the caliph or other matters in both Alid and Muʿtazilite circles at this time, see van Ess 2017: III, 417–19.

86. MS XII. 14 (IV, 520 / III, 70).

everything in Dionysius' narrative at face value, including his assertion that the caliph and his judges listened to a lengthy speech about ecclesiology. Nevertheless, his account tells us much about how Dionysius envisaged the role of the Jacobite patriarch under Muslim rule. In his vision, patriarchal authority is central to the cohesion of the Christian community and the maintenance of a Christian morality with Christian laws. Those who oppose this authority are cast as contravening not only the will of the bishops, articulated through their patriarch, but also the fellowship of the Holy Spirit.

Mere monarchy, for Dionysius, is not to be compared to this priestly authority. Because they rely on inferior constrained authority, the leaders of other dhimmī groups, the Jews and the Zoroastrians, are not, in Dionysius' view, analogous to Christian leaders. Critically, in an era in which the caliph claimed a form of authority that was superior to the authority of earlier kings thanks to his status as imam, the patriarch mirrored Abbasid claims to rule by divine sanction. This in turn meant that the patriarch had the authority to discipline dissenters like Lazarus, and the narrative of his encounter with al-Ma'mun disseminates his backing for this centralized model of Christian government. Through this narrative, Dionysius projects the image of himself as the most capable intercessor the Christians could hope for and the worthy object of the support of his co-religionists.

9

Conceptions of Suryaya Identity in the Sixth to Ninth Centuries

DIONYSIUS AND OTHER Jacobite authors generated texts that described the Jacobites as a single community. Commentators on the liturgy emphasized their common purpose in a Christian life that was centred on the Eucharist and led by priests and bishops. Patriarchal legislators emphasized the boundaries of the community against marriage or socialization with outsiders. And Dionysius' history of his own time described the threats to the community's property and its people from avaricious Muslim outsiders and from dissenters such as Abiram within the church.

This chapter describes a further use of history, namely the invocation of ancient history to argue that those who spoke Syriac, the Suryaye, were a distinct people who possessed famous kings and cultural achievements just like the Arabs, the Persians and the Greeks. In the last two chapters we saw how Dionysius engaged with Islamic history to argue for a specific kind of Christian-Muslim relations through the discourse surrounding the dhimma and through the notion of the imamate. Here we see him engaged in a third Islamicate discourse, namely the use of ancient history to compare different peoples.

In his history, Dionysius includes an important essay on the Suryaye and their past.[1] It is an essay that has a self-conscious sense of the Suryaye as a people apart. It has few precedents in earlier literature and served as a model

---

1. I have decided to keep the term Suryaya/Suryaye untranslated to stress that it is an emic term, used by the texts themselves with a shifting meaning, rather than a term I have imposed through translation. I am wary of the translation 'Syrian' because the latter can also refer to the inhabitants of a province of the Roman empire, centred on Antioch, or of the caliphate, centred on Damascus (the *bilād al-Shām*).

for later authors who wished to argue along similar lines, right into the twentieth century.[2]

Dionysius argues that the name 'Syria' should properly be used for the lands west of the Euphrates, in contrast to Mesopotamia. However, he also argues that the Suryaye were a people with kings, listing biblical figures from Damascus and Babylonia as well as other kings from Assyria and Edessa. Finally, he claims that Edessa, a city famous in earlier Syriac chronicles, was the home of the Syriac language. This chapter shows how Dionysius reused the Old Testament to assert the existence of a distinctive Suryaya people, with its own prestigious history.

I will examine Dionysius' essay in greater detail below, but we should note here how disjointed his three claims are. They are based on different criteria (territory, kingship and language) and do not align neatly to describe the same population or the same period of history. I suggest, therefore, that we are dealing with claims that were not widely acknowledged at the time when Dionysius wrote but instead were rather novel.

In this chapter I seek to trace how these three discourses of territory, kinship and language were asserted and how Dionysius came to combine them in the context of Arab Muslim rule. I also consider what he jettisoned in his essay, namely the ascetic culture that had once been a distinctive feature of Syriac Christianity and the assertions of ancient astrological knowledge, which seem to have had unsavoury, pagan connotations for Dionysius. I attempt to set out these developments chronologically.

'Ethnies' before Modernity

The historian of nationalism Antony Smith has suggested that it is possible to recognize the roles that myths and symbols play in emphasizing the differences between peoples in the premodern world without labelling these groups 'nations' or the process 'nationalism'. He proposes the term 'ethnie' for a group united by a shared self-definition (such as an ethnonym), shared myths (especially stories of common descent), public culture, legal standardization and a notion of territory.[3]

---

2. Michael uses Dionysius' essay as his main source for an appendix (MS IV, 748–51 / III, 442–47) on the Suryaye. Barsoum 2003 can be read as a modern example of this tradition.

3. A. Smith 2004: 15–18.

I follow Smith's definition here, but with four important caveats. The first is that an ethnie is also like a nation in that it binds together a number of different forms of belonging. The ethnonym (in our case 'Suryaye') acts as a magnet around which other forms of identity are gathered. Second, much of the evidence studied in this chapter is the work of ethnic or sectarian entrepreneurs:[4] men such as Dionysius who tried to appeal to preexisting facets of identity or attachment (such as language use or established custom) and tie them to other forms of identity or justify them through an appeal to the past. The texts rarely show us the straightforward existence of ethnies; rather, they are attempts to will ethnies into existence through identitarian discourse.

Third, although we do find some evidence of shared public culture and legal standardization among speakers of Syriac in the early Islamic period, the texts I examine here do not make very much of these features. So, even if, as we saw in chapter 6, legal codification was an important part of churchmanship (and of the definition of confessional groupings) in this period, I do not see this vocabulary in Dionysius' definition of the Suryaye as an ethnic group. On the other hand, what is found in the early medieval sources is an interest in marriage. Smith emphasizes a sense of common descent as an aspect of ethnie, but this sense may entail a tacit presumption of persistent ethnic endogamy, which is rendered explicit when it is challenged by powerful or wealthy outsiders. The need to defend marriage boundaries is an important trigger for an ethnic consciousness. In a similar vein, exclusion from systems of redistribution or specific ethnic/religious penalties may also clarify a sense of group difference.[5]

Fourth, ethnies, like nations, can be involved in mutual comparison, in which ethnies are placed in a hierarchy and/or certain characteristics are deemed to qualify a group as a people or a civilization. We see such comparison, for instance, in the discussion of the Muslim humanist Mas'udi, who compares the Muslim umma to other *ummāt* of the past and present, such as the Persians, the Assyrians and the Chaldeans, on the basis of the groups' discoveries and achievements.[6] Other Islamicate conceptions of the world are more clearly divided according to political claims, such as the eight monarchs depicted on the walls of the late Umayyad bathhouse at Qusayr 'Amra.

4. For this terminology, see Mathiesen 2015.
5. Wimmer 2013: 103–4. Also note Wimmer 2013: 71 for the role of the state in breaking up interethnic marriages, a phenomenon discussed below.
6. Cooperson 2015.

The images show simultaneously the universal claims of the caliphs and the division of the Umayyad world according to the kingdoms that existed at the appearance of Islam.[7] Arguments about the 'peoplehood' of various groups were not isolated from one another but rather proceeded according to rules set for one people that were then exported to others.[8] In our case, these trend-setting peoples were the Greeks and the Arabs.

The Spread of Syriac in the Fourth and Fifth Centuries

Syriac, the dialect of Aramaic native to Edessa, was unusual among the languages of the eastern Roman empire in that it avoided the common fate of disappearance in the face of the ever-expanding use of Greek. The expansion of the Greek Bible concluded a long process in which languages such as Isaurian, Lydian and Galatian, and with them any distinctive historical traditions that they might have preserved, were forgotten.[9] Syriac's resistance must owe something to its prestige as a missionary language through which Christianity was spread into the Caucasus and Mesopotamia, and as a scriptural language.[10] In particular, Tatian's (d. c. 180) Gospel harmony, the *Diatessaron*, was composed in Syriac and emphasized ascetic, renunciant strands in the preaching of Jesus.[11] This harmony achieved widespread fame, in spite of the controversy it would later attract.

One of the most striking marks of Syriac's new prominence was the spread of Syriac south and west of the Euphrates, where it can be observed in both epigraphy and manuscript production in the fifth century.[12] Inscriptions in Syriac remained vastly outnumbered by inscriptions in Greek. Nevertheless, Syriac's prominence is striking given that building inscriptions are highly public, politicized statements and the inscriptions are found in a region in which Greek had monopolized this kind of display for centuries. David Taylor has persuasively argued that the spread of Syriac reflects the adoption of Edessene Aramaic and its distinctive script as a high dialect by speakers of the many

---

7. Fowden 2004: ch. 7.

8. I have been influenced by contemporary debates in the study of religion, where it is increasingly recognized that the term 'religion' is loaded by its reference to an archetypal religion, which is often Protestant Christianity. See Asad 1993; Bayly 1988; Masuzawa 2005; Nongbri 2013.

9. Millar 1996; Trombley 1994: II, 104.

10. Wood 2010: 78–79.

11. Petersen 1994.

12. Millar 2015d: 534–38.

other forms of Aramaic that were spoken around the Fertile Crescent from Sinai to the Persian frontier.[13] A similar argument might be made for the use of Syriac in the Sasanian world at this time, though we do not have the epigraphic evidence to allow us to track its spread in the same way.[14]

A second indication of the new significance of Syriac was that Christian writings in the language were widely recognized. For instance, the church historians refer to the writings of the fourth-century poet-theologian Ephrem, especially his hymns, which were translated into and imitated in Greek and continued in Syriac by men such as Cyrillonas, Narsai (d. 502) and Jacob of Serug (d. 521).[15] The hagiographies of Theodoret of Cyrrhus (d. 457) popularized the achievements of ascetics in Syria and Mesopotamia (while still warning the reader of the presence of heterodox or extreme ideas in the region).[16]

A further example of the recognition of a claim made in Syriac by Greek writers is the record of the so-called *Abgar Legend* by Eusebius of Caesarea (d. 340). Eusebius claims to have found this letter in the archives of Edessa. He approvingly quotes its claim that a first-century king of Edessa, Abgar 'the Black', corresponded with Jesus and offered to rescue him from the Jews in Jerusalem.[17] Even though some modern historians have called into question whether Eusebius actually did see such a document in Edessa,[18] his endorsement of the story in his *Ecclesiastical History* essentially placed Edessa on the pilgrimage route as an extension of the Holy Land itinerary[19] and gave a seal of approval to the archive of Edessa, which in turn made it an attractive and prestigious source for future historians.[20]

13. Taylor 2002.

14. Briquel-Chatonnet 2001 stresses the fact that the scripts used to write Syriac in the east are derived from Edessene estrangela and are not related to scripts used locally in the third century, such as those of Ashur or Hatra.

15. For Ephrem Graecus, see Lash 2003. The literature on Ephrem and his school is vast, but see Brock 1992.

16. Wood 2010: ch. 2.

17. Desreumaux 1990; Drijvers 1990; Griffith 2003; Wood 2010: 82–95.

18. Millar 2015e: 568.

19. See Egeria, *Itinerarium*, §7 for her visits to Edessa and Harran.

20. For this archive in the third century, see Segal 1970: 20–21. For the use of the archive for sixth-century histories, such Pseudo-Joshua the Stylite's account of the war of 502–6 and the *Chronicle of Edessa*, see Debié 1999–2000; Desreumaux 1990; Witakowski 1984–86. For the derivation of the Abgarid king lists from these archives, see Luther 1999; Witakowski 1987: 77.

Writing in Syriac in the fifth century capitalized on the new fame of Edessa as an ancient Christian centre in various ways. The Syriac *Doctrina Addai*, probably composed in the mid-fifth century, continues the *Abgar Legend* by describing the mission of the apostle Addai to the court of Abgar after the Crucifixion and the conversion of the whole city to Christianity. It reports how the ancestors of prominent families in the fifth century greeted Addai and how he read to them from the *Diatessaron* and instituted ascetic orders in the city, the *bnay qyama*, a distinctively Mesopotamian form of ascetic life that predated Egyptian-style cenobitic monasticism. The *Doctrina Addai* also celebrates a letter sent by Jesus to Abgar in which Jesus promises that the city will remain invulnerable—a useful boast indeed for a city located on Rome's frontier with Sasanian Iran.[21]

The *Doctrina Addai* thus builds on the Eusebian endorsement of the *Abgar Legend* to assert its apostolic foundation and its wholly Christian character (conveniently ignoring the continued presence of both Jews and pagans). It uses the story of very early conversion to claim preeminence alongside the other great cities of the empire. And it justifies the endurance of distinctive ascetic customs as ordained by an apostle.

However, we should also recognize what the *Doctrina Addai* does not do: there is no sense of wider peoplehood here, or use of a distinctive ethnonym such as 'Suryaye'. And there is no emphasis on the Syriac language. The interest group for which it speaks is the Edessene aristocracy, who claimed descent from the courtiers of Abgar and who used this story of conversion to project their own authority back into the past.[22] We can find an interest in language and, perhaps implicitly, in ethnicity in one contemporary saint's life, the *Life of Euphemia and the Goth*, a cautionary tale against marriage to foreigners who do not speak Syriac.[23] And the ethnonym 'Suryaya' is employed in a fifth-century translation of Eusebius' *Ecclesiastical History*.[24] But we should acknowledge that at this point, pride in the city of Edessa and its antiquity or in the distinctive customs of Mesopotamia did not equate to the notion of a distinct Suryaye people with their own customs, language and territory.

21. Wood 2010: 82–95.
22. Wood 2010: 93–95, 99–100.
23. Wood 2010: 95–98.
24. See Wright and Maclean 1898: 183 for the description of the philosopher Bardaisan as a Suryaya.

The Sixth Century and the Miaphysite Movement

The sixth century saw the composition of significant writings in Syriac that were linked to the Severan Miaphysite movement. I have argued that some of these texts, such as the anonymous *Julian Romance* and John of Ephesus' (d. 588) *Lives of the Eastern Saints*, deployed tropes of ascetic superiority, partially inherited from earlier Syriac literature, in order to criticize the Chalcedonians. These texts perpetuated a notion of Edessa's religious purity as the first Christian city and as the preserver of an apostolic ascetic tradition. In an environment of periodic Chalcedonian persecution, Miaphysite writers emphasized the preservation of an orthodox Christianity in the places in which Christianity had first taken root: in the city of Edessa (in the case of the *Julian Romance*) and among the ascetics of Mesopotamia (in the case of John of Ephesus). In both cases, an ascetic tradition that was sometimes considered heteropraxy by church reformers of all confessions was represented as the guarantee of faithfulness to Christ's message and to orthodox belief. Furthermore, the claim that the holy men of John's Mesopotamia constituted a bastion of true belief in the face of heretical persecution also allowed authors to criticize Roman emperors and to show how the latter had failed to deserve the support of the people.[25]

Fergus Millar has drawn attention to a second important feature of Syriac writing in this period, namely the translation into Syriac from Greek of numerous works of Miaphysite theology, especially the works of Severus of Antioch, and the composition of histories and works of theology for the Miaphysite community. He observes that the manuscript evidence for sixth-century Syriac demonstrates the role of the language 'in the creation of a sectarian . . . collective history of the "orthodox", and in the establishment of an orthodox canon of literature, in the form of letters, homilies, biographies and ecclesiastical histories'.[26] There is some indication that Syriac acquired Miaphysite connotations in the fact that another dialect of Aramaic (Christian Palestinian Aramaic) was endorsed as an alternative high dialect among Chalcedonians in Palestine[27] (though Chalcedonians further north continued to use Syriac until well after Dionysius' lifetime).[28] None of this implies an intrinsic

25. Wood 2010: chs. 5 and 6.

26. Millar 2015f: 674.

27. Desreumaux 1987.

28. See, e.g., manuscripts copied in Melkite circles in Edessa in the sixth and eighth centuries: Mouterde 1932; Thomson 1962.

connection between speakers of Syriac and Miaphysitism. As Millar notes, 'we need not insist on any explanation [for the translation of Severus et al.] beyond the need to make such works available to a Syriac-speaking public'.[29] Rather, the displacement of the Miaphysite leadership into rural monasteries and the fact that these happened to be in areas in which Syriac was used explain the linguistic shift in Miaphysite writings.[30]

Some writers employ 'Suryaye' as an ethnonym in this period. An important example is John of Ephesus' *Lives of the Eastern Saints*, though we should note that he uses the term only on a handful of occasions. However, the text does not dwell on ethnic difference, and John's use of ethnic language seems incidental and not particularly loaded.

Muriel Debié has argued that John of Ephesus employs 'Suryaye' with a religious connotation and restricts it to Miaphysites.[31] But I do not think that we can credit John with using an 'ethno-confessional' term. Although most of the figures he refers to in his hagiography are Miaphysite, there are no cases of speakers of Syriac being discounted as Suryaye because of their religious beliefs, which is what one might expect if John were actually creating or enforcing an ethno-confessional boundary in a culturally mixed region.

John's criteria for membership of the Suryaye, insofar as he has any, are likely to be linguistic. In one hagiography, the *Life of John of Beth Urtaya*, he says that the saint was given this name because he spoke Urtaya, a rarely attested language of the Caucasus, though he was 'by race a Suryaya'.[32] John does not display any animus toward speakers of Greek; indeed, he was likely bilingual himself and saw bilingualism as an important pastoral tool. But he does seem to use native language as a proxy for ethnic membership, although, as the example of John of Beth Urtaya shows, this was not always easy to establish.

John uses the term 'Suryaya' for the following:

1. the holy man Zuʿra, a native of Sophanene in Armenia IV, while in Constantinople;[33]
2. himself ('John the Suryaya, the converter of the pagans');[34]

29. Millar 2015f: 675.
30. Frend 1972: 294–95; Wood 2010: 175.
31. Debié 2009b: 109.
32. John of Ephesus, *Lives of the Eastern Saints*, PO 19:208.
33. John of Ephesus, *Lives of the Eastern Saints*, PO 17:27; PO 17:35; PO 18:528.
34. John of Ephesus, *Lives of the Eastern Saints*, PO 19:157.

3. deacons in Ingilene, Persia, Armenia and Maypherkat;[35]
4. John of Beth Urtaya;
5. the missionary John Hephaestu, whom he describes as 'by race a Suryaya, that is a Palestinian from the city of Gaza'.[36]

I think that he identifies the ethnicity of individuals when it is unexpected or noteworthy, as it is in the case of himself and Zuʿra as members of a Syriac-speaking community in Constantinople. Zuʿra's ethnicity was contentious since it was mentioned by his opponents in order to blacken his name ('the Suryaya deceiver'),[37] so John may have felt obliged to mention it in order to exonerate the saint by reference to his pious life.

E. W. Brooks dismissed John's use of the term 'Suryaye' for the deacons of Ingilene, Persia, Armenia and Maypherkat as a slip of the pen, but I am not sure that we should be so hasty. It now seems more likely to me that John wanted to emphasize that these deacons, like John of Beth Urtaya, were native users of Syriac (whether they had moved to these territories or been brought up there is not mentioned).[38]

The reference to John Hephaestu is interesting, since it shows that John subsumed other Aramaic-speaking populations into the Suryaye. Given the geographical focus of his work, the effect is to make Palestinians part of a greater Suryaye population centred on Mesopotamia. It is worth stressing the difference between this inclusive vision and the more precise divisions of Aramaic-speaking people and languages by other writers. Theodoret of Cyrrhus, for example, had specified that the different populations in the Levant (Phoenicians, Palestinians, Mesopotamians, etc.) each had their own form of Aramaic.[39] The claim that John of Ephesus makes over the Palestinians may be rooted in the greater prestige of Syriac compared to Palestinian Aramaic. This analysis would support Desreumaux's hypothesis that Christian Palestinian Aramaic, with its own distinctive script, was developed deliberately in order to create a prestigious form of Aramaic without Mesopotamian or Miaphysite connotations.[40]

35. John of Ephesus, *Lives of the Eastern Saints*, PO 18:659.
36. John of Ephesus, *Lives of the Eastern Saints*, PO 19:527.
37. John of Ephesus, *Lives of the Eastern Saints*, PO 17:27.
38. Wood 2010: 179 n. 61.
39. Butcher 2003: 485.
40. Desreumaux 1987.

In John's usage, the term 'Suryaye' is vague and capacious, and it can consequently encompass a wide diaspora and claim all Aramaic-speaking peoples under its umbrella. However, it is important to note that John never expressly theorizes or justifies his use of ethnic or linguistic terminology, and we would be unwise to set too much store on individual examples. We should also note that some authors placed greater emphasis on the distinctive prestige of Edessa or on the Syriac language than John did: Syriac could be the language of religion, uncorrupted by the worldly advantages of Greek,[41] and Edessa the bastion of orthodoxy against pagans, heretics and Jews,[42] the land of Abraham[43] or a second Jerusalem.[44] John does not mention these tropes, perhaps because he was a native of Amida, which, unlike Edessa, was a fourth-century foundation, or because he wrote for a network that lay across the Mediterranean and was embedded in a Greek-speaking Constantinopolitan world.

The Eighth and Ninth Centuries: Jacob of Edessa and the *Chronicle to 819*

The Arab conquests introduced demographic changes that gave speakers of Syriac a much clearer sense of their differences with other populations. This period also witnessed wider debates about peoplehood, in which various attempts were made to use the pre-monotheist past to claim peoplehood in the present. Before we turn to Dionysius himself and attempt to situate his ideas within these processes, we should emphasize the fact that other writers reflected on the Syriac literary legacy or the issue of Suryaya peoplehood much less self-consciously than Dionysius did. But we can nonetheless ask important questions of these writers, namely what their reception of historical information and the terminology they use say about the importance of different kinds of identity categories.

The *Chronicle to 819* provides a good example of the enduring importance of Edessa for shaping Syriac historical writing. The bishops of Edessa were not major participants in the politics of the ninth-century Jacobite church.[45] But

41. Elias, *Life of John of Tella*, 39–42.

42. *Julian Romance.*

43. *Life of John bar Aphthonia*, 2 (114).

44. Anonymous, *Life of Jacob Baradeus* (published with John of Ephesus, *Lives of the Eastern Saints*, PO 19:259).

45. Honigmann 1954: 123.

the city remained a major centre for the production of manuscripts. Lawrence Conrad has observed that Edessa was a more vibrant scholarly centre than was either Antioch or Constantinople, in part because it had not been devastated by war and because it lay far from the loci of government (and therefore government taxation).[46]

Though composed in Qartmin, the *Chronicle to 819* illustrates Edessa's role in the imagination of the past, especially the third and fourth centuries. It devotes scenes to Abgar, to the heresies opposed by Ephrem, to the buildings of Abgar in Edessa and to the fourth-century bishops of Edessa. These scenes dominate the *Chronicle to 819*'s account of the fourth century, renouncing the broad vision of the same period espoused in Eusebius' *Ecclesiastical History* and by his Greek continuators in favour of an Edessene history, seen through the deeds of the Abgarids and the biography of Ephrem and probably drawing on a local chronicle tradition. Though Edessa is not very prominent in the *Chronicle to 819*'s account of the eighth and ninth centuries, the chronicler's sources funnel the geographical scope of the text's narrative of the formative period of Christianity onto the region of Mesopotamia and onto Edessa in particular.

We find a somewhat analogous pattern in Jacob of Edessa's continuation of the *Chronicle* of Eusebius. Eusebius had recorded the succession of the kings of the world, annotated with notes on contemporary events. Over time these regnal succession lists in the *Chronicle* of Eusebius are gradually whittled down, leaving only the Romans.[47] It is implied that the Roman empire was the end of history, a source of improvement for humankind that came to fruition with the appearance of Constantine.[48]

By contrast, Jacob's continuation of the *Chronicle* of Eusebius adds the kings of Persia, Armenia and Osrhoene to the regnal lists of the past and inserts a new kingdom, that of the Arabs, into the kingdoms of his own day.[49] A major implication of this approach is to reduce the eschatological significance of Rome, as even if Rome were to fall to the Arabs, the succession of human empires would continue. But Jacob also undermines Eusebius' notion of the

---

46. Conrad 1999.

47. Debié 2015a: 303–10 and Fowden 2014: 73. See further Keseling 1927 on the translation of the *Chronicle* into Syriac (now updated by Debié 2015a) and Mosshammer 1979 on Eusebius' working methods.

48. In general, see Cranz 1952; Schott 2008: 155–65; Wood 2010: 22–24, 31.

49. Witakowski 2008.

end of history. If we use Eusebius' *Ecclesiastical History* and his *Life of Constantine* to understand his *Chronicle*, the reduction of the number of empires seems to imply a reduction in war and anarchy, and the emergence of a single ruler of the world anticipates the worship of a single God.[50] The coming of the Arabs and their creation of a permanent empire obviously rendered such claims obsolete.[51] Jacob's inclusion of other empires in the pre-Islamic past seems designed to mitigate the sting of this sudden political change: in Jacob's new schema, there had, in fact, always been multiple centres of political authority.

Jacob's decision to include Persia was an obvious recognition of the political realities of the fourth to sixth centuries, and the evenly matched competition between Rome and Persia is a marked feature of the Syriac sources' reporting of the sixth century. Armenia and Osrhoene are less obvious candidates for inclusion, and it may be that Jacob was implicitly diminishing the uniqueness of Constantine's conversion, and hence of the importance of Rome, by celebrating other royal dynasties that had also converted, the Abgarids and the Arsacids. At any rate, the mention of Osrhoene alongside much more famous empires is a testimony to the imprint that stories like the *Abgar Legend* made on Jacob's image of the past. Other dynasties from the independent states between Rome and Persia, such as Hatra, Palmyra and Petra, are not given this prominence.

The Eighth and Ninth Centuries: The *Chronicle of Zuqnin*

The *Chronicle of Zuqnin* uses the ethnonym 'Suryaye' much more frequently than earlier chronicle sources do, but the term features only in reports of local political and social history toward the end of the *Chronicle*. The chronicler does not attempt to trace the history of the Suryaye before his own day, or to retroject a sense of ethnic difference onto his sources (chiefly Eusebius, Socrates and John of Ephesus). And he does not use his text to justify or explain the boundaries between the Suryaye and their neighbours. Rather, he finds the ethnonym a self-evident means of describing the world around him.

50. Debié 2009a: 23. For the alignment of monotheism and monarchy, see O'Meara 2005: 146–50 and Fowden 2014: 71–72.
51. See further Palmer et al. 1993 for the impact of the conquests on Syriac historiography.

The references to the Suryaye in the *Chronicle of Zuqnin* for the period about 690–750 highlight the distinction between them and other populations, especially the Tayyaye (in this context, Syrian Arab Muslims). These are

1. 'Abd al-Malik's census among the Suryaye;[52]
2. the solar calendar used by the Suryaye, which contrasts with the lunar calendar used by the Tayyaye;[53]
3. the Suryaya background of Leo III, the Roman emperor;[54]
4. Yazid II's order that a Tayyaya witness be given precedence over a Suryaya witness and that a Suryaya be paid only half of the blood money of a Tayyaya;[55]
5. the rebellion of the Tayyaye of Maypherkat against the central government and their oppression of the Suryaye, leading to the uprising of John of Pheison in about 750;[56]
6. the entrance of famine-stricken Armenians and Urtaye into the lands of the Suryaye, also called the territory of the 'people of the mountain'[57] (later we are told that both Urtaye and Suryaye inhabit the mining district of Tutis in the old Roman province of Armenia IV).[58]

I believe that the increased prominence of ethnic vocabulary stems in part from the movement of peoples into the region[59] and from the ensuing competition for resources. Comments later in the *Chronicle of Zuqnin* indicate that the Tayyaye who entered the area had been seminomadic but had begun to settle in the generation before the *Chronicle*'s completion, and the difference in lifestyle must have been a key feature that distinguished the Tayyaye and the Suryaye. Chase Robinson has noted that the use of Arabic tribal names for the *kuwar* of Diyar Bakr, Diyar Rabi'a and Diyar Mudar in the tenth century has no

---

52. *Chronicle of Zuqnin*, 154/147.

53. *Chronicle of Zuqnin*, 156/150.

54. *Chronicle of Zuqnin*, 157/151. On this issue in particular, see Gero 1973: ch. 1. He argues that the Greek sources are confused on this point and that the Syriac and Arabic traditions are correct in placing his birthplace east of the frontier, in Marash/Germanicia (e.g., Mas'udi, *Muruj*, II, 336).

55. *Chronicle of Zuqnin*, 163/155.

56. *Chronicle of Zuqnin*, 196 / 181ff.

57. *Chronicle of Zuqnin*, 199/183 and 205/188.

58. *Chronicle of Zuqnin*, 350/300. The text explicitly refers to the Roman province.

59. Normally simply called 'the land' in the *Chronicle*. Occasionally it is contrasted with 'the land of the Turks', as in the discussion of an invasion by Maslama: *Chronicle of Zuqnin*, 168/159.

precedent in Roman administrative units and contrasts with the customary use of cities to name *junds* (army districts) further south. He argues that this pattern may be linked to the settlement of frontier regions by nomadic Arabs who were paid in spoils and the relative weakness of city-based caliphal government in the region.[60] The danger posed by Tayyaye rebels, as evidenced by the Maypherkat rebellion, further suggests that military expertise was often something that set the Tayyaye apart from their Suryaya neighbours.

Most of the extracts do not call attention to religious differences between the Suryaye and the Tayyaye.[61] In his report of the Maypherkat rebellion the chronicler does equate Suryaye and Christians; but he does not dwell on the substance of religious disagreement. (There is no sense that we are dealing with Christian Tayyaye such as the Banu Taghlib.)

The tension between the local population and outsiders was heightened by the actions of the government. The Suryaye were subjected to a census and to taxation, whereas the Tayyaye were not, and the former were also granted more limited rights in terms of witness testimony and blood money.[62] In addition, though it is not mentioned here, the Tayyaye would have received payments from the dīwān.[63] The Marwanid period has been seen as a time when the caliphate used the powers of the government to emphasize its Islamic character through the construction of monumental buildings, reforms in coinage, the Arabization of the bureaucracy and some regionalized examples of iconoclasm and anti-Christian symbolism.[64] The reforms of ʿAbd al-Malik and Yazid II that the chronicler highlights may have been inspired by a wish at the level of the state to highlight the superiority of Muslims over non-Muslims.

60. Robinson 1996: 429; Robinson 2000: 61–62; Shaban 1971: 145. For the weakness of government from Mosul in this period (a government 'by Kufans for Kufans'), see Robinson 2000: 35.

61. However, Penn 2015a: 77–78 is right to point out that the *Chronicle* is, at times, conscious of the Muslims' bearing a distinct religion, with distinct beliefs, rituals and a holy book, and of the role of Muhammad in determining ideal Muslim behaviour.

62. See Friedmann 2003: 48–50 on the different levels of diya for Muslims and dhimmīs and 35 on the ability of dhimmīs to provide legal witness. The schools of law differ on both of these issues, but none of them had crystallized at this early date.

63. Kennedy 2001: esp. 88; Hoyland 2015: 99–100, 157.

64. Donner 2010: 208–10, 221; Hoyland 2015: 140, 195–200, 213–14; Howard-Johnston 2010: 498; Robinson 2005a; Heilo 2016: 52–60. For iconoclasm, see Sahner 2017. Levy-Rubin 2016 and Yarbrough 2016a debate the existence of the *shurūṭ ʿUmar* in this period.

The chronicler represents Muslims and non-Muslims as ethnic categories, Tayyaye and Suryaye, in his account of these reforms, reflecting a world in which conversion to Islam and the claims to new rights that might follow were, as yet, rare. But the government's differential treatment of the Tayyaye and the Suryaye as recipients and payers of taxes made these obvious categories for our chronicler to use.[65]

I have argued previously that the *Chronicle of Zuqnin* is a layered text that was composed in various stages, which can be discerned in the points at which the chronicle doubles back on its chronological sequence and adds new events for years that it has previously covered.[66] If my argument is correct, the ethnonyms 'Suryaye' and 'Tayyaye' may reflect late Marwanid usage before the *Chronicle* was continued after the Abbasid revolution.

The period 752–75 is covered in much greater detail. Here the *Chronicle* describes the arrival of new populations from the east, especially 'Persians', and the imposition of new tax structures by the Abbasids through governors based in Mosul. The representation of the relationship between the Tayyaye and the Suryaye changes markedly at this point: whereas before the Tayyaye had been the recipients of advantages from the government, now they are stripped of them and suffer alongside the Suryaye. The tax collectors prevent everyone, 'whether Tayyaya or Suryaya', from taking in the harvest;[67] goods are seized from both groups;[68] the Tayyaye are subjected to a census, just as the Suryaye were;[69] and the Tayyaye's stipends are stopped.[70] The phrase 'Tayyaye and Suryaye' is now used to mean all the people of the land. Thus the chronicler reports, 'The tax collectors detained everyone: Tayyaye and Suryaye, rich and poor'.[71]

The chronicler expresses sympathy for the Tayyaye, who have become fellow victims of an oppressive government. But although the Tayyaye have lost their position at the summit of the ethnic hierarchy, the government also seems keen to act against the settlement or assimilation of the Tayyaye. When the governor Musa ibn Mus'ab discovers that Tayyaye men have taken wives from among the Suryaye, sired children and mixed with them 'so that no one

---

65. The *Chronicle* seems unaware that Muslims did pay a charity tax (zakāt).
66. Wood 2011.
67. *Chronicle of Zuqnin*, 271/239.
68. *Chronicle of Zuqnin*, 292/255.
69. *Chronicle of Zuqnin*, 298/259.
70. *Chronicle of Zuqnin*, 381/321. Cf. Kennedy 2001: 97.
71. *Chronicle of Zuqnin*, 312/270. Also note similar phrases at 316/274.

could distinguish them from the Aramaye', he removes the men from the villages (and, it is implied, breaks up their families).[72] Likewise, in Mardin, the governor Khalil son of Zaydan finds that Tayyaye have taken over farmland abandoned by Suryaye who fled from tax collectors; 'he confiscated their property and made them roam again'.[73]

The Tayyaye are displaced as 'others' in the narrative by the newly arrived 'Persians'. The actual ethnic composition of the Abbasid movement's leadership and its armies has triggered much debate, but Étienne de la Vaissière's placement of the rebellion's origins in Merv is convincing.[74] This city, on the borderlands of the former Sasanian empire, had seen unprecedented levels of conversion and intermarriage.[75] As a consequence, many of the Abbasid abnā' may have seen themselves as Arabs and often claimed Arab patrilineal descent, but they also had many Persian grandparents and spoke Persian. Nimrod Hurvitz has suggested that men such as the hadith scholar Ahmad ibn Hanbal embodied several of the contradictions of this community: though Ahmad spoke Persian as well as Arabic from childhood, he was an advocate of Arab endogamy, even vis-à-vis other Muslims.[76]

However, to the chronicler of Zuqnin, and probably to Syrian Arabs as well, these eastern intruders were simply 'Persians': 'The Persian people invaded the land of Syria, subdued the Tayyaye and ruled over it in their place'.[77] After routing Marwan II, 'they flew across the land like evening wolves and eagles hungry for food'.[78] The term 'Tayyaya' is here reserved for the supporters of the Umayyads, and there is no sense in the *Chronicle* that any Tayyaye collaborated with the invaders.[79] The caliph is simply 'the king of the Persians'.[80] The

72. *Chronicle of Zuqnin*, 256/226. For Musa's later career in Egypt, where he also implemented harsh tax policies, see Kennedy 1998: 78.

73. *Chronicle of Zuqnin*, 269/237. The extent to which these exactions reflected state policy is unclear.

74. De la Vaissière 2017. See also earlier discussions in Wellhausen 1927; Shaban 1971; Agha 2003.

75. Shaban 1971: 173.

76. Hurvitz 2002: 28–31.

77. *Chronicle of Zuqnin*, 192/178. Note Kennedy 2001: 96 for the settlement of the Abbasid *abnā' al-dawla* on the Mesopotamian frontier.

78. *Chronicle of Zuqnin*, 194/180.

79. See *Chronicle of Zuqnin*, 194/181, for the pro-Umayyad rebellions of the Tayyaye. See also Cobb 2001: 44–51 on Umayyad revolts in the generation after the Abbasid revolution.

80. *Chronicle of Zuqnin*, 215/196.

'Persians', as a group, are the source of the torments of overtaxation and exploitation that occur toward the end of the *Chronicle*, and individual tax collectors are often identified as Persians.[81]

To summarize, the chronicler employs ethnic terminology much more frequently than his predecessors such as John of Ephesus did. The increase seems to reflect the influx of new populations, who played different social roles and spoke different languages and, perhaps most importantly, were favoured by the government. In much of the final part of the chronicle, the central groups described are the Suryaye, the Tayyaye and the Persians.

One difference between these populations concerned religion, but it is only right at the end of the *Chronicle*, with the martyrdom of Cyrus of Harran, that we get much of a sense of Islam as a distinct religion.[82] When discussing Suryaye who converted to Islam, the chronicler remarks that they became 'Aydoule', a hybrid community that he does not recognize as Tayyaya.[83] There are a couple of occasions on which he uses 'Suryaya' and 'Christian' interchangeably, as when John of Pheison summons the Christians to his banner in a local rebellion and when the chronicler speaks of the cemeteries of the Jews, the Suryaye and the Tayyaye,[84] but in these instances religion is an aspect of communal membership, not a thing that is chosen or reflected on. The Mesopotamia described by the chronicler was certainly not solely Jacobite, but the *Chronicle* is mostly uninterested in confessional divisions between Christians[85] and in the kinds of interconfessional conflict reported by John of Ephesus. So if we can speak of the *Chronicle* using 'Suryaye' as an ethnoconfessional term, it is only with reference to its presumption that all speakers of Syriac will naturally be Christians of some sort (but not specifically Jacobites).

81. *Chronicle of Zuqnin*, 375/317: 'The law of the Persians was, from the start, long-lasting and merciless imprisonment'. For governors, see 269/237 (the unnamed Persian official at Mardin), 273/240 (Abu ʿAwn in the Jazira), 375/317 (Khalil son of Zaydan).

82. *Chronicle of Zuqnin*, 393 / 330ff. See the discussion in Harrak 2003.

83. *Chronicle of Zuqnin*, 392/329.

84. *Chronicle of Zuqnin*, 366/310; see also 318/275 for Jews, Suryaye and Tayyaye imploring God in their different ways to end a drought.

85. One exception is the record of an earthquake on Mount Qardu, which killed 'Nestorians' gathered for a feast (*Chronicle of Zuqnin*, 227/204). There may be an implication that the earthquake was a sign of divine disapproval at their heresy. Nevertheless, judging by his discussion of manmade and natural disasters, the chronicler imagines that God was far more inclined to punish greed and avarice than 'heresy'.

Dionysius of Tel-Mahre

Dionysius devotes a section in his history to the geography of Syria and the language of the Suryaye that is explicitly quoted by Michael. This section directly addresses the puzzle of why the term 'Syria' applies to the region southwest of the Euphrates while the Syriac language comes from Mesopotamia.

Dionysius begins by differentiating Syria from Mesopotamia, which he identifies with the Arabic Jazira. However, he contends that the name 'Syria' is a general appellation for a territory that can be divided into two regions and that the Suryaye proper inhabit the region stretching from Mount Amanus to the border of Palestine and from the sea to the Euphrates. Dionysius' definition of Syria, therefore, matches the Roman administrative units of Syria and Phoenicia. Dionysius may have been motivated to provide this definition by the increased use of the ethnonym 'Suryaye', as seen in the *Chronicle of Zuqnin*, though he employs the term in a different way.

Dionysius justifies his definition with an ethnic foundation story of the kind found in the work of the sixth-century Antiochene historian John Malalas. He reports that in the time of the Israelites, two brothers, Cilikos and Suros, divided the land between them and placed a border at Mount Amanus, with Suros taking all the land to the south. After him, the area was divided into many different kingdoms.

There then follows a biblical section of Dionysius' argument, which is framed as a response to critics who argue that there was never a king of the Suryaye. He claims that when the Israelites entered the Promised Land and the Tyrians formed their own kingdom, there was a kingdom of the Idumeans at Damascus, and the Idumean kings were called kings of the Suryaye, 'as we find in the Septuagint'. He goes on to cull other references to the kings of the Suryaye from the book of Kings.

Next Dionysius turns to the lands east of the Euphrates. These, he argues, can be called 'Suryaya' metaphorically, as one would call anyone 'who speaks the Aramaic language, whether in the east or in the west, that is, from the sea up to Persia'. In this region, he says, there have been numerous kings, such as the family of Abgar at Edessa, the family of Sanatruq at Hatra, the family of Bel and Ninus at Nineveh and the family of Nebuchadnezzar at Babylon.

Dionysius concludes his presentation thus: 'We have said these things to show that the Suryaye are properly westerners and the Mesopotamians are those who are east of the Euphrates. And the root and foundation of the Syriac language, which is Aramaic, is Edessa'.[86] As an Edessene aristocrat, Dionysius had a vested interest in reasserting the Edessene origin of the Syriac language, which had been widely endorsed since Roman times. It was a claim that buttressed his own cultural capital as a bearer of a purer Syriac language than that represented by potential rivals.[87]

Dionysius makes a self-conscious attempt to understand the relationship between land, territory and language.[88] His prime targets are those who misuse geographical and ethnic names and those who say that the Suryaye have never had a kingdom. He also makes a point of emphasizing the importance of Edessa as the home of the Syriac language. To address these issues, Dionysius seeks to reconcile seven different pieces of information:

1. the contemporary geographical boundaries of Syria and Mesopotamia;
2. the foundation story of Cilikos and Suros;
3. the references to the kings of the Syrians in the Bible;
4. the dynasties of kings in Edessa and Hatra;
5. the figures Bel and Ninus, known from Hellenistic literature and referred to in Eusebius' *Chronicle*;
6. the fact that Nebuchadnezzar spoke Aramaic;
7. the origin of Syriac in Edessa and the identification of Syriac with Aramaic.

The result of his efforts is rather jagged, which suggests that Dionysius may have been one of the first to try to systematize these different ideas.

The definition of Syria that Dionysius puts forward is consistent with the geographical distinctions made in the eighth- and ninth-century sections of the *Chronicle* of Michael the Syrian. In these passages, Syria is most frequently defined in contrast to Mesopotamia, and both are depicted as higher-order

86. MS XII. 17 (IV, 523–24 / III, 76–78).

87. Nevertheless, we should note that Dionysius makes no claim for Edessa as the home of a more pure, ascetic Christianity and does not attempt to defend the distinctive forms of asceticism mentioned in the *Doctrina Addai* or in John of Ephesus. Such idiosyncrasies seem to have been abandoned as potential sources of opposition to episcopal governance or to avoid accusations of heteropraxy from other Christian confessions. For the winnowing of the ascetic tradition in Syriac literature and the view of links to 'traditional' Egyptian cenobitism, see Butts 2017; S. Johnson 2015: 55–58; Becker 2006: 172–75; Van Rompay 2000; Wood 2012.

88. It is difficult to determine exactly how this extract was contextualized in Dionysius' own chronicle. Michael places it next to sections discussing the reign of al-Maʾmun, but none of that narrative seems to be related to the debates about the nature of the Suryaye.

regions that transcend ecclesiastical provinces and the old Roman provincial structures. In other words, the territories are a greater Syria and a greater Mesopotamia, rather than the more restricted Roman provinces centred on Antioch and Apamea (Syria I and II) and on Amida and Dara (Mesopotamia I and II).[89] Occasionally, there is a further contrast between Syria, Mesopotamia and Assyria, and together these constitute the three major regions of the Jacobite church.[90] The reason that we hear less of Assyria and that it is omitted from Dionysius' definition above may reflect his focus on the patriarch and his limited jurisdiction and activity in the east. The fact that the geographical terms 'Syria' and 'Mesopotamia' began to carry broader meanings than they had in the past gave rise to struggles over authority in the eighth century, when Athanasius Sandalaya claimed superiority over other bishops as 'metropolitan of Mesopotamia'; this geographical controversy may have been stimulated by the existence of larger administrative units in the caliphate.[91] At any rate, by Dionysius' time, he was able to explicitly identify 'Mesopotamia' with 'the Jazira', though he was probably aware of the shift in usage.

The story that he uses at the start of his discussion to justify the division between Syria and Mesopotamia is a poor fit, since it is primarily concerned with the division of Syria and Cilicia. Cilicia had been a pair of Roman provinces, with capitals at Seleucia and Mopsuestia, but neither was a city of significance in the Arab period, and 'Cilicia' appears very rarely as a toponym in the seventh- to tenth-century material preserved in Michael the Syrian. However, the story of Cilikos and Suros is found in the *Chronicle* of John Malalas.[92]

89. Sixth-century sources apply such a higher-order usage alongside a more precise usage rooted in Roman administrative terms. Witness, for instance, MS IX. 14 (IV, 266 / II, 170) and XI. 1 (IV, 404 / II, 401), which describe Chalcedonian persecution and pillaging by Persian armies and use the territorial labels of Roman administration (Antioch, Euphratensia, Osrhoene and Mesopotamia in the first case and Cilicia, Palestine, Mesopotamia and Syria in the second). But terms such as Mesopotamia are increasingly used in a wider sense in the seventh-century material (Edessa as a city of Mesopotamia or Mesopotamia employed in distinction to Syria): MS XI. 13 and 14 (IV, 441 / II, 463). The bishoprics of Mesopotamia are listed as Edessa, Harran, Callinicum, Circesium, 'Armenia', Serug, Samosata, Melitene, Amida, Tella, Resh-Kepha, Arzun, Mardin and Hasn-Keph (MS XI, 23 [IV, 470 / II, 516]), a list that extends well beyond the Roman administrative unit around Amida and Dara.

90. See, e.g., MS XII. 7 (IV, 526 / III, 25); XII. 6 (IV, 490 / III, 23). The idea of these three regions of the Jacobite world comes chiefly from descriptions of the eighth century and after.

91. Robinson 2000: 39.

92. The euhemerist version found in Malalas II, 8 (30/14), describes Syros, Kilix, Phoinix and Cadmos as the sons of Agenor and Tyro and the grandchildren of Poseidon. Dionysius'

It seems likely that this narrative originated in Antioch, both because of the Greek names it features and because of its interest in Mount Amanus, which lies just outside the city.

The second set of ancient narratives, culled from the Old Testament, are given as reports concerning the descendants of Suros. Dionysius' aim here is partly to support his assertion of a greater Syria stretching from Mount Amanus to Palestine. By claiming that Bar Haddad was king of Damascus, he may be trying to align biblical data with Arab provincial geography, in which Damascus is the capital of Sham. He then supplements this material with other sources to claim Edessa, Hatra, Nineveh and Babylon as Suryaya kingdoms as well, though these were located outside the greater Syria that he has defined at the start of the section.

However, Dionysius' main agenda in this second passage is to show that the Syrians had kings in the past. This agenda is given priority over his initial emphasis on distinguishing Syria clearly from Mesopotamia, and examples from the whole of the Fertile Crescent are included to support his claims about ancient kingship. It is notable that these examples are broader than those that might have been easily taken from Jacob of Edessa and Eusebius, especially in that they include Damascus and Hatra. His choice of examples suggests that Dionysius has personally undertaken research on this issue.

Dionysius wrote in an era of multiethnic superstates, but this passage on the kings of the past indicates that he and his interlocutor agreed that past kingship was a sign of distinct peoplehood. His hypothetical opponent in this debate may have been an Arab, who could obviously boast of the greatest current empire in the world, but Dionysius could also have been engaging with the kinds of claims that might have been made by a Persian, a Roman, a speaker of Greek within the caliphate, or a Jew, all of whom might have laid claim to a 'kingdom' in the recent or more distant past.

Dionysius' assertion of past Syrian kingdoms deserves special attention because it coincided with an important moment in Muslim cultural history, the emergence of the so-called *shu ʿūbiyya*.[93] In this controversial movement, recent Persian converts to Islam asserted their superiority over Arab Muslims (even if most of them wrote in Arabic). They argued that whereas the

---

version of the story has removed Phoinix and Cadmos and made the brothers the grandchildren of Noah.

93. Savant and Webb (2017: xvi) note problems in the translation of the term *shu ʿūbī*, which they render 'bigot'.

Arabs' ancestors had been Bedouin who lived barbarous lives in the desert, theirs had been kings who had epitomized virtues, founded cities and created prosperity.[94] Sarah Savant has traced the various ways in which these celebrations of Persian superiority filtered through to later generations, including the centrality of Iranian kings to the Muslim imagination of the pre-Islamic past and the collection of ideal behaviours attributed to Persian monarchs.[95]

Other peoples also featured in these surveys of the pre-Islamic past. Partly in rebuttal of earlier Persian claims, some Muslim authors recast pre-Islamic history as a contest between Persians and Arabs, linking the kings of city-states such as Palmyra and Hatra to the Arabian peninsula and giving them Arab genealogies.[96] Others inserted the Arabs into biblical narratives, making them into enemies of Nebuchadnezzar and allies of the people of Israel.[97] Nevertheless, an important result of the shuʿūbiyya controversy was an increased interest in the pre-Islamic past on the part of Muslims and a reframing of this past as the histories of kings.[98]

This interest in pre-Islamic history made Eusebius' *Chronicle* and the Bible useful sources for Muslim intellectuals such as Masʿudi and Biruni, both of whom recognized the importance of the kingdoms of the Babylonians and the Assyrians.[99] For instance, Masʿudi discusses King Nimrod in Babel;[100] Sumeida, king of Sham, who fought Joshua;[101] the ancient kings of the *Suriyāniyyūn*;[102] and the kings of Nineveh and Mosul, whom he identifies as ʿNabat and

---

94. Good examples of this genre are the poems of Abu Nuwas and Bashar ibn Burd. Bashar, for instance, tells his readers, 'I am the son of Khusrau and of Qaysar. . . . I did not dig for and eat lizards from the stony ground / nor did my father warm himself standing astride a flame': Schoeler 1990: 280. The stress on kings makes a notable contrast to the egalitarian ethos of much Islamic writing: Marlow 1997.

95. Savant 2013: 34, 39–49, especially on Tabari. On Dinawari, see Yücesoy 2007.

96. For sources and discussion, see Webb 2016: 251. As Webb argues, the notion of an 'Arab' identity in the third century is likely an anachronism. On third-century Hatra, see Schmitt 2012. Also note the celebration of pre-Islamic Christian Arab kings such as the Jafnids and the Nasrids: Webb 2015; Toral-Niehoff 2014.

97. Webb 2016: 254.

98. Cf. Cooperson 2015. Tabari's history, the *History of Prophets and Kings*, is a particularly important example.

99. For Masʿudi's use of the Bible, see Shboul 1979: 291–92.

100. Masʿudi, *Muruj*, I, 82–84.

101. Masʿudi, *Muruj*, I, 98.

102. Masʿudi, *Muruj*, II, 78. Cf. Yaʿqubi I, 90 (1:344).

Suriyāniyyūn.'[103] In the case of Mas'udi, at least, it seems that claims of a politically autonomous past for the Suryaye, such as those made by Dionysius, had been accepted and that the 'Suriyāniyyūn' constituted an umma in Mas'udi's eyes, analogous to the Romans ('the Rūm'), the Arabs and the Persians.[104]

Severus of Sebokht: Civilization and the Suryaye

I have argued that Dionysius attempts in his history to assert Syriac people-hood by pointing to Syriac kingship in the past. But there were also parallel discourses that compared peoples with reference to their intellectual achieve-ments. Such discourses were a prominent feature of Abbasid Baghdad in the ninth and tenth centuries, when Christians and Sabians achieved fame through their mastery of medicine and astronomy, respectively (and incurred the re-sentment of some Muslim Arab competitors for their perceived unfair advantage).[105] In the case of the Christians, the belle-lettrist al-Jahiz was keen to deny that their medical abilities stemmed from the ancestral achievements of Christians as heirs to the Greek classical legacy. The 'Rūm' of his own day, he argued, were not the same as the ancient Greeks whose accomplishments in science and philosophy so impressed the patrons of Baghdad; rather, they were mere translators: 'they [the ancient Greeks] are scholars whereas this lot [contemporary Christians] are [only] workmen!'[106]

It is interesting that Dionysius does not attempt to defend the distinctive-ness or importance of the Suryaye on the basis of their mastery of science or medicine, especially since there are examples of such claims from earlier au-thors. The third-century writer Tatian, to whom the *Diatessaron* is attributed, lambasted the Greeks for claiming intellectual feats that properly belonged to other peoples, including the Egyptians, the Persians and the Babylonians, 'leading foreign words in triumph and wearing their plumes like jackdaws.'[107]

---

103. Mas'udi, *Muruj*, II, 92–94. Cf. Ya'qubi I, 91 (1:345).

104. It may be that Mas'udi's omission of Hatra as a city of Suriyāniyyūn reflects the success of the narratives that gave it an Arab genealogy, which contrast with Dionysius' claims of Hatra as an Aramaic-speaking city.

105. Putman 1975: 93–108; Richter-Bernburg 1989; Roberts 2017: 269.

106. Al-Jahiz, *Refutation of the Christians*, 4.8; Gibson 2015: 119–25.

107. Tatian, *Oratio ad Graecos*, 26. See further Wood 2010: 41–42 and Droge 1989: 85–110 for the wider discussion of the relationships among cultures and the position of Christianity with regard to the cultures of the empire.

Tatian had described himself as 'a philosopher among the barbarians, born in the land of the Assyrians'.[108]

However, we find an explicit defence of the Suryaye as a people of science in the works of the seventh-century intellectual Severus of Sebokht. Severus was a monk of Qenneshre, and in addition to his involvement in disputations with the Maronites, he was famous for his works on astronomy,[109] medicine, philosophy and mathematics. He is perhaps most noteworthy for having been the first to recognize the importance of the figure zero in Indian mathematics and for importing this concept to the Levant.[110] A native of Nisibis on the eastern side of the old Roman-Persian frontier, he is also remembered as the teacher of two other Qenneshrite intellectuals, Jacob of Edessa and the patriarch Athanasius of Balad.[111]

Severus' interest in the history of astronomy leads him to admonish those who imagine that all knowledge comes from the Greeks (*Yawnāyē*):

> Certain people believe that the Greeks alone know how to perform astronomical calculations. But all the Greek writers recognize that the Babylonians and the Egyptians preceded the Greeks and that the Babylonians are Suryaye. Ptolemy in his *Syntax* shows more: that the computation of the sun, the moon and stars occurred under Nebuchadnezzar, king of the Assyrians, and not under the Greeks. . . . The Greek oracles also showed that wisdom is found among the Chaldeans, and these are the Babylonians and the Suryaye. . . . There are those who think they have reached the limits of science because they speak Greek . . . but there are also others who know things, not only the Greeks, but also men who speak other languages. I do not say this to undermine the science of the Greeks, but to show that science is a common [enterprise].[112]

He adopts a similar stance in his treatise on the constellations:

---

108. Tatian, *Oratio ad Graecos*, 42.

109. Note his discussions on the calculation of the date of Easter and the calculation of solar eclipses: Nau 1910: 228 and 230.

110. Nau 1910: 227.

111. Hugonnard-Roche 2016; Hoyland 1997: 21. See Tannous 2013: 94 and Brock 1982a: 23–24 for Severus' circle in seventh-century Qenneshre. See also Debié 2014 on Syriac scientific achievements more generally, especially for the social role of intellectuals and the overlap between theology and science.

112. Nau 1910: 249.

That the Babylonians were Suryaye, I hope no one will deny. By their example, it shows that they defeat the argument of those who say it is not possible for Suryaye to know such a thing, for the Suryaye were the inventors and first masters of such matters.[113]

For our purposes, the most striking features of Severus' history are that it celebrates astronomy as one of the sciences that mark a civilization, that it identifies the ancient peoples of Iraq as Suryaye and that the opponents of this discourse are the Greeks, as they were with Tatian.

It is worth stressing, therefore, that the genre of civilizational comparison in which Dionysius engaged had other incarnations in the attempts of non-Greeks to undermine Greek claims to unique achievement. John Watt has recently pointed out that the Syriac translation movement preceded the interest of Muslim patrons in commissioning translations from Arabic into Greek via Syriac intermediaries. Instead, the translations of the seventh century reflect the demand of Syriac-speaking elites for knowledge that had become inaccessible as Greek education became less and less commonplace.[114]

Severus wrote in a Hellenophile intellectual world: he exchanged texts of Aristotle with his correspondents and esteemed Plato.[115] Many of the intellectual innovations of his pupil Jacob of Edessa can be linked to this background and to the wish to bring Syriac up to the standard of Greek, whether by producing accurate Bible translations,[116] by codifying the rules of grammar[117] or by importing Greek vowels to facilitate the accurate reading of Syriac.[118] Jack Tannous has argued that it was in this period (the mid-seventh century), in the monastery of Qenneshre and its circle, that the Greek patristic canon was first translated into Syriac.[119] Indeed, Qenneshre may have been an outlier as a peculiarly Hellenophile intellectual centre, and Jacob was ultimately forced to

113. Nau 1930: 332–33.

114. Watt 2014. For the translation movement as a whole, see Gutas 1998. At 21–22, Gutas is notably more downbeat about the achievements of Syriac translators in the sixth and seventh centuries: 'Compare their relative failure with the similar project undertaken by Arabic philosophers and its brilliant success. . . . The former worked without a supporting social, political and scientific context that would demand such a task'.

115. Hugonnard-Roche 2016.

116. Salvesen 2015.

117. Van Ginkel 2005: 73.

118. Segal 1953: 41–42.

119. Tannous 2013; D. King 2013.

leave the Syrian monastery of Eusebona for his attempts to introduce a Greek teaching curriculum to the monks there.[120]

We should see Severus' comments, therefore, as intended for a very small audience of Hellenophile Qenneshre monks whose native language was Syriac. Severus' message to them was to take pride in the achievements of other Suryaye before them and not to presume that they should not search out other forms of knowledge (such as the Indian mathematics that Severus was famous for).

But if there was a Qenneshrite tradition of pride in distinctively Suryaye intellectual achievements, why did Dionysius not make use of it two centuries later? Of course, he may simply have been ignorant of the details of Severus' writings. But there is also an edge to Severus' thought that may have seemed dangerously relativistic. Severus writes in neutral terms about the notorious third-century 'heresiarch' Bardaisan, who was accused of fatalistic astrological beliefs,[121] and even praises him as an astronomer.[122] And Severus' admiration of the Egyptians, the Babylonians and the Assyrians ignores the role that these people played as archetypal idolaters and persecutors of the Israelites.

When writing for a broader audience, Dionysius could not afford to appear favourable to known enemies of God's people. The image of the Assyrians as a scourge on the Israelites was an active memory: it is a recurrent theme in the *Chronicle of Zuqnin*, for instance.[123] And when Dionysius discusses the Pyramids during his visit to Egypt, he has to defend Christ's failure to destroy them by arguing that they had been allowed to stand as a reminder of the power of demons.[124] The pre-Christian past in the Near East was a dangerous thing when it seemed to celebrate polytheist religion, and the relics of past cultures, whose writings were no longer understood,[125] were symbols of an attractive but contaminating power that was still sought by people who consorted with

120. Salvesen 2015: 339.
121. Drijvers 1966.
122. Nau 1910: 227.
123. Cf. Harrak 2005. For appeals to Assyrian identity in the hagiography of the Church of the East, note Brock 1982b: 17; Walker 2006: 210, 277; Walker 2007; Becker 2008; Payne 2015: ch. 2.
124. MS XII. 17 (IV, 526 / III, 81).
125. On hieroglyphics, see Cooperson 2010. On cuneiform, see Geller 1997. For the general amnesia of ancient Assyria and Babylonia (except through the medium of the Old Testament), see Witakowski 1987: 76.

demons.[126] Engagement in demonology continued to be a charge levied against Christian clergy and monks in this period.[127] Fear of such accusations may explain why Severus' ideas were not taken up more widely in Qenneshre and form no part of Dionysius' defence of Suryaya civilization.

Conclusions

Dionysius' conception of a Syriac heritage was rooted in territory, language and a history of kingship. It provided an inspiration for later ethnic entrepreneurs such as Michael the Syrian and, through him, the 'Assyrian' nationalists of the early twentieth century.[128] But at the time when he wrote, Dionysius was highly atypical in his attempt to reconcile the territory of Syria, the Syriac language and the biblical kings of Aram. His essay on the Suryaye reflects his own status as an Edessene aristocrat, a product of a monastery that lay in Syria proper and a member of the court of the caliph. Each of these roles brought with it a peculiar perspective on the Syriac heritage that Dionysius attempted to reconcile into a single whole. But we should be aware that most Syriac speakers did not use the ethnonym 'Suryaye' in this way: for the chronicler of Zuqnin it did not possess the intricate intellectual hinterland that Dionysius gave it, and it seems to have developed as the antithesis of Tayyaye and Persians. Nor was Dionysius' conception of the Suryaya past the only possible option, as others made much more of the martial or scientific legacy of the Assyrians or the Babylonians.

126. Magic is condemned in the Jacobite canons (e.g., George canon 12); for examples of church legislation against sorcery in the Church of the East, see Wood 2013: 144. For the magical incantation bowls found in Iraq, inscribed in Hebrew and Syriac characters, see Shaked and Naveh 1985 and 1993. For the connection between ancient ruins and demons, note the *Life of Theodore of Sykeon*, 43, which describes demons being released by treasure hunters; Thomas of Marga VI, 6 (344/599), which has demons living on the site of a ruined fire temple; and *Life of Samuel of Qartmin*, XXVIII, where demons are released from a demolished ancient building.

127. See, e.g., the accusations made against the monks of Mar Mattai in *Life of Rabban Hormizd*, 80/108.

128. Atto 2011; Becker 2015.

Conclusions

THE ABBASID REVOLUTION OF 750 was a sign of the importance of the eastern half of the caliphate. The Abbasids' Khurasanian supporters were installed in new cities such as Baghdad and Raqqa/Rafiqa. The subsequent war between al-Amin and al-Ma'mun confirmed this eastern dominance, and numerous Khurasanians would find employment in the western governates of Egypt, Syria and the Jazira during al-Ma'mun's reign.[1]

The shift in the centres of power undoubtedly benefited some parts of the Jacobite church. The widespread influence of Takritians in church politics and theology owes much to the economic development of southern Iraq more generally.[2] And Dionysius' defeat of Abiram and the Gubbites depended on his connections in Raqqa and his access to ʿAbd Allah ibn Tahir, through whom he claimed to reach the ear of the caliph in Baghdad and reestablish links with Egypt.[3] Places such as Palestine and Central Asia receive very little notice in his history, and their neglect reflects a church structure dominated by a small number of well-connected monasteries.[4]

One factor in Dionysius' ability to acquire political influence was his command of Arabic. It is something that seems to distinguish him from his less politically accomplished predecessors such as George of Beltan.[5] A recurrent feature of Dionysius' history is his skilful remoulding of the vocabulary of Islamic political thought to benefit his co-religionists (and himself). He asserts the rights due to all dhimmīs when he tries to protect the Biamaye.[6] He appeals to the apostolic foundations of the patriarchate to fashion himself as the

1. Chapter 7; Hagemann 2019.
2. Chapter 5.
3. Chapters 4 and 7.
4. Chapter 4.
5. Chapter 2.
6. Chapter 7.

imam of the Christians before the caliph in an effort to prevent the atomization of Jacobite interests at court.[7] And he champions the claims of the Suryaye to have possessed a kingdom in the past and to be considered a distinct 'people' in their own right in terms that are similar to those used in debates about the Arab and Persian past.[8]

Dionysius' own political acumen is a leitmotif of the last part of his history. We should keep in mind that in spite of his protestations, he was more interested in showing his own talents than in giving an unvarnished picture of reality. Nevertheless, his conception of himself as a particularly qualified patriarch may owe something to his aristocratic heritage, which included powerful laymen in government service. At a time when the Abbasid government was becoming ever more effective in extracting taxes, a church position offered a chance to protect the investments of families such as his own through influence at court.[9] Though our sources do not give any direct indication that other aristocrats also sought episcopal careers, it would seem likely that other families were faced with similar challenges and opportunities and that some of Dionysius' readers shared his appreciation for an aristocratic education and savoir-faire.

I have stressed that the church became an increasingly lucrative institution in the Abbasid period, as the caliph propped up the patriarch's authority against critics and empowered the patriarch to collect tithes.[10] Why, then, did Jacobite laypeople tolerate the situation? One answer, from the point of view of aristocrats, is that the patriarch claimed to be able to secure good treatment and lower taxes for them from Muslim rulers and that the patriarch's authority was endorsed by the rulers.[11] Another answer, from the perspective of heads of households, is that patriarchal legislation provided clear endorsement of the rights of parents to nominate spouses for their children and of the need to marry only co-religionists during a period of Arab settlement in the countryside. Finally, all Christians would have been aware that the patriarch presided over a hierarchy that linked the great monasteries to rural communities. Through his canons, the patriarch ratified the authority of every Jacobite parish priest, and they, in turn, prayed for him during the liturgy.[12]

7. Chapter 8.
8. Chapter 9.
9. Chapters 1 and 3.
10. Chapters 2 and 3.
11. Chapters 3, 4 and 7.
12. Chapter 6.

A powerful patriarch also seems to have been beneficial to the caliph. Dionysius presented himself as a force for the good order of the state, and the caliph could use him to smooth over political disputes, even in areas where his military power was contested, as in the case of the Biamaye revolts. The patriarchs' own vested interest in the stability of al-Ma'mun's rule is apparent from the destabilization of patriarchal authority during the fourth fitna, when Dionysius and Cyriacus were challenged by the Gubbites and by Takritian dissenters and when links to Egypt were disrupted.

But Dionysius' self-representation to the caliph is not simply one of personal dependence. He also endorses the status of the Christians of the caliphate as a disarmed population that is reliant on the goodwill of the caliph for protection from the caliph's servants and their exactions. Muriel Debié and David Taylor have written of Syriac historical writing as a non-*étatiste* tradition.[13] But in the case of Dionysius, the situation is more complex. For although he inherits a Jacobite tradition that was critical of the Roman state, he defends the authority of his patron, al-Ma'mun.

Dionysius was critical of Christian lay elites like Shmuna who might have wanted to collaborate with the Byzantines, and Dionysius closes off any conceptual space for a Christian martial identity of the kind that had once been held by Christian Arabs and was still pursued by some highland Christian populations.[14] Denying the legitimacy of such an identity might have fostered an environment in which membership of the clergy and service to government administration became the most logical roles for Christian elites. But the realities of preindustrial society meant that it also eliminated Christian populations' ability to resist the government, limiting their political agency and the esteem in which they were held by their Muslim co-citizens.

13. Debié and Taylor 2012: 156.

14. Chapters 3 and 7. For the military role of the Christian Arabs under Mu'awiya see R. S. Humphreys 2006: esp. 61–62.

REGNAL TABLES

Roman Emperors

Justinian 527–65
Justin II 565–78
Tiberius 578–82
Maurice 582–602
Phocas 602–10
Heraclius 610–41
Constans II 641–68
Constantine IV 668–85
Justinian II 685–95 and 705–11
Leontius 695–98
Tiberius III 698–705
Philippikos 711–13
Anastasius II 713–15
Theodosius III 715–17
Leo III 717–41
Constantine V 741–75
Leo IV 775–80
Constantine VI 780–97
Irene 797–802
Nikepheros 802–11
Michael I 811–13
Leo V 813–20
Michael II 820–29
Theophilus 829–41

Rashidun Caliphs

Abu Bakr 632–34
Umar I 634–44

Uthman 644–56
'Ali 656–61

Sufyanid Caliphs

Mu'awiya I 661–80
Yazid I 680–83
Mu'awiya II 683–84

Marwanid Caliphs

Marwan I 684–85
'Abd al-Malik 685–705
Al-Walid I 705–15
Sulayman 715–17
Umar II 717–20
Yazid II 720–24
Hisham 724–43
Al-Walid II 743–44
Yazid III 744
Marwan II 744–50

Abbasid Caliphs

Al-Saffah 750–54
Al-Mansur 754–75
Al-Mahdi 775–85
Al-Hadi 785–86
Al-Rashid 786–809
Al-Amin 809–13
Al-Ma'mun 813–33
Al-Mu'tasim 833–42
Al-Wathiq 842–47
Al-Mutawakkil 847–61

Jacobite Patriarchs of Antioch
(after Hage 1964 and Nabe-von Schönberg 1977)

Athanasius I Gamala (595–631)
John Sedra (631–48)

Theodore (649–67)

Severus bar Mashqa (667–81)

Athanasius II of Balad (683–86)

Julian Romaya (688–708)

Elias (709–23)

Athanasius III (724–40)

Iwannis (740–54)

Ishaq of Harran (754–55)

Athanasius Sandalaya (755–58)

John of Callinicum (758–66)

David of Dara (766–75)

George of Beltan (758–66 and 775–90)

Joseph of Gubba Barraya (790–93)

Cyriacus of Takrit (793–817)

Dionysius of Tel-Mahre (817–45)

Yohannan (846–73)

Ignatius (878–83)

Theodosius (887–96)

Dionysius II (897–909)

(Datings for the patriarchal reigns are approximate.)

LIST OF FRAGMENTS OF DIONYSIUS OF TEL-MAHRE

(Peter Van Nuffelen, Maria Conterno, Marianna Mazzola)

T1

MS XII. 21 (IV, 544 / III, 111).

Ecclesiastical Fragments

F1: Preface

MS X. 20 (IV, 378 / II, 357–58).

F2: Election of Peter of Callinicum

X1234 (II, 257.23–258.7 / 193.30–194.6).

Parallel: MS X. 21 (IV, 379 / II, 360–61).

F3: Probus and John Barbour

MS Vat. Syr. 144, fol. 89 (Assemani 1721: 72–77).

Parallels: MS X. 21 (IV, 379–82 / II, 360–64); X1234 (II, 259.3–19 / 195.1–14).

F4: The schism between Damian and Peter

MS X. 22 (IV, 382–85 / II, 364–67).

F5: Origin of the domination of the 'Nestorians' in the Persian empire

Mich. Syr. VIII. 14 (IV, 239–40 / II, 123–24).

Parallels: X1234 (II, 260–61 / 196.18–36); MS XI. 4 (IV, 413–14 / II, 414–17).

F6: The union of 616
MS X. 26 (IV, 392–99 / II, 381–94).

F7: Severus of Samosata
MS XI. 7 (IV, 417–21 / II, 427–29).

F8: Election of Iwannis of Eusebona
MS XI. 21 (IV, 462–63 / II, 503–5).
Parallel: X1234 (I, 313.11–15 / 244.14–17).

F9: Death of Iwannis
Elias Nis., AH 138 = AG 1066 (174–75 / 83).
Parallels: MS XI. 25 (IV, 473 / II, 523); X813 (243/185).

F10: Election of George and schism of John of Callinicum
Elias Nis., AH 142 = AG 1074 (176/84).
Parallels: MS XI. 25 (IV, 473–76 / II, 523–25); X813 (243–46 / 185–87).

F11: Death of John of Callinicum
Elias Nis., AH 146 = AG 1074 (177/84).
Parallel: MS XI. 25 (IV, 476 / II, 525).

F12: Dionysius' election
MS XII. 10 (IV, 502–5 / III, 41–45).

F13: Philoxenus of Nisibis, Abiram
X1234 (II, 263–64 / 198–99).

F14: Trouble in Takrit
MS XII. 11 (IV, 505–7 / III, 47–49).
Parallel: X1234 (II, 265.1–6 / 199.20–25).

F15: Dionysius, Abiram and the emir ʿAbd Allah
MS XII. 12 (IV, 508–13 / III, 55–59); X1234 (II, 268.29–270.24 /
    202.25–203.35).

F16: Visit to Egypt (AG 1136)
MS XII. 13 (IV, 513–13 / III, 60–64); X1234 (II, 147 / 204.1–205.13).

F17: Debate with al-Maʾmun
MS XII. 14 (IV, 516–20 / III, 64–70).

F18: Basil of Takrit
MS XII. 15 (IV, 520–22 / III, 72–73).

F19: Salomon of Edessa and the false antichrist

X1234 (II, 265.10–28 / 199.29–200.15).

Parallel: MS XII. 16 (IV, 522 / III, 73).

F20: The meaning of Syria; prodigies

MS XII. 16 (IV, 522–25 / III, 76–79).

F21: Visit to Egypt (AG 1141)

MS XII. 16–17 (IV, 522–27 / III, 76–83); X1234 (II, 17.3–19.17 / 11.35–13.29);
    X1234 (II, 20.3–22.7 / 14.22–15.7).

F22: A great fish in Egypt

MS XII. 12 (IV, 508 / III, 55); X1234 (II, 19.17–20.2 / 13.29–14.5).

F23: Dionysius travels to Baghdad; solution to schisms in Nisibis and Mosul

MS XII. 18 (IV, 528–30 / III, 85–87); X1234 (II, 272.21–26 /
    205.14–205.18).

F24: Dionysius meets Abu Ishaq and the Nubian prince George

MS XII. 19 (IV, 530–34 / III, 90–94); X1234 (II, 272.26–273.19 / 205.19–
    206.5) (cf. X1234 [II, 33.9–13 / 23.27–30]).

F25: Death of Abiram; his brother Simeon; end of schism

MS XII. 19 (IV, 530–33 / III, 90–93); X1234 (II, 273.20–274.14 /
    206.6–206.26).

Fragments from Secular History

F26: Sergius and Iwannis Rusafaya

MS XI. 3 (IV, 408–49 / II, 411).

Parallels: MS X. 25 (IV, 390–91 / II, 379–81); X1234 (I, 221.18–224.11 /
    230.30–231.13; 174.11–176.14 / 181.4–17).

F27: Athanasius bar Gumaye

MS XI. 16 (IV, 448–49 / II, 475–77).

Parallel: X1234 (I, 294.13–295.29 / 229.8–230.16).

F28: Second siege of Constantinople; foundation of Constantinople

MS XI. 18 (IV, 452–55 / II, 486–88).

Parallel: X1234 (I, 142.8–145.6 / 113–115.11).

F29: Arab succession; death of Iwannis, patriarch of the Jacobites
Elias Nis., AH 138 = AG 1066 (174–75 / 83).
Parallel: MS XI. 25 (IV, 473 / II, 523).

F30: Pilgrimage of al-Mansur; siege of Theodosiopolis in Armenia
Elias Nis., AH 140 = AG 1068 (175/83).
Parallel: MS XI. 24 (IV, 472 / II, 518).

F31: Election of George; schism John of Callinicum
Elias Nis., AH 142 = AG 1070 (176/84).
Parallel: MS XI. 25 (IV, 475–76 / II, 525).

F32: Foundation of Baghdad by al-Mansur; death of John of Callinicum
Elias Nis., AH 146 = AG 1074 (177/84).
Parallel: MS XI. 25 (IV, 474 / II, 522).

F33: Revolt of Magi against al-Mansur
Elias Nis., AH 152 = AG 1080 (180/85).
Parallel: MS XI. 25 (IV, 475 / II, 522–23).

F34: Al-Mansur to Jerusalem; victory over Magi
Elias Nis., AH 153 = AG 1081 (180 / 85–86).
Parallel: MS XI. 25 (IV, 475 / II, 522–23).

F35: The usurper Elpidius; attempted attack on Sicily
MS XII. 3 (IV, 483–84 / III, 9).

F36: Treasure found at Edessa
MS XII. 4 (IV, 485–86 / III, 13–14).

F37: Meeting with Uthman
MS XII. 9 (IV, 500 / III, 36).

F38: Siege of Edessa
MS XII. 9 (IV, 499–500 / III, 37–39).

F39: On Leo V, Michael II, Theophilus
MS XII. 15 (IV, 520–22 / III, 70–72).

F40: End of *Chronicle*
MS XII. 21 (IV, 538–43 / III, 104–11).
Parallel: X1234 (II, 36.9–39.5 / 26.3–28.7).

BIBLIOGRAPHY

Primary Sources

Abū Yūsuf, *Kitāb al-kharāj*, ed. and tr. E. Fagnan (Paris: Librairie orientaliste / Geuthner, 1921).

Agapius, *Kitāb al- 'unwān* (part 2.2), ed. and tr. A. Vasiliev, Patrologia Orientalis [PO] 8.

'Amr ibn Mattā, *Kitāb al-majdal*, ed. and tr. H. Gismondi, *Maris, Amri, et Slibae: De patriarchis nestorianorum commentaria I: Amri et Salibae textus arabicus et versio latina* (Rome: De Luigi, 1896–99).

BH Chron = Bar Hebraeus, *Chronography*, ed. E.A.W. Budge, *The Chronography of Gregory Abu'l Faraj the Son of Aaron, the Hebrew Physician Commonly Known as Bar Hebraeus, Being the First Part of His Political History of the World* (London: Oxford University Press, 1932); tr. P. Talon (Fernelmont: EME, 2013).

BH HE = Bar Hebraeus, *Ecclesiastical History*, ed. and tr. D. Wilmshurst (Piscataway, NJ: Gorgias, 2015).

al-Azdī, *Futūḥ al-Shām*, ed. W. Less (Calcutta: Asiatic Society of Bengal, 1854).

al-Azdī, *Tārīkh al-Mawṣil*, ed. A. Habibah (Cairo: n.p., 1967).

al-Balādhurī, *Kitāb futūḥ al-buldān*, ed. M. J. de Goeje, *Liber expugnationis regionum* (Leiden: Brill, 1863, reprint 2014), tr. F. C. Murgotten, *The Origins of the Islamic State* (New York: Columbia University Press, 1924); tr. P. Hitti, *The Origins of the Islamic State* (New York: Columbia University Press, 1916).

al-Bīrūnī, *al-Āthār al-bāqiya*, tr. E. Sachau, *The Chronology of Ancient Nations* (London: Allen, 1879).

Chronicle of Seert, ed. A. Scher and tr. R. Griveau et al., PO 4, 5, 7, 13.

Chronicle of Zuqnin, ed. J.-B. Chabot, *Incerti auctoris chronicon Pseudo-Dionysianum vulgo dictum*, CSCO 91, 104, Scriptores Syri 43, 53 (Paris: E Typographeo Reipublicae, 1927–33), tr. A. Harrak, *The Chronicle of Zuqnin Parts III and IV: AD 488–775* (Toronto: Pontifical Institute of Medieval Studies, 1999); tr. W. Witakowski, *Pseudo-Dionysius, Chronicle (Also Known as the Chronicle of Zuqnin): Part III* (Liverpool: Liverpool University Press, 1996).

Chronicle to 813, ed. E. W. Brooks, *Chronica Minora III* CSCO 5, Scriptores Syri 5, 243–60, and tr. E. W. Brooks, CSCCO 6, Scriptores Syri 6, 183–96.

Chronicle to 819, ed. J.-B. Chabot, *Chronicon anonymum ad annum Christi 1234 pertinens*, CSCO 81, Scriptores Syri 36 (Leuven: Durbecq, 1916), 3–22, and tr. CSCO 109, Scriptores Syri 56 (1937).

Chronicle to 846, ed. E. W. Brooks, *Chronica Minora II* (Leipzig: Harrassowitz, 1904), 157–238, tr. J.-B. Chabot (Leuven: Durbecq, 1904), 121–80.

Chronicle to 1234, ed. J.-B. Chabot, *Chronicon anonymum ad annum Christi 1234 pertinens*, 2 vols., CSCO 81–82, Scriptores Syri 36–37 (Leuven: Durbecq, 1916–20); tr. J.-B. Chabot, CSCO 109, Scriptores Syri 56 (Leuven: Durbecq, 1937), and A. Abouna, CSCO 354, Scriptores Syri 154 (1974).

CJ = *Corpus Iuris Civilis*, ed. and tr. P. Krueger, 15th ed. (Berlin: Weidmann, 1970).

al-Dīnawarī, *al-Akhbār al-ṭiwāl*, ed. V. Guirgass (Leiden: Brill, 1888).

Doctrina Addai, tr. A. Desreumaux, *Histoire du roi Abgar et de Jésus* (Turnhout: Brepols, 1993).

Egeria, *Itinerarium*, tr. A. McGowan, *The Pilgrimage of Egeria: A New Translation of the Itinerarium Egeriae with Introduction and Commentary* (Collegeville, MN: Liturgical Press Academic, 2018).

Elias, *Life of John of Tella*, tr. J. Ghanem (PhD diss., University of Wisconsin at Madison, 1968).

Elias of Nisibis, *Chronography*, ed. and tr. E. W. Brooks and J.-B. Chabot, *Opus Chronologicum*, CSCO 62–63, Scriptores Syri, 3rd ser., 7–8 (Paris: E Typographeo Reipublicae, 1910).

Eusebius, *Chronicle* [Armenian version], ed. and tr. J. Aucher (Venice: St. Lazarus, 1818).

Eusebius, *Ecclesiastical History*, ed. G. Bardy, SC 31, 41, 55, 73 (Paris: Cerf, 1952–60), ed. and tr. H. Lawlor and J. Oulton, Loeb ed. (Cambridge, MA: Harvard University Press, 1973).

Eusebius, *Syriac Translation of the Ecclesiastical History*, ed. and tr. W. Wright and N. Maclean (London: n.p., 1898).

al-Hamadhānī, *Kitāb al-buldān*, tr. H. Massé, *Abrégé du livre des pays* (Damascus: Institut français de Damas, 1973).

History of Karka de Beth Slouq, ed. P. Bedjan, *Acta Martyrorum et Sanctorum* II (Leipzig: Harrassowitz, 1908), 507–35.

History of the Patriarchs of the Coptic Church of Alexandria, ed. and tr. B. Evetts, PO 1, 5, 10.

Ibn Jarīr, *Book of the Guide*, partial tr. G. Khoury-Sarkis, 'Le livre du guide de Yahya ibn Jarir', *L'Orient syrien* 12 (1967), 303–54, 421–80.

Ibn Shaddād, *al-Aʿlāq al-khaṭīra fī dhikr umarāʾ al-Shām wa-l-Jazīra: Taʾrīkh Ḥalab*, ed. D. Sourdel (Beirut: Institut français de Damas, 1953).

Ishodnah of Basra, *The Book of Chastity*, ed. and tr. J.-B. Chabot, *Mélanges d'archéologie et de l'histoire* 16 (1896), 225–90.

Ishoyahb III, *Letters*, ed. and tr. R. Duval, *Ishoyahb Patriarchae III: Liber Epistularum*, CSCO 11–12 (Leuven: Peeters, 1962).

Jacob of Edessa, *Chronicle*, ed. E. W. Brooks, *Chronica Minora* III (Leipzig: Harrassowitz, 1905), 261–330.

al-Jāḥiz, *Refutation of the Christians (Raḍḍ al-naṣāra)*, ed. and tr. J. Montgomery (unpublished).

John of Dara, *On Demons*, tr. E. L. Anderson (published on academia.edu).

John of Dara, *On Oblation*, tr. E. L. Anderson (published on academia.edu).

John of Dara, *On Priesthood*, tr. E. L. Anderson (published on academia.edu).

John of Dara, *On the Celestial Priesthood*, tr. E. L. Anderson (published on academia.edu).

John of Ephesus, *Ecclesiastical History: Part Three*, ed. and tr. E. W. Brooks (Leuven: Peeters, 1935–36).

John of Ephesus, *Lives of the Eastern Saints*, ed. and tr. E. W. Brooks, PO 17–19.

John of Nikiu, *Chronicle*, tr. R. H. Charles (London: Williams and Norgate, 1916).

John of Phenek, *Book of the Main Points*, ed. and tr. A. Mingana, *Sources syriaques* (Leipzig: Harrassowitz, 1908), partial tr. in Brock 1987.

Pseudo-Joshua the Stylite, *Chronicle*, tr. F. R. Trombley and J. W. Watt (Liverpool: Liverpool University Press, 2000).

Julian Romance, ed. and tr. M. Sokoloff (Piscataway, NJ: Gorgias, 2016).

Laws of the Christian Kings, ed. and tr. A. Vööbus, *The Synodicon in the West Syrian Tradition* (Leuven: CSCO, 1975–76).

Łewond Vardapet, *History*, tr. R. Bedrosian, http://www.tertullian.org/fathers/ghewond_01 _history.htm (2006).

Life of Ahudemmeh, ed. and tr. F. Nau, PO 3.

Life of Gabriel of Qartmin, ed. and tr. A. Palmer (microfiche attachment to Palmer 1990).

Life of Jacob Baradeus, ed. and tr. E. W. Brooks, PO 19.

Life of John bar Aphthonia, ed. and tr. F. Nau, *Revue de l'Orient chrétien* 7 (1902), 113–35.

Life of Marutha of Takrit, ed. and tr. F. Nau, PO 3.

Life of Rabban Bar 'Idta, ed. and tr. E. A. Wallis-Budge, *The Histories of Rabban Hôrmîzd the Persian and Rabban Bar 'Idtâ* (London: Luzac, 1904).

Life of Rabban Hormizd, ed. and tr. E. A. Wallis-Budge, *The Histories of Rabban Hôrmîzd the Persian and Rabban Bar 'Idtâ* (London: Luzac, 1904).

Life of Samuel of Qartmin, ed. and tr. A. Palmer (microfiche attachment to Palmer 1990).

Life of Stephen the Sabaite, ed. and tr. J. Lamoureaux, CSCO 578–79, Ar. 50–51 (Leuven: Peeters, 1999).

Life of Theodore of Sykeon, tr. E. Dawes and N. Baynes, *Three Byzantine Saints: Contemporary Biographies of St. Daniel the Stylite, St. Theodore of Sykeon and St. John the Almsgiver* (Oxford: Blackwell, 1948).

Life of Theodota of Amida, ed. A. Palmer, tr. J. Tannous (unpublished).

Life of Timothy of Kakushta, ed. and tr. J. Lamoureaux and C. Cairala, PO 48.

Madrashe on Cyriacus, ed. and tr. in Oez 2012.

Malalas, *Chronicle*, ed. L. Dindorf (Bonn: Weber, 1831), tr. E. Jeffreys, M. Jeffreys and R. Scott (Melbourne, 1986).

al-Ma'mūn, *Letter to the Army of Khurasan*, ed. and tr. in Arazi and Elad 1987 and 1988.

Mārī ibn Sulaymān, *Kitāb al-majdal*, ed. and tr. H. Gismondi, *Maris, Amri, et Slibae: De patriarchis nestorianorum commentaria II; Amri et Salibae textus arabicus et versio latina* (Rome: De Luigi, 1896–99).

Maronite Chronicle, ed. E. W. Brooks, *Chronica Minora* II (Leipzig: Harrassowitz, 1904), 43–74.

al-Mas'ūdī, *Kitāb al-tanbīh wa-l-ishrāf* (Leiden: Brill, 1894), tr. B. Carra de Vaux (Paris: Imprimerie nationale, 1896).

al-Mas'ūdī, *Murūj al-dhahab wa-ma'ādin al-jawhar*, ed. and tr. C. Barbier de Meynard and P. de Courteille (Paris: Société asiatique, 1861–77).

Moses bar Kepha, *On Baptism*, tr. B. Varghese, 'Moses bar Kepha's *Commentary on Baptism*', *The Harp* 24 (2009), 55–84.

Moses bar Kepha, *On Myron*, tr. B. Varghese, *Commentary on the Myron* (Piscataway, NJ: Gorgias, 2014).

Moses bar Kepha, *On the Eucharist*, tr. B. Varghese, *Commentary on the Eucharist* (Kottayam: Malankara Orthodox Church Publications, 2014).

MS = Michael the Syrian, *Chronicle*, reproduced (vol. 4) and tr. J.-B. Chabot (vols. 1–3) (Paris: Leroux, 1899–1924); Edessa-Aleppo codex ed. G. Yuhanna Ibrahim, *Texts and Translations of Michael the Great* (Piscataway, NJ: Gorgias, 2009), vol. 1.

al-Muqaddasī, *Aḥṣan al-taqāsīm fī ma ʾrifat al-aqālīm*, tr. B. Collins, *The Best Divisions for Knowledge of the Regions* (Reading: Garnet, 2001).

Piacenza Pilgrim, tr. A. Stewart, *Of the Holy Places Visited by Antoninus Martyr* (London: Adelphi, 1887).

Samaritan Chronicle, tr. M. Levy-Rubin, *The Continuatio of the Samaritan Chronicle of Abū l-Fatḥ al-Sāmirī al-Danafī* (Princeton, NJ: Darwin, 2002).

Severus Sebokht, *On Cosmography*, ed. and tr. F. Nau, 'La cosmographie au VIIe siècle chez les Syriens', *Revue de l'Orient chrétien* 5 (1910), 225–54.

Severus Sebokht, *On the Constellations*, ed. and tr. F. Nau, 'Le traité sur les "constellations" écrit, en 661, par Sévère Sébokt, évêque de Qennesrin', *Revue de l'Orient chrétien* 28 (1929–30), 327–410, and 29 (1931–32), 85–100.

Synodicon Orientale, ed. and tr. J.-B. Chabot (Paris: Imprimerie catholique, 1902).

al-Ṭabarī, *Tārīkh al-rusul wa-l-mulūk*, ed. M. J. de Goeje, *Annales quos scripsit Abu Djafar Mohammad ibn Djarir al-Tabari* (Leiden: Brill, 1879–1901), tr. E. Yarshater et al., *The History of al-Ṭabarī* (Albany: State University of New York Press, 1985–99).

Tatian, *Oratio ad Graecos*, ed. and tr. J. Trelenberg (Tübingen: Mohr Siebeck, 2012).

Theophanes, *Chronographia*, ed. J. Classen (Bonn: Weber, 1839–41), tr. C. Mango and R. Scott, *Theophanes Confessor: Byzantine and Near Eastern History AD 284–813* (Oxford: Clarendon, 1997).

Thomas of Marga, *Book of Governors*, ed. and tr. E. A. Wallis-Budge (London: Kegan, 1893).

West Syrian Synodicon, ed. and tr. A. Vööbus (Leuven: CSCO, 1975–76).

X1234, see *Chronicle to 1234*.

X813, see *Chronicle to 813*.

al-Yaʿqūbī, *Ta ʾrīkh*, ed. M. Houtsma (Leiden: Brill, 1883), tr. M. Gordon et al. (Leiden: Brill, 2017).

Secondary Sources

Abramowski, L., 1960, 'Diodore de Tarse', in A. Baudrillart et al. (eds.), *Dictionnaire d'histoire et de géographie ecclésiastiques*, vol. 14 (Paris: Letouzey et Ané), 496–504.

Abramowski, R., 1940, *Dionysius von Tell Mahre, jakobitischer Patriarch von 818–845: Zur Geschichte der Kirche unter dem Islam* (Leipzig: Brockhaus).

Adams, R. M., 1965, *Land behind Baghdad: A History of Settlement on the Diyala Plains* (Chicago: University of Chicago Press).

Agha, S. S., 2003, *The Revolution Which Toppled the Umayyads: Neither Arab nor ʿAbbāsid* (Leiden: Brill).

Ahmed, S., 2016, *What Is Islam? The Importance of Being Islamic* (Princeton, NJ: Princeton University Press).

Alpi, F., 2009, *La route royale: Sévère d'Antioche et les églises d'Orient (512–518)* (Beirut: Institut français du Proche-Orient).

Anderson, E. L., 2016, 'The Interpretation of Pseudo-Dionysius in the Works of John of Dara' (PhD diss., Yale University).

Anigbo, O.A.C., 1978, 'The Changing Pattern of Ostracism in an Igbo Community', *Africa: Rivista trimestrale di studi e documentazione dell'Istituto italiano per l'Africa e l'Oriente* 33, 419–25.

Anthony, S., 2010, 'The Syriac Account of Dionysius of Tell Maḥrē concerning the Assassination of ʿUmar b. al-Khaṭṭāb', *Journal of Near Eastern Studies* 69, 209–24.

Arazi, A., and A. Elad, 1987, '"L'épître à l'armée": Al-Maʾmūn et la seconde Daʿwa' (part 1), *Studia Islamica* 66, 27–70.

Arazi, A., and A. Elad, 1988, '"L'épître à l'armée": Al-Maʾmūn et la seconde Daʿwa' (part 2), *Studia Islamica* 67, 29–73.

Arjomand, S., 1994, 'ʿAbd Allah Ibn al-Muqaffaʿ and the ʿAbbasid Revolution', *Iranian Studies* 27, 9–36.

Asad, T., 1993, *Genealogies of Religion: Discipline and Reasons of Power in Christianity and Islam* (Baltimore: Johns Hopkins University Press).

Assemani, J. S., 1721, *Bibliotheca Orientalis: De Scriptoribus Syris Monophysitis* (Vatican City: Society for the Propagation of the Faith).

Assmann, J., 2006, *Religion and Cultural Memory: Ten Studies*, tr. R. Livingstone (Stanford, CA: Stanford University Press).

Assmann, J., 2011, *Cultural Memory and Early Civilization: Writing, Remembrance, and Political Imagination* (Cambridge: Cambridge University Press).

Astren, F., 2003a, 'Islamic Contexts of Medieval Karaism', in M. Polliack (ed.), *Karaite Judaism: A Guide to Its History and Literary Sources* (Leiden: Brill), 145–77.

Astren, F., 2003b, 'Karaite Historiography and Historical Consciousness', in M. Polliack (ed.), *Karaite Judaism: A Guide to Its History and Literary Sources* (Leiden: Brill), 25–69.

Atto, N., 2011, *Hostages in the Homeland, Orphans in the Diaspora: Identity Discourses among the Assyrian/Syriac Elites in the European Diaspora* (Leiden: Leiden University Press).

Banaji, J., 2001, *Agrarian Change in Late Antiquity: Gold, Labour, and Aristocratic Dominance* (Oxford: Oxford University Press).

Banaji, J., 2016, *Exploring the Economy of Late Antiquity: Selected Essays* (Cambridge: Cambridge University Press).

Barkey, K., 2005, 'Islam and Toleration: Studying the Ottoman Imperial Model', *International Journal of Politics, Culture and Society* 19, 5–19.

Barkey, K., and G. Gavrilis, 2016, 'The Ottoman Millet System: Non-territorial Autonomy and Its Contemporary Legacy', *Ethnopolitics* 15, 24–42.

Barsoum, I. A., 2003, *The Scattered Pearls: A History of Syriac Literature and Sciences*, rev. ed., tr. M. Moosa (Piscataway, NJ: Gorgias).

Bartelink, G.J.M., 1970, *Quelques observations sur parrhēsia dans la littérature paléo-chrétienne* (Nijmegen: Dekker en van de Vegt).

Barton, S., 2015, *Conquerors, Brides and Concubines: Interfaith Relations and Social Power in Medieval Iberia* (Philadelphia: University of Pennsylvania Press).

Bates, M. L., 1994, 'Byzantine Coinage and Its Imitations, Arab Coinage and Its Imitations: Arab-Byzantine Coinage', *Aram* 6, 381–403.

Baumstark, A., 1922, *Geschichte der syrischen Literatur, mit Ausschluß der christlich-palästinensischen Texte* (Bonn: Marcus und Weber).

Bayly, C. A., 1988, *Indian Society and the Making of the British Empire*, vol. 2, pt. 1 of *The New Cambridge History of India* (Cambridge: Cambridge University Press).

Beaumont, M., 2018a, ''Ammār al-Baṣrī: Ninth Century Christian Theology and Qur'anic Pre-suppositions', in M. Beaumont (ed.), *Arab Christians and the Qur'an from the Origins of Islam to the Medieval Period* (Leiden: Brill), 83–105.

Beaumont, M. (ed.), 2018b, *Arab Christians and the Qur'an from the Origins of Islam to the Medieval Period* (Leiden: Brill).

Becker, A. H., 2003, 'Beyond the Spatial and Temporal *Limes*: Questioning the "Parting of the Ways" outside the Roman Empire', in A. H. Becker and A. Y. Reed (eds.), *The Ways That Never Parted* (Tübingen: Mohr Siebeck), 373–92.

Becker, A. H., 2006, *Fear of God and the Beginning of Wisdom: The School of Nisibis and Christian Scholastic Culture in Late Antique Mesopotamia* (Philadelphia: University of Pennsylvania Press).

Becker, A. H., 2008, 'The Ancient Near East in the Late Antique Near East: Syriac Christian Appropriation of the Biblical East', in G. Gardner and K. L. Osterloh (eds.), *Antiquity in Antiquity: Jewish and Christian Pasts in the Greco-Roman World* (Tübingen: Mohr Siebeck), 394–416.

Becker, A. H., 2015, *Revival and Awakening: American Evangelical Missionaries in Iran and the Origins of Assyrian Nationalism* (Chicago: University of Chicago Press).

Benedetto, R. (ed.), 2008, *The New SCM Dictionary of Church History*, vol. 1, *From the Early Church to 1700* (London: SCM).

Benga, D., 2013, 'Defining Sacred Boundaries, Processes of Delimitation from the Pagan Society in Syrian Christianity according to the Didadscalia Apostolorum', *Zeitschrift für Antikes Christentum* 17, 526–59.

Berger, P. L., and T. Luckmann, 1966, *The Social Construction of Reality: A Treatise in the Sociology of Knowledge* (Garden City, NY: Anchor Books).

Bernheimer, T., 2013, *The 'Alids: The First Family of Islam 750–1200* (Edinburgh: Edinburgh University Press).

Berthier, S., 2001, *Peuplement rural et aménagements hydroagricoles dans la moyenne vallée de l'Euphrate, fin VIIᵉ–XIXᵉ siècle* (Damascus: Institut français de Damas).

Berti, V., 2009, *Vita e studi di Timotheo I (†823), patriarca cristiano di Baghdad: Ricerche sull'epistolario e sulle fonti contigue* (Paris: Association pour l'avancement des études iraniennes).

Bessard, F., 2020, *Caliphs and Merchants: Cities and Economies of Power in the Near East (700–950)* (Oxford: Oxford University Press).

Bingham, J., 1722, *Antiquities of the Christian Church*, 2 vols., reprinted 1852 (London: Henry Bohn).

Blanchard, M., 1995, 'Moses of Nisibis (fl. 906–943) and the Library of Deir Suriani', in L.S.B. MacCoull (ed.), *Studies in the Christian East in Memory of Mirrit Boutros Ghali* (Washington, DC: Society for Coptic Archaeology), 13–24.

Blankinship, K. Y., 1994, *The End of the Jihâd State: The Reign of Hishām ibn 'Abd al-Malik and the Collapse of the Umayyads* (Albany: State University of New York Press).

Blaudeau, P., 1996, 'Timothée Aelure et la direction ecclésiale de l'Empire post-chalcédonien', *Revue des études byzantines* 54, 107–33.

Blaudeau, P., 1997, 'Le voyage de Damien d'Alexandrie vers Antioche puis Constantinople (579–580): Motivations et objectifs', *Orientalia Christiana Periodica* 63, 333–61.

Blaudeau, P., 2006, *Alexandrie et Constantinople (451–491): De l'histoire à la géo-ecclésiologie* (Rome: École française de Rome).

Blaudeau, P., 2016, 'Faut-il s'interdire de parler de miaphysisme? Quelques suggestions d'un historien intéressé à la géo-ecclésiologie de la période tardo-antique', *Cristianesimo nella storia* 37, 7–18.

Bonner, M., 1996, *Violence and Holy War: Studies on the Jihad and the Arab-Byzantine Frontier* (New Haven, CT: American Oriental Society Monograph Series).

Booth, P., 2013a, *Crisis of Empire: Doctrine and Dissent at the End of Late Antiquity* (Berkeley: University of California Press).

Booth, P., 2013b, 'Sophronius of Jerusalem and the End of Roman History', in P. Wood (ed.), *History and Identity in the Late Antique Near East* (New York: Oxford University Press), 1–27.

Bosworth, C. E., 1992, 'Naṣr b. Shabath', in P. Bearman et al. (eds.), *Encyclopaedia of Islam*, 2nd ed. (Leiden: Brill).

Bowden, W., 2001, 'A New Urban Elite? Church Builders and Church Building in Late-Antique Epirus', in L. Lavan (ed.), *Recent Research in Late-Antique Urbanism* (Portsmouth, RI: Journal of Roman Archaeology), 57–68.

Braude, B. (ed.), 2014, *Christians and Jews in the Ottoman Empire: The Abridged Edition* (Boulder, CO: Lynne Rienner).

Briquel-Chatonnet, F., 2001, 'De l'écriture édessénienne à l'estrangelâ et au sertô', *Semitica* 50, 81–90.

Briquel-Chatonnet, F., et al., 2000, 'Lettre du patriarche Timothée a Maranzekha, évêque de Ninive', *Journal Asiatique* 288, 1–13.

Brock, S., 1972, 'Studies in the Early History of the Syrian Orthodox Baptismal Liturgy', *Journal of Theological Studies*, new ser., 23, 16–64.

Brock, S., 1973, 'An Early Syriac Life of Maximus the Confessor', *Analecta Bollandiana* 91, 299–346.

Brock, S., 1979, 'The Fenqitho of the Monastery of Mar Gabriel in Tur Abdin', *Ostkirchliche Studien* 28, 168–82.

Brock, S., 1982a, 'From Antagonism to Assimilation: Syriac Attitudes to Greek Learning', in S. Brock, *Syriac Perspectives on Late Antiquity* (Aldershot: Ashgate), ch. 5.

Brock, S., 1982b, 'Christians in the Sasanian Empire: A Case of Divided Loyalties', in S. Brock, *Syriac Perspectives on Late Antiquity* (Aldershot: Ashgate), ch. 6.

Brock, S., 1987, 'North Mesopotamia in the Late Seventh Century: Book XV of John Bar Penkāyē's *Rīš Mellē*', *Jerusalem Studies in Arabic and Islam* 9, 51–75.

Brock, S., 1990, 'Syriac Manuscripts Copied on the Black Mountain, near Antioch', in R. Schulz and M. Görg (eds.), *Lingua restituta orientalis: Festgabe für Julius Assfalg* (Wiesbaden: Harrassowitz), 59–67.

Brock, S., 1992, *The Luminous Eye: The Spiritual World Vision of St. Ephrem* (Kalamazoo, MI: Cistercian).

Brock, S., 2004, 'Without Mushê of Nisibis, Where Would We Be? Some Reflections on the Transmission of Syriac Literature', *Journal of Eastern Christian Studies* 56, 15–24.

Brock, S., 2007, 'A Syriac Intermediary for the Arabic Philosophy of Aristotle? In Search of a Chimera', in C. D'Ancona (ed.), *The Libraries of the Neoplatonists* (Leiden: Brill), 294–306.

Brock, S., 2009, 'Edessene Syriac Inscriptions in Late Antique Syria', in H. Cotton, R. Hoyland, J. Price and D. Wasserstein (eds.), *From Hellenism to Islam: Cultural and Linguistic Change in the Roman Near East* (Cambridge: Cambridge University Press), 289–302.

Brock, S., and L. Van Rompay, 2014, *Catalogue of the Syriac Manuscripts and Fragments in the Library of Deir al-Surian, Wadi al-Natrun (Egypt)* (Leuven: Peeters).

Brody, R., 1998, *The Geonim of Babylonia and the Shaping of Medieval Jewish Culture* (New Haven, CT: Yale University Press).

Brooks, E. W., 1900, 'A Syriac Fragment', *Zeitschrift der deutschen morgenländischen Gesellschaft* 54, 195–230.

Brooks, E. W., 1906, 'The Sources of Theophanes and the Syriac Chroniclers', *Byzantinische Zeitschrift* 15, 578–87.

Brooks, E. W., 1923, 'The Struggle with the Saracens 717–867', in J. Tanner, C. Previtte-Orton and Z. Brooke (eds.), *The Cambridge Medieval History IV* (Cambridge: Cambridge University Press), 119–38.

Brooks, E. W., 1929, 'The Patriarch Paul of Antioch and the Alexandrian Schism of 575', *Byzantinische Zeitschrift* 30, 468–76.

Brown, P., 1992, *Power and Persuasion in Late Antiquity: Towards a Christian Empire* (Madison: University of Wisconsin Press).

Brown, P., 2002, *Poverty and Leadership in the Later Roman Empire* (Hanover, NH: University Press of New England).

Bulliet, R., 2004, *The Case for Islamo-Christian Civilization* (New York: Columbia University Press).

Bundy, D., 1978, 'Jacob Baradaeus: The State of Research, a Review of Sources and a New Approach', *Le Muséon* 91, 45–86.

Butcher, K., 2003, *Roman Syria and the Near East* (London: British Museum Press).

Butts, A. M., 2017, 'Manuscript Tradition as Reception History: The Case of Ephrem the Syrian (d. 373)', *Journal of Early Christian Studies* 25, 281–306.

Byron, G., 2002, *Symbolic Blackness and Ethnic Difference in Early Christian Literature* (London: Routledge).

Cahen, C., 1954, 'Fiscalité, propriété, antagonismes sociaux en Haute-Mesopotamie au temps des premiers Abbāsides d'après Denys de Tell-Mahré', *Arabica* 1, 136–52.

Calder, N., 1993, *Studies in Early Muslim Jurisprudence* (Oxford: Clarendon).

Cameron, A., 1991, *Christianity and the Rhetoric of Empire: The Development of Christian Discourse* (Berkeley: University of California Press).

Campopiano, M., 2012, 'State, Land Tax and Agriculture in Iraq from the Arab Conquest to the Crisis of the Abbasid Caliphate (Seventh–Tenth Centuries)', *Studia Islamica*, new ser., 3, 1–37.

Canard, M., 1971, 'Ikritish', in P. Bearman et al. (eds.), *Encyclopaedia of Islam*, 2nd ed. (Leiden: Brill).

Carlson, T., 2018, *Christianity in Fifteenth-Century Iraq* (Cambridge: Cambridge University Press).

Catlos, B., 2014, 'Accursed, Superior Men: Ethno-religious Minorities and Politics in the Medieval Mediterranean', *Comparative Studies in Society and History* 56, 844–69.

Chabot, J.-B., 1899–1905, *Chronique de Michel le syrien, patriarche jacobite d'Antioche (1166–1199)* (Paris: Leroux).

Chamberlain, M., 1994, *Knowledge and Social Practice in Medieval Damascus, 1190–1350* (Cambridge: Cambridge University Press).

Cheikho, L., 1909, 'The Vows of the Prophet and Orthodox Caliphs to Christians' [in Arabic], *al-Machriq* 12, 609ff., 674ff.

Chokr, M., 1993, *Zandaqa et zindīqs en Islam au second siècle de l'hégire* (Damascus: Institut français de Damas).

Choksy, J., 1997, *Conflict and Cooperation: Zoroastrian Subalterns and Muslim Elites in Medieval Iranian Society* (New York: Columbia University Press).

Cobb, P. M., 2001, *White Banners: Contention in Abbasid Syria, 750–880* (Albany: State University of New York Press).

Connolly, R. H., and H. W. Codrington, 1913, *Two Commentaries on the Jacobite Liturgy by George Bishop of the Arab Tribes and Moses Bār Kēphā: Together with the Syriac Anaphora of St. James and a Document Entitled the Book of Life* (London: Williams and Norgate).

Conrad, L. I., 1981, 'A Nestorian Diploma of Investiture from the *Taḏkira* of Ibn Ḥamdūn: The Text and Its Significance', in W. al-Qadi (ed.), *Studia Arabica et Islamica: Festschrift for Ihsan ʿAbbas on His Sixtieth Birthday* (Beiruit: American University of Beirut Press), 83–104.

Conrad, L. I., 1991, 'Syriac Perspectives on Bilād al-Shām during the ʿAbbāsid Period', in M. A. al-Bakhit and R. Schick (eds.), *Bilad al-Sham during the Abbasid Period: Proceedings of the Fifth International Conference on the History of Bilad al-Sham* (Amman: History of Bilad al-Sham Committee), 1–44.

Conrad, L. I., 1999, '*Varietas syriaca*: Secular and Scientific Culture in the Christian Communities of Syria after the Arab Conquests', in G. Reinink and A. Klugkist (eds.), *After Bardaisan: Studies on Continuity and Change in Syriac Christianity in Honour of Professor Han J.-W. Drijvers* (Leuven: Peeters), 85–106.

Conterno, M., 2014, *La 'descrizione dei tempi' all' alba dell'espansione islamica: Un'indagine sulla storiografia greca, siriaca e araba fra VII e VIII secolo* (Berlin: De Gruyter).

Cook, M., 1980, 'The Origins of *Kalām*', *Bulletin of the School of Oriental and African Studies* 43, 32–43.

Cooperson, M., 2000, *Classical Arabic Biography: The Heirs of the Prophet in the Age of al-Maʾmun* (Cambridge: Cambridge University Press).

Cooperson, M., 2005, *Al-Maʾmun* (Oxford: Oneworld).

Cooperson, M., 2010, 'The Reception of Pharaonic Egypt in Islamic Egypt', in A. Bowman (ed.), *A Companion to Ancient Egypt* (Chichester: Blackwell), II, 1109–28.

Cooperson, M., 2015, '"Arabs" and "Iranians": The Uses of Ethnicity in the Early Abbasid Period', in B. Sadeghi et al. (eds.), *Islamic Cultures, Islamic Contexts: Essays in Honor of Professor Patricia Crone* (Leiden: Brill), 364–87.

Cooperson, M., 2016, 'An Early Arabic Conversion Story: The Case of al-Faḍl b. Sahl', in A. Korangy et al. (eds.), *Essays in Islamic Philology, History, and Philosophy: A Festschrift in Celebration and Honor of Professor Ahmad Mahdavi Damghani's 90th Birthday* (Berlin: De Gruyter), 386–99.

Cranz, F. E., 1952, 'Kingdom and Polity in Eusebius of Caesarea', *Harvard Theological Review* 45, 47–66.

Crone, P., 1980, *Slaves on Horses: The Evolution of the Islamic Polity* (Cambridge: Cambridge University Press).

Crone, P., 1989a, 'On the Meaning of the 'Abbasid Call to al-Riḍā', in C. E. Bosworth et al. (eds.) *The Islamic World from Classical to Modern Times: Essays in Honor of Bernard Lewis* (Princeton, NJ: Darwin), 95–111.

Crone, P., 1989b, *Pre-industrial Societies: Anatomy of the Pre-modern World* (Oxford: Blackwell).

Crone, P., 2004, *God's Rule: Government and Islam; Six Centuries of Medieval Islamic Political Thought* (New York: Columbia University Press).

Crone, P., 2007, 'Quraysh and the Roman Army: Making Sense of the Meccan Leather Trade', *Bulletin of the School of Oriental and African Studies* 70, 63–88.

Crone, P., 2012, *The Nativist Prophets of Early Islamic Iran: Rural Revolt and Local Zoroastrianism* (Cambridge: Cambridge University Press).

Crone, P., and M. Hinds, 1986, *God's Caliph: Religious Authority in the First Centuries of Islam* (Cambridge: Cambridge University Press).

Crone, P., and A. Silverstein, 2016, 'The Ancient Near East and Islam: The Case of Lot-Casting', in P. Crone, *Islam, the Ancient Near and Varieties of Godlessness*, vol. 3 of *Collected Studies in Three Volumes*, ed. H. Siurua (Leiden: Brill), 17–43.

Crum, W., 1908, 'A Greek Diptych of the Seventh Century', *Proceedings of the Society of Biblical Archaeology* 30, 255–65.

Daniel, E., 1979, *The Social and Political History of Khurasan under Arab Rule, 740–820* (Minneapolis: Bibliotheca Islamica).

Dauvillier, J., 1948, 'Les provinces chaldéennes "de l'extérieur" au môyen âge', in *Mélanges offerts au R. P. Ferdinand Cavallera* (Toulouse: Bibliothèque de l'Institut catholique), 261–316.

De Gifis, V., 2014, *Shaping a Qur'anic Worldview: Scriptural Hermeneutics and the Rhetoric of Moral Reform in the Caliphate of al-Ma'mun* (London: Routledge).

de Jong, A., 2016, 'The *Dēnkard* and the Zoroastrians of Baghdad', in A. Williams, S. Stewart and A. Hintze, *The Zoroastrian Flame: Exploring Religion, History and Tradition* (London: I. B. Tauris), 223–38.

de la Vaissière, É., 2007, *Samarcande et Samarra: Élites d'Asie centrale dans l'empire Abbasside* (Paris: Association pour l'avancement des études iraniennes).

de la Vaissière, É., 2017, 'The 'Abbāsid Revolution in Marw: New Data', *Der Islam* 95, 110–46.

de Vries, B., 1998, *Umm el-Jimal: A Frontier Town and Its Landscape in Northern Jordan* (Portsmouth, RI: Journal of Roman Archaeology).

de Vries, W., 1957, 'La conception de l'Église chez les Syriens séparés de Rome (Les Syriens du patriarcat d'Antioche)', *L'Orient Syrien* 2, 111–24.

Debié, M., 1999–2000, 'Record Keeping and Chronicle Writing in Antioch and Edessa', *Aram* 6–7, 409–17.

Debié, M., 2009a, 'L'héritage de l'historiographie grecque', in M. Debié (ed.), *L'historiographie syriaque* (Paris: Geuthner), 11–32.

Debié, M., 2009b, 'Syriac Historiography and Identity Formation', *Church History and Religious Culture* 89, 93–114.

Debié, M., 2010, 'Devenir chrétien dans l'Iran sassanide: La conversion à la lumière des récits hagiographiques', in S. Destephen, H. Inglebert and B. Dumézil (eds.), *Le problème de la christianisation du monde antique* (Paris: Picard), 329–58.

Debié, M., 2014, 'Sciences et savants syriaques: Une histoire multiculturelle', in E. Villey (ed.), *Les sciences en syriaque* (Paris: Geuthner), 9–66.

Debié, M., 2015a, *L'écriture de l'histoire en syriaque: Transmissions interculturelles et constructions identitaires entre hellénisme et l'islam* (Leuven: Peeters).

Debié, M., 2015b, 'Theophanes' Oriental Source: What Can We Learn from Syriac Historiography?', in M. Jankowiak and F. Montinaro (eds.), *Studies in Theophanes: Travaux et Mémoires* 19, 365–82.

Debié, M., 2016, 'Christians in the Service of the Caliph: Through the Looking Glass of Communal Identities', in A. Borrut and F. M. Donner (eds.), *Christians and Others in the Umayyad State* (Chicago: University of Chicago Press), 53–72.

Debié, M., and D. Taylor, 2012, 'Syriac and Syro-Arabic Historical Writing c. 500–c. 1400', in S. Foot and C. Robinson (eds.), *The Oxford History of Historical Writing*, vol. 2, *400–1400* (Oxford: Oxford University Press), 155–79.

Decker, M., 2009, *Tilling the Hateful Earth: Agricultural Production and Trade in the Late Antique East* (Oxford: Oxford University Press).

den Heijer, J., 1989, *Mawhūb ibn Manṣūr ibn Mufarrij et l'historiographie copto-arabe: Études sur la composition de l'Histoire des Patriarches d'Alexandrie* (Leuven: CSCO).

den Heijer, 1991, 'History of the Patriarchs', in A. Atiya (ed.), *Coptic Encyclopedia*, http://ccdl .libraries.claremont.edu/cdm/landingpage/collection/cce.

Desreumaux, A., 1987, 'La naissance d'une nouvelle écriture araméenne à l'époque Byzantine', *Semitica* 37, 95–107.

Desreumaux, A., 1990, 'La Doctrina Addaï: Le chroniqueur et ses documents', *Apocrypha* 1, 249–63.

Dickens, M., 2010, 'The Three Scythian Brothers: An Extract from the Chronicle of Michael the Great', *Parole de l'Orient* 35, 1–24.

Donner, F., 1981, *The Early Islamic Conquests* (Princeton, NJ: Princeton University Press).

Donner, F., 2010, *Muhammad and the Believers: At the Origins of Islam* (Cambridge, MA: Belknap Press of Harvard University Press).

Donner, F., 2011, 'Qur'ānicization of Religio-Political Discourse in the Umayyad Period', *Revue des mondes musulmans et de la Méditerranée* 129, 79–92.

Dorfmann-Lazarev, I., 2008, 'Beyond Empire I: Eastern Christianities from the Persian to the Turkish Conquest, 604–1071', in T. Noble and J. Smith (eds.), *The Cambridge History of Christianity*, vol. 1, *Early Medieval Christianities, c. 600–c. 1100* (Cambridge: Cambridge University Press), 65–85.

Draguet, R., 1941, 'Le Pacte de l'union de 797: Entre les Jacobites et les Julianistes du patriarcat d'Antioche', *Le Muséon* 54, 91–100.

Drake, H., 2000, *Constantine and the Bishops: The Politics of Intolerance* (Baltimore: University of Maryland Press).

Drijvers, H. J.-W., 1966, *Bardaisan of Edessa* (Groningen: Van Gorcum).

Drijvers, H. J.-W., 1967, 'Quq and the Quqites: An Unknown Sect in Edessa in the Second Century', *Numen* 14, 104–29.

Drijvers, H. J.-W., 1990, 'Apocryphal Literature in the Cultural Milieu of Osrhoëne', *Apocrypha* 1, 231–47.

Drijvers, H. J.-W., 1994, 'The Testament of Our Lord: Jacob of Edessa's Response to Islam', *Aram* 6, 104–14.

Droge, A., 1989, *Homer or Moses? Early Christian Interpretations of the History of Culture* (Tübingen: Mohr Siebeck).

Dunn, M., 1975, 'The Struggle for Abbasid Egypt' (PhD diss., University of Michigan).

Duri, A., 2011, *Early Islamic Institutions: Administration and Taxation from the Caliphate to the Umayyads and Abbasids*, tr. R. Ali (London: I. B. Tauris).

Dyakanov, A., 1912, *Cyrus of Batna: A Syrian Church Historian of the Seventh Century* [in Russian] (St. Petersburg: Типографія М. Меркушева).

Dye, G., 2011, 'Le Coran et son contexte: Remarques sur un ouvrage récent', *Oriens Christianus* 95, 247–70.

Dye, G., 2014, 'Réflexions méthodologiques sur la "rhétorique coranique"', in D. De Smet and M. A. Amir-Moezzi (eds.), *Controverses sur les écritures canoniques de l'islam* (Paris: Cerf), 147–76.

Ebied, R. Y., A. Van Roey and L. R. Wickham, 1981, *Peter of Callinicum: Anti-Tritheist Dossier* (Leuven: Peeters).

Eddé, A.-M., F. Micheau and C. Picard, 1997, *Communautés chrétiennes en pays d'islam: Du début du VIIᵉ siècle au milieu du XIᵉ siècle* (Paris: Sedes).

Edelby, N., 1950–51, 'L'autonomie législative des chrétiens en terre de l'Islam', *Archives d'histoire du droit oriental* 5, 307–51.

Eger, A., 2014, *The Islamic-Byzantine Frontier: Interaction and Exchange between Muslim and Christian Communities* (London: I. B. Tauris).

El-Cheikh, N.-M., 2004, *Byzantium Viewed by the Arabs* (Cambridge, MA: Harvard University Press).

El-Hibri, T., 1994, 'The Reign of the Abbasid Caliph al-Ma'mun' (PhD diss., Columbia University).

El-Hibri, T., 1999, *Reinterpreting Islamic Historiography: Harun al-Rashid and the Narrative of the Abbasid Caliphate* (Cambridge: Cambridge University Press).

Er, S., 2016, 'Commemoration of the Departed in the Eucharist according to Jacob of Serugh (d. 522), Jacob of Edessa (d. 708) and Moses Bar Kepho (d. 903)', in D. Winkler (ed.), *Syrische Studien: Beiträge zum 8. Deutschen Syrologie-Symposium in Salzburg 2014* (Vienna: LIT Verlag), 259–70.

Essid, Y., 1995, *A Critique of the Origins of Islamic Economic Thought* (Leiden: Brill).

Fattal, A., 1958, *Le statut légal des non-musulmans en pays d'islam* (Beirut: Imprimerie catholique).

Fedalto, G., 1988, *Hierarchia Ecclesiastica Orientalis: Series episcoporum ecclesiarum christianarum orientalium* (Padua: Massagero).

Fiey, J.-M., 1959, *Mossoul chrétienne: Essai sur l'histoire, l'archéologie et l'état actuel des monuments chrétiens de la ville de Mossoul* (Beirut: Imprimerie catholique).

Fiey, J.-M., 1963, 'Tagrit: Esquisse de l'histoire chrétienne', *L'Orient Syrien* 8, 289–342.

Fiey, J.-M., 1965–68, *Assyrie chrétienne: Contribution à l'étude de l'histoire et de la géographie ecclésiastiques et monastiques du nord de l'Iraq*, 3 vols. (Beirut: Imprimerie catholique).

Fiey, J.-M., 1967, 'Les étapes de la prise de conscience de son identité patriarcale par l'église syrienne orientale', *L'Orient Syrien* 12, 3–22.

Fiey, J.-M., 1970a, *Jalons pur un histoire de l'église en Iraq* (Leuven: CSCO).

Fiey, J.-M., 1970b, 'Les Marcionites dans les textes historiques de l'Église de Perse', *Le Muséon* 83, 183–88.

Fiey, J.-M., 1973, 'Chrétientés syriaques du Horasan et du Segestan', *Le Muséon* 86, 75–104.

Fiey, J.-M., 1980, *Chrétiens syriaques sous les Abbassides surtout à Bagdad (749–1258)* (Leuven: CSCO).

Fiey, J.-M., 1992, 'Syriaques occidentaux de "pays des perses": Ré-union avec Antioche et "grand-métropolitat" de Takrit en 628/9?', *Parole de l'Orient* 17, 113–26.

Fiey, J.-M., 1993, *Pour un Oriens Christianus Novus: Répertoire des diocèses syriaques orientaux et occidentaux* (Beirut: Franz Steiner Verlag).

Finkel, J., 1927, 'A Risāla of al-Jāḥiẓ', *Journal of the American Oriental Society* 47, 311–34.

Fiori, E., 2011, 'The Topic of Mixture as a Philosophical Key to the Understanding of the Divine Names: Dionysius and the Origenist Monk Stephen bar Sudaili', in L. Karfíková and M. Havrda (eds.), *Nomina Divina: Colloquium Dionysiacum Pragense (Prag, den 30.–31. Oktober 2009)* (Fribourg: Academic), 71–88.

Fiori, E., 2014, 'Un intellectuel alexandrin en Mésopotamie: Essai d'une interprétation d'ensemble de l'œuvre de Sergius de Rešʿaynā', in E. Coda and C. Martini Bonadeo (eds.), *De l'Antiquité tardive au Moyen Âge: Études de logique aristotélicienne et de philosophie grecque, syriaque, arabe et latine offertes à Henri Hugonnard-Roche* (Paris: Vrin), 59–90.

Fisher, G., et al., 2015, 'Arabs and Christianity', in G. Fisher (ed.), *Arabs and Empires before Islam* (Oxford: Oxford University Press), 276–372.

Florovsky, G., 1972, *Bible, Church, Tradition: An Eastern Orthodox View*, vol. 1 (Belmont, MA: Nordland).

Forand, P., 1969, 'The Governors of Mosul according to al-Azdī's *Taʾrīkh al-Mawṣil*', *Journal of the American Oriental Society* 89, 88–105.

Foss, C., 1997, 'Syria in Transition, A.D. 550–750: An Archaeological Approach', *Dumbarton Oaks Papers* 51, 189–269.

Foucault, M., 2001, *Fearless Speech*, ed. J. Pearson (Los Angeles: Semiotext[e]), https://monoskop.org/images/b/ba/Foucault_Michel_Fearless_Speech.pdf.

Fowden, G., 2004, *Qusayr ʿAmra: Art and the Umayyad Elite in Late Antique Syria* (Berkeley: University of California Press).

Fowden, G., 2014, *Before and after Muhammad: The First Millennium Refocused* (Princeton, NJ: Princeton University Press).

Frend, W.H.C., 1972, *The Rise of the Monophysite Movement* (New York: Cambridge University Press).

Frézouls, E., 1954–55, 'Recherches historiques et archeologiques sur la ville de Cyrrhus', *Annales archeologiques de la Syrie* 4–5, 89–128.

Friedmann, Y., 2003, *Tolerance and Coercion in Islam: Interfaith Relations in the Muslim Tradition* (Cambridge: Cambridge University Press).

Gaddis, M., 2005, *'There Is No Crime for Those Who Have Christ': Religious Violence in the Christian Roman Empire* (Berkeley: University of California Press).

Gagos, T., and P. van Minnen, 1994, *Settling a Dispute: Toward a Legal Anthropology of Late Antique Egypt* (Ann Arbor: University of Michigan Press).

Gatier, P.-L., 2011, 'Inscriptions grecques, mosaïques et églises des débuts de l'époque islamique au Proche-Orient (VIIe–VIIIe siècles)', in A. Borrut et al. (eds.), *Le Proche-Orient de Justinien aux Abbassides: Peuplement et dynamiques spatiales* (Turnhout: Brepols), 7–28.

Geller, M., 1997, 'The Last Wedge', *Zeitschrift für Assyriologie und vorderasiatische Archäologie* 87, 43–95.

Gellner, D., 1997, 'For Syncretism: The Position of Nepal and Japan Compared', *Social Anthropology* 5, 277–91.

Genequand, D., 2012, *Les établissements des élites omeyyades en Palmyrène et au Proche-Orient* (Beirut: Institut français du Proche-Orient).

Gero, S., 1973, *Byzantine Iconoclasm during the Reign of Leo III: With Particular Attention to the Oriental Sources* (Leuven: CSCO).

Gero, S., 1982, 'The Status of the Patriarchs of Seleucia-Ctesiphon', in N. Garsoïan, Th. F. Mathews and R. W. Thomson (eds.), *East of Byzantium: Syria and Armenia in the Formative Period* (Washington, DC: Dumbarton Oaks), 45–51.

Giardina, A., 2000, 'The Family in the Late Roman World', in A. Cameron, B. Ward-Perkins and M. Whitby (eds.), *The Cambridge Ancient History*, vol. 14, *Late Antiquity: Empire and Successors, A.D. 425–600*, 392–415.

Gibb, H.A.R., 1955, 'The Fiscal Rescript of ʿUmar II', *Arabica* 2, 1–16.

Gibson, N., 2015, 'Closest in Friendship? Al-Jāḥiẓ' Profile of Christians in Abbasid Society in "The Refutation of the Christians" (*Al-Radd ʿalā al-Naṣārā*)' (PhD diss., Catholic University of America).

Gil, M., 2003, 'The Origins of the Karaites', in M. Polliack (ed.), *Karaite Judaism: A Guide to Its History and Literary Sources* (Leiden: Brill), 73–118.

Gil, M., 2004, *Jews in Islamic Countries in the Middle Ages* (Leiden: Brill).

Gilliot, C., 1991–92, 'Ṭabarī et les chrétiens taġlibites', *Annales du département des lettres arabes, Université Saint-Joseph* 6B, 145–59.

Goitein, S., 1963, 'Evidence on the Muslim Poll Tax from Non-Muslim Sources', *Journal of the Economic and Social History of the Orient* 6, 278–95.

Goitein, S., 1970, 'Minority Self-Rule and Government Control in Islam', *Studia Islamica* 31, 101–16.

Golitzin, A., 1994, *Et introibo ad altare Dei: The Mystagogy of Dionysius Areopagita, with Special Reference to Its Predecessors in the Eastern Christian Tradition* (Thessaloniki: Patriarchikon Idruma Paterikon Meleton).

Goody, J., 1976, *Production and Reproduction: A Comparative Study of the Domestic Domain* (Cambridge: Cambridge University Press).

Goody, J., 1983, *Development of the Family and Marriage in Europe* (Cambridge: Cambridge University Press).

Goody, J., 2000, *The European Family: An Historico-anthropological Essay* (Oxford: Blackwell).

Gordon, M. M., 1964, *Assimilation in American Life: The Role of Race, Religion and National Origins* (New York: Oxford University Press).

Graumann, T., 2013, 'Theodosios II and the Politics of the First Council of Ephesus', in C. Kelly (ed.), *Theodosius II: Rethinking the Roman Empire in Late Antiquity* (Cambridge: Cambridge University Press), 109–29.

Gregg, R., 2015, *Shared Stories, Rival Tellings: Early Encounters of Jews, Christians and Muslims* (Oxford: Oxford University Press).

Gribomont, J., 1974, 'Documents sur les origines de l'église maronite', *Parole de l'Orient* 5, 95–132.

Griffith, S. H., 1988, 'Jews and Muslims in Christian Syriac and Arabic Texts of the Ninth Century', *Jewish History* 3, 65–94.

Griffith, S. H., 2002a, 'Comparative Religion in the Apologetics of the First Christian Arabic Theologians', in S. H. Griffith, *The Beginnings of Christian Theology in Arabic: Muslim-Christian Encounters in the Early Islamic Period* (Aldershot: Ashgate), ch. 1.

Griffith, S. H., 2002b, 'Ḥabīb ibn Ḥidmah Abū Ra'iṭah, a Christian *Mutakallim* of the First Abbasid Century', in S. H. Griffith, *The Beginnings of Christian Theology in Arabic: Muslim-Christian Encounters in the Early Islamic Period* (Aldershot: Ashgate), ch. 2.

Griffith, S. H., 2002c, ''Ammār al-Baṣrī's *Kitāb al-Burhān*: Christian Kalām in the First Abbasid Century', in S. H. Griffith, *The Beginnings of Christian Theology in Arabic: Muslim-Christian Encounters in the Early Islamic Period* (Aldershot: Ashgate), ch. 3.

Griffith, S. H., 2002d, 'The Apologetic Treatise of Nonnus of Nisibis', in S. H. Griffith, *The Beginnings of Christian Theology in Arabic: Muslim-Christian Encounters in the Early Islamic Period* (Aldershot: Ashgate), ch. 4.

Griffith, S. H., 2002e, 'Disputes with Muslims in Syriac Christian Texts: From Patriarch John (d. 648) to Bar Hebraeus (d. 1286)', in S. H. Griffith, *The Beginnings of Christian Theology in Arabic: Muslim-Christian Encounters in the Early Islamic Period* (Aldershot: Ashgate), ch. 5.

Griffith, S. H., 2002f, 'Muslims and Church Councils: The Apology of Theodore Abū Qurrah', in S. H. Griffith, *The Beginnings of Christian Theology in Arabic: Muslim-Christian Encounters in the Early Islamic Period* (Aldershot: Ashgate), ch. 6.

Griffith, S. H., 2002g, 'From Aramaic to Arabic: The Languages of the Monasteries of Palestine in the Byzantine and Early Islamic Periods', in S. H. Griffith, *The Beginnings of Christian Theology in Arabic: Muslim-Christian Encounters in the Early Islamic Period* (Aldershot: Ashgate), ch. 10.

Griffith, S. H., 2002h, *Yaḥyā ibn 'Adī: The Reformation of Morals* (Provo, UT: Brigham Young University Press).

Griffith, S. H., 2003, 'The Doctrina Addai as a Paradigm of Christian Thought in Edessa in the Early Fifth Century', *Hugoye* 6, 269–92.

Griffith, S. H., 2007, 'The Syriac Letters of Patriarch Timothy I and the Birth of Christian *Kalām* in the Mu'tazilite Milieu of Baghdad and Baṣrah in Early Islamic Times', in W. J. van Bekkum, J.-W. Drijvers and A. C. Klugkist (eds.), *Syriac Polemics: Studies in Honour of Gerrit Jan Reinink* (Leuven: Peeters), 103–32.

Griffith, S. H., 2008a, *The Church in the Shadow of the Mosque* (Princeton, NJ: Princeton University Press).

Griffith, S. H., 2008b, 'John of Damascus and the Church in Syria in the Umayyad Era: The Intellectual and Cultural Milieu of Orthodox Christians in the World of Islam', *Hugoye* 11, 207–37.

Griffith, S. H., 2013, *The Bible in Arabic: The Scriptures of the 'People of the Book' in the Language of Islam* (Princeton, NJ: Princeton University Press).

Griffith, S. H., 2016, 'The Manṣūr Family and Saint John of Damascus: Christians and Muslims in Umayyad Times', in A. Borrut and F. M. Donner (eds.), *Christians and Others in the Umayyad State* (Chicago: University of Chicago Press), 29–52.

Griffith, S. H., 2018, 'The Qur'an in Christian Arabic Literature: A Cursory Overview', in M. Beaumont (ed.), *Arab Christians and the Qur'an from the Origins of Islam to the Medieval Period* (Leiden: Brill), 1–19.

Grillmeier, A., 1987, *From the Council of Chalcedon (451) to Gregory the Great (590–604)*, tr. P. Allen and J. Cawte, vol. 2, pt. 1 of *Christ in Christian Tradition* (London: Mowbray).

Grillmeier, A., and T. Hainthaler, 1996, *The Church of Alexandria with Nubia and Ethiopia after 451*, tr. O. Dean, vol. 2, pt. 4 of *Christ in Christian Tradition* (London: Mowbray).

Grillmeier, A., and T. Hainthaler, 2013, *The Churches of Jerusalem and Antioch from 451 to 600*, tr. M. Ehrhardt, vol. 2, pt. 3 of *Christ in Christian Tradition* (Oxford: Oxford University Press).

Guidetti, M., 2009, 'The Byzantine Heritage in the *Dār al-Islām*: Churches and Mosques in al-Ruha between the Sixth and Twelfth Centuries', *Muqarnas* 26, 1–36.

Gutas, D., 1998, *Greek Thought, Arabic Culture: The Graeco-Arabic Translation Movement in Baghdad and Early ʿAbbāsid Society (2nd–4th/8th–10th Centuries)* (London: Routledge).

Hage, W., 1966, *Die syrisch-jakobitische Kirche in frühislamischer Zeit nach orientalischen Quellen* (Wiesbaden: Harrassowitz).

Hagemann, H.-L., 2019, 'Muslim Elites in the Early Islamic Jazīra: The *Qāḍīs* of Ḥarrān, al-Raqqa, and al-Mawṣil', in H.-L. Hagemann and S. Heidemann (eds.), *Transregional and Regional Elites: Connecting the Early Islamic Empire* (Berlin: De Gruyter), 331–58.

Halbertal, M., 1997, *The People of the Book: Canon, Meaning and Authority* (Cambridge, MA: Harvard University Press).

Haldon, J., 1992, 'The Works of Anastasius of Sinai: A Key Source for the History of Seventh-Century East Mediterranean Society and Belief', in A. Cameron and L. I. Conrad (eds.), *The Byzantine and Early Islamic Near East* (Princeton, NJ: Darwin), I, 107–47.

Haldon, J., 2016, *The Empire That Would Not Die: The Paradox of Eastern Roman Survival, 640–740* (Cambridge, MA: Harvard University Press).

Harrak, A., 1998, 'Arabisms in Part IV of the Chronicle of Zuqnin', in R. Lavenant (ed.), *Symposium Syriacum VII* (Rome: Pontificio Istituto Orientale), 469–98.

Harrak, A., 2003, 'Piecing Together the Fragmentary Account of the Martyrdom of Cyrus of Harran', *Analecta Bollandiana* 121, 297–328.

Harrak, A., 2005, 'Ah! The Assyrian Is the Rod of My Hand! Syriac View of History after the Advent of Islam', in J. J. van Ginkel, H. L. Murre-van den Berg and T. M. van Lint (eds.), *Redefining Christian Identity: Cultural Interaction in the Middle East since the Rise of Islam* (Leuven: Peeters), 45–65.

Harrak, A., 2015, 'Dionysius of Tell-Maḥrē: Patriarch, Diplomat, and Inquisitive Chronicler', in M. Doerfler, E. Fiano and K. Smith (eds.), *Syriac Encounters: Papers from the Sixth North American Syriac Symposium, Duke University, 26–29 June, 2011* (Paris: Peeters), 215–35.

Harries, J., 2001, *Law and Empire in Late Antiquity*, 2nd ed. (Cambridge: Cambridge University Press).

Hayek, M., 1986, ʿ*Ammar al-Basri: Apologie et controverses* (Beirut: Dar el-Machreq).

Hayes, E., 2017, 'Alms and the Man: Fiscal Sectarianism in the Legal Statements of the Shiʿi Imams', *Journal of Arabic and Islamic Studies* 17, 280–98.

Heather, P., 2005, *The Fall of the Roman Empire: A New History of Rome and the Barbarians* (London: Macmillan).

Heidemann, S., 2003, 'Die Geschichte von ar-Raqqa/ar-Rāfiqa', in S. Heidemann and A. Becker (eds.), *Raqqa II: Die islamische Stadt* (Mainz: Von Zabern), 9–56.

Heidemann, S., 2006, 'The History of the Industrial and Commercial Area of ' Abbāsid al-Raqqa, Called al-Raqqa al-Muḥtariqa', *Bulletin of the School of Oriental and African Studies* 69, 33–52.

Heidemann, S., 2011, 'The Agricultural Hinterland of Baghdād, al-Raqqa and Sāmarrā ': Settlement Patterns in the Diyār Muḍar', in A. Borrut et al. (eds.), *Le Proche-Orient de Justinien aux Abbasides: Peuplement et dynamiques spatiales* (Turnhout: Brepols), 43–57.

Heidemann, S., 2015, 'How to Measure Economic Growth in the Middle East?', in D. Talmon-Heller and K. Cytryn-Silverman (eds.), *Material Evidence and Narrative Sources: Interdisciplinary Studies of the History of the Muslim Middle East* (Leiden: Brill), 30–58.

Heilo, O., 2016, *Eastern Rome and the Rise of Islam: History and Prophecy* (London: Routledge).

Heiming, O., 1970, 'Ein jakobitisches Doppellektionar des Jahres 824 aus Harran in den Handschriften British Museum Add. 14485 bis 14487', in P. Granfield and J. Jungman (eds.), *Festschrift Quasten II* (Munich: Aschendorff), 768–90.

Herman, G., 2012, *A Prince without a Kingdom: The Exilarch in the Sasanian Era* (Tübingen: Mohr Siebeck).

Herrin, J., 1987, *The Formation of Christendom* (Oxford: Blackwell).

Hilkens, A., 2014, 'The Anonymous Syriac Chronicle up to the Year 1234 and Its Sources' (PhD diss., Ghent University).

Hilkens, A., 2018, *The Anonymous Chronicle of 1234 and Its Sources* (Leuven: Peeters).

Hodgson, M., 1974, *The Venture of Islam: Conscience and History in a World Civilization*, vol. 1, *The Classical Age of Islam* (Chicago: University of Chicago Press).

Honigmann, E., 1954, *Le couvent de Barṣaumā et le patriarcat jacobite d'Antioche et de Syrie* (Leuven: Durbecq).

Horn, C., 2006, *Asceticism and Christological Controversy in Fifth-Century Palestine: The Career of Peter the Iberian* (Oxford: Oxford University Press).

Howard-Johnston, J. D., 2010, *Witnesses to a World Crisis: Historians and Histories of the Middle East in the Seventh Century* (Oxford: Oxford University Press).

Hoyland, R. G., 1991, 'Arabic, Syriac and Greek Historiography in the First Abbasid Century: An Inquiry into Inter-cultural Traffic', *Aram* 3, 211–33.

Hoyland, R. G., 1997, *Seeing Islam as Others Saw It: A Survey and Evaluation of Christian, Jewish and Zoroastrian Writing on Early Islam* (Princeton, NJ: Darwin).

Hoyland, R. G., 2004, 'Language and Identity: The Twin Histories of Arabic and Aramaic (and: Why Did Aramaic Succeed Where Greek Failed?)', *Scripta Classica Israelica* 23, 183–99.

Hoyland, R. G. (tr.), 2011, *Theophilus of Edessa's Chronicle and the Circulation of Historical Knowledge in Late Antiquity and Early Islam* (Liverpool: Liverpool University Press).

Hoyland, R. G., 2015, *In God's Path: The Arab Conquests and the Creation of an Islamic Empire* (Oxford: Oxford University Press).

Huebner, S. R., 2009, 'Currencies of Power: The Venality of Office in the Later Roman Empire', in A. Cain and N. Lenski (eds.), *The Power of Religion in Late Antiquity* (Farnham: Ashgate), 167–80.

Hughes, A., 2015, *Shared Identities: Medieval and Modern Imaginings of Judeo-Islam* (Oxford: Oxford University Press).

Hugonnard-Roche, H., 2016, 'Sévère Sebokht', in R. Goulet (ed.), *Dictionnaire des philosophes antiques*, vol. 6 (Paris: CNRS).

Humfress, C., 2007, *Orthodoxy and the Courts in Late Antiquity* (Oxford: Oxford University Press).

Humphreys, M., 2014, *Law, Power and Imperial Ideology in the Iconoclast Era* (Oxford: Oxford University Press).

Humphreys, R. S., 1988, *Islamic History: A Framework for Enquiry* (Minneapolis: Bibliotheca Islamica).

Humphreys, R. S., 2006, *Mu'awiya ibn Abi Sufyan: The Savior of the Caliphate* (London: Oneworld).

Humphreys, R. S., 2014, 'Consolidating the Conquest: Arab-Muslim Rule in Syria and the Jazīrah, 630–775 CE', in J. Dijkstra and G. Fisher (eds.), *Inside and Out: Interactions between Rome and the Peoples on the Arabian and Egyptian Frontiers in Late Antiquity* (Leuven: Peeters), 391–406.

Hurvitz, N., 2002, *The Formation of Ḥanbalism: Piety into Power* (New York: Routledge).

Immerzeel, M., 2004, 'The Stuccoes of Deir al-Surian: A *Waqf* of the Takritans in Fustat?', in M. Immerzeel and J. van der Vliet (eds.), *Coptic Studies on the Threshold of a New Millennium II: Proceedings of the Seventh International Congress of Coptic Studies, Leiden* (Leuven: Peeters), 1303–20.

Immerzeel, M., 2008, 'Playing with Light and Shadow: The Stuccoes of Deir al-Surian and Their Historical Context', *Eastern Christian Art* 5, 59–74.

Innemée, K. C., 2015, 'The Doors of Deir al-Surian Commissioned by Moses of Nisibis: Some Observations on the Occasion of Their Restoration', in M. E. Doerfler, E. Fiano and K. R. Smith (eds.), *Syriac Encounters: Papers from the Sixth North American Syriac Symposium, Duke University, 26–29 June 2011* (Leuven: Peeters), 193–214.

Innemée, K. C., 2016, 'Dayr al-Suryan: New Discoveries', in K. Torjesen and G. Gabra (eds.), *Claremont Coptic Encyclopedia*, http://ccdl.libraries.claremont.edu/cdm/ref/collection/cce/id/2137.

Innemée, K. C., G. Ochała and L. Van Rompay, 2015, 'Project Report: A Memorial for Abbot Maqari of Deir al-Surian (Egypt); Wall-Paintings and Inscriptions in the Church of the Virgin Discovered in 2014', *Hugoye* 18, 147–90.

Innemée, K. C., and L. Van Rompay, 1998, 'La présence des Syriens dans le Wadi al-Natrun (Égypte): À propos des découvertes récentes de peintures et de textes muraux dans l'Église de la Vierge du Couvent des Syriens', *Parole de l'Orient* 23, 167–202.

Jankowiak, M., 2009, 'Essai d'histoire politique du monothélisme à partir de la correspondance entre les empereurs byzantins, les patriarches de Constantinople et les papes de Rome' (PhD thesis, École pratique des hautes études, Paris).

Janos, D., 2014, 'Al-Ma'mun's Patronage of Astrology', in J. J. Scheiner and D. Janos (eds.), *The Place to Go: Contexts of Learning in Baghdād, 750–1000 C.E.* (Princeton, NJ: Darwin), 389–454.

Johnson, M. E., 2013, *Praying and Believing in Early Christianity: The Interplay between Christian Worship and Doctrine* (Collegeville, MN: Liturgical).

Johnson, S. F., 2015, 'Introduction: The Social Presence of Greek in Eastern Christianity, 200–1200 CE', in S. F. Johnson (ed.), *Languages and Cultures of Eastern Christianity: Greek* (Aldershot: Ashgate), 1–122.

Jones, A.H.M., 1964, *The Later Roman Empire: A Social, Economic and Administrative Survey*, 3 vols. (Oxford: Blackwell).

Joosse, N. P., 2011, 'Between Enigma and Paradigm: The Reception of Aristotle's Politica in the Near East: The Arabic and Syriac-Aramaic Traditions', in V. Syros (ed.), *Well Begun Is Only Half Done: Tracing Aristotle's Political Ideas in Medieval Arabic, Syriac, Byzantine and Jewish Sources* (Tempe: Arizona Centre for Medieval and Renaissance Studies), 97–120.

Jugie, M., 1937, 'Gainaites', *Dictionnaire de théologie catholique* (Paris: Letouzey et Ané).

Jullien, C., 2008, *Le monachisme en Perse: La réforme d'Abraham le Grand, père des moines de l'Orient* (Leuven: Peeters).

Kalmijn, M., 1998, 'Intermarriage and Homogamy: Causes, Patterns, Trends', *Annual Review of Sociology* 24, 395–421.

Karamustafa, A., 2001, 'Community', in J. Elias (ed.), *Keywords for Islam* (Oxford: Oneworld).

Katbi, G. K., 2010, *Islamic Land Tax—al-Kharāj: From the Islamic Conquests to the Abbasid Period* (Beirut: I. B. Tauris / Centre for Arab Unity Studies).

Kaufhold, H., 2012, 'Sources of Canon Law in the Eastern Churches', in W. Hartmann and K. Pennington (eds.), *The History of Byzantine and Eastern Canon Law to 1500* (Washington, DC: Catholic University of America Press), 215–342.

Keating, S. T., 2006, *Defending the 'People of Truth' in the Early Islamic Period: The Christian Apologies of Abū Rā'iṭah* (Leiden: Brill).

Kelly, C., 2004, *Ruling the Later Roman Empire* (Cambridge, MA: Belknap Press of Harvard University Press).

Kennedy, H., 1986, *The Early Abbasid Caliphate: A Political History* (London: Croom Helm).

Kennedy, H., 1998, 'Egypt as a Province in the Islamic Caliphate, 641–868', in C. Petry (ed.), *The Cambridge History of Egypt*, vol. 1 (Cambridge: Cambridge University Press), 62–86.

Kennedy, H., 2001, *The Armies of the Caliphs: Military and Society in the Early Islamic State* (London: Routledge).

Kennedy, H., 2002, 'Military Pay and the Economy of the Early Islamic State', *Historical Research* 75, 155–69.

Kennedy, H., 2006, 'From Shahrestan to Medina', *Studia Islamica* 102, 5–35.

Kennedy, H., 2008, 'Inherited Cities', in S. Jayyusi (ed.), *Cities in the Islamic World* (Leiden: Brill), 93–113.

Kennedy, H., 2011, 'The Feeding of the Five Hundred Thousand: Cities and Agriculture in Early Islamic Mesopotamia', *Iraq* 73, 177–99.

Kennedy, H., 2015, 'The Middle East in Islamic Late Antiquity', in A. Monson and W. Scheidel (eds.), *Fiscal Regimes and the Political Economy of Premodern States* (Cambridge: Cambridge University Press), 390–403.

Keseling, P., 1927, 'Die Chronik von Eusebius in der syrischen Überlieferung', *Oriens Christianus*, 3rd ser., 1, 23–48, and 2, 33–56.

Keser-Kayaalp, E., 2013, 'Églises et monastères de Tur 'Abdin', in F. Briquel-Chatonnet (ed.), *Les églises en monde syriaque* (Paris: Geuthner), 269–88.

Keser-Kayaalp, E., 2016, 'Patronage of Churches in Late Antique Northern Mesopotamia', in C. Kapitoğlu, E. Yavuz and B. Tabib (eds.), *Spaces/Times/Peoples: Patronage and Architectural History* (Ankara: Odtü), 43–56.

Keser-Kayaalp, E., 2018, 'Church Building in the Ṭur ʿAbdin in the First Centuries of Islamic Rule', in A. Delattre, M. Legendre and P. Sijpesteijn (eds.), *Authority and Control in the Countryside: From Antiquity to Islam in the Mediterranean and Near East (Sixth–Tenth Century)* (Leiden: Brill), 176–209.

Khoury-Sarkis, G., 1967, 'Le livre du guide de Yahya ibn Jarir', *L'Orient syrien* 12, 303–54, 421–80.

King, D., 2013, 'Why Were the Syrians Interested in Greek Philosophy?', in P. Wood (ed.), *History and Identity in the Late Antique Near East* (Oxford: Oxford University Press), 61–82.

King, D., 2014, 'Continuities and Discontinuities in the History of Syriac Philosophy', in E. Coda and C. Martini Bonadeo (eds.), *De l'Antiquité tardive au Moyen Âge: Études de logique aristotélicienne et de philosophie grecque, syriaque, arabe et latine offertes à Henri Hugonnard-Roche* (Paris: Vrin), 225–43.

King, R., 1999, 'Orientalism and the Modern Myth of Hinduism', *Numen* 46, 146–85.

Kitchen, R., 2017, 'Trying to Fix What Is Broken in a Broken Age: Syrian Orthodox Synodical Canons (628–896)', *Journal of the Canadian Society for Syriac Studies* 17, 3–20.

Krakowski, E., 2017, *Coming of Age in Medieval Egypt: Female Adolescence, Jewish Law and Ordinary Culture* (Princeton, NJ: Princeton University Press).

Krueger, D., 2014, *Liturgical Subjects: Christian Ritual, Biblical Narrative, and the Formation of the Self in Byzantium* (Philadelphia: University of Pennsylvania Press).

Lamoureaux, J. C., and C. Cairala, 2001, *The Life of Timothy of Kakushta*, Patrologia Orientalis 48 (Turnhout: Brepols).

Lapidus, I., 1972, 'The Conversion of Egypt to Islam', *Israel Oriental Studies* 2, 248–62.

Lapidus, I., 1975, 'The Separation of State and Religion in the Development of Early Islamic Society', *International Journal of Middle East Studies* 6, 363–85.

Lapin, H., 2012, *Rabbis as Romans: The Rabbinic Movement in Palestine, 100–400 C.E.* (Oxford: Oxford University Press).

Lash, E., 2003, 'The Greek Writings Attributed to Saint Ephrem the Syrian', in J. Behre and A. Louth (eds.), *Abba: The Tradition of Orthodoxy in the West; Festschrift for Bishop Kallistos (Ware) of Diokleia* (New York: St. Vladimir's Seminary Press), 81–98.

Lassner, J., 1980, *The Shaping of ʿAbbāsid Rule* (Princeton, NJ: Princeton University Press).

Latham, J. D., 1990, 'Ibn al-Muqaffaʿ and Early ʿAbbasid Prose', in J. Ashtiany et al. (eds.), *ʿAbbasid Belles-Lettres*, vol. 2 of *The Cambridge History of Arabic Literature* (Cambridge: Cambridge University Press), 48–77.

Lebon, J., 1909, *Le monophysisme sévérien: Étude historique, littéraire et théologique sur la résistance monophysite au Concile de Chalcédoine jusqu' à la constitution de l'église jacobite* (Leuven: Peeters).

Leclerq, H., 1928, 'Katholikoi', *Dictionnaire d'archéologie chrétienne et de liturgie* (Paris: Letouzey et Ané).

Lee, D., 1988, 'Close-Kin Marriage in Late Antique Mesopotamia', *Greek, Roman and Byzantine Studies* 29, 403–13.

Legendre, M.A.L., and K. Younes, 2015, 'The Use of Terms Ǧizya and Ḫarāǧ in the First 200 Years of Hiǧra in Egypt', Formation of Islam project website, https://www.universiteitleiden.nl/en/research/research-projects/humanities/formation-of-islam-topics#the-use-of-terms-izya-and-ar-in-the-first-200-years-of-hi-ra-in-egypt.

Lev, Y., 2012, 'Coptic Rebellions and the Islamization of Medieval Egypt (8th–10th Century): Medieval and Modern Perceptions', *Jerusalem Studies in Arabic and Islam* 39, 303–42.

Levy-Rubin, M., 2011, *Non-Muslims in the Early Islamic Empire: From Surrender to Coexistence* (New York: Cambridge University Press).

Levy-Rubin, M., 2016, ' 'Umar II's *Ghiyār* Edict: Between Ideology and Practice', in A. Borrut and F. M. Donner (eds.), *Christians and Others in the Umayyad State* (Chicago: University of Chicago Press), 157–72.

Lewin, A., 1989, 'Roman Urban Defences in the East in Late Antiquity: The Case of the Negev', in D. H. French and C. S. Lightfoot (eds.), *The Eastern Frontier of the Roman Empire* (Oxford: BAR), 267–75.

Lewis, B., 1992, *Race and Slavery in the Middle East* (Oxford: Oxford University Press).

Liebeschuetz, J.H.W.G., 1972, *Antioch: City and Imperial Administration in the Later Roman Empire* (Oxford: Clarendon).

Liu, X., 1988, *Ancient India and Ancient China: Trade and Religious Exchanges AD 1–600* (Delhi: Oxford University Press).

Lloyd, S., and W. Brice, 1951, 'Harran', *Anatolian Studies* 1, 77–111.

Louth, A., 1989, *Denys the Areopagite* (London: Continuum).

Louth, A., 2009, 'The Reception of Dionysius in the Byzantine World: Maximus to Palamas', in S. Coakley and C. M. Stang (eds.), *Re-thinking Dionysius the Areopagite* (Oxford: Wiley-Blackwell), 55–70.

Luther, A., 1999, 'Elias von Nisibis und die Chronologie der edessenischen Könige', *Klio* 81, 180–98.

Lyman, R., 2003, 'Hellenism and Heresy', *Journal of Early Christian Studies* 11, 209–22.

Maas, M., 2003, 'Delivered from Their Ancient Customs: Christianity and the Question of Cultural Change in Early Byzantine Ethnography', in A. Grafton and K. Mills (eds.), *Conversion in Late Antiquity and the Early Middle Ages* (Rochester, NY: University of Rochester Press), 152–88.

Mabra, J., 2017, *Princely Authority in the Early Marwānid State: The Life of 'Abd al-'Azīz ibn Marwān* (Piscataway, NJ: Gorgias).

Macomber, W., 1968, 'The Authority of the Catholicos-Patriarch of Seleucia-Ctesiphon', *Orientalia Christiana Analecta* 181, 179–200.

Magness, J., 2003, *The Archaeology of the Early Islamic Settlement in Palestine* (Winona Lake, IN: Eisenbrauns).

Markus, R., 1990, *The End of Ancient Christianity* (Cambridge: Cambridge University Press).

Marlow, L., 1997, *Hierarchy and Egalitarianism in Islamic Thought* (Cambridge: Cambridge University Press).

Marsham, A., 2009, *Rituals of Islamic Monarchy: Accession and Succession in the First Muslim Empire* (Edinburgh: Edinburgh University Press).

Masuzawa, T., 2005, *The Invention of World Religions, or How European Universalism Was Preserved in the Language of Pluralism* (Chicago: University of Chicago Press).

Mathiesen, T., 2015, *Sectarian Gulf: Bahrain, Saudi Arabia and the Arab Spring That Wasn't* (Stanford, CA: Stanford University Press).

Mattson, I., 2003, 'Status-Based Definition of Need in Early Islamic *Zakat* and Maintenance Laws', in M. Bonner, M. Ener and A. Singer (eds.), *Poverty and Charity in Middle Eastern Contexts* (Albany: State University of New York Press), 31–51.

Mayerson, P., 1978, 'Anti-Black Sentiment in the *Vitae Patrum*', *Harvard Theological Review* 71, 304–11.

Mazza, R., 2011, 'Households as Communities? *Oikoi* and *Poleis* in Late Antique and Byzantine Egypt', in O. M. van Nijf and R. Alston (eds.), *Political Culture in the Greek City after the Classical Age* (Leuven: Peeters), 263–86.

Mazzola, M., 2017, 'A "Woven-Texture" Narration: On the Compilation Method of the Syriac Renaissance Chronicles (Twelfth–Thirteenth Centuries)', *Sacris Erudiri* 55, 445–63.

Meinardus, O., 1967, 'The Nestorians in Egypt', *Oriens Christianus* 15, 114–29.

Melchert, C., 2006, *Ahmad ibn Hanbal* (Oxford: Oneworld).

Menze, V.-L., 2008, *Justinian and the Making of the Syrian Orthodox Church* (Oxford: Oxford University Press).

Meyendorff, J., 1989, *Imperial Unity and Christian Divisions: The Church 450–680 AD* (Crestwood, NY: St. Vladimir's Seminary Press).

Michelson, D. A., 2014, *The Practical Christology of Philoxenus of Mabbug* (Oxford: Oxford University Press).

Mikhail, M., 2016, *Byzantine to Islamic Egypt: Religion, Identity and Politics after the Arab Conquest* (London: I. B. Tauris).

Millar, F., 1996, *The Roman Near East, 31 BC–AD 337* (Cambridge, MA: Harvard University Press).

Millar, F., 2015a, 'Imperial Government and the Maintenance of Orthodoxy: Justinian I and Irregularities at Cyrrhus in 520', in F. Millar, *Empire, Church and Society in the Late Roman East: Greeks, Jews, Syrians and Saracens* (Leuven: Peeters), 93–120.

Millar, F., 2015b, 'Community, Religion and Language in the Middle Euphrates Zone in Late Antiquity', in F. Millar, *Empire, Church and Society in the Late Roman East: Greeks, Jews, Syrians and Saracens* (Leuven: Peeters), 177–212.

Millar, F., 2015c, 'Libanius and the Near East', in F. Millar, *Empire, Church and Society in the Late Roman East: Greeks, Jews, Syrians and Saracens* (Leuven: Peeters), 213–44.

Millar, F., 2015d, 'The Syriac Acts of the Second Council of Ephesus', in F. Millar, *Empire, Church and Society in the Late Roman East: Greeks, Jews, Syrians and Saracens* (Leuven: Peeters), 529–52.

Millar, F., 2015e, 'Greek and Syriac in Edessa and Osrhoene, 213–363', in F. Millar, *Empire, Church and Society in the Late Roman East: Greeks, Jews, Syrians and Saracens* (Leuven: Peeters), 553–76.

Millar F., 2015f, 'The Evolution of the Syrian Orthodox Church in the Pre-Islamic Period: From Greek to Syriac?', in F. Millar, *Empire, Church and Society in the Late Roman East: Greeks, Jews, Syrians and Saracens* (Leuven: Peeters), 631–78.

Moorhead, J., 1981, 'Monophysite Responses to the Arab Invasions', *Byzantion* 51, 579–91.

Morony, M., 1984, *Iraq after the Muslim Conquests* (Princeton, NJ: Princeton University Press).

Morony, M., 2005, 'History and Identity in the Syrian Churches', in J. J. van Ginkel, H. L. Murre-van den Berg and T. M. van Lint (eds.), *Redefining Christian Identity: Cultural Interaction in the Middle East since the Rise of Islam* (Leuven: Peeters), 1–35.

Mortley, R., 1986, *From Word to Silence: The Way of Negation, Christian and Greek* (Bonn: Hanstein).

Moss, Y., 2016a, 'Controverses christologiques au sein de la tradition miaphysite: Sur l'incorruptibilité du corps du Christ et autres questions', in F. Ruani (ed.), *Les controverses religieuses en syriaque* (Paris: Geuthner), 119–36.

Moss, Y., 2016b, 'Fish Eats Lion Eats Man: Saadia Gaon, Syriac Christianity, and the Resurrection of the Dead', *Jewish Quarterly Review* 106, 494–520.

Moss, Y., 2016c, *Incorruptible Bodies: Christology, Society, and Authority in Late Antiquity* (Berkeley: University of California Press).

Moss, Y., 2018, review of M. Penn, *Envisioning Islam, Der Islam* 95, 250–53.

Mosshammer, A. A., 1979, *The Chronicle of Eusebius and Greek Chronographic Tradition* (Lewisburg, PA: Bucknell University Press).

Mounayer, J., 1963, *Les synodes syriens jacobites* (Beirut: n.p.).

Mouterde, P., 1932, 'Les versions syriaques du Tome de saint Léon', *Mélanges de l'Université Saint-Joseph* 19, 119–62.

Nabe-von Schönberg, I., 1977, 'Die Westsyrische Kirche im Mittelalter (800–1150)' (PhD diss., Heidelberg University).

Nasrallah, J., 1976, *L'église melchite en Iraq, en Perse et en Asie Centrale* (Jerusalem: n.p.).

Nau, F., 1910, 'La cosmographie au VIIe siècle chez les Syriens', *Revue de l'Orient chrétien* 5, 225–54.

Nau, F., 1930, 'Le traité sur les "constellations" écrit, en 661, par Sévère Sébokt, évêque de Qennesrin', *Revue de l'Orient chrétien* 28, 327–410.

Nawas, J., 1992, 'Al-Ma᾽mun: Mihna and Caliphate' (Phd dissertation, University of Nijmegen).

Nawas, J., 2010, 'All in the Family? Al-Muʿtaṣim's Succession to the Caliphate as Denouement to the Lifelong Feud between al-Maʾmūn and His ʿAbbasid Family', *Oriens* 38, 77–88.

Nemoy, L., 1930, 'Al-Qirqisānī's Account of the Jewish Sects and Christianity', *Hebrew Union College Annual* 7, 317–97.

Neuwirth, A., 2010, *Der Koran als Text der Spätantike: Ein europäischer Zugang* (Berlin: Verlag der Weltreligionen).

Neuwirth, A., 2014, *Scripture, Poetry, and the Making of a Community: Reading the Qurʾan as a Literary Text* (Oxford: Oxford University Press).

Nongbri, B., 2013, *Before Religion: A History of a Modern Concept* (New Haven, CT: Yale University Press).

Norton, P., 2007, *Episcopal Elections 250–600: Hierarchy and Popular Will in Late Antiquity* (Oxford: Oxford University Press).

Nováček, K., et al., 2017, *Medieval Urban Landscape in Northeastern Mesopotamia* (Oxford: Archaeopress).

Oez, M., 2012, *Cyriacus of Tagrit and His Book on Divine Providence*, 2 vols. (Piscataway, NJ: Gorgias).

Omar, F., 2012, 'Ibrāhīm b. Muḥammad', in P. Bearman et al. (eds.), *Encyclopaedia of Islam*, 2nd ed. (Leiden: Brill).

Omar, H., 2013, '"The Crinkly-Haired People of the Black Earth": Examining Egyptian Identities in Ibn ʿAbd al-Ḥakam's *Futūḥ*', in P. Wood (ed.), *History and Identity in the Late Antique Near East* (Oxford: Oxford University Press), 149–67.

O'Meara, D., 2005, *Platonopolis: Platonic Political Philosophy in Late Antiquity* (Oxford: Clarendon).

Ortiz de Urbina, I., 1965, *Patrologia Syriaca* (Rome: Pontificio Istituto Orientale).

Osti, L., 2010, 'The Practical Matters of Culture in Pre-Madrasa Baghdad', *Oriens* 38, 145–64.

Palmer, A., 1990, *Monk and Mason on the Tigris Frontier: The Early History of Ṭur ʿAbdin* (Cambridge: Cambridge University Press).

Palmer, A., 1990–91, 'The Garshūnī Version of the Life of Theodotos of Amida', *Parole de l'Orient* 16, 253–59.

Palmer, A., 2006, 'Āmīd in the Seventh-Century Life of Theodūṭē', in E. Grypeou, M. N. Swanson and D. Thomas (eds.), *The Encounter of Eastern Christianity with Early Islam* (Leiden: Brill), 111–38.

Palmer, A., with S. Brock and R. Hoyland, 1993, *The Seventh Century in the West-Syrian Chronicles* (Liverpool: Liverpool University Press).

Palumbo, A., 2015, 'From Constantine the Great to Emperor Wu of the Liang: The Rhetoric of Imperial Conversion and the Divisive Emergence of Religious Identities in Late Antique Eurasia', in A. Papaconstantinou, N. McLynn and D. L. Schwartz (eds.), *Conversion in Late Antiquity: Christianity, Islam, and Beyond* (Farnham: Ashgate), 95–122.

Papaconstantinou, A., 2008, 'Between *Umma* and *Dhimma*: The Christians of the Middle East under the Umayyads', *Annales Islamologiques* 42, 127–56.

Papaconstantinou, A., 2009, 'What Remains Behind? Hellenism and Romanitas after the Arab Conquest', in H. Cotton et al. (eds.), *From Hellenism to Islam: Cultural and Linguistic Change in the Roman Near East* (Cambridge: Cambridge University Press), 447–66.

Papaconstantinou, A., 2010, 'Administering the Early Islamic Empire: Insights from the Papyri', in J. Haldon (ed.), *Money, Power and Politics in Early Islamic Syria: A Review of Current Debates* (Farnham: Ashgate), 57–74.

Papaconstantinou, A., 2011, 'Saints and Saracens: On Some Miracle Accounts from the Early Islamic Period', in D. Sullivan, E. Fisher and S. Papaioannou (eds.), *Byzantine Religious Culture: Studies in Honor of Alice-Mary Talbot* (Leiden: Brill), 323–38.

Papaconstantinou, A., 2012, 'Why Did Coptic Fail Where Aramaic Succeeded? Linguistic Developments in Egypt and the Near East after the Arab Conquest', in A. Mullen and P. James (eds.), *Multilingualism in the Graeco-Roman Worlds* (Cambridge: Cambridge University Press), 58–76.

Papaconstantinou, A., 2013, review of R. Hoyland, *Theophilus of Edessa*, *Le Muséon* 126, 459–65.

Papaconstantinou, A., 2016, 'Credit, Debt, and Dependence in Early Islamic Egypt and Southern Palestine', *Travaux et Mémoires* 20, 613–42.

Papaconstantinou, A., 2020, '"Great Men", Churchmen and the Others: Forms of Authority in the Villages of the Umayyad Period', in D. Rathbone and M. Langelotti (eds.), *Village Institutions in Egypt from Roman to Early Arab Rule* (London: British Academy), 178–89.

Patlagean, E., 1977, *Pauvreté économique et pauvreté sociale à Byzance, 4ᵉ–7ᵉ siècles* (Paris: Mouton).

Payne, R., 2009, 'Persecuting Heresy in Early Islamic Iraq: The Catholicos Ishoyahb III and the Elites of Nisibis', in A. Cain and N. Lenski (eds.), *The Power of Religion in Late Antiquity* (Farnham: Ashgate), 397–410.

Payne, R., 2015, *A State of Mixture: Christians, Zoroastrians and Iranian Political Culture in Late Antiquity* (Berkeley: University of California Press).

Payne, R., 2016, 'Iranian Cosmopolitanism: World Religions at the Sasanian Court', in M. Lavan, R. Payne and J. Weiseweiler (eds.), *Cosmopolitanism and Empire: Universal Rulers, Local Elites and Cultural Integration in the Ancient Near East and Mediterranean* (Oxford: Oxford University Press), 209–30.

Payne-Smith, J., 1903, *A Compendious Syriac Dictionary* (Oxford: Clarendon).

Peeters, P., 1908, 'Le martyrologue de Rabban Slība', *Analecta Bollandiana* 27, 127–200.

Penn, M. P., 2015a, *Envisioning Islam: Syriac Christians and the Early Muslim World* (Philadelphia: University of Pennsylvania Press).

Penn, M. P., 2015b, *When Christians First Met Muslims: A Sourcebook of the Earliest Syriac Writings on Islam* (Berkeley: University of California Press).

Petersen, W., 1994, *Tatian's* Diatessaron: *Its Creation, Dissemination and Significance in Scholarship* (Leiden: Brill).

Piccirillo, M., 2002, *L'Arabie chrétienne*, tr. É. Schelstraete and M.-P. Duverne (Paris: Mengès).

Platti, E., 2015, 'Yaḥyā ibn ʿAdī, Disciples and Masters: On Questions of Religious Philosophy', in D. Pratt et al. (eds.), *The Character of Christian-Muslim Encounter: Essays in Honour of David Thomas* (Leiden: Brill), 60–84.

Pohlmann, K.-F., 2013, *Die Entstehung des Korans: Neue Erkenntnisse aus Sicht der historisch-kritischen Bibelwissenschaft* (Darmstadt: Wissenschaftlicher Buchgesellschaft).

Poirier, P.-H., 1987, 'Les discours sur la Providence de Lazare bar Sabta', *Journal of Theological Studies*, new ser., 38, 431–35.

Polliack, M., 2006, 'Rethinking Karaism: Between Judaism and Islam', *Association for Jewish Studies Review* 30, 67–93.

Posner, N., 1985, 'The Muslim Conquest of Northern Mesopotamia: An Introductory Essay into Its Historical Background and Historiography' (PhD diss., New York University).

Possekel, U., 2013, 'Julianism in Syriac Christianity', in P. Bruns and H. Luthe (eds.), *Orientalia Christiana: Festschrift für Hubert Kaufhold zum 70. Geburtstag* (Wiesbaden: Harrassowitz), 437–58.

Possekel, U., 2015, 'Christological Debates in Eighth-Century Harran: The Correspondence of Leo of Harran and Eliya', in M. E. Doerfler, E. Fiano and K. R. Smith (eds.), *Syriac Encounters: Papers from the Sixth North American Syriac Symposium, Duke University, 26–29 June 2011* (Leuven: Peeters), 345–68.

Pradines, J., 1975, 'Récherches sur la role des chrétiens à la cour des umayyades et des premiers abbasides (661–861)' (PhD thesis, University of Toulouse).

Price, R., and M. Whitby (eds.), 2010, *Chalcedon in Context: Church Councils 400–700* (Liverpool: Liverpool University Press).

Putman, H., 1975, *L'Église et l'Islam sous Timothée I (780–823): Études sur l'église nestorienne au temps des premiers ʿAbbāsides avec nouvelle édition et traduction du dialogue entre Timothée et al-Mahdī* (Beirut: Dar el-Machreq).

Rapp, C., 2000, 'The Elite Status of Bishops in Late Antiquity in Ecclesiastical, Spiritual and Social Contexts', *Arethusa* 33, 379–99.

Rapp, C., 2005, *Holy Bishops in Late Antiquity: The Nature of Christian Leadership in an Age of Transition* (Berkeley: University of California Press).

Rapp, C., 2016, *Brother-Making in Late Antiquity and Byzantium: Monks, Laymen and Christian Ritual* (London: Oxford University Press).

Rassi, S., 2015, 'Justifying Christianity in the Islamic Middle Ages: The Apologetic Theology of ʿAbdīshōʿ bar Brīkhā (d. 1318)' (DPhil thesis, University of Oxford).

Reeves, J., 2011, *Prolegomena to the History of Islamicate Manichaeism* (Sheffield: Equinox).

Reinink, G. J., 1999, '"Origenism" in Thirteenth-Century Northern Iraq', in G. Reinink and A. Klugkist (eds.), *After Bardaisan: Studies on Continuity and Change in Syriac Christianity in Honour of Professor Han J.-W. Drijvers* (Leuven: Peeters), 237–52.

Reynolds, D., n.d., 'Silent Partners: Christians in the Economy of Early Islamic Palestine'. Unpublished manuscript.

Reynolds, G. S., 2004, *Muslim Theologian in the Sectarian Milieu: ʿAbd al-Jabbār and the Critique of Christian Origins* (Leiden: Brill).

Rickards, R. R., 1974, 'The Hexaemeron of Moses bar Kepha: A Critical Analysis and Translation of the Second Memra' (PhD thesis, University of Melbourne).

Roberts, A., 2017, 'Being a Sabian at Court in Tenth-Century Baghdad', *Journal of the American Oriental Society* 137, 253–77.

Robinson, C., 1996, 'Tribes and Nomads in Early Islamic Mesopotamia', in K. Bartl and S. Hauser (eds.), *Continuity and Change in Northern Mesopotamia from the Hellenistic to the Early Islamic Period* (Berlin: Reimer), 429–52.

Robinson, C., 2000, *Empire and Elites after the Muslim Conquest: The Transformation of Northern Mesopotamia* (Cambridge: Cambridge University Press).

Robinson, C., 2005a, *ʿAbd al-Malik* (London: Oneworld).

Robinson, C., 2005b, 'Neck-Sealing in Early Islam', *Journal of the Economic and Social History of the Orient* 48, 401–41.

Robinson, C., 2016, 'Al-ʿAṭṭāf b. Sufyān and Abbasid Imperialism', in A. Korangy et al. (eds.), *Essays in Islamic Philology, History, and Philosophy: A Festschrift in Celebration and Honor of Professor Ahmad Mahdavi Damghani's 90th Birthday* (Berlin: De Gruyter), 357–85.

Roggema, B., 2009, *The Legend of Sergius Baḥīrā: Eastern Christian Apologetics and Apocalyptic in Response to Islam* (Leiden: Brill).

Roques, R., 1954, *L'univers dionysien: Structure hiérarchique du monde selon le Pseudo-Denys* (Paris: Aubier).

Rudolph, C., 1994, 'Christliche Bibelexegese und Muʿtazilitische Theologie: Der Fall des Moses bar Kepha (gest. 903 n.Chr.)', *Oriens* 34, 299–313.

Ruffini, G., 2011, 'Village Life and Family Power in Late Antique Nessana', *Transactions of the American Philological Association* 141, 201–35.

Sahner, C. C., 2016, 'Swimming against the Current: Muslim Conversion to Christianity in the Early Islamic Period', *Journal of the American Oriental Society* 136, 265–84.

Sahner, C. C., 2017, 'The First Iconoclasm in Islam: A New History of the Edict of Yazid II (AH 104 / AD 723)', *Der Islam* 94, 5–56.

Sahner, C. C., 2018, *Christian Martyrs under Islam: Religious Violence and the Making of the Muslim World* (Princeton, NJ: Princeton University Press).

Saint-Laurent, J.-N. M., 2015, *Missionary Stories and the Formation of the Syriac Churches* (Berkeley: University of California Press).

Sako, L., 1986, *Le rôle de la hiérarchie syriaque orientale dans les rapports diplomatiques entre la Perse et Byzance aux Vᵉ–VIIᵉ siècles* (Paris: Université de Paris IV).

Salaymeh, L., 2016, 'Taxing Citizens: Socio-legal Constructions of Late Antique Muslim Identity', *Islamic Law and Society* 23, 333–67.

Salvesen, A. G., 2015, 'Scholarship on the Margins: Biblical and Secular Learning in the Work of Jacob of Edessa', in M. E. Doerfler, E. Fiano and K. R. Smith (eds.), *Syriac Encounters:*

Papers from the Sixth North American Syriac Symposium, Duke University, 26–29 June 2011 (Leuven: Peeters), 327–44.

Sarris, P., 2006, *Economy and Society in the Age of Justinian* (Cambridge: Cambridge University Press).

Sarris, P., 2011a, *Empires of Faith: The Fall of Rome to the Rise of Islam, 500–700* (Oxford: Oxford University Press).

Sarris, P., 2011b, 'Restless Peasants and Scornful Lords: Lay Hostility to Holy Men and the Church in Late Antiquity and the Early Middle Ages', in P. Sarris, M. Dal Santo and P. Booth (eds.), *An Age of Saints? Power, Conflict and Dissent in Early Medieval Christianity* (Leiden: Brill), 1–10.

Sarris, P., 2017, 'Emperor Justinian', in J. White and G. Hauk (eds.), *Christianity and Family Law: An Introduction* (Cambridge: Cambridge University Press), 100–114.

Sartre, M., 1985, *Bostra: Des origines à l'Islam* (Paris: Geuthner).

Savant, S. B., 2013, *The New Muslims of Post-conquest Iran: Tradition, Memory and Conversion* (Cambridge: Cambridge University Press).

Savant, S. B., and P. Webb, 2017, *Ibn Qutaybah: The Excellence of the Arabs* (New York: New York University Press).

Schenke, G., 2018, 'Monastic Control over Agriculture and Farming: New Evidence from the Monastery of Apa Apollo at Bawit concerning the Payment of APARCHE', in A. Delattre, M. Legendre and P. Sijpesteijn (eds.), *Authority and Control in the Countryside: From Antiquity to Islam in the Mediterranean and Near East (Sixth-Tenth Century)* (Leiden: Brill), 420–31.

Schick, R., 1995, *The Christian Communities of Palestine from Byzantine to Islamic Rule: A Historical and Archaeological Study* (Princeton, NJ: Darwin).

Schmitt, R., 2012, 'Hatra', in E. Yarshater (ed.), *Encyclopedia Iranica*.

Schoeler, G., 1990, 'Bashshār b. Burd, Abū ʾl-ʿAtāhiyah and Abū Nuwās', in J. Ashtiany et al. (eds.), *ʿAbbasid Belles-Lettres*, vol. 2 of *The Cambridge History of Arabic Literature* (Cambridge: Cambridge University Press), 275–99.

Schor, A., 2011, *Theodoret's People: Social Networks and Religious Conflict in Late Roman Syria* (Berkeley: University of California Press).

Schott, J., 2008, *Christianity, Empire and the Making of Religion in Late Antiquity* (Philadelphia: University of Pennsylvania Press).

Schrier, O. J., 1991, 'Chronological Problems concerning the Lives of Severus bar Mašqā, Athanasius of Balad, Julianus Romāyā, Yohannān Sābā, George of the Arabs and Jacob of Edessa', *Oriens Christianus* 75, 62–90.

Schulze, W., 2017, 'The Standing Caliph Coins with the Mint Name Qūrus', in T. Goodwin (ed.), *Coinage and History in the Seventh Century Near East 5* (London: Archetype), 141–51.

Segal, J. B., 1953, *The Diacritical Point and the Accents in Syriac* (Oxford: Oxford University Press).

Segal, J. B., 1970, *Edessa: The Blessed City* (Oxford: Clarendon).

Segovia, C. A., 2019, *The Qurʾanic Jesus: A New Interpretation* (Berlin: De Gruyter).

Selb, W., 1989, *Orientalisches Kirchenrecht II: Die Geschichte des Kirchenrechts der Westsyrer (von den Anfängen bis zur Mongolenzeit)* (Vienna: Verlag der Österreichischen Akademie der Wissenschaften).

Seleznyov, N. N., 2013, 'Jacob and Jacobites: The Syrian Origin of the Name and Its Egyptian Interpretations', *Scrinium* 9, 382–98.

Shaban, M. A., 1971, *Islamic History: A New Interpretation*, vol. 1, A.D. 600–750 (A.H. 132) (Cambridge: Cambridge University Press).

Shaked, S., and J. Naveh, 1985, *Amulets and Magic Bowls: Aramaic Incantations of Late Antiquity* (Jerusalem: Magnes).

Shaked, S., and J. Naveh, 1993, *Magic Spells and Formulae: Aramaic Incantations of Late Antiquity* (Jerusalem: Magnes).

Sharon, M., 1983, *Black Banners from the East: The Establishment of the ʿAbbāsid State—Incubation of a Revolt* (Jerusalem: Magnes).

Shaw, R., and C. Stewart, 2003, *Syncretism/Anti-syncretism: The Politics of Religious Synthesis* (London: Routledge).

Shboul, A.M.H., 1979, *Al-Masʿūdī and His World: A Muslim Humanist and His Interest in Non-Muslims* (London: Ithaca).

Signes-Codoñer, J., 2014, *The Emperor Theophilos and the East, 829–842: Court and Frontier in Byzantium during the Last Phase of Iconoclasm* (Farnham: Ashgate).

Sijpesteijn, P. M., 2007, 'Creating a Muslim State: The Collection and Meaning of Ṣadaqa', in B. Palme (ed.), *Akten des 23. internationalen Papyrologenkongresses Wien, 22.–28. Juli 2001* (Vienna: Verlag der Österreichischen Akademie der Wissenschaften), 661–74.

Sijpesteijn, P. M., 2009, 'Landholding Patterns in Early Islamic Egypt', *Journal of Agrarian Change* 9, 120–33.

Sijpesteijn, P. M., 2013, *Shaping a Muslim State: The World of a Mid-Eighth-Century Egyptian Official* (Oxford: Oxford University Press).

Sijpesteijn, P. M., 2017, 'Delegation of Judicial Power in Abbasid Egypt', in M. van Berkel, L. Buskens and P. Sijpesteijn (eds.), *Legal Documents as Sources for the History of Muslim Societies: Studies in Honour of Rudolph Peters* (Leiden: Brill), 61–84.

Silverstein, A. J., 2007, *Postal Systems in the Pre-modern Islamic World* (Cambridge: Cambridge University Press).

Simonsohn, U., 2010, 'The Christians Whose Force Is Hard: Non-ecclesiastical Judicial Authorities in the Early Islamic Period', *Journal of the Economic and Social History of the Orient* 53, 579–620.

Simonsohn, U., 2011, *A Common Justice: The Legal Allegiances of Christians and Jews under Early Islam* (Philadelphia: University of Pennsylvania Press).

Simonsohn, U., 2013a, 'Blessed Are the Peacemakers: An Ecclesiastical Definition of Authority in the Early Islamic Period', in D. Shulman (ed.), *Meditations on Authority* (Jerusalem: Magnes), 101–27.

Simonsohn, U., 2013b, '"Halting between Two Opinions": Conversion and Apostasy in Medieval Islam', *Medieval Encounters* 19, 342–70.

Simonsohn, U., 2015, 'Justice', in A. J. Silverstein and G. G. Stroumsa (eds.), *The Oxford Handbook of the Abrahamic Religions* (Oxford: Oxford University Press), 137–65.

Simonsohn, U., 2016a, 'Communal Membership despite Religious Exogamy: A Critical Examination of East and West Syrian Legal Sources of the Late Sasanian and Early Islamic Periods', *Journal of Near Eastern Studies* 75, 249–66.

Simonsohn, U., 2016b, 'The Introduction and Formalization of Civil Law in the East Syrian Church in the Late Sasanian–Early Islamic Periods', *History Compass* 14, 231–43.

Sizgorich, T., 2009, *Violence and Belief in Late Antiquity: Militant Devotion in Christianity and Islam* (Philadelphia: University of Pennsylvania Press).

Sklare, D., 1996, *Samuel ben Hofni Gaon and His Cultural World: Texts and Studies* (Leiden: Brill).

Smith, A. D., 2004, *The Antiquity of Nations* (Cambridge: Polity).

Smith, J. Z., 1982, *Imagining Religion: From Babylon to Jonestown* (Chicago: University of Chicago Press).

Smith, W. C., 1991, *The Meaning and End of Religion*, reprint (Minneapolis: Fortress).

Sokoloff, M., 2009, *A Syriac Lexicon: A Translation from the Latin, Correction, Expansion and Update of C. Brockelmann's Lexicon Syriacum* (Piscataway, NJ: Gorgias).

Sourdel, D., 1959–60, *Le vizirat ʿabbaside de 749 à 936 (132 à 324 de l'hégire)* (Damascus: Institut français de Damas).

Sourdel, D., 1999, *L'État impérial des califes abbassides, VIIIᵉ–Xᵉ siècle* (Paris: Presses universitaires de France).

Stark, R., 1996, *The Rise of Christianity: A Sociologist Reconsiders History* (Princeton, NJ: Princeton University Press).

Straughn, I. B., 2006, 'Materializing Islam: An Archaeology of Landscape in Early Islamic Period Syria (c. 600–1000 CE)' (PhD diss., University of Chicago).

Stroumsa, G., 2015, *The Making of Abrahamic Religions in Late Antiquity* (Oxford: Oxford University Press).

Stroumsa, S., 1999, 'The Religion of the Freethinkers in Medieval Islam', in F. Niewöhner and O. Pluta (eds.), *Atheismus im Mittelalter und in der Renaissance* (Wiesbaden: Harrassowitz), 44–58.

Sundermann, W., 1991, 'Christianity: V. Christ in Manichaeism', in E. Yarshater (ed.), *Encyclopaedia Iranica*.

Taft, R. F., 1991, *A History of the Liturgy of St. John Chrysostom*, vol. 4, *The Diptychs* (Rome: Pontificio Istituto Orientale).

Taft, R. F., 2000, *A History of the Liturgy of St. John Chrysostom*, vol. 5, *The Precommunion Rites* (Rome: Pontificio Istituto Orientale).

Taft, R. F., 2008, *A History of the Liturgy of St. John Chrysostom*, vol. 6, *The Communion, Thanksgiving and Concluding Rites* (Rome: Pontificio Istituto Orientale).

Tannous, J., 2013, 'You Are What You Read: Qenneshre and the Miaphysite Church in the Seventh Century', in P. Wood (ed.), *History and Identity in the Late Antique Near East* (Oxford: Oxford University Press), 83–102.

Tannous, J., 2016, 'The *Life of Simeon of the Olives*: A Christian Puzzle from Islamic Syria', in J. Kreiner and H. Reimitz (eds.), *Motions of Late Antiquity: Essays on Religion, Politics and Society in Honour of Peter Brown* (Turnhout: Brepols), 309–30.

Tannous, J., 2018, *The Making of the Medieval Middle East: Religion, Society and Simple Believers* (Princeton, NJ: Princeton University Press).

Tarán, L., and D. Gutas, 2012, *Aristotle, Poetics: Editio Maior of the Greek Text with Historical Introductions and Philological Commentaries* (Leiden: Brill).

Tas, L., 2010, 'The Myth of the Ottoman Millet System', *Journal of Minority and Group Rights* 21, 497–526.

Tate, G., 1992, *Les campagnes de Syrie du nord du IIᵉ au VIIᵉ siècle: Exemple d'expansion démographique et économique à la fin de l'Antiquité* (Paris: Geuthner).

Taylor, D.G.K., 2002, 'Bilingualism and Diglossia in Late Antique Syria and Mesopotamia',
in J. Adams, S. Swain and M. Janse (eds.), *Bilingualism in Ancient Society: Language Contact
and the Written Word* (Oxford: Oxford University Press), 298–331.

Taylor, D.G.K., 2015, 'The Syriac Baptism of St. John: A Christian Ritual for Protection for
Muslim Children', in R. Hoyland (ed.), *The Late Antique World of Early Islam: Muslims among
Christians and Jews in the East Mediterranean* (Princeton, NJ: Darwin), 47–95.

Tchalenko, G., 1953–58, *Villages antiques de la Syrie du Nord: Le massif du Bélus à l'époque romaine*
(Paris: Geuthner).

Thomas, D., 2008, *Christian Doctrines in Islamic Theology* (Leiden: Brill).

Thomson, R. W., 1962, 'An Eighth-Century Melkite Colophon from Edessa', *Journal of Theological Studies* 13, 249–68.

Tillier, M., 2009, *Les cadis d'Iraq et l'état abbasside (132/750–334/945)* (Damascus: Institut français du Proche-Orient).

Toral-Niehoff, I., 2014, *Al-Ḥīra: Eine arabische Kulturmetropole im spätantiken Kontext* (Leiden:
Brill).

Toubert, P., 1973, *Les structures du Latium médiéval: Le Latium méridional et la Sabine du IXᵉ à la
fin du XIIᵉ siècle* (Rome: École française de Rome).

Treiger, A., 2014a, 'Origins of *Kalām*', in S. Schmidtke (ed.), *The Oxford Handbook of Islamic
Theology* (Oxford: Oxford University Press), https://www.oxfordhandbooks.com/view/10
.1093/oxfordhb/9780199696703.001.0001/oxfordhb-9780199696703-e-001.

Treiger, A., 2014b, 'Unpublished Texts from the Arab Orthodox Tradition (1): On the Origins
of the Term "Melkite" and On the Destruction of the Maryamiyya Cathedral in Damascus',
Chronos 29, 7–37.

Tritton, A. S., 1930, *The Caliphs and Their Non-Muslim Subjects: A Critical Study of the Covenant
of Umar* (London: Oxford University Press).

Trombley, F., 1994, *Hellenic Religion and Christianization, c. 370–529*, 2 vols. (Leiden: Brill).

Troupeau, G., 1991, 'Le rôle des syriaques dans la transmission et l'exploitation du patrimoine
philosophique et scientifique grec', *Arabica* 38, 1–10.

Turner, B. S., 2013, *Sociology of Islam: Collected Essays of Bryan S. Turner* (Farnham: Ashgate).

Turner, J., 2013, *Inquisition in Early Islam: The Contention for Political and Religious Authority in
the Abbasid Empire* (London: I. B. Tauris).

Vacca, A., 2016, *Non-Muslim Provinces under Early Islam: Islamic Rule and Iranian Legitimacy in
Armenia and Caucasian Albania* (Cambridge: Cambridge University Press).

Vailhé, S., 1908, 'Cyrrhus', in *Catholic Encyclopedia* (New York: Robert Appleton), http://
catholicencyclopedia.newadvent.com/cathen/04597a.htm.

van Bekkum, W. J., 2007, 'The Karaite Jacob al-Qirqisani (Tenth Century) on Christianity and
the Christians', in W. J. van Bekkum, J. W. Drijvers and A. C. Klugkist (eds.), *Syriac Polemics:
Studies in Honour of Gerrit Jan Reinink* (Leuven: Peeters), 173–92.

van Berkel, M., 2013, 'Archives and Chanceries: Pre-1500, in Arabic', *Encyclopedia of Islam*, 3rd ed.
(Leiden: Brill).

van Bladel, K., 2009, *The Arabic Hermes: From Pagan Sage to Prophet of Science* (Oxford: Oxford
University Press).

van den Berghe, P. L., 1987, *The Ethnic Phenomenon* (Westport, CT: Praeger).

van Esbroeck, M., 1991, 'Primauté, patriarcats, catholicossats, autocéphalies en Orient', in M. Maccarrone (ed.), *Il primato del vescovo di Roma nel primo millennio: Richerche e testimonianze* (Vatican City: Libreria Editrice Vaticana), 493–521.

van Ess, J., 2006, *The Flowering of Muslim Thought* (Cambridge, MA: Harvard University Press).

van Ess, J., 2017, *Theology and Society in the Second and Third Centuries of the Hijra*, 2 vols. (Leiden: Brill).

van Ginkel, J. J., 1998, 'Making History: Michael the Syrian and His Sixth-Century Syriac Sources', in R. Lavenant (ed.), *Symposium Syriacum VII* (Rome: Pontificio Istituto Orientale), 351–58.

van Ginkel, J. J., 2005, 'History and Community: Jacob of Edessa and the West Syrian Identity', in J. J. van Ginkel, H. L. Murre-van den Berg and T. M. van Lint (eds.), *Redefining Christian Identity: Cultural Interaction in the Middle East since the Rise of Islam* (Leuven: Peeters), 67–75.

van Ginkel, J. J., 2006, 'Michael the Syrian and His Sources: Reflections on the Methodology of Michael the Great as a Historiographer and Its Implications for Modern Historians', *Journal of the Canadian Society for Syriac Studies* 6, 53–60.

van Ginkel, J. J., 2010, 'A Man Is Not an Island: Reflections on the Historiography of the Early Syriac Renaissance', in H. Teule et al. (eds.), *The Syriac Renaissance* (Leuven: Peeters), 113–21.

van Leeuwen, M.H.D., and I. Maas, 2005, 'Endogamy and Social Class in History: An Overview', *International Review of Social History* 50, suppl. 13, 1–23.

Van Nuffelen, P., 2011, 'The Rhetoric of Rules and the Rules of Consensus', in P. Van Nuffelen, J. Leemans, S. Keogh and C. Nicolaye (eds.), *Episcopal Elections in Late Antiquity* (Boston: De Gruyter), 243–58.

Van Nuffelen, P., forthcoming, 'Conflict, Debate and Authority in the History of Dionysius of Tell-Mahre', in B. Roggema and I. Papadogiannakis, eds., *Patterns of Argumentation and Exchange of Ideas in Late Antiquity and Early Islam* (Routledge).

Van Nuffelen, P., M. Conterno and M. Mazzola, n.d., 'The Chronicle of Dionysius of Tel-Mahre'. Unpublished manuscript.

Van Rompay, L., 1999, 'Syriac Inscriptions in Deir al-Surian: Some Reflections on Their Writers and Readers', *Hugoye* 2, 189–202.

Van Rompay, L., 2000, 'Past and Present Perceptions of Syriac Literary Tradition', *Hugoye* 3, 71–301.

Varghese, B., 1989, *Les onctions baptismales dans la tradition syrienne* (Leuven: Peeters).

Varghese, B., 2004, *West Syrian Liturgical Theology* (Aldershot: Ashgate).

Vevaina, Y., 2015, 'Theology and Hermeneutics', in Y. Vevaina and M. Stausberg (eds.), *The Wiley-Blackwell Companion to Zoroastrianism* (Chichester: John Wiley and Sons), 211–34.

Vollandt, R., 2015, *Arabic Versions of the Pentateuch: A Comparative Study of Jewish, Christian, and Muslim Sources* (Leiden: Brill).

Vööbus, A., 1975, 'New Manuscript Discoveries for the Literary Legacy of Mōšē bar Kēphā: The Genre of Theological Writings', *Harvard Theological Review* 68, 377–84.

Vööbus, A., 1975–76, *The Synodicon in the West Syrian Tradition* (Leuven: CSCO).

Walker, J., 2006, *The Legend of Mar Qardagh: Narrative and Christian Heroism in Late Antique Iraq* (Berkeley: University of California Press).

Walker, J., 2007, 'The Legacy of Mesopotamia in Late Antique Iraq: The Christian Martyr Shrine at Melqi (Neo-Assyrian Milqia)', *Aram* 19, 483–508.

Walmsley, A., 2007, *Early Islamic Syria: An Archaeological Assessment* (London: Duckworth).

Ware, K., 1990, 'The Meaning of Divine Liturgy for the Byzantine Worshipper', in R. Morris (ed.), *Church and People in Byzantium* (Birmingham: Centre for Byzantine, Ottoman and Modern Greek Studies, University of Birmingham), 7–28.

Wasserstein, D., 2003, 'Why Did Arabic Succeed Where Greek Failed?', *Scripta Classica Israelica* 22, 257–72.

Watt, J. W., 2011, 'Anṭun of Tagrit', in S. P. Brock et al. (eds), *Gorgias Encyclopedic Dictionary of the Syriac Heritage*.

Watt, J. W., 2014, 'Why Did Ḥunayn, the Master Translator into Arabic, Make Translations into Syriac? On the Purpose of the Syriac Translations of Ḥunayn and His Circle', in J. J. Scheiner and D. Janos (eds.), *The Place to Go: Contexts of Learning in Baghdād, 750–1000 C.E.* (Princeton, NJ: Darwin), 363–88.

Webb, P., 2015, 'Pre-Islamic al-Shām in Classical Arabic Literature: Spatial Narratives and History-Telling', *Studia Islamica* 110, 135–64.

Webb, P., 2016, *Imagining the Arabs: Arab Identity and the Rise of Islam* (Cambridge: Cambridge University Press).

Weitz, L., 2016, 'Shaping East Syrian Law in Abbasid Iraq', *Le Muséon* 129, 71–116.

Weitz, L., 2018, *Between Christ and Caliph: Law, Marriage and Christian Community in Early Islam* (Philadelphia: University of Pennsylvania Press).

Wellhausen, J., 1927, *The Arab Kingdom and Its Fall* (Calcutta: University of Calcutta Press).

Weltecke, D., 2003, *Die 'Beschreibung der Zeiten' von Mōr Michael dem Großen (1126–1199): Eine Studie zu ihrem historischen und historiographiegeschichtlichen Kontext* (Leuven: Peeters).

Weltecke, D., 2010, 'Michael the Syrian', in R. G. Dunphy (ed.), *The Encyclopedia of the Medieval Chronicle* (Leiden: Brill).

Wheatley, P., 2001, *The Places Where Men Pray Together: Cities in Islamic Lands in the Seventh through Tenth Centuries* (Chicago: University of Chicago Press).

Whitcomb, D., 1994, 'Amsar in Syria? Syrian Cities after the Conquest', *Aram* 6, 13–33.

White, H. E., 1932–33, *The Monasteries of the Wâdi Natrûn*, 3 vols. (New York: Metropolitan Museum of Art).

Whittow, M., 1996, *The Making of Orthodox Byzantium, 600–1025* (Basingstoke: Macmillan).

Wickham, C., 2005, *Framing the Early Middle Ages: Europe and the Mediterranean, 400–800* (Oxford: Oxford University Press).

Wickham, C., 2011, 'Tributary Empires: Late Rome and the Caliphate', in P. Bang and C. Bayly, *Tributary Empires in Global History* (Basingstoke: Macmillan), 205–13.

Wickham, C., 2015, 'Administrators' Time: The Social Memory of the Early Medieval State, East and West', in A. Ahmed, B. Sadeghi, R. Hoyland and A. Silverstein (eds.), *Islamic Cultures, Islamic Contexts* (Leiden: Brill), 430–67.

Wickham, C., 2016, 'The Comparative Method and Early Medieval Religious Conversion', in R. Flechner and M. Ní Mhaonaigh (eds.), *The Introduction of Christianity into the Early Medieval Insular World: Converting the Isles I* (Turnhout: Brepols), 13–40.

Wimmer, A., 2013, *Ethnic Boundary Making: Institutions, Power, Networks* (Oxford: Oxford University Press).

Winkler, D. W., 1997, 'Miaphysitism: A New Term for Use in the History of Dogma and in Ecumenical Theology', *Harp* 10, 33–40.

Winkler, D. W., 1999, 'Theodosios von Alexandrien: Ökumenischer Patriarch der Miapysiten',
Zeitschrift für katholische Theologie 121, 396–412.

Wipszycka, E., 1972, *Les ressources et les activités économiques des églises en Égypte du IVe au VIIIe
siècle* (Brussels: Fondation Égyptologique Reine Élisabeth).

Wipszycka, E., 2011, 'The Economics of Egyptian Monasticism', *Journal of Juristic Papyrology* 41,
159–263.

Wissa, M., 2016, 'Yusab of Alexandria, Dionysius of Tel-Mahre, al-Ma'mun of Baghdad, the
Bashmurites and the Narrative of the Last Rebellion in 'Abbasid Egypt: Re-considering
Coptic and Syriac Historiography', in P. Buzi, A. Camplani and F. Contardi (eds.), *Coptic
Society, Literature and Religion from Late Antiquity to Modern Times* (Leuven: Peeters),
1045–62.

Witakowski, W., 1984–86, 'Chronicles of Edessa', *Orientalia Suecana* 33–35, 487–98.

Witakowski, W., 1987, *The Syriac Chronicle of Pseudo-Dionysius of Tel-Maḥrē: A Study in the History of Historiography* (Uppsala: Almqvist och Wiksell).

Witakowski, W., 2008, 'The Chronicle of Jacob of Edessa', in B. ter Haar Romeny (ed.), *Jacob of
Edessa and the Syriac Culture of His Day* (Leiden: Brill), 25–43.

Wood, P., 2010, *'We Have No King but Christ': Christian Political Thought in Greater Syria on the
Eve of the Arab Conquest (c. 400–585)* (Oxford: Oxford University Press).

Wood, P., 2011, 'The Chroniclers of Zuqnin and Their Times, c. 720–775', *Parole de l'Orient* 36,
549–68.

Wood, P., 2012, 'Syriac and the "Syrians"', in S. F. Johnson (ed.), *The Oxford Handbook of Late
Antiquity* (Oxford: Oxford University Press), 170–95.

Wood, P., 2013, *The Chronicle of Seert: Christian Historical Imagination in Late Antique Iraq* (Oxford: Oxford University Press).

Wood, P., 2018a, 'Christians in Umayyad Iraq: Decentralization and Expansion (600–750)', in
A. Marsham and A. George (eds.), *Power, Patronage and Memory in Early Islam: Perspectives
on Umayyad Elites* (Oxford: Oxford University Press), 255–74.

Wood, P., 2018b, 'The Idea of Freedom in the Writings of Non-Chalcedonian Christians in the
Fifth and Sixth Centuries', *History of European Ideas* 44, 774–94.

Wood, P., 2019, 'Changing Geographies: West Syrian Ecclesiastical History, AD 700–850', in
P. Van Nuffelen (ed.), *Historiography and Space in Late Antiquity* (Cambridge: Cambridge
University Press), 136–63.

Woolf, G., 1997, 'The Roman Urbanization of the East', in S. Alcock (ed.), *The Early Roman
Empire in the East* (Oxford: Oxbow), 1–15.

Woolf, G., and P. Garnsey, 1989, 'Patronage of the Rural Poor', in A. Wallace-Hadrill (ed.),
Patronage in Ancient Society (London: Routledge), 153–71.

Wright, W., 1870, *Catalogue of Syriac Manuscripts in the British Museum Acquired since the Year
1838*, 3 vols. (London: British Museum).

Wright, W., 2001, *A Short History of Syriac Literature*, reprint (Piscataway, NJ: Gorgias).

Wright, W., and N. Maclean, 1898, *The Ecclesiastical History of Eusebius in Syriac* (Oxford: Oxford
University Press).

Yarbrough, L., 2016a, 'Did ʿUmar b. ʿAbd al-ʿAzīz Issue an Edict concerning Non-Muslim Officials?', in A. Borrut and F. M. Donner (eds.), *Christians and Others in the Umayyad State* (Chicago: University of Chicago Press), 173–206.

Yarbrough, L., 2016b, review of M. Penn, *Envisioning Islam, Church History* 85, 827–30.

Yücesoy, H., 2007, 'Ancient Imperial Heritage and Islamic Universal Historiography: Al-Dīnawarī's Secular Perspective', *Journal of Global History* 2, 135–55.

Zaman, M. Q., 1997, *Religion and Politics under the Early ʿAbbāsids: The Emergence of the Proto-Sunnī Elite* (Leiden: Brill).

Zellentin, H. M., 2013, *The Qurʾān's Legal Culture: The Didascalia Apostolorum as a Point of Departure* (Tübingen: Mohr Siebeck).

Zerbini, A., 2013, 'Society and Economy in Marginal Zones: A Study of the Levantine Agricultural Economy (1st–8th c. AD)' (PhD thesis, Royal Holloway, University of London).

Zychowicz-Coghill, E., 2017, 'Conquests of Egypt: Making History in ʿAbbāsid Egypt' (DPhil thesis, University of Oxford).

INDEX

Abbasid revolution, 162–63, 183n90, 203, 235

ʿAbd al-Malik, 4, 52–55, 58, 220–21

ʿAbd Allah ibn Tahir: as governor of Syria, Jazira and Egypt, 71, 93, 116, 182; links with Dionysius, 39, 71, 85, 93, 116, 171–76, 182; role in fourth *fitna*, 165–71

ʿAbdun of Takrit (martyr), 85

Abgar V (king of Edessa), 53, 104, 212–13, 218–19, 225

Abraham of Qartmin (Abiram), 3, 71; in audience with ʿAbd Allah ibn Tahir, 172–74; in comparison to Numbers 16, 150; complaints about to al-Maʾmun, 197; as leader of the opposition to Cyriacus, 115–16, 119

Abu al-Wazir (commander), 178, 181

Abu Bakr (caliph), 163

Abu Hanifa (jurist), 189

Abu Raʾita (theologian), 125

Abu Sufyan (opponent of Muhammad), 163

Abu Yusuf, 84, 200–202

Addai (apostle to Edessa), 213

Afshin (general), 178–81, 183, 185

ʿAhd Ardashir, 205

Al-Amin, 162–64, 166–67, 203–5

Al-Fadl ibn Sahl (vizier), 167

Al-Mahdi, 29, 92n68, 103

Al-Maʾmun, 1–2, 25–26, 31, 35, 37–40, 71, 73, 96, 161, 170, 235; in Egypt, 178–85; endorsement of Dionysius, 90, 93, 161, 172–74; legislation for *dhimmīs*, 187–88; personal meetings with Dionysius, 192–201; propaganda as caliph, 203–5; war with al-Amin, 162–66

Al-Mansur (ʿAbd Allah), 1, 33, 56, 65–67, 71, 81, 89, 91, 170

Al-Muʾtasim (Abu Ishaq), 26, 36–37, 90, 181–85

Al-Mutawakkil, 88n48

Al-Wathiq, 37, 91

Alexandria, 83n25, 124, 133, 175, 195–96

ʿAli, general of al-Amin, 166

ʿAli, governor of Damascus, 91

ʿAli, governor of the Jazira, 74, 103

ʿAli al-Rida, 164, 167

ʿAli ibn Abi Talib, 173–74, 202–3

Alids, 164

Ambrose of Milan, 96

Amida, 18, 24, 47–50, 65, 88, 98n6, 119, 119n94, 126, 217, 227

amṣār, 98

Anan, 189–91

Anastasius (emperor), 15

Anastasius of Sinai, 138n4

Angels, 140, 147–48

Antioch: city of, 7, 19, 25, 88, 99–100, 106, 168, 179, 208, 218, 227–28; patriarchate of, 10, 14–16, 19–23, 31, 100, 175, 195–96

Apamea, 19, 99–100, 118, 168, 227

Arabs: Bedouin groups, 94–95, 168, 171, 211; Christian Arabs, 32–33, 120; conquests and treaties, 180, 196; cultural achievement, 211, 229; in the succession of kingdoms, 218–19; terminology and definition, 168n38, 220–24

Aristotle, 5, 199, 232

Armenians, 24, 43n12, 52, 56

Arzun, 126, 227

GPSR Authorized Representative: Easy Access System Europe - Mustamäe tee 50, 10621 Tallinn, Estonia, gpsr.requests@easproject.com